JDBC 4.0 and Oracle JDeveloper for J2EE Development

A J2EE developer's guide for using Oracle JDeveloper's integrated database features to build data-driven applications

Deepak Vohra

PUBLISHING

BIRMINGHAM - MUMBAI

JDBC 4.0 and Oracle JDeveloper for J2EE Development

First published: April 2008

First reprint: May 2009

Production Reference: 2290409

Published by Packt Publishing Ltd.
32 Lincoln Road
Olton
Birmingham, B27 6PA, UK.

ISBN 978-1-847194-30-5

www.packtpub.com

Cover Image by Vinayak Chittar (vinayak.chittar@gmail.com)

Credits

Author

Deepak Vohra

Reviewer

Frank Nimphius

Acquisition Editor

Shayantani Chaudhuri

Development Editor

Ved Prakash Jha

Technical Editors

Akshara Aware

Rashmi Balachandran

Code Testing

Rashmi Balachandran

Copy Editing

Sumathi Sridhar

Editorial Team Leader

Mithil Kulkarni

Project Manager

Abhijeet Deobhakta

Project Coordinator

Lata Basantani

Indexer

Monica Ajmera

Proofreaders

Chris Smith

Camille Guy

Production Coordinator

Shantanu Zagade

Cover Work

Shantanu Zagade

About the Author

Deepak Vohra is a consultant and a principal member of the NuBean software company. Deepak is a Sun Certified Java Programmer and Web Component Developer, and has worked in the fields of XML and Java programming and J2EE for over five years. Deepak is the co-author of the APress book, *Pro XML Development with Java Technology* and was the technical reviewer for the OReilly book, *WebLogic: The Definitive Guide*. Deepak was also the technical reviewer for the Course PTR book, *Ruby Programming for the Absolute Beginner*, and the technical editor for the Manning Publications book, *Prototype and Scriptaculous in Action*.

About the Reviewer

Frank Nimphius is a Principal Product Manager for application development tools at Oracle Corporation since 1999. Working from Germany, Frank actively contributes to the development of Oracle JDeveloper and the Oracle Application Development Framework (ADF). As a conference speaker, Frank represents the Oracle J2EE development team at J2EE conferences world wide, including various Oracle user groups and the Oracle Open World conference

Table of Contents

Preface

Data retrieval and storage are one of the most common components of J2EE applications. JDBC (Java DataBase Connectivity) is the Java API for accessing a Structured Query Language (SQL) relational database and adding, retrieving, and updating data in the database. JDBC 3.0 specification is the current specification implemented by most application servers. JDBC 4.0 specification became available in December 2006, but is not yet implemented by most application servers such as Oracle Application Server, WebLogic Server, JBoss Application Server, and WebSphere Application Server.

To connect with a SQL relational database, a JDBC driver is required; and most databases provide a JDBC 4.0 driver. We will use the Oracle JDeveloper 10.1.3 IDE to develop most of the J2EE applications in the book. We have chosen JDeveloper, because it includes an embedded J2EE server, the Oracle Containers for J2EE (OC4J) server, to run J2EE applications. JDeveloper also provides built-in support to connect to any of the commonly used application servers such as Oracle Application Server, WebLogic Server, JBoss Application Server, Tomcat server, and WebSphere Application Server and deploy applications to these servers. Another advantage of using JDeveloper is that JDeveloper provides built-in support for JDBC. JDeveloper also provides support for JSF; JSF user-interface components may be selected from a component palette and added to a J2EE application.

What This Book Covers

In *Chapter 1* we discuss the JDBC 4.0 specification. We discuss the commonly used interfaces and classes in the JDBC API. We also discuss the new features in JDBC 4.0 specification.

In *Chapter* 2 we configure JDBC in JDeveloper IDE. JDeveloper provides a built-in library for the Oracle database and may be configured with third-party databases also. We connect to MySQL database using the JDBC 4.0 driver for MySQL. We also discuss connection pooling and data sources and the new connection pooling and statement pooling features in JDBC 4.0. We run a web application in the embedded OC4J server to connect with the MySQL database and retrieve and display data from the database.

In *Chapter 3* we discuss the JavaServer Pages Standard Tag Library (JSTL) SQL tags. JDeveloper 10.1.3 provides a Component Palette for JSTL SQL tags. We create a database table, add data to the database table, update the database table, and query the database table, all with the JSTL SQL tag library.

In *Chapter 4*, we discuss configuring JDBC in JBoss Application Server, one of the most commonly used open-source J2EE application server. We develop a web application to connect to MySQL database, and retrieve and display data from the database, in JDeveloper and deploy the web application to JBoss server. We also discuss the JDBC 4.0 version of the web application. We configure data sources in JBoss with Oracle database, MySQL database, DB2 database, PostgreSQL database, and SQL Server.

In *Chapter 5* we configure JDBC in BEA's WebLogic Server 9.x. WebLogic Server 9 provides some new JDBC features such as additional connection pool properties, which improve data source performance, and support for multi-data sources. We configure a data source with Oracle database. We also develop a web application to retrieve and display data from Oracle database in JDeveloper and deploy the web application to WebLogic server. We also discuss the JDBC 4.0 version of the web application.

In *Chapter 6* we configure JDBC in IBM's WebSphere application server. WebSphere has a built-in support to configure a JDBC Provider and data source with commonly used databases. We configure a JDBC Provider and data source with IBM's DB2 UDB database. We also develop a web application in JDeveloper to connect with IBM's DB2 UDB database and retrieve and display data from the database. We run the web application in WebSphere Application Server. We also discuss the JDBC 4.0 version of the web application.

In *Chapter 7*, we discuss Oracle's XML SQL Utility (XSU) to map an XML document to a database table and map a database table to an XML document. We also update and delete data in the database using the XML SQL Utility. We develop the XSU application in JDeveloper using the JDBC 4.0 driver for Oracle database.

In *Chapter 8*, we discuss the XSQL Pages Publishing Framework support in JDeveloper 10.1.3. We generate an XML document using an SQL query with XSQL. We also transform the output from an XSQL query using Extensible Stylesheet Language Transformations (XSLT). We also discuss the JDBC 4.0 features that may be availed of in a XSQL application.

In *Chapter 9*, we discuss Oracle JDBC's implementation of a new feature in JDBC 3.0 specification, Web RowSet. A Web RowSet object is an XML representation of a RowSet, which is a container for ResultSet data that may operate without being connected to the data source. Oracle Web RowSet is Oracle database 10g driver's implementation of Web RowSet. We develop an Oracle Web RowSet web application in JDeveloper to create, read, update, and delete a row in Oracle database. We also discuss the JDBC 4.0 version of the Oracle Web RowSet web application.

In *Chapter 10* we create a JSF Data Table from Oracle database in JDeveloper. We display database data in a JSF data table using a static SQL query and a dynamically specified SQL query. We also discuss the JDBC 4.0 version of the JSF application to create a data table.

In *Chapter 11*, we discuss another JSF UI Component, Panel Grid, to display and update database data. We also use JSF validators and converters to convert and validate input data being stored in a database. We develop the JSF Panel Grid application in JDeveloper and also discuss the JDBC 4.0 version of the Panel Grid application.

In *Chapter 12*, we develop a PDF report and an Excel spreadsheet report with JasperReports reporting tool using JDBC to retrieve data for the report from a database. We develop the JasperReports web application in JDeveloper and also discuss the JDBC 4.0 version of the web application.

In *Chapter 13*, we create an Excel spreadsheet from database data using the Apache POI HSSF library. We create the report in JDeveloper using JDeveloper's built-in support to connect with a database. We also discuss the JDBC 4.0 version of the Apache POI application.

In *Chapter 14*, we discuss Business Component for Java (BC4J) layer of Oracle's Application Developer Framework (ADF). Business Components are based on JDBC and consist of view objects, entity objects, and application modules. We develop a web application using the Oracle ADF Model and Business Components API in JDeveloper.

In *Chapter 15*, we discuss Hibernate, an object/relational persistence and query service for Java. We create a database table, add data to the table, retrieve data from the table, update data in the table and delete table data, all using Hibernate. We will develop the Hibernate application in JDeveloper.

Who is This Book for

This book is for J2EE developers. Most J2EE applications have a database component and the book is specially suited for database-based J2EE development.

Conventions

In this book, you will find a number of styles of text that distinguish between different kinds of information. Here are some examples of these styles, and an explanation of their meaning.

There are three styles for code. Code words in text are shown as follows: "A `managed-data-source` element is added to the `data-sources.xml` file."

A block of code will be set as follows:

```
<resource-ref>
 <res-ref-name>jdbc/OracleDataSource</res-ref-name>
 <res-type>javax.sql.DataSource</res-type>
 <res-auth>Container</res-auth>
</resource-ref>
```

Any command-line input and output is written as follows:

```
CREATE TABLE OE.Catalog(Journal VARCHAR(25), Publisher Varchar(25),
  Edition VARCHAR(25), Title Varchar(45), Author Varchar(25));
```

New terms and **important words** are introduced in a bold-type font. Words that you see on the screen, in menus or dialog boxes for example, appear in our text like this: " In the **Create Project** window specify a **Project Name** and click on **Next**".

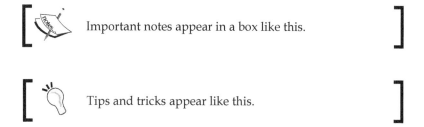

Important notes appear in a box like this.

Tips and tricks appear like this.

Reader Feedback

Feedback from our readers is always welcome. Let us know what you think about this book, what you liked or may have disliked. Reader feedback is important for us to develop titles that you really get the most out of.

To send us general feedback, simply drop an email to feedback@packtpub.com, making sure to mention the book title in the subject of your message.

If there is a book that you need and would like to see us publish, please send us a note in the **SUGGEST A TITLE** form on www.packtpub.com or email suggest@packtpub.com.

If there is a topic that you have expertise in and you are interested in either writing or contributing to a book, see our author guide on www.packtpub.com/authors.

Customer Support

Now that you are the proud owner of a Packt book, we have a number of things to help you to get the most from your purchase.

Downloading the Example Code for the Book

Visit http://www.packtpub.com/files/code/4305_Code.zip to directly download the example code.

The downloadable files contain instructions on how to use them.

Errata

Although we have taken every care to ensure the accuracy of our contents, mistakes do happen. If you find a mistake in one of our books—maybe a mistake in text or code—we would be grateful if you would report this to us. By doing this you can save other readers from frustration, and help to improve subsequent versions of this book. If you find any errata, report them by visiting http://www.packtpub.com/support, selecting your book, clicking on the **Submit Errata** link, and entering the details of your errata. Once your errata are verified, your submission will be accepted and the errata added to the list of existing errata. The existing errata can be viewed by selecting your title from http://www.packtpub.com/support.

Questions

You can contact us at questions@packtpub.com if you are having a problem with some aspect of the book, and we will do our best to address it.

1
JDBC 4.0

The Java Database Connectivity API is used to access a SQL database from a Java application. JDBC also supports tabular data sources, such as a spreadsheet. We will constrain our discussion to SQL relational databases. Using JDBC API, SQL statements can be run in a database. JDBC started as JDBC 1.0 API; JDBC 1.0 covered the basics of establishing a connection with a database, running SQL statements, retrieving values from result sets, and using transactions. JDBC 2.0 introduced scrollable result sets, JDBC methods to update a result set or a database table, batch updates, and SQL3 data types such as, BLOB, CLOB, Array, Ref, and Struct. JDBC 3.0 introduced savepoints, connection pooling of prepared statements, multiple open ResultSet objects, BOOLEAN data type, and an interface for parameter metadata and for retrieving database metadata. JDBC 4.0 specifications added some new features, which we will discuss in this chapter.

The JDBC API provides various interfaces and classes for accessing a database; creating tables in the database; and adding, updating, deleting data, in the database tables. In the following sections, we will discuss some of the JDBC classes and interfaces. We will also discuss the new methods added to these classes or interfaces, in JDBC 4.0 specifications. To run a JDBC 4.0 application, install a RDBMS database such as the open-source MySQL database or the commercial Oracle database. A JDBC driver class is required to establish a connection with the database. JDBC drivers are vendor-specific. A JDBC driver class implements the java.sql.Driver interface.

DriverManager Class

The DriverManager class is used to obtain a connection with a database. A JDBC driver is required to be loaded before obtaining a connection with the database. In JDBC 3.0, a JDBC driver can be loaded either by specifying it in the jdbc.drivers system property, or by using the Class.forName() method. We require invoking the Class.forName() method by loading the Oracle JDBC driver, oracle.jdbc. OracleDriver, using JDBC 3.0.

```
Class.forName("oracle.jdbc.OracleDriver");
```

In JDBC 4.0 specifications, the `DriverManager` class has added support to `getConnection()` and `getDrivers()` methods, for the **Java SE** (Service Provider) mechanism. By using these methods, JDBC drivers may be loaded automatically. The `Class.forName()` method is not required to be invoked. Loading drivers using the Java SE Service Provider mechanism will be discussed in the *Automatic SQL Driver Loading* section.

A JDBC connection is represented by a `java.sql.Connection` object, and may be obtained from a `DriverManager` by calling the overloaded static `getConnection()` methods. The `getConnection()` method is listed in following table:

getConnection() Method	Description
getConnection(String url)	Obtains a connection with the specified database URL.
getConnection(String url, Properties properties)	Username and password may be specified in the Properties Hashtable.
getConnection(String url, String user, String password)	Obtains a connection with a URL username, and password.

For example, a connection with the Oracle database may be obtained as shown below:

```
String url="jdbc:oracle:thin:@localhost:1521:ORCL";
Connection connection = DriverManager.getConnection(url, "oe", "pw");
```

Connection Interface

The `Connection` interface represents a connection with the database. SQL statements may be run in a connection session by using a `Statement` object. A `Connection` object is in `auto-commit` mode, by default. In the `auto-commit` mode, changes are committed to the database after an SQL statement is executed. The `auto-commit` mode can be modified by calling the `setAutoCommit(boolean autoCommit)` method. For example, `auto-commit` may be set to `false`:

```
connection.setAutoCommit(false);
```

If `auto-commit` is set to `false`, it would be required to commit changes by calling the `commit()` method:

```
connection.commit();
```

A `Connection` object can be set to read-only by calling the `setReadOnly()` method:

```
connection.setReadOnly(true);
```

If a `Connection` object is not required, close the connection by calling the `close()` method:

```
connection.close();
```

The following table discusses the methods in JDBC 4.0 that have been added to the `Connection` interface.

Method	Description
`createArrayOf()`	Creates a java.sql.Array object. java.sql.Array is the Java mapping for the SQL data type, ARRAY. The SQL3 data type ARRAY stores an array in a column.
`createBlob()`	Creates a Blob object.
`createClob()`	Creates a Clob object.
`createNClob()`	Creates an NClob object.
`createSQLXML()`	Creates a SQLXML object.
`createStruct()`	Creates a Struct object.
`isValid()`	Tests the validity of a connection.
`getClientInfo()`	Overloaded method returns a client info property, or a list of client info properties. Client info represents information, such as user name and application name about the client.
`setClientInfo()`	Overloaded method sets client info.

Transactions

A transaction is a group of one or more statements run as a unit. If the default value of `auto-commit` is set to `true`, then each `Statement` that would be run represents a transaction. After each statement is run, changes to the database are made with the `auto-commit` set to `true`. Set the `auto-commit` to false, if a developer requires a group of statements to be run together. Changes to the database are not made till each of the statement has run. If `auto-commit` is set to `false`, the changes to the database are committed with the `commit()` method. The `commit()` method commits the SQL statements run after the previous commit to the database was made. The group of statements run between two consecutive commits to the database represents a transaction. The `rollback()` method rolls back the changes made in the current transaction. A transaction may be required to be rolled back, if an error or a `SQLException` is generated.

```
connection.rollback();
```

While one transaction is modifying a database table, another transaction could be reading from the same table. The type of read can be dirty-read, a non-repeatable read, or a phantom read. A dirty-read occurs when a row has been modified by a transaction, but has not been committed, and is being read by a different transaction. If the transaction that modifies the row rolls back the transaction, then the value retrieved by the second transaction would be erroneous. A non-repeatable transaction occurs when one transaction reads a row while the other transaction modifies it. The first transaction re-reads the row obtaining a different value. A phantom read occurs when one transaction retrieves a result set with a WHERE condition, while the other transaction adds a row that meets the WHERE condition. The first transaction re-runs to generate a result set that has an additional row. The default transaction level can be obtained with the getTransactionLevel() method:

```
int transactionLevel=connection. getTransactionIsolation();
```

The different transaction isolation levels are listed in following table:

Transaction Isolation Level	Description
TRANSACTION_NONE	Transactions are not supported.
TRANSACTION_READ_COMMITTED	Dirty-reads cannot be done. Non-repeatable reads and phantom reads can be done.
TRANSACTION_REPEATABLE_READ	Dirty reads and non-repeatable reads cannot be done. Phantom reads can be done.
TRANSACTION_SERIALIZABLE	Dirty-reads, non-repeatable reads and phantom reads cannot be done.

The transaction isolation level can be set with the setTransactionIsolation(int level) method:

```
connection.setTransactionIsolation(level);
```

Savepoint Interface

Savepoint is a new interface in JDBC 3.0 specification. A **Savepoint** is a point within a transaction up to which the changes made in the transaction are rolled back, if the transaction is rolled back with the rollback() method. All changes before the savepoint are implemented when a transaction is rolled back. A savepoint is set with the overloaded setSavepoint() method:

```
Savepoint savepoint=connection.setSavepoint();
Savepoint savepoint=connection.setSavepoint("savepointName");
```

The `getSavepointId()` method returns the savepoint id, and the `getSavepointName()` method returns the savepoint name.

Statement Interface

The `Statement` interface runs SQL statements in a database and returns the result sets. A Statement object is obtained from a `Connection` object with the overloaded `createStatement()` method. Before enumerating the different `createStatement()` methods, we will discuss about the result set type, result set concurrency, and result set holdability. There are three result set types:

1. TYPE_FORWARD_ONLY
2. TYPE_SCROLL_INSENSITIVE
3. TYPE_SCROLL_SENSITIVE

The `TYPE_FORWARD_ONLY` result set is not scrollable. Its cursor moves only in the forward direction. The rows in the result set satisfies the query, either at the time when the query is executed, or when the rows are retrieved.

The `TYPE_SCROLL_INSENSITIVE` result set is scrollable. The rows in the result set do not reflect the changes made in the database. The rows in the result set satisfy the query, either at the time when the query is executed, or when the rows are retrieved.

The `TYPE_SCROLL_SENSITIVE` result set is scrollable, and reflects the changes made to the database while the result set is open.

Result set concurrency specifies the level of updatability. There are two concurrency levels:

1. CONCUR_READ_ONLY
2. CONCUR_UPDATABLE

`CONCUR_READ_ONLY` is the default concurrency level. The `CONCUR_READ_ONLY` concurrency specifies a result set that is not updatable, and `CONCUR_UPDATABLE` concurrency specifies a result set that is updatable.

Holdability specifies that the result set objects are to be kept open when the `commit()` method is invoked. There are two holdability values:

1. HOLD_CURSORS_OVER_COMMIT
2. CLOSE_CURSORS_AT_COMMIT

If `HOLD_CURSORS_OVER_COMMIT` is specified, the result set objects (that is cursors) are kept open after the `commit()` method is called. If `CLOSE_CURSORS_AT_COMMIT` is specified, the result set objects are closed at the `commit()` method.

The different createStatement() methods, which are used to create a Statement object from a Connection object are discussed in following table:

Create Statement Method	Description
createStatement()	A Statement object is created with result set of type TYPE_FORWARD_ONLY, and of concurrency CONCUR_READ_ONLY.
createStatement(int resultSetType, int resultSetConcurrency)	A Statement object is created with the specified result set type and result set concurrency. Implementation dependent, resultSetHoldability is used.
createStatement(int resultSetType, int resultSetConcurrency, int resultSetHoldability)	A Statement object is created with the specified result set type, concurrency, and holdability.

Different execute() methods are available to run an SQL statement that may return multiple results. The execute(String sqlStatement) method runs an SQL statement and returns a boolean, which indicates whether the first result is a ResultSet object, or an update count. If true is returned, the first result is a ResultSet object. If false is returned, the first result is an update count. If the first result is a ResultSet object, then the ResultSet object can be obtained with the getResultSet() method. If the first result is an update count, then the update count can be obtained with the getUpdateCount() method:

```
Statement stmt=connection.createStatement();
boolean resultType=stmt.execute("SQL Statement");
if(resultType==true)
ResultSet resultSet=stmt.getResultSet();
else
int updateCount=stmt.getUpdateCount();
```

Multiple results can be returned by the execute() method. To obtain additional results, invoke the getMoreResults() method. The return value of the getMoreResults() method is similar to that of the execute() method. JDBC 3.0 introduced the getMoreResults(int) method to specify whether the current result set should be closed before opening a new result set. The getMoreResults(int) method parameter value can be CLOSE_ALL_RESULTS, CLOSE_CURRENT_RESULT, or KEEP_CURRENT_RESULT. If the parameter value is CLOSE_ALL_RESULTS, then all the previously opened ResultSet objects would be closed. If the value is CLOSE_CURRENT_RESULT, only the current ResultSet object is closed. If the value is KEEP_CURRENT_RESULT, the current ResultSet object is not closed.

The setQueryTimeout(int) method specifies the timeout, in seconds, for a Statement object to execute. The executeQuery(String sql) executes an SQL query and returns a single ResultSet object. The executeUpdate(String sql) method executes an SQL statement, which is either a **DML** (INSERT, UPDATE, or DELETE) statement or a **DDL** statement. If the SQL string is a DML statement, the executeUpate(String) method returns the number of rows modified. If the SQL string is a DDL statement, the method returns the value, "0". SQL statements can also be run in a batch with the executeBatch() method. Add SQL commands to run a batch with the addBatch(String sql) method:

```
stmt.addBatch("SQL command");
stmt.executeBatch();
```

The executeBatch() method returns an int [] value of update counts. The batch SQL commands can be cleared with the clearBatch() method. If a Statement object is not being used, it is closed automatically. It is recommended to close the Statement object with the close() method:

```
stmt.close();
```

When a Statement object is closed, the database and the JDBC resources associated with that object are also closed. Further, the ResultSet object associated with the Statement object is also closed.

In JDBC 4.0, the new methods discussed in following table have been added to the Statement interface:

Method	Description
isClosed()	Tests, if the Statement object has been closed.
isPoolable()	Tests, if the Statement object is poolable.
setPoolable()	Sets the Statement object as poolable. By default, a Statement object is not set to poolable. The method is only a hint to the statement pooling implementation. Statement pooling provides a better management for statement pooling resources.

ResultSet Interface

A `ResultSet` is a table of data, which is a database result set. The result set types, concurrency and holdability were discussed in the previous section. A `ResultSet` object can be created to scroll, update, and keep the cursors open, when a commit is done:

```
Statement stmt=connection.createStatement(
     ResultSet.TYPE_SCROLL_INSENSITIVE, ResultSet.CONCUR_UPDATABLE,
     ResultSet.HOLD_CURSORS_OVER_COMMIT);
ResultSet rs=stmt.execute("sql");
```

A `ResultSet` has a cursor, which points to the current row. Initially, the cursor points before the first row. The `next()` method moves the cursor to the next row. The `previous()` method shifts the cursor to the previous row. The `ResultSet` interface provides different methods to position the cursor. If the `ResultSet` is scrollable, then the result set type is TYPE_SCROLL_INSENSITIVE, or TYPE_SCROLL_SENSITIVE and the cursor can be shifted to a specified position. Some of the methods to position a `ResultSet` cursor are listed in following table:

ResultSet Method	Description
absolute(int row)	Positions the cursor to the specified row. Index for the First row is 1. If the index is a –ve number, then the cursor is positioned with respect to the end of the result set. –1 index, positions the cursor to the last row. If the index is more than the number of rows in the ResultSet, then the cursor is positioned at the end of the ResultSet. If the –ve index is less than the number of rows, then the cursor is positioned before the first row. The method returns the value as true, if the cursor is in the ResultSet.
afterLast()	Positions the cursor after the last row.
beforeFirst()	Positions the cursor before the first row. SQLException is generated, if the ResultSet is TYPE_FORWARD_ONLY
first()	Positions the cursor on the first row in the ResultSet. Returns the value as true, if cursor is on a valid row.
last()	Positions the cursor on the last row in the ResultSet.
relative(int rows)	Positions the cursor to a relative number of rows from the current row. If the relative position is before or after the current row, the cursor is positioned before or after the current row.

For an updatable result set, the method `moveToInsertRow()` moves the cursor to the insert row, which is a buffer, to insert a new row. The cursor can be shifted back to the current row with the method, `moveToCurrentRow()`. The `ResultSet` interface has methods, which are used to obtain the position of the cursor, and are listed in following table:

Method Name	Description
`isAfterLast()`	Returns true, if the cursor's position is after the last row.
`isFirst()`	Returns true, if the cursor's position is in the first row.
`isLast()`	Returns true, if the cursor's position is in the last row.
`isBeforeFirst()`	Returns true, if the cursor's position is before the first row.

The `ResultSet` column values are obtained with the help of getter methods. The `ResultSet` interface has a 'getter' method for each of the Java data types that map to the database data type. If the database data type is mappable to the Java data type, the Java data type is returned. A getter method with a column index position and column name are included for each of the data types. The getter method with the column index position is more efficient. An `int` column value is retrieved with the index position, and a `String` column value is retrieved with the column name as follows:

```
ResultSet rs;
Int intColumnValue=rs.getInt(1);
String stringColumnValue=rs.getString("column name");
```

The `ResultSet` interface has updater methods to update column values in a row. An 'updater' method is included for each of the Java data types that map to the database data type. If the `ResultSet` is updatable, then the column values in a row can be updated, or a new row can be added. To update a row, move the cursor to the row to be updated. For example, shift the cursor to the tenth row. Update a column value with an updater method. For example, update a `String` column, `column1` to the value `col1val`. Also update the row in the database:

```
rs.absolue(10);
rs.updateString("column1", "col1val");
rs.updateRow();
```

The method `updateRow()` updates the database. To add a new row, shift the cursor to the insert row with the `moveToInsertRow()` method. Add column values with the updater methods, and insert a row in the database with the `insertRow()` method. Shift the cursor to the current row with the `moveToCurrentRow()` method:

```
rs.moveToInsertRow();
rs.updateString(1, "JDBC4.0");
rs.updateInt(2,16);
```

```
rs.updateBoolean(3, true);
rs.insertRow();
rs.moveToCurrentRow();
```

The current row in a `ResultSet` can be deleted with the `deleteRow()` method. A `ResultSet` object is automatically closed and the associated resources are released when the `Statement` object that had created the `ResultSet` object is being closed. However, it is recommended to close the `ResultSet` object using the `close()` method.

```
rs.close();
```

In JDBC 4.0, the methods discussed in following table have been added to the `ResultSet` interface:

Method	Description
getHoldability()	Returns the holdability of the ResultSet object.
getRowId()	Overloaded method returns the row id of the specified column.
updateRowId()	Overloaded method updates the row id for the specified RowId of an object.
getNClob()	Overloaded method returns the specified column as an NClob object.
isClosed()	Returns a Boolean value to indicate if the ResultSet object is closed.
getNString()	Overloaded method returns the specified column as a String object, which is used with NCHAR, NVARCHAR and LONGNVARCHAR columns.
getNCharacterStream()	Overloaded method returns the specified column value as a java.io.Reader object, which is used with NCHAR, NVARCHAR and LONGNVARCHAR columns.
updateNString()	Overloaded method updates the specified column with the specified String value, which is used with NCHAR, NVARCHAR and LONGNVARCHAR columns.
updateNCharacterStream()	Overloaded method updates the specified column with the specified character stream, and the specified String value. It is used with NCHAR, NVARCHAR and LONGNVARCHAR columns.
getSQLXML()	Overloaded method returns the specified column as an SQLXML object. SQLXML Java data type is discussed in a later section, in this chapter.
updateSQLXML()	Overloaded method updates the specified column with the specified SQLXML value.
updateNClob()	Overloaded method updates the specified column with the specified Reader object.

The `updateObject()` method in the `ResultSet` interface has been modified to support the new data types, `NClob` and `SQLXML` in JDBC 4.0. The updater methods in the table do not update the underlying database. To update the database, the `insertRow()` or `updateRow()` method is required to be invoked.

PreparedStatement Interface

A `PreparedStatement` object represents a precompiled SQL statement. The `PreparedStatement` interface extends the `Statement` interface. The precompiled SQL statement has `IN` parameters for which values are being set with the setter methods of the `PreparedStatement` interface. A 'setter' method is included for each of the Java data types that map to a SQL data type. The JDBC driver converts the Java data type to an SQL data type. The `IN` parameter values are set with parameter index. For example, update a `Catalog` table with the following definition using `PreparedStatement`:

```
CatalogId NUMBER
Journal VARCHAR(255)
Publisher VARCHAR(255)
Title VARCHAR(255)
Author VARCHAR(255)
```

Set `Publisher` column value to `Oracle Publishing`, and `Journal` column values to `Oracle Magazine`, where `CatalogId` is 1, referred to the code below:

```
PreparedStatement pstmt = connection.prepareStatement("UPDATE CATALOG
SET Journal=? AND Publisher=? WHERE CatalogId=?");
pstmt.setString(1, "Oracle Magazine");
pstmt.setString(2, "Oracle Publishing");
pstmt.setInt(3, 1);
pstmt.executeUpdate();
```

If the database supports statement pooling, `PreparedStatement` objects are pooled by default. In JDBC 4.0, the methods discussed in the following table have been added to the `PreparedStatement` interface:

Method	Description
`setRowId()`	Sets the specified parameter to the specified RowId value. The driver converts the value to the SQL type ROWID.
`setNString()`	Sets the specified parameter to the specified String value. The driver converts the value to NCHAR, NVARCHAR, or LONGNVARCHAR SQL date type.

Method	Description
setNClob()	Overloaded method sets the specified parameter to the specified NClob object or Reader object. The driver converts the value to SQL type NCLOB.
setNCharacterStream()	Overloaded method sets the specified parameter to the specified Reader object.
setSQLXML()	Sets the specified parameter to the specified SQLXML value. The driver converts the value to the SQL type XML.

Database Metadata

Different RDBMS databases in combination with the database-specific JDBC drivers usually support, and implement features differently. It also supports different SQL data types. An application that is used with different databases would be required to obtain database-specific information. For example, an application could be required to retrieve information about all the SQL data types, which are being supported with a database. An application that implements batch updates would be required to find out if a database supports batch updates. The DatabaseMetaData interface represents the database metadata. The database metadata is obtained from the Connection object:

```
DatabaseMetaData metadata = currentConnection.getMetaData();
```

The SQL data type supported by a database can be obtained using the getTypeInfo() method:

```
ResultSet resultSet=metadata.getTypeInfo();
```

To find out if a database supports batch update, invoke the supportsBatchUpdates() method:

```
metadata.supportsBatchUpdates();
```

To find out if a database supports transactions, invoke the supportsTransactions() method, and to find out if a database supports savepoints, invoke the supportsSavepoints() method:

```
metadata.supportsTransactions();
metadata.supportsSavepoints();
```

Support for a ResultSet type can be checked using the supportsResultSetType() method, while support for a concurrency type, in combination with a result set type, can be checked with the supportsResultSetConcurrency() method. Support for a result set holdability can be checked with the supportsResultSetHoldability() method:

```
metadata.supportsResultSetType(ResultSet.TYPE_SCROLL_INSENSITIVE);
metadata.supportsResultSetConcurrency(ResultSet.
    TYPE_SCROLL_INSENSITIVE, ResultSet.CONCUR_UPDATABLE);
metadata.supportsResultSetHoldability(ResultSet.
    CLOSE_CURSORS_AT_COMMIT);
```

The database metadata also includes information about the different SQL clauses supported by the database. Support for the GROUP BY clause is checked with the supportsGroupBy() method; support for SELECT FOR UPDATE is checked with the supportsSelectForUpdate() method; support for UNION clause is checked with the supportsUnion() method; support for ALTER TABLE with add column is checked with the supportsAlterTableWithAddColumn() method; and support for mixed case SQL identifiers is checked with the storesMixedCaseIdentifiers() method. Also, the maximum number of columns that can be specified in a SELECT statement is obtained with the getMaxColumnsInSelect() method.

The database metadata also provides information about the JDBC driver and the database. The database product name, the database major version, the driver major version, the driver name, the driver version, and the JDBC major version supported by the driver are obtained as follows:

```
String database=metadata.getDatabaseProductName();
int databaseMajorVersion=metadata.getDatabaseMajorVersion();
int driverMajorVersion=metadata.getDriverMajorVersion();
String driverName=metadata.getDriverName();
int driverVersion=metadata.getDriverVersion();
int jdbcMajorVersion=metadata.getJDBCMajorVersion();
```

Metadata about a database table is obtained with the getTables(String catalog, String schemaPattern, String tableNamePattern, String[] types) method. The parameter, catalog, is a catalog name in the database. SchemaPattern is the Schema pattern. TableNamePattern is the table name pattern and the types represents the table type. Table types include TABLE, VIEW, SYSTEM TABLE, GLOBAL TEMPERORY, LOCAL TEMPERORY, ALIAS, and SYNONYM. Obtain all the tables of type, TABLE:

```
String[] names = {"TABLE"};
ResultSet tables = metadata.getTables(null,"%", "%", names);
```

Obtain the table name and table schema from the table's metadata:

```
while (tables.next()) {
  String tableName = tables.getString("TABLE_NAME");
  String tableSchema = tables.getString("TABLE_SCHEM");
}
```

Metadata about the columns can be obtained with the `getColumns(String catalog,String schemaPattern,String tableNamePattern,String columnNamePattern)` method. Obtain the column's metadata for the table name obtained from the table's metadata:

```
ResultSet columns = metadata.getColumns(null, "%", tableName, "%");
```

Obtain the column name, column type, column size, and column nullable:

```
while (columns.next()) {
    String columnName = columns.getString("COLUMN_NAME");
    String datatype = columns.getString("TYPE_NAME");
    int datasize = columns.getInt("COLUMN_SIZE");
    int nullable = columns.getInt("NULLABLE");
}
```

The procedures in the database can be obtained from the `getProcedures(String catalog,String schemaPattern, String procedureNamePattern)` method:

```
ResultSet procedures=metadata.getProcedures(null,"%", "%");
```

Obtain the procedure name, procedure type, and procedure schema:

```
while (procedures.next())
{
  String procedureName = procedures.getString("PROCEDURE_NAME");
  String procedureSchema = procedures.getString("PROCEDURE_SCHEM");
  String procedureType = procedures.getString("PROCEDURE_TYPE");
}
```

In JDBC 4.0, the methods discussed in the following table have been added to the `DatabaseMetaData` interface:

Method	Description
`getRowIdLifetime()`	Indicates if the database supports SQL data type ROWID, and the duration for which a RowId object is valid. The value returned is one of the following:
	RowIdLifetime.ROWID_UNSUPPORTED.
	RowIdLifetime.ROWID_VALID_OTHER.
	RowIdLifetime.ROWID_VALID_SESSION.
	RowIdLifetime.ROWID_VALID_TRANSACTION.
	RowIdLifetime.ROWID_VALID_FOREVER.

Method	Description
autoCommitFailureClosesAllResultSets()	Indicates if all the ResultSets are closed, and if an SQLException is generated for an autocommit that was set as true.
getFunctions()	Retrieves a ResultSet of system and user functions in the specified catalog.
	Functions and Procedures are outside the scope of this book.
getFunctionColumns()	Retrieves a ResultSet of the system and the user parameters for a specified catalog.
getClientInfoProperties()	Retrieves a ResultSet of the client info properties supported by the JDBC driver.
supportsStoredFunctionsUsingCallSyntax()	Indicates if the database supports the invoking functions using the CALL syntax.

The getSchemas() method in the DatabaseMetaData interface has been overloaded to support a catalog name and a schema pattern.

JDBC Exceptions

SQLException is the main Exception that is generated in a JDBC application. The detail of an SQL exception can be obtained from an SQLException object using the SQLException methods, some of which are discussed in following table:

Method	Description
getMessage()	Returns a textual description of the error.
getSQLState()	Returns a SQLState for the SQLException.
getErrorCode()	Returns the implementation-specific error code for the SQLException object.
getCause()	Returns the cause of the SQLException or null, if the cause is not specified or not known.
getNextException()	Returns an exception chained to the SQLException. All the chained exceptions can be retrieved by invoking the getNextException() method recursively. Returns null, if no chained exception occurs.
getMessage()	Returns a textual description of the error.

When an SQLException occurs, it is likely that one or more SQLExceptions chained to it, have also occurred. The chained exceptions can be retrieved by invoking the getNextException() method recursively, until the method returns null. The cause of an SQLException can be retrieved using the getCause() method. The chained causes can be also be retrieved by invoking the getCause() method recursively, until the value, null, is returned.

If SQLException is generated output the exception message using the getMessage() method, output the exception causes using the getCause() method recursively, and retrieve exceptions chained to the exception using the getNextException() method recursively:

```
catch(SQLException e)
{
 while(e != null)
 {
  System.out.println("SQLException Message:" + e.getMessage());
  Throwable t = e.getCause();
  while(t != null)
  {
   System.out.println("SQLException Cause:" + t);
   t = t.getCause();
  }
  e = e.getNextException();
 }
}
```

Some of the subclasses in the SQLException class are listed in following table:

SQLException	Description
javax.sql.rowset.RowSetWarning	Database warning on a RowSet object.
javax.sql.rowset.serial.SerialException	Indicates an error in the serialization and de-serialization of SQL types such as: BLOB, CLOB, STRUCT, ARRAY.
Java.sql.SQLWarning	Database access warning.
Java.sql.DataTruncation	Indicates data truncation.
Java.sql.BatchUpdateException	Represents an error in a batch update operation.

JDBC 4.0 has added support for categorization of SQLExceptions and enhanced support for chained SQLExceptions, which we will discuss in a later section.

New Features in JDBC 4.0

JDBC 4.0 specification was made available in December 2006. Most databases provide at least a partial support for the JDBC 4.0 specification, in their JDBC drivers. JDBC 4.0 specification is implemented in JDK 6.0. Some of the new features of JDBC 4.0 specification, and the database support for JDBC 4.0 specification are discussed in the following sections.

Automatic SQL Driver Loading

JDBC 4.0 has facilitated the loading of a JDBC driver. In JDBC 3.0, a JDBC driver is loaded with the `Class.forName(String)` method. The Oracle JDBC driver is loaded in the following manner:

```
Class.forName("oracle.jdbc.OracleDriver");
```

In JDBC 4.0, a JDBC driver is loaded automatically with the Java **Standard Edition Service Provider** mechanism. The JDBC driver is loaded when the `java.sql.DriverManager.getConnection()` method is invoked. To load a JDBC driver with the Service Provider mechanism, JDBC 4.0 drivers should include the `META-INF/services/java.sql.Driver` file. In the `java.sql.Driver` file, specify the JDBC driver class to load. If the `oracle.jdbc.OracleDriver` is to be loaded then specify the following line in the `java.sql.Driver` file:

```
oracle.jdbc.OracleDriver
```

Multiple driver classes can be specified in a `java.sql.Driver` file, each on a separate line. A list of JDBC drivers available to a `DriverManager` can be obtained with the `getDrivers()` method:

```
Enumeration<Driver> drivers=DriverManager.getDrivers();
```

A JDBC connection can be obtained using the `getConnection()` method of the `DriverManager` class:

```
String url="jdbc:oracle:thin:@localhost:1521:ORCL";
Connection connection = DriverManager.getConnection(url,"oe", "pw");
```

Enhanced Data Type Support

JDBC 4.0 has added support for some new SQL data types. The `ROWID` SQL data type, which identifies a row in a table, is mapped to the `java.sql.RowId` Java data type. The Reader method, `readRowId()` has been added to the `SQLInput` interface, and the writer method, `writeRowId()`, has been added to the `SQLOutput` interface to read, and write `ROWID` values.

In JDBC 3.0, JDBC drivers supported only Unicode character set. SQL: 2003 standard has added support for SQL types, NCAHR, NVARCHAR, LONGVARCHAR, and NCLOB in which values are encoded using the **National Character Set (NCS)**. The National Character Set SQL data type values were converted to the Unicode Character Set values with a JDBC 3.0 driver. The NCS data types can be more suitable if extensive character processing operations are required. Support for National Character Set database data types, NCHAR, NVARCHAR, LONGNVARCHAR, and NCLOB have been added in JDBC 4.0.

Setter methods, setNString(), setNCharacterStream(), and setNClob() have been added to the PreparedStatement and CallableStatement interfaces. Getter method, getNString(), getNCharacterStream(), and getNClob() have been added to the CallableStatement and ResultSet interfaces. Updater methods, updateNString(), updateNCharacterStream(), and updateNClob() have been added to the ResultSet interface. To create a NClob object, createNClob() method has been added to the Connection interface. Reader methods, readNString() and readNClob() have been added to the SQLInput interface to read the NCHAR, NVARCHAR, LONGNVARCHAR, and NCLOB values. Writer methods, writeNClob() and writeNString() have been added to the SQLOutput interface to write the NCHAR, NVARCHAR, LONGNVARCHAR, and NCLOB values.

In JDBC 4.0, support for BLOB and CLOB SQL data types have been enhanced. To create java.sql.Blob and java.sql.Clob objects, methods such as createBlob() and createClob() have been added to the Connection interface. In the PreparedStatement and CallableStatement interfaces, setBlob() method has been overloaded to set the Blob values from an InputStream, and setClob() method has been overloaded to set the Clob values from a Reader. In the ResultSet interface, the updater method, updateBlob(), has been overloaded to update a column from an InputStream and the updater method, updateClob(), has been overloaded to update a column from a Reader. To free resources in Blob and Clob objects, a method, free(), has been added to the Blob and Clob interfaces.

The setAsciiStream, setBinaryStream, and setCharacterStream methods in the CallableStatement and PreparedStatement interfaces have been overloaded. These interfaces have been overloaded to support the length parameter of type long in addition to the length parameter of type int. The length parameter specifies the length in bytes or characters of the InputStream or Reader object. Also, the setAsciiStream, setBinaryStream, and setCharacterStream methods in the CallableStatement and PreparedStatement interfaces have been overloaded with versions without the length parameter.

The setBlob() method in the CallableStatement and PreparedStatement interfaces has been overloaded with the other two methods to set parameter values from the InputStream object, one with a length parameter for the length of the binary stream, and the other without a length parameter. If the InputStream length does not match the specified length, an SQLException is generated. The setClob() method in the CallableStatement and PreparedStatement interfaces has been overloaded with other two methods to set parameter values from the Reader object, one with a length parameter for the number of characters in the Reader object and the other without a length parameter.

If the number of characters in the Reader object does not match the specified length, an SQLEception is generated. Similar to the setter methods in the PreparedStatement/CallableStatement, the updateAsciiStream, updateBinaryStream, updateBlob, updateCharacterStream, and updateClob methods in the ResultSet interface have been overloaded. Unlike the setBlob and setClob methods of the PreparedStatement and CallableStatement interfaces, the updateBlob and updateClob methods of the ResultSet interface do not generate an SQLException, if the InputStream/Reader length does not match the specified length.

SQL: 2003 XML Data Type Support

The SQL: 2003 standard supports a new data type, XML, for storing XML documents. With the XML data type, an XML document can be stored in a database table column similar to the other data types. JDBC 4.0 supports the SQL: 2003 standard. The java. sql.SQLXML object is the Java mapping for the database type, XML. Prior to the SQLXML Java data type, an XML type column value could be retrieved only as a String or CLOB, which did not include the functionality to access different nodes in an XML document.

An XML type database column can be mapped to a Java data type with the help of SQLXML data type. In JDBC 4.0 specification, a java.sql.Connection object has the provision to create an SQLXML object that initially does not have any data. The data can be added with the setString() method or the setBinaryStream(), setCharacterStream(),and setResult() methods. An SQLXML object can be retrieved from a ResultSet or a CallableStatement by using the overloaded getSQLXML() method. The data in an SQLXML object can be retrieved by using the getString() method or the getBinaryStream(), getCharacterStream(), and getSource() methods. An SQLXML object can be stored in a database table column of type XML, which is similar to any other data type using the setSQLXML() method of the PreparedStatement interface.

SQL Server 2005 EXPRESS supports the XML data type whereas, SQL Server 2000 does not. IBM's DB2 UDB V 9 also supports the XML data type. To find out if a database supports the XML data type, obtain the database metadata from the Connection object:

```
DatabaseMetaData metadata= connection.getMetaData();
```

The data types are supported with the `getTypeInfo()` method, as shown below:

```
ResultSet rs=metadata.getTypeInfo();
```

Iterate over the data type result set and output the `TYPE_NAME` column, as shown below:

```
System.out.println("TYPE_NAME:"+rs.getString("TYPE_NAME"));
```

For SQL Server 2005 and IBM's DB2 UDB v9, the `XML TYPE_NAME` is output:

TYPE_NAME: XML

In the following subsections, the procedures to create an XML document, store it in a database that supports the `XML` data type, and retrieve it from the database will be discussed.

Generating an XML Document

We will discuss the procedure to create and initialize an `SQLXML` object. Import the `java.sql` package, and the `javax.xml.stream` package:

```
import java.sql.*;
import javax.xml.stream.*;
```

The Java representation of an XML document in a database table is the `SQLXML` object. Create an `SQLXML` object from the Connection object with the `createSQLXML()` method, as shown below:

```
SQLXML sqlXML=connection.createSQLXML();
```

An `SQLXML` object can be initialized using one of the `setString()`, `setBinaryStream()`, `setCharacterStream()`, or `setResult()` methods. An `SQLXML` object can be initiated using the `setResult()` method and the `StAXResult` class. Create an `XMLStreamWriter` object from a `StAXResult` object, as shown below:

```
StAXResult staxResult = sqlXML.setResult(StAXResult.class);
XMLStreamWriter xmlStreamWriter = staxResult.getXMLStreamWriter();
```

The `SQLXML` object becomes non-writable after the `setResult()` method is invoked. Add the start of an XML document with the `writeStartDocument(String,String)` method, as shown below:

```
xmlStreamWriter.writeStartDocument("UTF-8","1.0");
```

The encoding and version of the XML document is specified in the `writeStartDocument` method. Add the start of an element with the `writeStartElement(String localName)` method, as shown below:

```
xmlStreamWriter.writeStartElement("catalog");
```

Add the element attributes by using the `writeAttribute(String localName, String value)` method. Add an element of text by using the `writeCharacters(String text)` method. Each start element would have a corresponding end element tag. Add an end element by using the `writeEndElement()` method. The `writeEndElement()` method does not specify the element name as the `writeStartElement(String)` method:

```
xmlStreamWriter.writeEndElement();
```

Add end of the document by using the `writeEndDocument()` method:

```
xmlStreamWriter.writeEndDocument();
```

A `SQLXML` object can also be initiated using the `SAXResult` class. Create a `SAXResult` object using the `setResult()` method of the `SQLXML` interface. Subsequently, obtain the `ContentHandler` result using the `getHandler()` method:

```
SAXResult saxResult = sqlXML.setResult(SAXResult.class);
ContentHandler contentHandler= saxResult.getHandler();
```

Specify the start of an XML document using the `startDocument()` method:

```
contentHandler.startDocument();
```

Specify the start of an element using the `startElement(String uri,String localName,String qName,Attributes atts)` method in which the parameter `uri` specifies the element namespace, parameter `localName` specifies the element local name, parameter `qName` specifies the element qualified name and parameter `atts` of type `Attributes` specifies the element attributes. An `Attributes` object can be created using the `org.xml.sax.helpers.AttributesImpl` class, which implements the `Attributes` interface. An attribute can be added to the `AttributesImpl` object using the `addAttribute(String uri, String localName, String qName, String type, String value)` method:

```
AttributesImpl.AttributesImpl() attrs=new AttributesImpl();
attrs.addAttribute("","","journal","StringType","OracleMagazine");
contentHandler.startElement("","","catalog",attrs);
```

The end of an element is specified with the `endElement(String uri,String localName,String qName)` method. Also specify the end of the document with the `endDocument()` method:

```
contentHandler.endElement("","","catalog");
contentHandler.endDocument();
```

An `SQLXML` object can also be initiated using the `setCharacterStream()` method. Create a `Writer` object from the `SQLXML` object using the `setCharacterStream()` method. Create a `BufferedReader` object from an input XML file. Read from the `BufferedReader`, and output to the `Writer` object:

```
Writer writer= sqlXML.setCharacterStream();
BufferedReader bufferedReader = new BufferedReader(new FileReader(new
File("C:/catalog.xml")));
String line= null;
while((line = bufferedReader.readLine() != null) {
writer.write(line);
}
```

The `SQLXML` object becomes non-writable after the `setCharacterStream()` method is invoked. An XML document can also be added to an `SQLXML` object with the `setString()` method, as shown below:

```
sqlXML.setString("xmlString");
```

The `SQLXML` object becomes non-writable after invoking the `setString()` method. If the `setString()`, `setBinaryStream()`, `setCharacterStream()`, or `setResult()` method is invoked on an `SQLXML` object that has been previously initiated, a `SQLException` is generated. If any of the `setBinaryStream()`, `setCharacterStream()`, or `setResult()` methods are invoked more than once, a `SQLException` is generated, and the previously returned `InputStream`, `Writer`, or `Result` object is not effected.

Storing an XML Document

The `SQLXML` Java data type is stored in an XML document, just like any other Java data type. Create a database table with an `XML` type column. Run the SQL statement to create a database table, and obtain a `Statement` object from the `Connection` object, as shown below:

```
Statement stmt=connection.createStatement();
```

Create a database table, `Catalog` with an `XML` type column, as shown below:

```
stmt.executeUpdate("CREATE Table Catalog(CatalogId int, Catalog
XML)");
```

Create a `PreparedStatement` object to add values to a database table, as shown in the following listing:

```
PreparedStatement statement=connection.prepareStatement("INSERT INTO
CATALOG(catalogId, catalog) VALUES(?,?)");
```

Set the `int` value with the `setInt()` method and the `SQLXML` value with the `setSQLXML()` method, as shown below:

```
stmt.setInt(1, 1);
stmt.setSQLXML(2, sqlXML);
```

Update the database with the `executeUpdate()` method:

```
stmt.executeUpdate();
```

Retrieving an XML Document

An `XML` database data type row is retrieved as an `SQLXML` Java data type. Create a `PreparedStatement` for a `SELECT` query, as shown below:

```
PreparedStatement stmt=connection.prepareStatement("SELECT * FROM
CATALOG WHERE catalogId=?");
```

Specify the `catalogId` value for which an XML document is to be retrieved:

```
stmt.setInt(1, 1);
```

Obtain a result set with the `executeQuery()` method:

```
ResultSet rs=stmt.executeQuery();
```

Obtain the `SQLXML` object for the `catalog` column of type `XML`, as shown below:

```
SQLXML sqlXML=rs.getSQLXML("Catalog");
```

Output the XML document in the `SQLXML` object by using the `getString()` method:

```
System.out.println(sqlXML.getString());
```

Accessing an XML Document Data

The `XMLStreamReader` interface can be used to read an XML document with an event iterator. An `XMLStreamReader` object is obtained from a `SQLXML` object, as shown below:

```
InputStream binaryStream = sqlXML.getBinaryStream();
XMLInputFactory factory = XMLInputFactory.newInstance();
XMLStreamReader xmlStreamReader = factory.createXMLStreamReader(binar
yStream);
```

The `SQLXML` object becomes non-readable after calling the `getBinaryStream()` method. The next event is obtained by using the `next()` method, as shown below:

```
while(xmlStreamReader.hasNext())
{
  int parseEvent=xmlStreamReader.next();
}
```

The `next()` method returns an `int` value that corresponds to an `XMLStreamConstants` constant, which represents an event type. Some of the return values of the `next()` method are listed in following table:

Event Type	Description
ATTRIBUTE	Specifies an attribute.
CDATA	Specifies a Cdata.
CHARACTERS	Text.
COMMENT	An XML document comment.
NOTATION_DECLARATION	Specifies a notation declaration.
START_DOCUMENT	Specifies the start of a document
START_ELEMENT	Specifies the start of an element.
END_ELEMENT	Specifies the end of an element.
ENTITY_DECLARATION	Specifies an entity declaration.
ENTITY_REFERENCE	Specifies an entity reference.
NAMESPACE	Specifies a namespace declaration.
SPACE	Specifies an ignorable white space.

If the return value is ELEMENT, then the local name, prefix, and namespace can be obtained by using the `getLocalName()`, `getPrefix()`, and `getNamespaceURI()` methods, as shown below:

```
System.out.println("Element Local Name: "+xmlStreamReader.
getLocalName());
System.out.println("Element Prefix: "+xmlStreamReader.getPrefix());
System.out.println("Element Namespace:"+xmlStreamReader.
getNamespaceURI());
```

The attribute count in an element is obtained by using the `getAttributeCount()` method. Iterate over the attributes and obtain the attribute local name by using the `getAttributeLocalName()` method, the attribute value with the `getAttributeValue()` method, the attribute prefix with the `getAttributePrefix()` method, and the attribute namespace with the `getAttributeNamespace()` method:

```
for(int i=0; i<xmlStreamReader.getAttributeCount();i++){
System.out.println("Attribute Prefix:"+xmlStreamReader.
getAttributePrefix(i));
System.out.println("Attribute Namespace:"+xmlStreamReader.getAttribute
Namespace(i));
System.out.println("Attribute Local Name:"+xmlStreamReader.getAttribut
eLocalName(i));
System.out.println("Attribute Value:"+xmlStreamReader.
getAttributeValue(i));
}
```

Support for Wrapper Pattern

Some vendor-specific JDBC resources that provide nonstandard JDBC methods are wrapped for architectural reasons. Such JDBC resources can be unwrapped to access instances with the wrapper pattern. Support for wrapper pattern is implemented in the `Wrapper` interface. With the `Wrapper` interface, resources that are wrapped as proxy classes can be accessed. The objective of the `Wrapper` interface is to provide a standard method to access vendor-specific extensions inside standard JDBC objects, such as, `Connections`, `Statements`, and `ResultSets`. The `Wrapper` interface is extended by the following interfaces:

- java.sql.Connection
- java.sql.DataSource
- java.sql.ResultSet
- java.sql.Statement
- java.sql.DatabaseMetaData
- java.sql.ResultSetMetaData
- java.sql.ParameterMetaData

The `Wrapper` interface provides the methods `isWrapperFor(Class<?>)` and `unwrap(Class<?>)`. The `unwrap()` method takes an interface as a parameter, and returns an `Object` that implements the interface. The object that is returned is either the object found to implement the specified interface, or a proxy for that object. The `isWrapperFor()` method returns a `boolean`. This method is used to find out if an instance implements the specified interface, or if an instance is a wrapper for an object that implements the specified interface. If the object implements the specified interface the value returned is `true`. If the object is a wrapper for the specified interface, the `isWrapperFor()` method is invoked recursively on the wrapped object. If the object does not implement the interface and is not a wrapper for the interface, the value returned is `false`. The `unwrap()` method should be invoked, if the `isWrapperFor()` method returns `true`.

Create an object of type, java.sql.PreparedStatement and check if the object is a wrapper for the Oracle JDBC specific interface, oracle.jdbc. OraclePreparedStatement using the isWrapperFor() method. If the object is a wrapper for the interface, create an instance of the oracle.jdbc. OraclePreparedStatement JDBC interface using the unwrap() method:

```
String url="jdbc:oracle:thin:@localhost:1521:ORCL";
Connection connection = DriverManager.getConnection(url,"oe", "pw");
String sql="INSERT INTO CATALOG(catalogId, journal) VALUES(?,?)"
java.sql.PreparedStatement stmt = connection.prepareStatement(sql);
Class class = Class.forName("oracle.jdbc.OraclePreparedStatement");
if(stmt.isWrapperFor(class))
{
 OraclePreparedStatement ops = (OraclePreparedStatement)stmt.
unwrap(class);
 ops.defineColumnType(2, oracle.jdbc.OracleTypes.VARCHAR,4000);
}
```

Enhancements in SQLException

An error in interaction with the datasource is represented with the SQLException class. JDBC 4.0 has enhanced support for navigation of chained SQLExceptions with the iterator() method in the SQLException class. A chained SQLException is an Exception that is linked with other Exceptions. The iterator() method iterates over the chained exceptions and the chained causes. Chained exceptions can be retrieved and iterated over (without having to invoke the getNextException() and getCause() methods recursively) using the enhanced For-Each loop introduced in J2SE 5. When an SQLException is generated using the For-Each loop, the chained exceptions can be output as shown below:

```
catch(SQLException sqlException)
{
 for(Throwable e : sqlException )
 {
  System.out.println("Error encountered: " + e);
 }
}
```

In JDBC 4.0, four constructors have been added to the SQLException class with the Throwable cause as one of the parameters. The getCause() method can return non-SQLExceptions. In JDBC 4.0, three new categories of SQLExceptions have been added, which are as follows:

- SQLTransientException
- SQLNonTransientException
- SQLRecoverableException

Categorization of the SQLExceptions facilitates the portability of error handling code. SQLTransientException and SQLNonTransientException classes have subclasses, which map to common SQLState class values. SQLState class provides JDBC application's return code information about the most recently executed SQL statement. The return code is sent by the database manager after the completion of each SQL statement. The SQLState class values are defined in the SQL: 2003 specification.

A SQLTransientException indicates that the operation that generates the exception could succeed, if retried. Subclasses of the SQLTransientException class are discussed in following table:

SQLException	SQLState Class Value	Description
SQLTransient ConnectionException.	08	Represents that a connection operation that failed could succeed, if the operation is retried.
SQLTransaction RollbackException.	40	Represents that a current Statement was rolled back.
SQLTimeoutException.	Does not correspond to a standard SQLState.	Represents that a Statement has timed out.

SQLNonTransientException indicates the operation, which generates the exception that will not succeed without the cause of the SQLException being rectified. Subclasses of the SQLNonTransientException are discussed in following table:

SQLException	SQLState Class Value	Description
SQLFeatureNotSupported Exception.	0A	Represents that a JDBC driver does not support a feature.
SQLNonTransientConnection Exception.	08	Represents that a connection operation that failed will not succeed if retried, without the cause of the exception being corrected.
SQLDataException.	22	Represents various data errors including non allowable conversion and division by 0.
SQLIntegrityConstraint ViolationException.	23	Represents an integrity constraint exception.
SQLInvalidAuthorization SpecException.	28	Represents an authorization exception.
SQLSyntaxErrorException.	42	Represents an error in the SQL syntax.

The SQLRecoverableException indicates that the operation that throws the Exception can succeed, if the application performs some recovery steps and retries the entire transaction(or the transaction branch in the case of a distributed transaction). The recovery steps include at the least, closing the current connection and obtaining a new connection.

A new subclass of the SQLException class, SQLClientInfoException, has been added in the JDBC 4.0 specification. The SQLClientInfoException is generated, if one or more client info properties could not be set on a Connection. The SQLClientInfoException also lists the client info properties, which were not set. Some databases that do not allow multiple client info properties to be set atomically can generate the SQLClientInfoException exception after one or more client info properties have been set. The client info properties that were not set can be retrieved by using the getFailedProperties() method.

Connection Management

Connection pooling improves the performance and scalability of the connections by providing a cache of the connections that are reusable across client sessions. Connection pooling reduces the overhead of opening, initializing and closing connections. One of the drawbacks of the connection pooling is that when a connection in a connection pool becomes stale and unusable, the application performance is reduced. JDBC 3.0 specification did not have the provision to track connection state. Connection state tracking has been added to the Connection interface in the JDBC 4.0 to find out if a connection is valid. The isValid(int timeout) method returns true, if the connection is valid. The isValid() method validates a connection with a SQL query, or another mechanism. If a connection is not valid, the connection can be closed, thus reducing the accumulation of unusable connections. The Connection object conn can be closed, if it is not in use:

```
if(!conn.isClosed())
if(!conn.isValid())
conn.close();
```

Connection state tracking and closing of invalid connections are implemented by the connection pool manager. Another drawback of connection pooling has been that one or more connections assigned from a connection pool in a web or application server can bog down an application. JDBC 3.0 does not have the provision to identify the connections that use the excess of CPU time. JDBC 4.0 has added the setClientInfo() and getClientInfo() methods to the Connection interface using which, client specific information can be specified on a Connection object, when a Connection is assigned to an application. Client specification information includes user name and application name. The DatabaseMetaData interface in JDBC 4.0 provides a new method, getClientInfoProperties(). Client info properties supported by a JDBC driver can be obtained using the `getClientInfoProperties()` method. When one or more connections bog down the application, the `getClientInfo()` method can be used to identify which connections could be causing the reduction in performance. Some standard client info properties that a JDBC driver can support are discussed in the following table:

Client Info Property	Description
ApplicationName.	The name of the application that is using the connection.
ClientUser.	The name of the user.
ClientHostname.	The hostname on which the application is running.

Similar to connection pooling, JDBC 4.0 provides `Statement` pooling to reduce the overheads of opening, initiating, and closing `Statement` objects. Frequently used `Statement` objects can be pooled using the `setPoolable(boolean poolable)` method. The `isPoolable()` method is used to check if a `Statement` object is poolable. The `Statement` object, `stmt` can be pooled, if poolable:

```
if(stmt.isPoolable())
stmt.setPoolable(true);
```

Scalar Functions

Most databases support numeric, string, time, date, system, and conversion functions on the scalar values. SQL statements run using the `Statement` object, and can include the scalar functions using the JDBC escape syntax. JDBC 4.0 provides some new scalar function, which are discussed in the following table:

Scalar Function	Description
CHAR_LENGTH CHARACTER_LENGTH	Returns the length of a string expression.
CURRENT_DATE	Returns the current date.
CURRENT_TIME	Returns the current time.
CURRENT_TIMESTAMP	Returns the current timestamp.
EXTRACT	Extracts a field from a datetime value.
OCTET_LENGTH	Returns the length of a string expression in octets (bytes).

JDBC 4.0 support in Oracle Database

Support for JDBC 4.0 specification is a JDBC driver feature, and not a database feature. Oracle Database 11g JDBC drivers support JDBC 4.0 specification. Add the ojdbc6.jar file to the CLASSPATH environment variable to use the JDBC 4.0 features. JDK 6.0 is required for JDBC 4.0 support. Oracle database 11g JDBC drivers can be used with the Oracle database 9i and the later versions. Oracle database 11g JDBC drivers support all the JDBC 4.0 features except the SQLXML Java data type that is used to access the SQL data type XML. Oracle database 11g JDBC drivers support the wrapper pattern to access non-standard Oracle JDBC resources. Oracle extensions to the JDBC are available in the oracle.jdbc package.

The oracle.jdbc.OracleStatement interface can be unwrapped using the unwrap() method to create a oracle.jdbc.OracleStatement object. As the Statement interface extends the Wrapper interface, create a Statement object from a Connection object, conn. Check if the Statement object is a wrapper for the oracle.jdbc.OracleStatement interface using the isWrapperFor() method. Obtain a OracleStatement object from the interface using the unwrap() method to use the methods of the OracleStatement interface:

```
Statement stmt = conn.createStatement();
Class class = Class.forName("oracle.jdbc.OracleStatement");
if(stmt.isWrapperFor(class))
{
 OracleStatement oracleStmt = (OracleStatement)stmt.unwrap(class);
 oracleStmt.defineColumnType(1, Types.NUMBER);
}
```

Oracle database 11g JDBC drivers support the enhanced chained exceptions in the JDBC 4.0 SQLException class. JDBC 4.0 has added a distinction between the permanent errors and transient errors. Permanent errors are errors that occur in the correct operation of the database system and continue to recur, until the cause of the error is removed. Transient errors are errors occurring due to the failure of some segment of the system, or due to timeouts, and these may not recur if the operation that generated the error is retried. Oracle database 11g JDBC drivers support the different categories of SQLException.

Oracle database 11g JDBC drivers support the ROWID SQL data type. Each table in an Oracle database has a ROWID pseudocolumn that identifies a row in a table. The SQL data type of the ROWID column is ROWID. Usually a rowid uniquely identifies a row in a database. But rows in different tables that are stored in a cluster may have the same rowid. Rowids should not be used as the primary key for a database table. If a row is deleted and reinserted using an Import or Export utility, its rowid may get modified. If a row is deleted, its rowid can be assigned to a row added later. The ROWID pseudocolumn can be used in the SELECT and WHERE clauses. Rowid values have the following applications:

1. Rowids are the fastest way to access a row in a database table.

2. Rowids are unique identifiers for rows in a table.

3. Rowids represent how rows are stored in a table.

A ROWID column value can be retrieved using the getter methods in the ResultSet and CallableStatement interfaces. Retrieve the ROWID column value for the current row in a ResultSet object, rs, as shown below:

```
java.sql.RowId rowid=rs.getRowId();
```

A RowId object is valid till the identified row is not deleted. A RowId duration of the validity can be obtained using the getRowIdLifetime() method of the DatabaseMetaData interface. The duration of validity can be one of the int values in the following table:

int Value	Description
ROWID_UNSUPPORTED	Databases do not support the ROWID SQL data type.
ROWID_VALID_TRANSACTION	Valid for the duration of transaction in which it is created.
ROWID_VALID_SESSION	Valid for the duration of a session in which it is created across all transactions.
ROWID_VALID_FOREVER	Valid across all sessions.
ROWID_VALID_OTHER	Validity not known.

A RowId value can be used with a parameterized PreparedStatement to set a parameter value with a RowId object. A RowId value can also be used with an updatable ResultSet to update a column with a RowId object.

Oracle database 11g JDBC drivers support the **National Character Set** (NCS) data types NCHAR, NVARCHAR, LONGNVARCHAR, and NCLOB. Oracle database 11g drivers also support **Large Object data types** (LOBs). The Connection interface provides createBlob, createClob, and createNClob methods to create Blob, Clob, and NClob objects. Create a Blob object as shown below:

```
String url="jdbc:oracle:thin:@localhost:1521:ORCL";
Connection connection = DriverManager.getConnection(url,"oe", "pw");
Blob aBlob = connection.createBlob();
```

The LOB objects created do not contain any data. Data can be added using the setter methods in the Blob, Clob, and NClob interfaces. To add data to the Blob object, obtain an OutputStream object from the Blob object:

```
OutputStream outputStream=aBlob.setBinaryStream(1);
```

LOB objects can be used as input parameters with a `PreparedStatement` object using the `setBlob`, `setClob`, and `setNClob` methods. The `Blob` object created previously can be set as a parameter value on a `PreparedStatement` object, `pstmt`, as follows:

```
pstmt.setBlob(2,aBlob);
```

For an updatable `ResultSet`, the `updateBlob`, `updateClob`, and `updateNClob` methods can be used to update a `Blob`, `Clob`, or `NClob` column value. Update a `ResultSet` object, `rs`, of column type, `BLOB`, with the `Blob` object already created:

```
rs.updateBlob(3,aBlob);
```

`Blob`, `Clob`, and `NClob` data can be retrieved using the `getBlob`, `getClob`, and `getNClob` methods in the `ResultSet` and `CallableStatement` interfaces. Retrieve a `Blob` object corresponding to a `BLOB` column from a `ResultSet` object, `rs`:

```
Blob blob=rs.getBlob(2);
```

Either the entire data in a `Blob` object can be retrieved using the `getBinaryStream()` method, or the partial data in the `Blob` object can be retrieved using the `getBinaryStream(long pos,long length)` method. Here, the parameter, `pos`, specifies the offset position for start of data retrieval and the `length` parameter specifies the length in bytes of the data to be retrieved. Retrieve 100bytes of data from the `Blob` object that was created previously with an offset position of 200:

```
InputStream inputStream = aBlob.getBinaryStream(200, 100);
```

LOBs are valid at least for the duration of the transaction in which it is created. For long running transactions, it can be better to release LOB resources using the `free()` method:

```
aBlob.free();
```

JDBC 4.0 support in MySQL Database

MySQL database server provides support for the JDBC 4.0 specification in the Connector/J 5.1 JDBC drivers. MySQL's Connector/J 5.1 supports the JDBC 4.0 features, listed below:

1. Auto-registration of the JDBC driver with the `DriverManager` via the J2SE Service Provider mechanism.

2. Connection validity check using the `isValid()` method of the `Connection` interface.

3. Categorized `SQLException`s based on recoverability or retry-ability, and class of the underlying error.

4. Unwrapping of MySQL-specific extensions for JDBC.

5. Support for SQLXML. MySQL database does not support the SQL: 2003 SQL data type XML. JDBC 4.0 specification does not specify that the SQL data type to store a SQLXML object is required to be the SQL: 2003 XML data type. MySQL's Connector/J 5.1 JDBC driver supports the SQLXML Java data type.

6. Support for setting per-connection client info using the setClientInfo() method of the Connection interface.

7. Support for National Character Set data types NCHAR, NVARCHAR, LONGNVARCHAR, and NCLOB.

JDBC 4.0 support in IBM's DB2 UDB

IBM Data Server Driver for JDBC and SQLJ Version 4.0 supports the JDBC 4.0 specification. To use the JDBC 4.0 features, add the db2jcc4.jar file to the CLASSPATH environment variable. The JDBC 4.0 driver name is,"IBM Data Server Driver for JDBC and SQLJ" instead of the previous, "IBM DB2 JDBC Universal Driver Architecture". IBM Data Server Driver for JDBC and SQLJ supports most of the JDBC 4.0 features.

JDBC support has been added for the JDBC 4.0 java.sql.RowId interface for updating and retrieving data in ROWID columns. JDBC support has also been added for the java.sql.SQLXML interface for storing, updating, and retrieving data in XML columns. The IBM Data Server Driver for JDBC and SQLJ supports the following client info properties to identify the client connections:

1. ApplicationName
2. ClientAccountingInformation
3. ClientHostname
4. ClientUser

IBM Data Server Driver for JDBC and SQLJ supports the new SQLException subclasses, in the JDBC 4.0 specification. It also supports chained exceptions. The wrapper pattern is supported to access vendor-specific resources. The following IBM Data Server Driver for JDBC and SQLJ-specific interfaces in the com.ibm.db2.jcc package extend the Wrapper interface:

1. DB2Connection
2. DB2BaseDataSource
3. DB2SimpleDataSource
4. DB2Statement

5. DB2ResultSet

6. DB2DatabaseMetaData

Example Connection using a JDBC 4.0 Driver

We will connect with a database using a JDBC 4.0 driver. We will use Java DB as the example database. Java DB is Sun's version of the open-source **Apache Derby** database. Java DB is a lightweight (only 2MB), yet fully transactional, secure, and standards-based component. It also supports the SQL, JDBC, and Java EE standards. Java DB is a 100% Java technology database, and since Java is portable across platforms, Java DB can be run on any platform and its applications can be migrated to other open standard databases. Java DB is packaged with JDK 6. Therefore, all that is required to install Java DB is to install JDK 6. We connect with Java DB database using the JDBC 4.0 driver. Create a Java application, JDBCConnection.java, in a directory, C:/JavaDB, and add the directory to the CLASSPATH system environment variable. Java DB can be started in the embedded mode or as network server. Embedded mode is used to connect to the Java DB from a Java application running in the same JVM as the Java DB database. Java DB as a network server is used to connect with the database from different JVMs across the network. We will start Java DB in embedded mode from the JDBCConnection.java application. We will load the JDBC 4.0 driver automatically using the Java SE Service Provider mechanism. For automatic loading of the JDBC driver, we need to add the Java DB JDBC 4.0 driver JAR file, C:/Program Files/Sun/JavaDB/lib/derby.jar to the CLASSPATH variable. Java DB provides a batch script, setEmbeddedCP.bat in the bin directory to set the CLASSPATH for the embedded mode. Run the setEmbeddedCP script from the directory from which the JDBCConnection.java application is to be run as follows:

```
"C:\Program Files\Sun\JavaDB\bin\setEmbeddedCP.bat"
```

JAR file, derby.jar is added to the CLASSPATH. The derby.jar file includes a directory structure, META-INF/services/, and a file, java.sql.Driver, in the services directory. The java.sql.Driver file specifies the following JDBC driver class for the Java DB that is to be loaded automatically using the Java SE Service Provider mechanism:

```
org.apache.derby.jdbc.AutoloadedDriver
```

In the JDBCConnection.java application, specify the connection URL for the Java DB database. Create a new database instance by specifying the database name, demodb, and the create attribute as, true:

```
String url="jdbc:derby:demodb;create=true";
```

Connect with the Java DB database using the getConnection() method of the DriverManager class:

```
Connection conn = DriverManager.getConnection(url);
```

The DriverManager automatically loads the JDBC 4.0 driver class, org.apache. derby.jdbc.AutoloadedDriver, which is specified in the java.sql.Driver file using the Java SE Service Provider mechanism. The JDBC driver is not required to be loaded using the Class.forName() method using a JDBC 3.0 driver. The JDBCConnection.java application is listed below:

```
import java.sql.*;
public class JDBCConnection
{
 public void connectToDatabase()
 {
  try
  {
   String url="jdbc:derby:demodb;create=true";
   Connection conn = DriverManager.getConnection(url);
   System.out.println("Connection Established");
  }
  catch (SQLException e)
  {
   System.out.println(e.getMessage());
  }
 }
 public static void main(String[] argv)
 {
  JDBCConnection jdbc = new JDBCConnection();
  jdbc.connectToDatabase();
 }
}
```

Other **Relational Database Management Systems** (RDBMS) databases provide a JDBC 4.0 driver that can be connected using the JDBC 4.0 driver, as discussed for the Java DB database. The connection URLs, and JDBC 4.0 drivers for some of the commonly used databases are discussed in following table:

Database	Connection URL	JDBC 4.0 Driver
MySQL (4.1, 5.0, 5.1 and the 6.0 alpha).	`jdbc:mysql:// localhost:3306/test`	MySQL Connector/J 5.1 (`http://dev.mysql.com/ downloads/connector/ j/5.1.html`) META-INF/ services/java.sql.Driver is required to be added to the CLASSPATH as it is not included in the driver JAR file.
Oracle Database (9.01 and later).	`jdbc:oracle:thin:@ localhost:1521:ORCL`	Oracle Database 11g JDBC Driver's (`http://www.oracle.com/ technology/software/tech/ java/sqlj_jdbc/htdocs/ jdbc_111060.html`) java.sql. Driver file is included in the JDBC JAR file, `ojdbc6.jar`.
IBM DB2 for Linux UNIX and Windows.	`jdbc:db2:// localhost:50000/SAMPLE`	IBM Data Server Driver for JDBC and SQLJ version 4.0's (`https:// www14.software.ibm. com/webapp/iwm/web/reg/ download.do?source=swg- informixfpd&S_ PKG=dl&lang=en_US&cp=UTF- 8`) java.sql.Driver file is not included in the JDBC JAR file, `db2jcc4.jar`.
SQL Server Database (MS SQL Server 6.5 - 2005 with all Service Packs).	`jdbc:inetdae7: localhost:1433`	i-net MERLIA JDBC 4.0 driver for MS SQL Database's (`http://www.inetsoftware. de/products/jdbc/mssql/ merlia/`) java.sql.Driver file is not included in the JDBC JAR file, `Merlia.jar`.

Summary

In this chapter, you have been introduced to the JDBC API and the new features in JDBC 4.0 specification. The DriverManager class is used to connect with a database. The Connection interface represents a database connection. The Savepoint interface represents a savepoint in a transaction. This is the point up to which the changes would be rolled back, if the transaction is rolled back. The Statement interface is used to run static SQL statements. The ResultSet interface represents the result set table generated by running SQL statements on a database. The PreparedStatement represents a compiled SQL statement that can be run more than once with different parameters. The DatabaseMetadata interface represents the database metadata, such as, table name, schema name, column name, and column type. The SQLException class represents the database access error or other SQL errors. JDBC 4.0 specification provides some new features to facilitate the development of JDBC applications. Support for new SQL data types has been added. The new features include, automatic SQL Driver loading, SQL: 2003 XML Data Type support, support for wrapper pattern, enhancements in SQLException, and enhanced connection management.

2
Configuring JDBC in Oracle JDeveloper

Oracle JDeveloper is a free **Integrated Development Environment** (IDE) for modeling, developing, debugging, optimizing, and deploying Java applications. JDeveloper 10g is used to develop J2EE applications comprising the JSPs, EJBs, Struts, Servlets, and the Java classes that may require accessing a database table in the Oracle 10g Database, or a third-party database. Unlike **Eclipse**, which requires a plugin, JDeveloper has a built-in provision to establish a JDBC connection with a database. JDeveloper is the only Java IDE with an embedded application server, the Oracle Containers for J2EE (OC4J). This database-based web application may run in JDeveloper without requiring a third-party application server. However, JDeveloper also supports third-party application servers. Starting with JDeveloper 11, application developers may point the IDE to an application server instance (or OC4J instance), including third-party application servers that they want to use for testing during development. JDeveloper provides connection pooling for the efficient use of database connections. A database connection may be used in an ADF BC application, or in a JavaEE application.

A database connection in JDeveloper may be configured in the Connections Navigator. A Connections Navigator connection is available as a `DataSource` registered with a JNDI naming service. The database connection in JDeveloper is a reusable named connection that developers configure once and then use in as many of their projects as they want. Depending on the nature of the project and the database connection, the connection is configured in the **bc4j.xcfg file** or a JavaEE data source. Here, it is necessary to distinguish between data source and `DataSource`. A data source is a source of data; for example an RDBMS database is a data source. A `DataSource` is an interface that represents a factory for JDBC `Connection` objects. JDeveloper uses the term Data Source or data source to refer to a factory for connections. We will also use the term Data Source or data source to refer to a factory for connections, which in the `javax.sql` package is represented by the

DataSource interface. A DataSource object may be created from a data source registered with the JNDI (Java Naming and Directory) naming service using JNDI lookup. A JDBC Connection object may be obtained from a DataSource object using the getConnection method. As an alternative to configuring a connection in the Connections Navigator a data source may also be specified directly in the data source configuration file data-sources.xml. In this chapter we will discuss the procedure to configure a JDBC connection and a JDBC data source in JDeveloper 10g IDE. We will use the MySQL 5.0 database server and MySQL Connector/J 5.1 JDBC driver, which support the JDBC 4.0 specification. In this chapter you will learn the following:

- Creating a database connection in JDeveloper Connections Navigator
- Configuring the Data Source and Connection Pool associated with the connection configured in the Connections Navigator
- The common JDBC Connection Errors
- Creating a Connection Pool and Data Source
- Connecting to a Database from a Web Application
- The JDBC 4.0 Version of the Web Application

Before we create a JDBC connection and a data source we will discuss connection pooling and DataSource.

Connection Pooling and DataSource

The javax.sql package provides the API for server-side database access. The main interfaces in the javax.sql package are DataSource, ConnectionPoolDataSource, and PooledConnection. The DataSource interface represents a factory for connections to a database. In Chapters 1 and 2, we obtained a Connection object using the DriverManager class. DataSource is an alternative and a preferred method of obtaining a JDBC connection. An object that implements the DataSource interface is typically registered with a Java Naming and Directory API-based naming service. DataSource interface implementation is driver-vendor specific. The DataSource interface has three types of implementations:

- **Basic implementation:** In basic implementation there is 1:1 correspondence between a client's Connection object and the connection with the database. This implies that for every Connection object, there is a connection with the database. With the basic implementation, the overhead of opening, initiating, and closing a connection is incurred for each client session.

- **Connection pooling implementation:** A pool of Connection objects is available, from which connections are assigned to the different client sessions. A connection pooling manager implements the connection pooling. When a client session does not require a connection, the connection is returned to the connection pool and becomes available to other clients. Thus, the overheads of opening, initiating, and closing connections are reduced.

- **Distributed transaction implementation:** Distributed transaction implementation produces a Connection object that is mostly used for distributed transactions and is always connection pooled. A transaction manager implements the distributed transactions.

An advantage of using a data source is that code accessing a data source does not have to be modified when an application is migrated to a different application server. Only the data source properties need to be modified. A JDBC driver that is accessed with a DataSource does not register itself with a DriverManager. A DataSource object is created using a JNDI lookup and subsequently a Connection object is created from the DataSource object. For example, if a data source JNDI name is jdbc/OracleDS a DataSource object may be created using JNDI lookup. First, create an InitialContext object and subsequently create a DataSource object using the InitialContext lookup method. From the DataSource object create a Connection object using the getConnection() method:

```
InitialContext ctx=new InitialContext();
DataSource ds=ctx.lookup("jdbc/OracleDS");
Connection conn=ds.getConnection();
```

The JNDI naming service, which we used to create a DataSource object is provided by J2EE application servers such as the Oracle Application Server Containers for J2EE (OC4J) embedded in the JDeveloper IDE.

A connection in a pool of connections is represented by the PooledConnection interface, not the Connection interface. The connection pool manager, typically the application server, maintains a pool of PooledConnection objects. When an application requests a connection using the DataSource.getConnection() method, as we did using the jdbc/OracleDS data source example, the connection pool manager returns a Connection object, which is actually a handle to an object that implements the PooledConnection interface. A ConnectionPoolDataSource object, which is typically registered with a JNDI naming service, represents a collection of PooledConnection objects. The JDBC driver provides an implementation of the ConnectionPoolDataSource, which is used by the application server to build and manage a connection pool. When an application requests a connection, if a suitable PooledConnection object is available in the connection pool, the connection pool manager returns a handle to the PooledConnection object as a Connection object. If a suitable

PooledConnection object is not available, the connection pool manager invokes the getPooledConnection() method of the ConnectionPoolDataSource to create a new PooledConnection object. For example, if connectionPoolDataSource is a ConnectionPoolDataSource object a new PooledConnection gets created as follows:

```
PooledConnection
pooledConnection=connectionPoolDataSource.getPooledConnection();
```

The application does not have to invoke the getPooledConnection() method though; the connection pool manager invokes the getPooledConnection() method and the JDBC driver implementing the ConnectionPoolDataSource creates a new PooledConnection, and returns a handle to it. The connection pool manager returns a Connection object, which is a handle to a PooledConnection object, to the application requesting a connection. When an application closes a Connection object using the close() method, as follows, the connection does not actually get closed.

```
conn.close();
```

The connection handle gets deactivated when an application closes a Connection object with the close() method. The connection pool manager does the deactivation. When an application closes a Connection object with the close() method any client info properties that were set using the setClientInfo method are cleared. The connection pool manager is registered with a PooledConnection object using the addConnectionEventListener() method. When a connection is closed the connection pool manager is notified and the connection pool manager deactivates the handle to the PooledConnection object, and returns the PooledConnection object to the connection pool to be used by another application. The connection pool manager is also notified if a connection has an error. A PooledConnection object is not closed until the connection pool is being reinitialized, the server is shutdown, or a connection becomes unusable.

In addition to connections being pooled, PreparedStatement objects are also pooled by default if the database supports statement pooling. It can be discovered if a database supports statement pooling using the supportsStatementPooling() method of the DatabaseMetaData interface. The PeparedStatement pooling is also managed by the connection pool manager. To be notified of PreparedStatement events such as a PreparedStatement getting closed or a PreparedStatement becoming unusable, a connection pool manager is registered with a PooledConnection manager using the addStatementEventListener() method. A connection pool manager deregisters a PooledConnection object using the removeStatementEventListener() method. Methods addStatementEventListener and removeStatementEventListener are new methods in the PooledConnection interface in JDBC 4.0. Pooling of Statement objects is another new feature in JDBC 4.0. The Statement interface has two new methods in JDBC 4.0 for Statement pooling: isPoolable() and setPoolable().

The `isPoolable` method checks if a `Statement` object is poolable and the `setPoolable` method sets the `Statement` object to poolable. When an application closes a `PreparedStatement` object using the `close()` method the `PreparedStatement` object is not actually closed. The `PreparedStatement` object is returned to the pool of `PreparedStatements`. When the connection pool manager closes a `PooledConnection` object by invoking the `close()` method of `PooledConnection` all the associated statements also get closed. Pooling of `PreparedStatements` provides significant optimization, but if a large number of statements are left open, it may not be an optimal use of resources. Thus, the following procedure is followed to obtain a connection in an application server using a data source:

1. Create a data source with a JNDI name binding to the JNDI naming service.

2. Create an `InitialContext` object and look up the JNDI name of the data source using the `lookup` method to create a `DataSource` object. If the JDBC driver implements the `DataSource` as a connection pool, a connection pool becomes available.

3. Request a connection from the connection pool. The connection pool manager checks if a suitable `PooledConnection` object is available. If a suitable `PooledConnection` object is available, the connection pool manager returns a handle to the `PooledConnection` object as a `Connection` object to the application requesting a connection.

4. If a `PooledConnection` object is not available the connection pool manager invokes the `getPooledConnection()` method of the `ConnectionPoolDataSource`, which is implemented by the JDBC driver.

5. The JDBC driver implementing the `ConnectionPoolDataSource` creates a `PooledConnection` object and returns a handle to it.

6. The connection pool manager returns a handle to the `PooledConnection` object as a `Connection` object to the application requesting a connection.

7. When an application closes a connection, the connection pool manager deactivates the handle to the `PooledConnection` object and returns the `PooledConnection` object to the connection pool.

`ConnectionPoolDataSource` provides some configuration properties to configure a connection pool. The configuration pool properties are not set by the JDBC client, but are implemented or augmented by the connection pool. The properties can be set in a data source configuration. Therefore, it is not for the application itself to change the settings, but for the administrator of the pool, who also happens to be the developer sometimes, to do so. Connection pool properties supported by `ConnectionPoolDataSource` are discussed in following table:

Connection Pool Property	Type	Description
maxStatements	int	Maximum number of statements the pool should keep open. 0 (zero) indicates that statement caching is not enabled.
initialPoolSize	int	The initial number of connections the pool should have at the time of creation.
minPoolSize	int	The minimum number of connections in the pool. 0 (zero) indicates that connections are created as required.
maxPoolSize	int	The maximum number of connections in the connection pool. 0 indicates that there is no maximum limit.
maxIdleTime	int	Maximum duration (in seconds) a connection can be kept open without being used before the connection is closed. 0 (zero) indicates that there is no limit.
propertyCycle	int	The interval in seconds the pool should wait before implementing the current policy defined by the connection pool properties.
maxStatements	int	The maximum number of statements the pool can keep open. 0 (zero) indicates that statement caching is not enabled.

Setting the Environment

Before getting started, we have to install the JDeveloper 10.1.3 IDE and the MySQL 5.0 database. Download JDeveloper from: http://www.oracle.com/technology/ software/products/jdev/index.html. Download the MySQL Connector/J 5.1, the MySQL JDBC driver that supports JDBC 4.0 specification. To install JDeveloper extract the JDeveloper ZIP file to a directory. Log in to the MySQL database and set the database to test. Create a database table, Catalog, which we will use in a web application. The SQL script to create the database table is listed below:

```
CREATE TABLE Catalog(CatalogId VARCHAR(25)
PRIMARY KEY, Journal VARCHAR(25), Publisher VARCHAR(25),
 Edition VARCHAR(25), Title Varchar(45), Author Varchar(25));
INSERT INTO Catalog VALUES('catalog1', 'Oracle Magazine',
 'Oracle Publishing', 'Nov-Dec 2004', 'Database Resource Manager',
'Kimberly Floss');
INSERT INTO Catalog VALUES('catalog2', 'Oracle Magazine', 'Oracle
Publishing', 'Nov-Dec 2004', 'From ADF UIX to JSF', 'Jonas Jacobi');
```

MySQL does not support `ROWID`, for which support has been added in JDBC 4.0. Having installed the JDeveloper IDE, next we will configure a JDBC connection in the **Connections** Navigator. Select the **Connections** tab and right-click on the **Database** node to select **New Database Connection**.

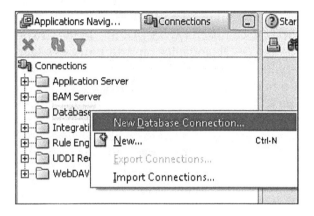

Click on **Next** in **Create Database Connection Wizard**. In the **Create Database Connection Type** window, specify a Connection Name—MySQLConnection for example—and set Connection Type to Third Party JDBC Driver, because we will be using MySQL database, which is a third-party database for Oracle JDeveloper and click on **Next**. If a connection is to be configured with Oracle database select Oracle (JDBC) as the Connection Type and click on **Next**.

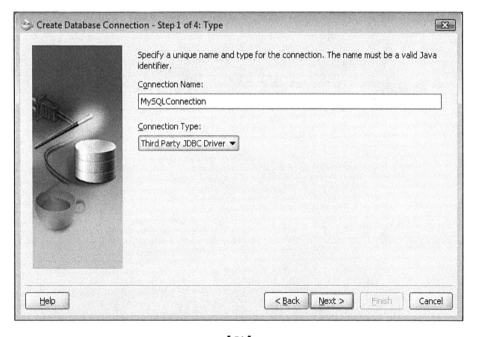

In the **Authentication** window specify **Username** as **root** (**Password** is not required to be specified for a root user by default), and click on **Next**. In the **Connection** window, we will specify the connection parameters, such as the driver name and connection URL; click on **New** to specify a Driver Class. In the **Register JDBC Driver** window, specify Driver Class as com.mysql.jdbc.Driver and click on **Browse** to select a Library for the Driver Class. In the **Select Library** window, click on **New** to create a new library for the MySQL Connector/J 5.1 JAR file. In the **Create Library** window, specify Library Name as MySQL and click on **Add Entry** to add a JAR file entry for the MySQL library. In the **Select Path Entry** window select mysql-connector-java-5.1.3-rc\mysql-connector-java-5.1.3-rc-bin.jar and click on **Select**. In the **Create Library** window, after a Class Path entry gets added to the MySQL library, click on **OK**. In the **Select Library** window, select the MySQL library and click on **OK**. In the **Register JDBC Driver** window, the MySQL library gets specified in the Library field and the mysql-connector-java-5.1.3-rc\mysql-connector-java-5.1.3-rc-bin.jar gets specified in the Classpath field. Now, click on **OK**. The Driver Class, Library, and Classpath fields get specified in the **Connection** window. Specify URL as jdbc:mysql://localhost:3306/test, and click on **Next**.

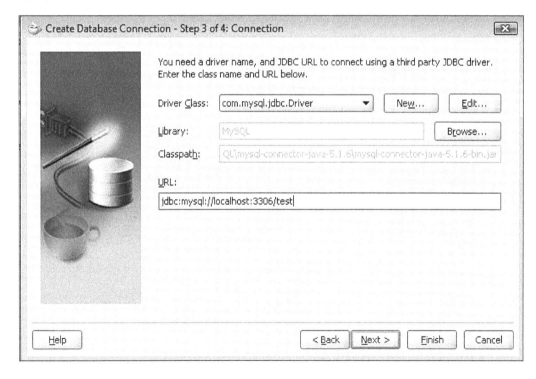

In the **Test** window click on **Test Connection** to test the connection that we have configured. A connection is established and a success message gets output in the Status text area. Click on **Finish** in the **Test** window. A connection configuration, **MySQLConnection**, gets added to the **Connections** navigator.

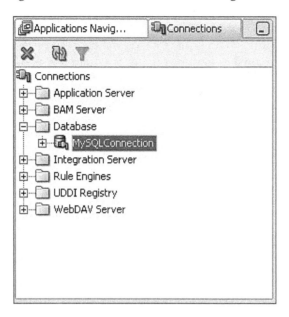

The connection parameters are displayed in the structure view. To modify any of the connection settings, double-click on the **Connection** node. The **Edit Database Connection** window gets displayed. The connection Username, Password, Driver Class, and URL may be modified in the Edit window.

A database connection configured in the Connections navigator has a JNDI name binding in the JNDI naming service provided by OC4J. Using the JNDI name binding, a `DataSource` object may be created in a J2EE application. To view, or modify the configuration settings of the JDBC connection select **Tools | Embedded OC4J Server Preferences** in JDeveloper. In the window displayed, select **Global | Data Sources** node, and to update the `data-sources.xml` file with the connection defined in the Connections navigator, click on the **Refresh Now** button. Checkboxes may be selected to **Create data-source elements where not defined,** and to **Update existing data-source elements**.

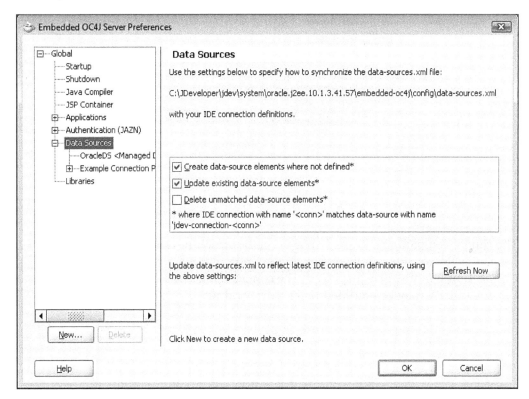

The connection pool and data source associated with the connection configured in the **Connections** navigator get listed. Select the **jdev-connection-pool-MySQLConnection** node to list the connection pool properties as **Property Set A** and **Property Set B**.

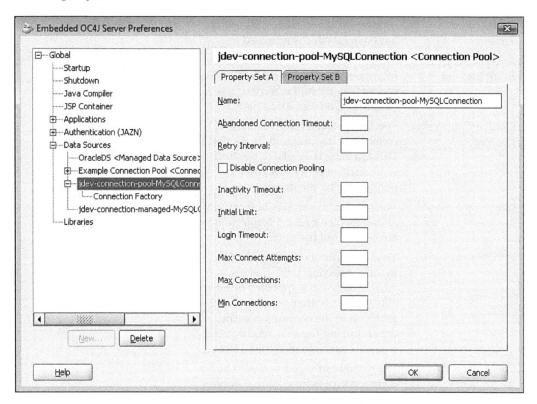

The tuning properties of the JDBC connection pool may be set in the **Connection Pool** window. The different tuning attributes are listed in following table:

Tuning Attribute	Attribute Description	Default Value
Abandoned Connection Timeout	Interval (seconds) after which a connection acquired by a user that has been inactive is returned to the cache.	-1 implies that the feature is not in effect.
Retry Interval	Interval (seconds) after which a failed connection attempt is retried. Used with Max Connect Attempts.	1
Disable Connection Pooling	Specifies if application server's connection pooling is to be disabled. This attribute is available because some drivers provide connection pooling inside the driver.	False
Inactivity Timeout	The number of seconds of inactivity after which an unused connection is removed from the pool.	Inactivity Timeout
Initial Limit	The initial number of connections in the connection pool. If value is greater than 0, the specified number of connections are pre-created and available in the connection cache, thus reducing the time required to build the cache to its optimal size.	0
Login Timeout	The number of seconds after which a login attempt is timed out. 0 implies that the system timeout value is used. If a system timeout is not defined, a login attempt is not timed out.	0
Max Connect Attempts	The maximum number of connection attempts to a database. Used in conjunction with retry interval.	3
Max Connections	The maximum number of available database connections in the connection pool. A value of 0 or less implies that there is no maximum limit.	0
Min Connections	The minimum number of database connections in the connection pool.	0

Select **Property Set B** to specify additional connection pool properties.

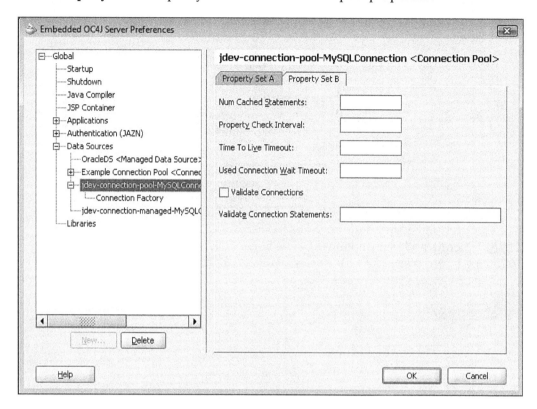

The connection pool properties in **Property Set B** are discussed in the following table:

Property	Description	Default Value
Num Cached Statements	Specifies the maximum number of prepared and callable statements that should be cached for each connection in each connection pool. Statement caching increases system performance. A value greater than 0 enables statement caching.	0
Property Check Interval	Specifies the time interval (seconds) after which property values are checked for new values, and time out limits are implemented.	900
Time to Live Timeout	Specifies the maximum number of seconds a used connection may be active, after which it is closed and returned to the connection pool. -1 indicates that the feature is not enabled.	-1

Property	Description	Default Value
Used Connection Wait Timeout	Number of seconds for which a used connection remains unused before being returned to the connection pool. Only applies if the maximum numbers of connections that a connection pool may cache have been acquired by clients, and a client requests a connection.	60
Validate Connections	Specifies if connections are to be validated, when given to a client. Used in conjunction with Validate Connection Statements.	False
Validate Connection Statements	Specifies the SQL statements used to validate connections before being acquired by a client.	None

The **Connection Factory** node specifies the Factory Class, User name, Password, Login Timeout, and connection URL. The factory class must implement one of the following interfaces: `java.sql.Driver`, `javax.sql.DataSource`, `javax.sql.ConnectionPoolDataSource`, `javax.sql.XADataSource`.

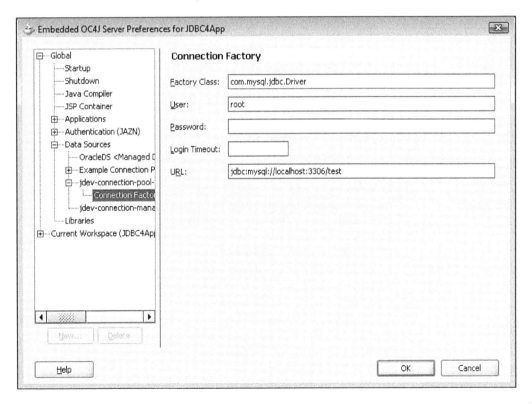

The **Managed DataSource** node specifies the managed data sources associated with the connection, and which are data sources managed by the OC4J. A managed data source is an OC4J implementation of the `javax.sql.DataSource` interface that wraps a JDBC driver class, or data source class. Even if the factory class does not implement the `javax.sql.DataSource` interface, the OC4J implementation of the factory class implements the `javax.sql.DataSource` interface. A managed data source supports connection caching, global transaction management, and error handling, all provided by the OC4J. A managed data source is associated with a connection pool, and thus has the advantage of being able to specify the tuning parameters. The **JNDI Name** of the data source is specified in the managed data source window. The **JNDI Name** is in the jdbc/MySQLConnectionDS format, with MySQLConnection being the connection name configured in the **Connections** navigator.

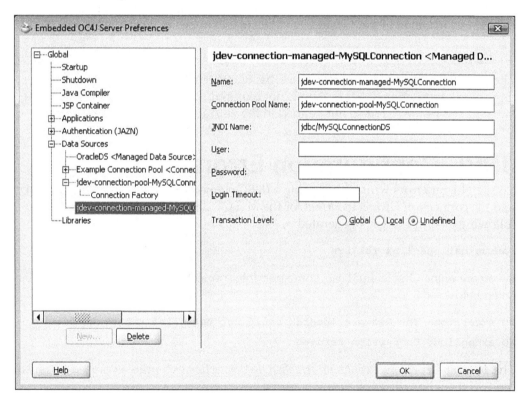

A connection `MySQLConnection` in the **Connections** navigator is available as a data source with the **JNDI Name** binding jdbc/MySQLConnectionDS. To obtain a connection from the data source, add a `resource-ref` element to the web application in which a connection is to be obtained. In a Servlet or JSP application, a connection may be obtained with the data source JNDI Name.

```
InitialContext initialContext = new InitialContext();
javax.sql.DataSource ds = (javax.sql.DataSource)
initialContext.lookup("java:comp/env/jdbc/MySQLConnectionDS");
java.sql.Connection conn = ds.getConnection();
```

JavaEE 5 defines annotations to support resource injection. Resource injection is the injection of external resources, such as a data source in a JEE 5 application using the javax.annotation.Resource annotation. JDeveloper 11 will support resource injection with annotations to obtain a handle of a data source. For example, define a `catalogDS` resource of the `javax.sql.DataSource` type, as shown below:

```
private @Resource DataSource catalogDS;
```

The `catalogDS` field of type `javax.sql.DataSource` is annotated with the `@Resource` annotation. JNDI lookup is not required with resource injection, and the `DataSource` resource is also not defined in the `web.xml` deployment descriptor.

JDBC Configuration Errors

You might get errors while configuring a JDBC connection. If you are using MySQL, and the connection URL is incorrect, or the MySQL database is not running, the following error message is generated:

`Communications link failure`

If you are using Oracle database, some possible connection configuration errors are listed below:

`IO exception: The Network Adapter could not establish the connection`

`IO exception: Connection refused`

The *The Network Adapter could not establish the connection* exception is caused by one or more of the following configuration errors:

1. The database host name, port number, or database instance name is wrong.

2. The database `TNSListener` has not been started. The `TNSListener` may be started with the `lsnrctl` utility.

    `C:\>lsnrctl start`

The *Connection refused* exception is caused by one or more of the following configuration errors:

1. The database **SID** specified is incorrect.

2. The database instance has not been started. To start the database instance connect to SQL*Plus as SYSDBA.

   ```
   C:\>sqlplus SYS/<pwd> AS SYSDBA
   ```

At the SQL prompt, start the database instance with the startup command.

```
SQL>startup
```

Creating a Managed Data Source

In the previous section, a JDBC connection was obtained in the **Connections** navigator. A corresponding JNDI managed data source becomes available for the **Connections** navigator connection. A data source object is configured with a JNDI Name binding in the OC4J server integrated with JDeveloper. A data source may also be configured in the **Embedded OC4J Server Preferences** window directly, or may be configured declaratively by modifying the data-sources.xml file. We will discuss each of these methods for creating a data source. A data source may be configured at the **Global** level or the Current Workspace level. A **Global** data source is available to all applications while a Current Workspace data source is available only in the current workspace. To create a new **Global** data source, select **Tools | Embedded OC4J Preferences** and select the **Global | Data Sources** node, and click on the **New** button.

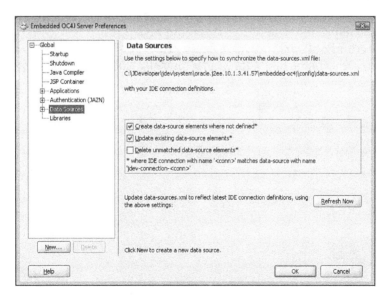

Before we are able to configure a managed data source, we need to configure a connection pool. In the **Create Data Source** window select **Transaction Level** as Connection Pool, specify a connection pool name, and click on the **OK** button.

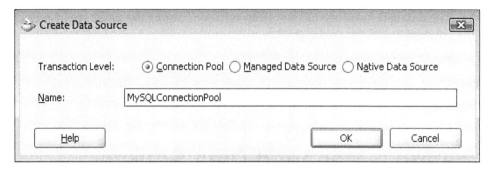

A new connection pool gets created and its tuning properties may be set, as required. In the **Connection Factory** window, specify a Factory Class, User name, Password, Login Timeout, and connection URL. The Factory Class is required to implement one of the following interfaces: `java.sql.Driver`, `javax.sql.DataSource`, `javax.sql.ConnectionPoolDataSource`, `javax.sql.XADataSource`. The **Factory Class** for a MySQL managed data source can be a MySQL class that implements the `javax.sql.DataSource` interface, for example the com.mysql.jdbc.jdbc2.optional.MysqlDataSource and com.mysql.jdbc.jdbc2.optional.MysqlConnectionPoolDataSource classes, or it can be a class that implements the `java.sql.Driver` interface, for example the com.mysql.jdbc.Driver class. Whether a class implementing the `java.sql.Driver` interface is used, or a class implementing the `javax.sql.DataSource` interface is used, the OC4J server wraps the class and provides an implementation of the `javax.sql.DataSource` interface. We will use the data source class **com.mysql.jdbc.jdbc2.optional.MysqlConnectionPoolDataSource**. A **Password** is not required for a root user, by default. Specify the connection **URL** as jdbc:mysql://localhost:3306/test. Click on **OK** to configure the connection pool.

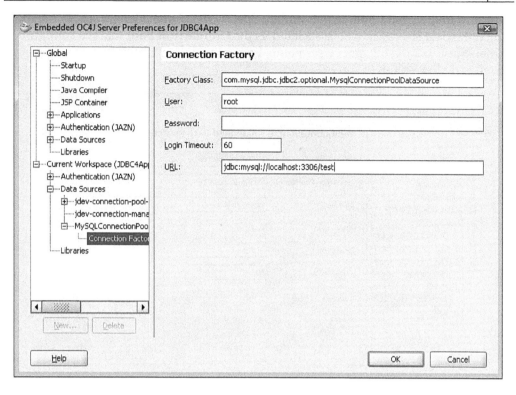

Create a data source by selecting the **Global | Data Sources** node, and click on **New**, as we did for creating a Connection Pool. In the **Create Data Source** window, select Transaction Level as Managed Data Source, specify a data source **Name** and click on **OK**. A data source may also be configured as a **Native Data Source**. The difference between a Managed Data Source and a Native Data Source is that the OC4J server does not wrap a Native Data Source. The OC4J server does not provide connection caching for a Native Data Source. A Native Data Source does not support global/distributed transactions. A distributed transaction is a transaction that spans over multiple database servers. If a Native Data Source is to be configured, specify a data source class that implements the `javax.sql.DataSource` interface. A **Connection Pool** is not to be configured for a Native Data Source.

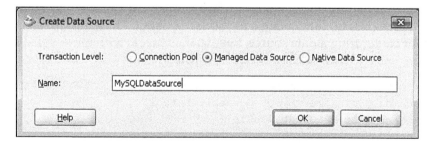

A new **Managed Data Source** gets added. Specify the Connection Pool Name with which the data source is to be associated as the **Connection Pool** that we configured earlier. Specify a JNDI Name, User name, Password, Login Timeout, Transaction Level, and click on **OK**.

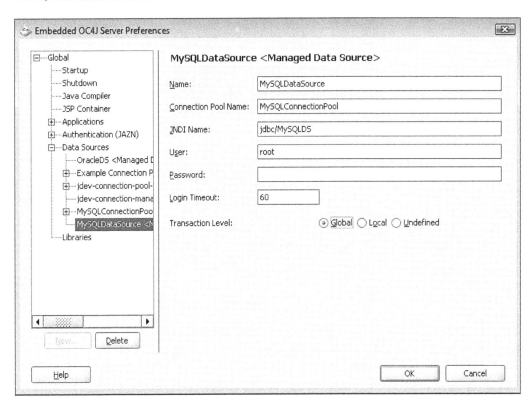

A Managed Data Source gets configured and updates the `data-sources.xml` file using the **Refresh** button. A Managed Data Source may also be created declaratively by modifying the `data-sources.xml` configuration file directly in the directory: C:\JDeveloper\jdev\system\oracle.j2ee.10.1.3.nn.nn\embedded-oc4j\config. `<JDeveloper10.1.3>` is the directory in which JDeveloper is installed. Add a `managed-data-source` element to the `data-sources.xml` file specifying the configuration of the `DataSource` object. The `managed-data-source` element includes the data source class used to obtain a `DataSource` object. The `managed-data-source` element for configuring a data source, `MySQLDataSource`, with the `MySQL` database, using `jndi-name jdbc/MySQLDataSource`, is listed below:

```
<managed-data-source name='MySQLDataSource'
connection-pool-name='MySQL Connection Pool'
jndi-name='jdbc/MySQLDataSource'/>
<connection-pool name='MySQL Connection Pool'>
```

```
<connection-factory factory-class='com.mysql.jdbc.jdbc2.optional.
MysqlConnectionPoolDataSource'
user='root'
password=''
url="jdbc:mysql://localhost:3306/test">
</connection-factory>
</connection-pool>
```

The elements in the `data-sources.xml` file are based on the XML Schema `http://www.oracle.com/technology/oracleas/schema/data-sources-10_1.xsd`. The `root` element is `data-sources`, and the `data-sources` element has one or more `managed-data-source`, `connection-pool`, and `native-data-source` elements. The `managed-data-source` element has the following attributes: `name`, `user`, `password`, `login-timeout`, `tx-level`, `schema`, `connection-pool-name`, and `jndi-name`. Each `managed-data-source` element is associated with a connection pool, which is specified in the `connection-pool` element. A `connection-pool` element has a `connection-factory` sub-element and attributes, which are discussed in following table:

Element	Description	Default Value
name	Connection pool name.	-1
min-connections	Minimum number of connections in the connection pool.	0
max-connections	Maximum number of open connections in a connection pool. Value of 0 or less indicates that there is no maximum limit.	0
initial-limit	Initial number of connections in the connection pool when created or reinitialized. Specifying an initial size of connection pool reduces ramp-up time to an optimal size.	0
used-connection-wait-timeout	When a connection pool has a maximum number of connections and all the connections in the pool are being used, the connection pool waits for the specified time for a client to release a connection to the connection pool.	60
inactivity-timeout	When a connection in a connection pool has been inactive for the inactivity timeout period (in seconds), the connection is removed.	60
login-timeout	Specifies the amount of time (in seconds), a data source waits to establish a connection with the database. A value of 0 specifies the default system timeout.	0

Element	Description	Default Value
connection-retry-interval	Specifies the interval (in seconds) to wait before retrying a connection with the database.	1
max-connect-attempts	Specifies the number of times to retry to connect to a database.	3
validate-connection	If set to true, this validates a connection with the database, when a connection is given to a client, using the SQL statement specified in the validate-connection-statement attribute.	False
validate-connection-statement	Statement runs when a connection is given to a client from the connection pool.	None
num-cached-statements	Specifies the maximum number of statements that are cached for a connection. A value greater than 0 enables statement caching.	0
time-to-live-timeout	Not enabled by default, this element specifies the maximum time (in seconds) a used connection may be active before being closed and returned to the connection pool. The statement handles are also closed, when a connection is closed.	-1
abandoned-connection-timeout	Supported with Oracle database only and not enabled by default, this element specifies inactivity timeout for used connections.	-1
disable-server-connection-pooling	Disables application server's connection pooling. The element is used with JDBC drivers that support connection pooling inside the driver. With Oracle JDBC driver using Implicit Connection Cache, its value is not used.	False
property-check-interval	Used with Oracle database only. This element specifies the time interval (in seconds), after which the time-outs are applied.	900
lower-threshold-limit	The lower threshold limit on the connection limit. Defaults to 20%.	20%

If a native data source is used, connection caching is performed mainly programmatically. The `OracleDataSource` provides connection caching using the methods `getConnectionCacheName()`, `setConnectionCacheName(String cacheName)`, `getConnectionCacheProperties()`, and `setConnectionCacheProperties(java.util.Properties cp)`. Alternatively, the connection cache manager class `OracleConnectionCacheManager` may be used to specify connection caching. The `OracleConnectionCacheManager` class provides the `getCacheManagerInstance()`, `createCache(String cacheName, javax.sql.DataSource ds, Properties cacheProperties)`, `createCache(javax.sql.DataSource ds, Properties cacheProperties)`, `removeCache(String cacheName, int mode)`, `refreshCache(String cacheName, int mode)`, and `getCacheProperties(String cacheName)` methods, to configure the connection cache. With a native data source, declarative connection caching may also be specified in the `native-data-source` element in the `data-sources.xml` file with the `property` elements. The connection cache properties that may be specified in a native data source are discussed in the following table:

Connection Cache Property	Type	Description
connectionCacheName	String	Cache Name.
connectionCachingEnabled	Boolean	Specifies if implicit connection caching is enabled.
fastConnectionFailoverEnabled	Boolean	Specifies if fast connection failover is enabled. Implicit connection caching should also be enabled to enable fast connection failover. Fast connection failover provides load balancing of available connections in the connection cache. Moreover, invalid connections are closed with fast connection failover.

The Managed Data Source is the preferred data source as the connection pooling is implemented by the OC4J server, and the developer does not have to implement the connection pooling. In the next section, we will develop a web application to retrieve data from MySQL database. Delete the managed data source, MySQLDataSource, and the connection pool, MySQLConnectionPool configured in this section by selecting the managed data source/connection pool in the **Tools | Embedded OC4J Server Preferences** window and by selecting the **Delete** button. Update the `data-sources.xml` configuration file using the **Refresh Now** button

Connecting to a Database from a Web Application

If a Java application is used to connect to a database, a JDBC connection may be obtained using the `getConnection()` method of the `DriverManager` class. If a JDBC connection is to be obtained in a web application, a data source with a JNDI naming service binding must be configured in an application server, such as the OC4J embedded in JDeveloper IDE. The data source object configured in `data-sources.xml` may be used in a Servlet or JSP in JDeveloper. In this section, we will connect to MySQL database using the managed data source we configured in the previous section. First, we need to create a project in JDeveloper with **File | New**. In the **New Gallery** window, select **General | Applications** in Categories and **Application** in

Items and click on **OK**. Specify the Application Name in the **Create Application** window and click on the **OK** button. Specify the Project Name in the **Create Project** window and click on the **OK** button. A new project is added to the Applications Navigator.

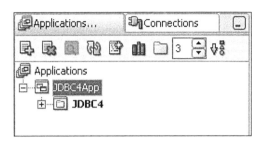

In the **Applications Navigator** window right-click on the Project node and select **New**. In the **New Gallery** window, select **Web Tier | JSP** in Categories, and **JSP** in Items, and click on **OK**.

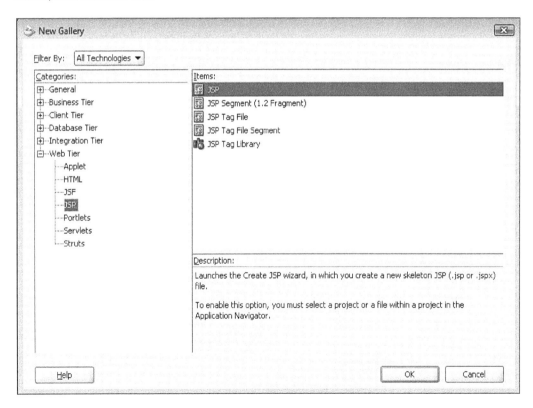

The **Create JSP Wizard** gets started. In the **Web Application** window, select J2EE 1.4 as the J2EE version and click on **Next**. In the **JSP File** window, specify a File Name and click on **Next**.

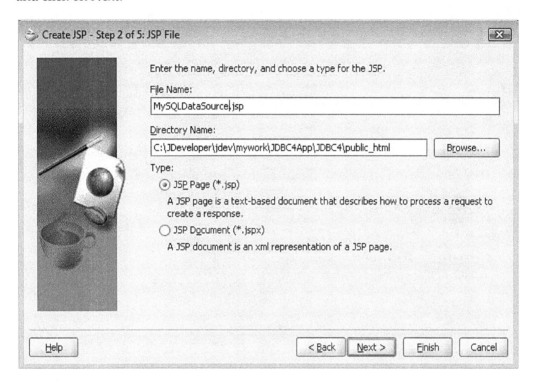

Select the default settings in the **Error Page Options** window, if an error page is not to be used to handle unhandled exceptions. If an error page is to be used to handle unhandled exceptions, select **Use an Error Page** and click on the **Next** button. Select the Default Settings in the **Tag Libraries** window as we will not be using any tag libraries in this chapter, and click on **Next**. Select the Default Settings in the **HTML Options** window, with the the HTML Version being 4.0.1 Transitional, and click on **Next**.

On clicking finish in the **Finish** window, a JSP gets added to the project. To the
`web.xml` file, add a `resource-ref` element in the Managed Data Source.

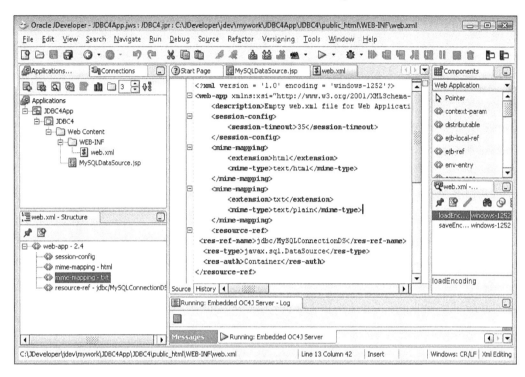

The `res-ref-name` specifies the JNDI name of the Managed Data Source. The
`resource-ref` element is listed below:

```
<resource-ref>
 <res-ref-name>jdbc/MySQLConnectionDS</res-ref-name>
  <res-type>javax.sql.DataSource</res-type>
  <res-auth>Container</res-auth>
</resource-ref>
```

We also need to copy `mysql-connector-java-5.1.3-rc-bin.jar` to the
`C:\JDeveloper\j2ee\home\applib` directory, which adds the MySQL Connector/J
JDBC 4.0 driver to the runtime class path of the web application.

Setting J2SE Version to JDK 6.0

JDBC 4.0 driver requires JDK 6.0. Therefore, we have to set the J2SE version for the JDBC4 project to J2SE 6.0. Select the Project node in the **Applications Navigator** and select **Tools | Project Properties**. In the **Project Properties** window, select the Libraries node. Click on the **Change** button for the J2SE Version field. In the **Edit J2SE Definition** window, click **New**.

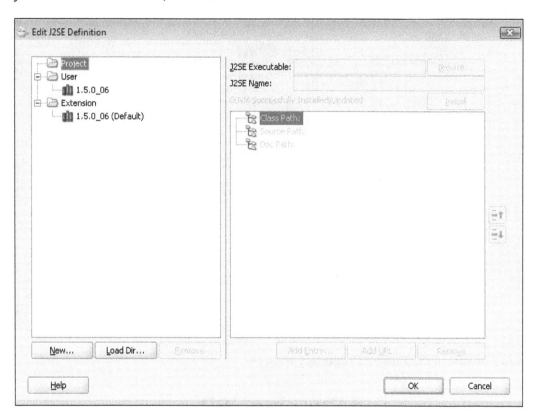

In the **Create J2SE** window, click on **Browse** to select a JDK 6.0 `java.exe` executable file. Specify a J2SE Name, and click on **OK**. A new J2SE Definition gets created in the **Edit J2SE Definition** window. Select the J2SE6.0 definition and click on **OK**.

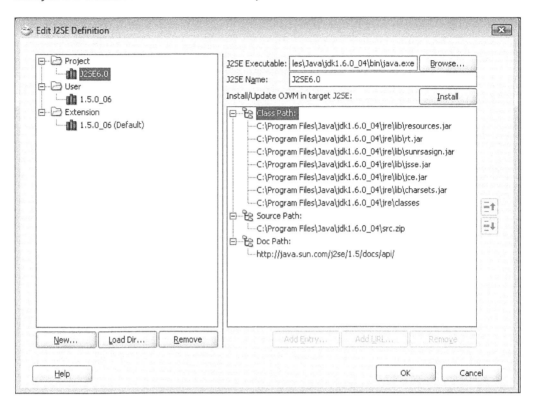

Click on **OK** in the **Project Properties** window.

Developing and Running JSP

Next, we will obtain a JDBC connection in the `MySQLDataSource` JSP, using the Managed Data Source configured in the previous section. The OC4J server embedded in JDeveloper 10.1.3 does not support JDBC 4.0. Therefore, we will not be able to use the JDBC 4.0 features in the web application. Most of the J2EE application servers such as WebLogic server, JBoss server, and WebSphere server do not support JDBC 4.0. **Sun Java System Application Server 9.1** is the only application server that supports JDBC 4.0.

However, we will use the JDBC 4.0 driver and the JDBC 4.0 features may be used with an application server that supports JDBC 4.0. Copy the MySQL JDBC 4.0 JAR file to the `<JDeveloper>\j2ee\home\applib` directory, `<JDeveloper>` being the

JDeveloper installation directory. All that is required for a developer to use JDBC 4.0 is an application server that supports the JDBC 4.0 driver. In the MySQLDataSource JSP, create a DataSource object from the Managed Data Source that we configured earlier. First, we have to create an InitialContext object and then create a javax. sql.DataSource object using the lookup() method to look up the data source resource, which is specified in the web.xml file as an external resource using the resource-ref element. We have to prefix the JNDI name jdbc/MySQLDS with the JNDI context java:comp/env. For a tutorial on JNDI Naming, refer to the JNDI Tutorial: http://java.sun.com/products/jndi/tutorial/.

```
InitialContext initialContext = new InitialContext();
javax.sql.DataSource ds = (javax.sql.DataSource) initialContext.
lookup("java:comp/env/jdbc/MySQLConnectionDS");
```

Obtain a JDBC connection from the DataSource object, using the getConnection() method.

```
java.sql.Connection connection = ds.getConnection();
```

Run an SQL query and create an HTML table from the result set of the query. Create a Statement object from the Connection object using the createStatement() method. Run an SQL query using the executeQuery() method of the Statement object. Iterate over the result set and retrieve column values from the result set rows, to create an HTML table. Close the ResultSet object, the Statement object, and the Connection object using the close() method, which is defined for each of these interfaces. The MySQLDataSource.jsp is listed below:

```
<%@ page contentType="text/html;charset=windows-1252"%>
<%@ page language="java" import="java.sql.*, javax.naming.*, javax.
sql.*" %>
<%
 InitialContext initialContext = new InitialContext();
 javax.sql.DataSource ds = (javax.sql.DataSource)
 initialContext.lookup("java:comp/env/jdbc/MySQLDS");
 java.sql.Connection connection = ds.getConnection();
 Statement stmt=connection.createStatement();
 ResultSet resultSet=stmt.executeQuery("Select * from Catalog");
%>
<table border="1" cellspacing="0">
 <tr>
  <th>CatalogId</th>
  <th>Journal</th>
  <th>Publisher</th>
  <th>Edition</th>
  <th>Title</th>
  <th>Author</th>
 </tr>
<%
```

```
while (resultSet.next())
  {
%>
 <tr>
  <td><%out.println(resultSet.getString(1));%></td>
  <td><%out.println(resultSet.getString(2));%></td>
  <td><%out.println(resultSet.getString(3));%></td>
  <td><%out.println(resultSet.getString(4));%></td>
  <td><%out.println(resultSet.getString(5));%></td>
  <td><%out.println(resultSet.getString(6));%></td>
 </tr>
<%
  }
%>
</table>
<%
 resultSet.close();
 stmt.close();
 if(!connection.isClosed())
 connection.close();
%>
```

Run the JSP, by right-clicking on the JSP node in the **Applications Navigator** and selecting **Run**.

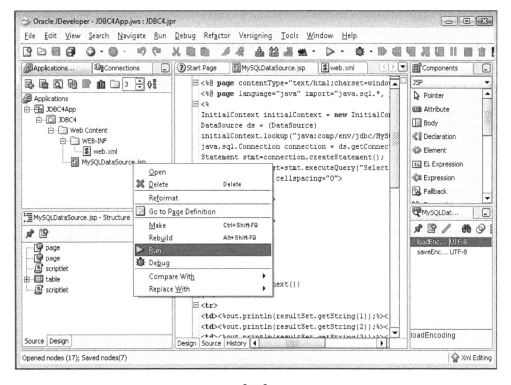

The output from the JSP gets displayed in the default browser:

CatalogId	Journal	Publisher	Edition	Title	Author
catalog1	Oracle Magazine	Oracle Publishing	Nov-Dec 2004	Database Resource Manager	Kimberly Floss
catalog2	Oracle Magazine	Oracle Publishing	Nov-Dec 2004	From ADF UIX to JSF	Jonas Jacobi

JDBC 4.0 Version

The OC4J embedded in JDeveloper 10g does not support JDBC 4.0. When support gets added for JDBC 4.0, JDBC 4.0's features may be added to the JSP web application that we have developed in the previous section. Provision to set client info properties on the `Connection` object is a new feature in JDBC 4.0. Client info properties may be set using the `setClientInfoProperty()` method of the `Connection` object. Set client info properties `ApplicationName`, `ClientUser`, and `ClientHostname` as follows:

```
connection.setClientInfo("ApplicationName","DataDirectApp");
connection.setClientInfo("ClientUser","DataDirect");
connection.setClientInfo("ClientHostname","DataDirectHost");
```

If the database supports statement caching, we can set statement pooling to `true`. To find out whether the database supports statement pooling create a `DatabaseMetaData` object. Using the `supportsStatementPooling()` method test if the database supports statement pooling. If the database supports statement pooling check if the `Statement` is poolable using the `isPoolable()` method. If the `Statement` object is poolable, set the `Statement` object to poolable using the `setPoolable()` method:

```
DatabaseMetaData metaData=connection.getMetaData();
if(metaData.supportsStatementPooling())
  {
  if(stmt.isPoolable())
  stmt.setPoolable(true);
  }
```

We may use support for the wrapper pattern with the `Wrapper` interface, which is extended by the `Statement` interface. Oracle's extensions to the JDBC API provide an `OracleStatement` interface that extends the `Statement` interface. Using the wrapper pattern create an object of type `OracleStatement` type. First we need to check if the `Statement` object is a wrapper for the `oracle.jdbc.OracleStatement` using the `isWrapperFor()` method. Subsequently create an object of type `OracleStatement` type using the `unwrap()` method:

```
OracleStatement oracleStmt=null;
Class class = Class.forName("oracle.jdbc.OracleStatement");
if(stmt.isWrapperFor(class))
 {
   oracleStmt = (OracleStatement)stmt.unwrap(class);
 }
```

The `OracleStatement` object may be used to set column types for different columns to be fetched from the database, using the `defineColumnType()` method. Also, the number of rows to be prefetched may be set, using the `setRowPrefetch()` method.

If the database supports `ROWID` of SQL type, we may add a column for the `ROWID` value of a row in the result set. A `ROWID` column value may be retrieved as a `java.sql.RowId` object using the `getRowId()` method. Oracle database 10g supports the `ROWID` data type. Therefore, modify the `SELECT` query to add a column for the `ROWID` pseudocolumn.

```
ResultSet resultSet= oracleStmt.executeQuery("Select ROWID, CATALOGID,
JOURNAL, PUBLISHER, EDITION, TITLE, AUTHOR from Catalog");
```

We also have to add a column of type `ROWID` to the HTML table created from the result set. A `ROWID` column value is retrieved from a `ResultSet` object using the `getRowId()` method. The `RowId` object may be converted to a `String` value using the `toString()` method:

```
<%out.println(resultSet.getRowId("ROWID").toString());%>
```

Enhanced support for chained exceptions in the `SQLException` interface may be used in the JSP web application. We need to specify an `errorPage` in the `input.jsp` for error handling:

```
<%@ page errorPage="errorpage.jsp" %>
```

In the `errorpage.jsp`, the enhanced **for-each loop** is used to retrieve the chained exceptions and chained causes.

```
<%@ page isErrorPage="true" %>
<%
 for(Throwable e : exception )
```

```
  {
   out.println("Error encountered: " + e);
  }
%>
```

The JDBC 4.0 version of the input.jsp, which may run in JDeveloper when supports get added for JDBC 4.0 in the OC4J server, is listed below:

```
<%@ page contentType="text/html;charset=windows-1252"%>
<%@ page language="java" import="java.sql.*, javax.naming.*, javax.
sql.*,oracle.jdbc.*" %>
<%@ page errorPage="errorpage.jsp" %>
<%
 InitialContext initialContext = new InitialContext();
 DataSource ds = (DataSource)
 initialContext.lookup("java:comp/env/jdbc/OracleDS");
 java.sql.Connection connection = ds.getConnection();
 connection.setClientInfo("ApplicationName","DataDirectApp");
 connection.setClientInfo("ClientUser","DataDirect");
 connection.setClientInfo("ClientHostname","DataDirectHost");
 Statement stmt=connection.createStatement();
 DatabaseMetaData metaData=connection.getMetaData();
 if(metaData.supportsStatementPooling())
  {
   if(stmt.isPoolable())
   stmt.setPoolable(true);
  }
 OracleStatement oracleStmt=null;
 Class class = Class.forName("oracle.jdbc.OracleStatement");
 if(stmt.isWrapperFor(class))
  {
   oracleStmt = (OracleStatement)stmt.unwrap(class);
   oracleStmt.defineColumnType(1, OracleTypes.VARCHAR);
   oracleStmt.defineColumnType(2, OracleTypes.VARCHAR);
   oracleStmt.defineColumnType(3, OracleTypes.VARCHAR);
   oracleStmt.defineColumnType(4, OracleTypes.VARCHAR);
   oracleStmt.defineColumnType(5, OracleTypes.VARCHAR);
   oracleStmt.defineColumnType(6, OracleTypes.VARCHAR);
   oracleStmt.defineColumnType(7, OracleTypes.VARCHAR);
   oracleStmt.setRowPrefetch(2);
  }
 ResultSet resultSet=oracleStmt.executeQuery("Select ROWID, CATALOGID,
JOURNAL, PUBLISHER, EDITION, TITLE, AUTHOR from Catalog");
%>
<table border="1" cellspacing="0">
```

```
<tr>
 <th>Row Id</th>
 <th>Catalog Id</th>
 <th>Journal</th>
 <th>Publisher</th>
 <th>Edition</th>
 <th>Title</th>
 <th>Author</th>
</tr>
<%
 while (resultSet.next())
   {
%>
<tr>
 <td><%out.println(resultSet.getRowId("ROWID").toString());%></td>
 <td><%out.println(resultSet.getString(1));%></td>
 <td><%out.println(resultSet.getString(2));%></td>
 <td><%out.println(resultSet.getString(3));%></td>
 <td><%out.println(resultSet.getString(4));%></td>
 <td><%out.println(resultSet.getString(5));%></td>
 <td><%out.println(resultSet.getString(6));%></td>
</tr>
<%
   }
%>
</table>
<%
 resultSet.close();
 oracleStmt.close();
 if(!connection.isClosed())
   connection.close();
%>
```

Summary

JDeveloper IDE provides a built-in **Connections** navigator to configure a connection with any relational database for which a JDBC driver is available. A connection configured in the **Connections** navigator is also available as a data source. In this chapter, we have configured a JDBC connection in JDeveloper with MySQL database using the MySQL Connector/J 5.1 JDBC 4.0 driver. We also created a managed data source in the OC4J embedded in JDeveloper and used the data source in a web application. Subsequently, we discussed the JDBC 4.0 version of the web application.

3

Connecting to a Database with JSTL SQL Tag Library

JSP 1.1 and the later versions of JSP support reusable modules called custom actions. A custom action is invoked with a custom tag in a JSP page. A collection of custom tags is called a tag library. Various SQL tag libraries are available for accessing a database. The **JavaServer Pages Standard Tag Library** (JSTL) is a tag library, which provides SQL tags for accessing a database. JSTL 1.1 requires a JSP container that supports Servlet specification 2.4 and JSP specification 2.0. In this chapter, we will discuss the JSTL SQL tag library and develop a JSTL SQL tag library application in JDeveloper 10.1.3 with embedded OC4J, which supports Servlet 2.4 and JSP 2.0 specifications. The JSTL SQL tag library was created before JDBC 4.0 specification became available. If you are using the JDBC 4.0 driver with JDK 6.0, you would still be able to use the JSTL SQL tag library. We will be using JDBC 4.0 with JDK 6.0 for accessing the Oracle database using the JSTL SQL tag library. First, let us discuss the JSTL SQL tag library tags.

Overview of JSTL SQL and Core Tags

The JSTL SQL tag library provides various tags for accessing a database, creating a database table, updating, deleting, and querying a database. The SQL tag library URI is: `http://java.sun.com/jsp/jstl/sql`. The syntax for including the JSTL SQL tag library in a JSP page is the `taglib` directive shown below. The URI is used to define a namespace for the tag library, which avoids conflicts that could occur if another tag library with similar names for their tags is used on the same JSP page.

```
<%@ taglib prefix="sql" uri=" http://java.sun.com/jsp/jstl/sql" %>
```

The different tags in the JSTL SQL tag library are discussed in the following table. All the tag attributes in the table are of `java.lang.String` type, unless specified to be of another type. Attributes are not required, unless specified to be required.

Tag Name	Description	Attributes
transaction	Creates a transaction in which a group of SQL statements are run. Establishes a transaction context for `sql:query` and `sql:update` subtags. The `sql:query` and `sql:update` tags within a `sql:transaction` tag must not specify a `dataSource` attribute. The `sql:transaction` tag commits or rollbacks (if a transaction occurs) the transaction by invoking the commit(), or rollback() method.	`dataSource`- Specifies a data source, which is either a relative path to a JNDI resource, or JDBC parameters to a DriverManager class. JDBC parameters are `driver` class, connection `url`, `user` name, and `password`. `isolation`- Specifies the transaction isolation level. Isolation level value may be "read_committed", "read_uncommitted", "repeatable_read", or "serializable". Isolation level values were discussed in Chapter 1. The default is the isolation level of the data source.
query	Runs a SQL query. The SQL query may be specified in the `sql` attribute, or in the query element. If `dataSource` is specified, query tag should not be within a transaction tag. The result of the query is stored in scoped variable `var`. If the query produces no results, an empty Result object is returned. The query statement may include parameter markers ("?") identifying `PreparedStatement` parameters. Order of rows in a result set may vary with RDBMS implementation, unless an `ORDER BY` clause is specified. If a `query` tag is specified in a `transaction` tag, the Connection object is obtained from the `transaction` tag.	`var`(required)- Scoped variable for the query. Var is of type, `javax.servlet.jsp.jstl.sql.Result`. scope- Scope of variable. Scope may be "page", "request", "session", or "application". `sql`-SQL query statement `dataSource`- Datasource associated with the query. The data source is either a relative path to a JNDI resource, or JDBC parameters to a DriverManager class. startRow- Specifies the start row of the Result returned by the query. The default is '0', which is also the index of the start row of the original result set. maxRows- The maximum number of rows in the query result set. The default includes all the rows. Value should be >-1. Value of –1 also includes all rows.

Tag Name	Description	Attributes
update	Runs a SQL statement. The SQL statement may be specified in the sql attribute or within update element tags. The SQL statement may be a CREATE, UPDATE, INSERT, or a DELETE statement. SQL DDL statements may also be run. The update statement may contain parameter markers ("?") identifying PreparedStatement parameters, whose value is specified using enclosed sql:param, or sql:dataParam tags. If scope is specified, var must also be specified. If dataSource is specified, sql:update tag should not be specified within a sql:transaction tag. If sql:update tag is specified in a sql:transaction tag, Connection object is obtained from the sql:transaction tag.	var- Scoped variable for the result of the SQL statement, which is the update count of the UPDATE, DELETE, INSERT statements. Attribute var is of Integer type. scope- Scope of variable. sql- SQL statement, which may be a CREATE, UPDATE, INSERT, or DELETE statement. dataSource- Datasource associated with the update statement. The data source is either a relative path to a JNDI resource or JDBC parameters to a DriverManager class.
param	Specifies the value of parameter markers ("?") in a SQL statement using a subtag of sql:query, and sql:update tags. Parameters are substituted in the order that they are specified. If the value is null, parameter is set to SQL NULL value.	value- Parameter value.
dateParam	Sets the value of parameter markers ("?") in a SQL statement for values of type java.util.Date parameter using subtag of sql:query, or sql:update tag.	value- Parameter value for DATE, TIME, or TIMESTAMP database. type- "date" "time" or "timestamp". If value is null, value is set to SQL NULL.

Tag Name	Description	Attributes
setDataSource	Creates and exports a data source as a scoped variable to be used in the JSP page.	var- Scoped variable for data source, which is either a relative path to a JNDI resource, or JDBC parameters to a DriverManager class. var is either of type String or DataSource.
		scope- Scope of variable.
		dataSource- Datasource. A relative path to a JNDI resource, or JDBC parameters to a DriverManager
		url- Database connection URL.
		user- Username.
		password- Password.

We will also be using some of the JSTL Core 1.1 tag library tags. JSTL Core 1.1 tag library provides tags for expression evaluation, loops, conditional evaluation, import of URL based resources, and output of the results of expression evaluation. Some familiarity with expression language (EL- http://www.oracle.com/technology/ sample_code/tutorials/jsp20/simpleel.html) is required to use the JSTL Core 1.1 tags. The JSTL Core 1.1 tag library tags are discussed in the following table. Attributes are not required, unless specified to be required.

Tag	Description	Attributes
catch	Catches a java.lang. Throwable thrown by any of its enclosed actions.	var (String)- Scoped variable representing the exception thrown by the enclosed action.
choose	Specifies the context for mutually exclusive conditional execution of operations marked by <when> and <otherwise>.	None.
forEach	Iterates over a collection of objects.	test (boolean)- Required attribute that specifies the test condition for evaluation of content.
		var (java.lang.String)- Name of the exported variable for the resulting value of test condition.
		scope (java.lang.String)- Scope of variable.

Tag	Description	Attributes
forTokens	Iterates over tokens.	items (java.lang.String)- Required attribute that specifies the tokens to iterate over.
		delims (java.lang.String)- Required attribute, which specifies the delimiters that separate the tokens.
		begin (int)- Specifies the index at which iteration is to begin. First token has index 0.
		end (int)- Specifies index at which iteration ends.
		step (int)- The step value to get the next token.
		var (String)- Name of the exported scoped variable for the current item of iteration.
		varStatus (String)- Name of the exported scoped variable for the status of the iteration.
if	Evaluates content if an expression evaluates to true.	test (Boolean)- Required attribute that specifies the test condition.
		var (String)- Name of the exported scoped variable for the resulting value under test condition.
		scope (String)- Scope of variable.
import	Imports the content of an URL-based resource.	All attributes are of the String type.
		url- Required attribute that specifies URL of the resource to import.
		var- Name of the exported scoped variable for the resources content.
		scope- Scope of the variable.
		varReader- Same as var, but of the Reader type.
		context- Name of the context for a relative URL.
		charEncoding- Character encoding of the content of the URL resource.

Tag	Description	Attributes
otherwise	Specifies the last alternative in a <c:choose> action.	None.
out	Evaluates an expression and outputs the result.	All attributes are of the String type.
		`value`- Required attribute that specifies expression to be evaluated.
		`default`- Default value if resulting value is null.
		escapeXml- Specifies if characters <, >, &, ', " in resulting string should be converted to their corresponding character entity codes.
param	Adds a parameter to an import tag containing URL.	name- Required attribute that specifies name of query string parameter.
		`value`- Value of parameter.
redirect	Redirects to a new URL.	All attributes are of String type.
		`url`- Redirects to the URL of the resource.
		context- Name of the context when redirecting to a relative URL.
remove	Removes a scoped variable.	All attributes are of String type.
		var- Required attribute that specifies the name of the scoped variable to be removed.
		scope- Scope of the variable.
set	Sets the result of an expression evaluation as a property of a target object.	All attributes are of String type.
		var- Name of the exported scoped variable that contains the resulting value of the expression evaluation.
		`value`- Expression to be evaluated.
		target- Target object whose value will be set.
		property- Property in the target object to be set.
		scope- Scope for variable.

Tag	Description	Attributes
url	Creates a URL with optional query parameters.	All attributes are of String type. var- Name of the exported scoped variable for the processed URL. scope- Scope of variable. value- URL to be processed. context- Context for a relative URL.
when	Subtag that would be evaluated, if a test condition evaluates to true.	test (boolean)- Required attribute that specifies the test condition.

Setting the Environment

Download JDeveloper 10.1.3 from: http://www.oracle.com/technology/ software/products/jdev/index.html. Extract the JDeveloper zip file to a directory, which installs the JDeveloper IDE. Download the Oracle database. Install the Oracle database including the sample schemas. We need to copy the Oracle database 11g JDBC drivers JAR file, ojdbc6.jar, for JDBC 4.0 to C:\JDeveloper\j2ee\ home\applib directory. Keep a copy of the JDBC JAR files and delete them from the C:\JDeveloper\jdbc\lib directory. Copy back the deleted JDBC JAR files to the directory after running the JSTL application. We also need to set the J2SE Version to JDK 6.0 as explained in Chapter 2. In JDeveloper, create a project for the JSTL SQL taglib. Select **File | New**, and in the **New Gallery** window, select **General** in the **Categories** list and **Application** in the **Items** list. Click on **OK** button. In the **Create Application** window, specify an Application Name, JSTLApp, and click on **OK**. In the **Create Project** window specify a Project Name, JSTLSQL, and click on **OK**. An Application and a Project node get added to the Applications Navigator.

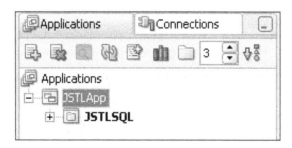

Select the project node and select **File | New**. In the **Categories,** select
Web Tier | JSP and select **JSP** in the **Items** listed, and click on **OK**. In the **Create
JSP Wizard,** click the next button. In the **Web Application** window, select J2EE 1.4
which is required for JSTL 1.1, and click on **Next**. In the **JSP File** window, specify a
File Name, catalog.jsp, and click on **Next**. Select the default setting, **Do Not Use an
Error Page to Handle Uncaught Exceptions** in This File, in the **Error Page Options**
window and click on **next**. In the **Tag Libraries** window, select the libraries JSTL
Core 1.1 and JSTL SQL 1.1 and click on the **Next** button.

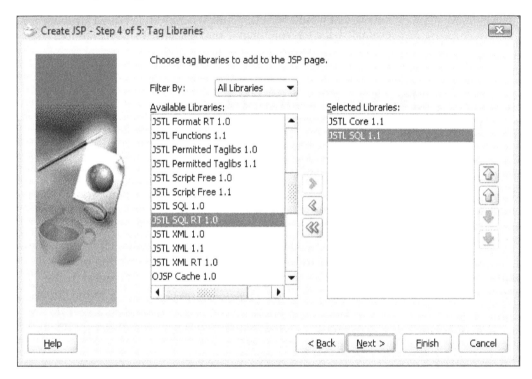

Select the default settings in the **HTML Options** window, and click on **Next**. Once
you click on **Finish** in the **Finish** window, a JSP and a web.xml get added to
the project.

After creating a project in JDeveloper in the **Applications-Navigator,** select the
project node and select **Tools | Project Properties**. Select the **Libraries** node in the
Project Properties window. The libraries should be listed in the project libraries.
If any of these libraries is not in the project libraries, add a library with the **Add
Library** button. For example, to add the JSTL 1.1 library, click on **Add Library** and
select the JSTL 1.1 library and then click on **OK**

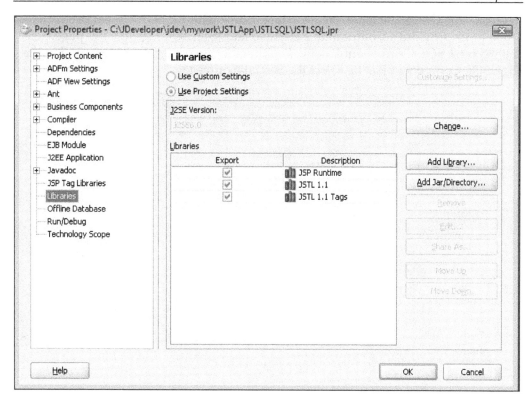

Creating a Database Table

In this section, we will create a database table in the Oracle database using the JSTL 1.1 SQL tags in JDeveloper 10.1.3 IDE. The database table will be created using the catalog.jsp JSP, which was created in the *Setting the Environment* section. The `taglib` directives for the JSTL SQL taglib and the JSTL Core taglib shown below get added to the catalog.jsp, because the JSTL SQL 1.1 and JSTL Core 1.1 taglibs were selected while creating the JSP.

```
<%@ taglib uri="http://java.sun.com/jsp/jstl/sql" prefix="sql"%>
<%@ taglib uri="http://java.sun.com/jsp/jstl/core" prefix="c"%>
```

To access the Oracle database, create a data source with the SQL tag `setDataSource`. JDeveloper provides a **Component Palette** to add JSTL SQL tags to a JSP page. Select the **JSTL 1.1 SQL** Component Palette. Position the cursor in the JSP page and in the JSTL SQL Component Palette select the SetDataSource tag.

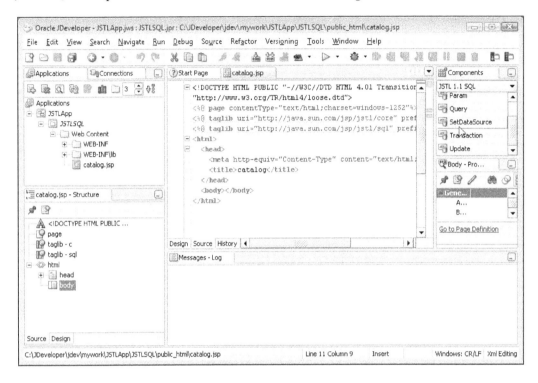

In the `setDataSource` tag specify the JDBC driver, `oracle.jdbc.OracleDriver`, in the `driver` attribute for the Oracle database. Specify the connection URL as: `jdbc:oracle:thin:@localhost:1521:ORCL` for the Oracle database. Also specify the username as `OE`, and the password. To add a tag attribute, press the space bar in the `setDataSource` tag and double-click on the attribute.

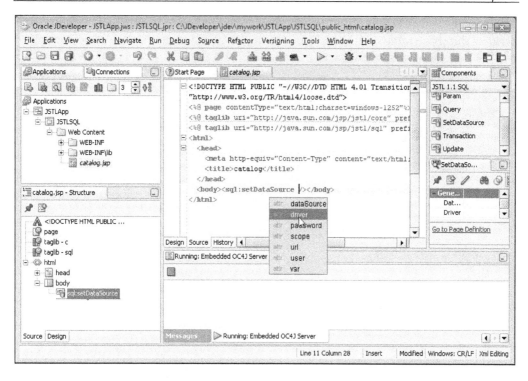

The `sql:setDataSource` tag with the added attributes, is shown below:

```
<sql:setDataSource driver="oracle.jdbc.OracleDriver" url="jdbc:oracle:
thin:@localhost:1521:ORCL" user="OE" password="pw"/>
```

Next, create a transaction with the `sql:transaction` tag to run SQL statements, to create a database table and to add rows to the database table. Position the cursor in the JSP page, and select Transaction in the **JSTL 1.1 SQL** Component Palette.

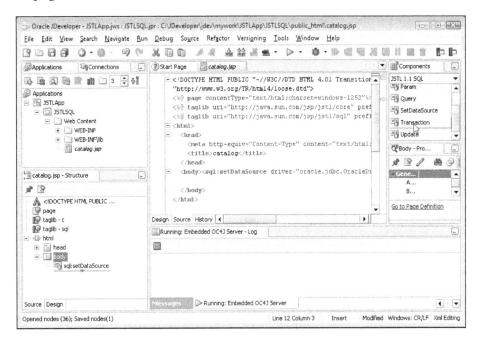

The `sql:transaction` tag provides dataSource and isolation attributes, which can be similarly added to the `setDataSource` tag attributes. Add the following `sql:transaction` tag to the JSP page.

```
<sql:transaction>
</sql:transaction>
```

The sql:update tag is used to create a database table and add rows to the database table. The sql:update tag is added within the sql:transaction tag. Position the cursor between the opening sql:transaction tag and the closing sql:transaction tag, and select the Update tag in the **JSTL 1.1 SQL** Component Palette.

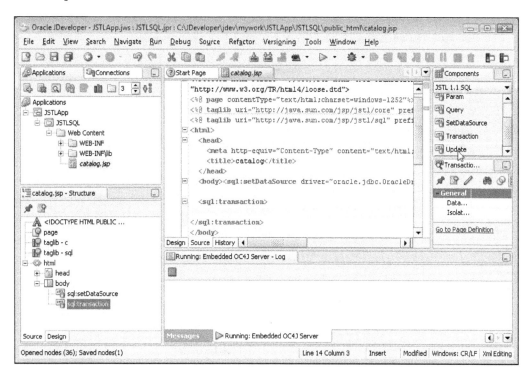

The `sql:update` may include the `sql`, `dataSource`, `var`, and scope attributes. First, create a database table with the JSTL SQL tags. The SQL CREATE statement is specified in the `sql` attribute of the `sql:update` tag. To add the `sql` attribute, press the space bar in the `sql:update` tag and double-click on the `sql` attribute in the attributes listed:

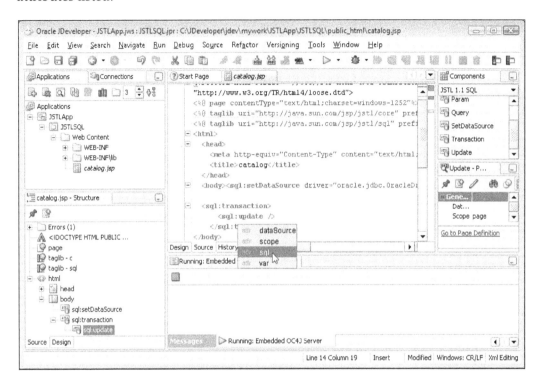

The `sql:update` tag to create a database table is as follows:

```
<sql:update   sql="CREATE TABLE OE.Catalog(CatalogId VARCHAR(25)
PRIMARY KEY, Journal VARCHAR(25), Publisher VARCHAR(25),
 Edition VARCHAR(25), Title Varchar(45), Author Varchar(25))">
</sql:update>
```

Next, add rows to the database table, with the `sql:update` tag. The INSERT statement is specified in the `sql` attribute of the `sql:update` tag.

```
<sql:update   sql="INSERT INTO OE.Catalog VALUES('catalog1', 'Oracle
Magazine', 'Oracle Publishing', 'Nov-Dec 2004', 'Database Resource
Manager', 'Kimberly Floss')">
</sql:update>
```

The **catalog.jsp** page needed to create a database table and to insert rows in the database table, is shown in the following listing:

```
<!DOCTYPE HTML PUBLIC "-//W3C//DTD HTML 4.01 Transitional//EN"
"http://www.w3.org/TR/html4/loose.dtd">
<%@ page contentType="text/html;charset=windows-1252"%>
<%@ taglib uri="http://java.sun.com/jsp/jstl/sql" prefix="sql"%>
<%@ taglib uri="http://java.sun.com/jsp/jstl/core" prefix="c"%>
<html>
  <head>
    <meta http-equiv="Content-Type" content="text/html;
charset=windows-1252"/>
    <title>catalog</title>
  </head>
  <body><sql:setDataSource driver="oracle.jdbc.OracleDriver"
url="jdbc:oracle:thin:@localhost:1521:ORCL" user="OE" password="pw"/>
    <sql:transaction>
<sql:update   sql="CREATE TABLE OE.Catalog(CatalogId VARCHAR(25)
PRIMARY KEY, Journal VARCHAR(25), Publisher VARCHAR(25),
 Edition VARCHAR(25), Title Varchar(45), Author Varchar(25))">
</sql:update>
<sql:update   sql="INSERT INTO OE.Catalog VALUES('catalog1', 'Oracle
Magazine', 'Oracle Publishing', 'Nov-Dec 2004', 'Database Resource
Manager', 'Kimberly
Floss')">
</sql:update>
<sql:update   sql="INSERT INTO OE.Catalog VALUES('catalog2', 'Oracle
Magazine', 'Oracle Publishing', 'Nov-Dec 2004', 'From ADF UIX to JSF',
'Jonas Jacobi')">
</sql:update>
<sql:update   sql="INSERT INTO OE.Catalog VALUES('catalog3', 'Oracle
Magazine',
'Oracle Publishing','March-April 2005','Starting with Oracle ADF',
'Steve Muench')">
</sql:update>
    </sql:transaction>
<%out.println("Database Table Created");%>
  </body>
</html>
```

Run the JSP, by right-clicking the JSP node in the **Applications Navigator** and selecting **Run**.

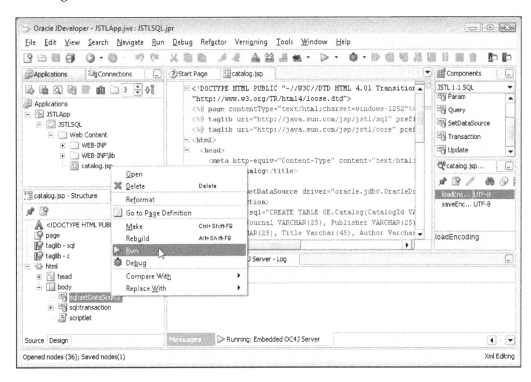

The database table gets created and rows get added to the database table.

Updating a Database Table

In this section, a database table row will be updated. Create a JSP **catalogUpdate. jsp** in the **JSTLSQL** project. As in the previous section, set the data source for the JSP page with the `setDataSource` tag. The UPDATE SQL statement is run with the `sql:update` tag. Add an Update tag to the JSP page from the Component Palette. The SQL statement has placeholders for specifying IN parameters for the UPDATE statement. Add the UPDATE SQL statement in the `sql` attribute of the `sql:update` tag.

```
<sql:update  sql="UPDATE OE.CATALOG SET TITLE=?, AUTHOR=?
WHERE CATALOGID=?">
</sql:update>
```

The values for the IN parameters are specified with the `sql:param` tags. Position the cursor in the `sql:update` statement, and select the Param tag in the **JSTL 1.1 SQL Component Palette**.

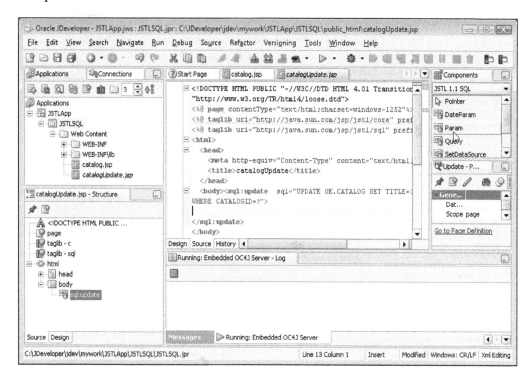

The param value is set with the `value` attribute in the `sql:param` tag. To add the `value` attribute, press the space bar in the `sql:param` tag and double-click on the **value** attribute.

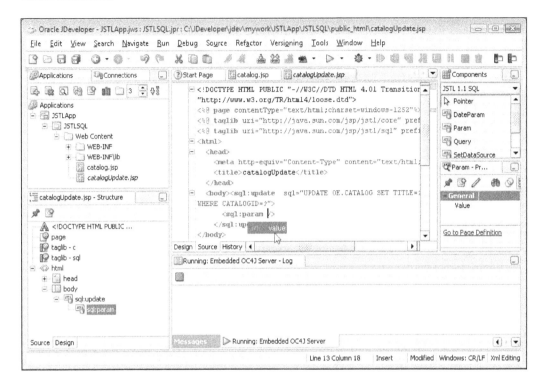

Specify the param `value` and similarly add `sql:param` tags to specify the param values corresponding to the IN parameters in the UPDATE SQL statement, as listed below:

```
<sql:param value="Introduction to ADF"/>
<sql:param value="Muench, Steve"/>
<sql:param value="catalog3"/>
```

The **catalogUpdate.jsp** is listed below:

```
<!DOCTYPE HTML PUBLIC "-//W3C//DTD HTML 4.01 Transitional//EN"
"http://www.w3.org/TR/html4/loose.dtd">
<%@ page contentType="text/html;charset=windows-1252"%>
<%@ taglib uri="http://java.sun.com/jsp/jstl/sql" prefix="sql"%>
<%@ taglib uri="http://java.sun.com/jsp/jstl/core" prefix="c"%>
<html>
  <head>
    <meta http-equiv="Content-Type" content="text/html;
```

```
charset=windows-1252"/>
    <title>catalogUpdate</title>
  </head>
  <body>
  <sql:setDataSource driver="oracle.jdbc.OracleDriver"
url="jdbc:oracle:thin:@localhost:1521:ORCL"  user="oe"
password="pw"/>
<sql:update  sql="UPDATE OE.CATALOG SET TITLE=?, AUTHOR=?
WHERE CATALOGID=?">
<sql:param value="Introduction to ADF"/>
<sql:param value="Muench, Steve"/>
<sql:param value="catalog3"/>
    </sql:update>
  </body>
  </html>
```

Run **catalogUpdate.jsp** by right-clicking on the JSP and selecting **Run**.

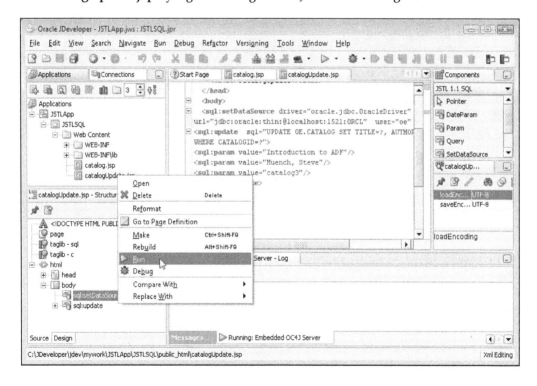

The database table gets updated.

Querying a Database Table

In this section, the database table created and modified in the previous sections will be queried, and the result is displayed in a HTML table. Create a JSP, **catalogQuery. jsp**. Select the **JSTL Core 1.1** and **JSTL SQL 1.1** tag libraries for the JSP. As in the previous sections, add a `setDataSource` tag for obtaining a connection with the Oracle database. The SQL `taglib` tag to query a database is `sql:query`. Position the cursor in the JSP page, and select Query tag in the SQL Component Palette.

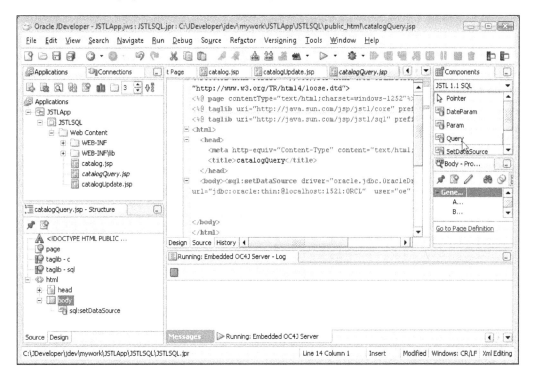

In the **Insert Query** window, specify the `var` attribute, which is a required attribute. The `var` attribute specifies the variable for the result set returned by the Query tag. Select the **Advanced Properties** tab.

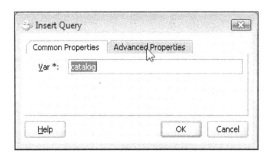

Specify the SQL query in the sql attribute field and click on the **OK** button.

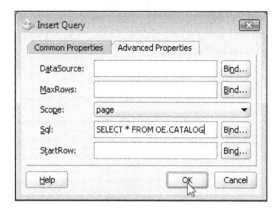

The `sql:query` tag gets added to the JSP page:

```
<sql:query  var="catalog" sql="SELECT * FROM CATALOG"/>
```

Add a `<table>` to display the result set of the Query tag. Add the table headers. A row will be added corresponding to each row in the result set. Select the **JSTL 1.1 Core** component library and add a ForEach tag to the **<table>**.

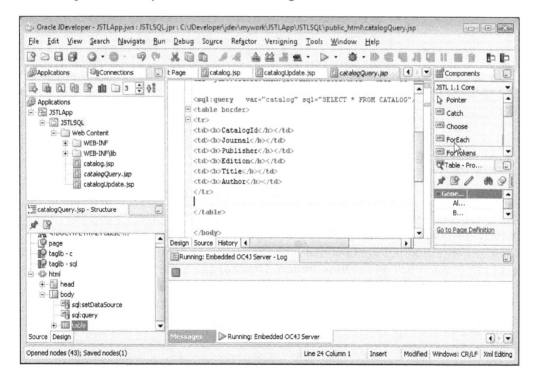

The `var` attribute of the `c:forEach` tag specifies the variable corresponding to a row in the result set. The `items` attribute specifies the EL binding to iterate over the rows in the result set returned by the Query tag. The rows in the result set returned by the `sql:query` tag are obtained with `${catalog.rows}` EL expression. The `c:forEach` tag in the **catalogQuery.jsp** JSP is as follows:

```
<c:forEach var="journal" items="${catalog.rows}">
</c:forEach>
```

Next, output the values corresponding to each column in a row to the JSP table. The JSP table values are added with the `c:out` tag. Add a `c:out` tag for each column from the **JSTL 1.1 Core** Component Palette, to the `c:forEach` tag.

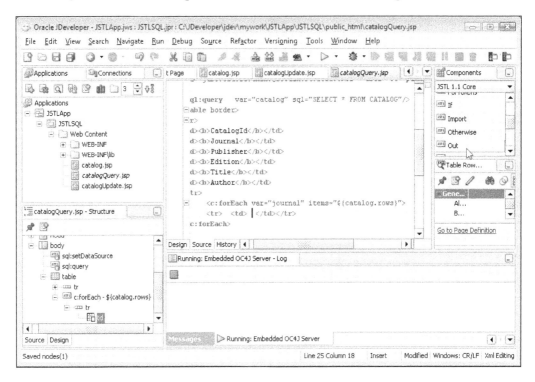

In the **Insert Out** window, specify the EL expression to bind a column Value. The column Value bindings are obtained with the column names in the result set. To bind a column Value, click on the **Bind** button. The `journal` is the variable corresponding to a row in the result set. For example, the EL expression to bind the `CatalogId` column is `${journal.CatalogId}`. Specify the EL expression in the Expression text area in the **Bind to Data** window, and click on the **OK** button.

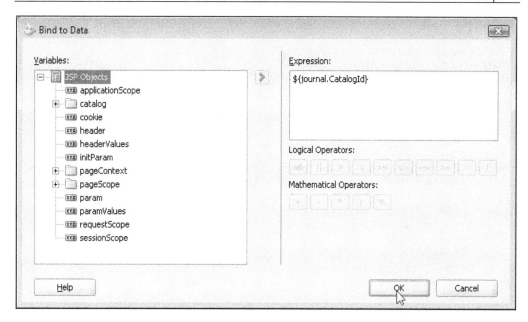

Click on the **OK** button in the **Insert Out** window.

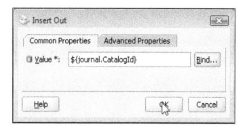

Similarly add c:out tags for the other columns in the result set. The **catalogQuery. jsp** is listed below:

```
<!DOCTYPE HTML PUBLIC "-//W3C//DTD HTML 4.01 Transitional//EN"
"http://www.w3.org/TR/html4/loose.dtd">
<%@ page contentType="text/html;charset=windows-1252"%>
<%@ taglib uri="http://java.sun.com/jsp/jstl/core" prefix="c"%>
<%@ taglib uri="http://java.sun.com/jsp/jstl/sql" prefix="sql"%>
<html>
  <head>
    <meta http-equiv="Content-Type" content="text/html;
charset=windows-1252"/>
    <title>catalogQuery</title>
  </head>
  <body><sql:setDataSource driver="oracle.jdbc.OracleDriver"
url="jdbc:oracle:thin:@localhost:1521:ORCL"  user="oe"
```

```
password="pw"/><sql:query var="catalog" sql="SELECT * FROM
OE.CATALOG"/>
<table border>
<tr>
    <td><b>CatalogId</b></td>
    <td><b>Journal</b></td>
    <td><b>Publisher</b></td>
    <td><b>Edition</b></td>
    <td><b>Title</b></td>
    <td><b>Author</b></td>
</tr>
<c:forEach var="journal" items="${catalog.rows}">
<tr>
    <td>
        <c:out value="${journal.CatalogId}"/>
    </td>
    <td><c:out value="${journal.Journal}"/></td>
    <td><c:out value="${journal.Publisher}"/></td>
    <td><c:out value="${journal.Edition}"/></td>
    <td><c:out value="${journal.Title}"/></td>
    <td><c:out value="${journal.Author}"/></td>
</tr>
</c:forEach>
</table>
</body>
</html>
```

To run the **catalogQuery.jsp,** right-click on the JSP and select **Run**:

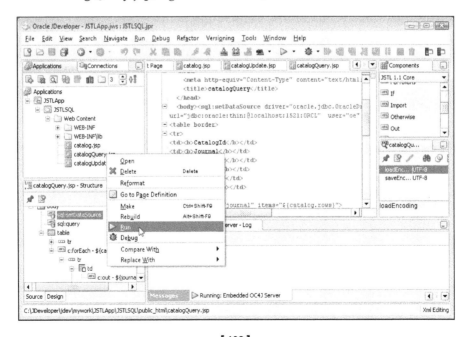

The result set obtained with the Query tag gets displayed in a HTML table.

CatalogId	Journal	Publisher	Edition	Title	Author
catalog1	Oracle Magazine	Oracle Publishing	Nov-Dec 2004	Database Resource Manager	Kimberly Floss
catalog2	Oracle Magazine	Oracle Publishing	Nov-Dec 2004	From ADF UIX to JSF	Jonas Jacobi
catalog3	Oracle Magazine	Oracle Publishing	March-April 2005	Introduction to ADF	Muench, Steve

Summary

The JSTL SQL tag library provides access to a database. JDeveloper 10.1.3 facilitates the development of a JSTL SQL application with a **Component Palette** for the **JSTL SQL 1.1** tags, from which tag library tags may be added to a JSP application. In this chapter, you have learnt to create an Oracle database table using JSTL SQL 1.1 tags in JDeveloper 10.1.3. You have also learnt to update the database table and query the database table using **JSTL SQL 1.1** tags.

4
Configuring JDBC in JBoss Application Server

JBoss 4.0 is an open-source application server configured to use **Hypersonic Database** (HSQLDB) by default. However, some **Java 2 Platform Enterprise Edition** (J2EE) developers would like to use databases other than Hypersonic Database to develop and deploy applications. The JBoss application server provides data source access for **Enterprise Java Beans** (EJB) persistence, and for J2EE applications. In this chapter, we will see how to configure JBoss to use other databases.

The JBoss 4.0 server makes use of Java Database Connectivity (JDBC) configuration files and data source files to configure the server with a database. To use the server with a database other than the default database, Hypersonic, the JDBC configuration files have to be modified and the data source file for the database has to be made available to the server. Download the JBoss 4.0 application server ZIP file from `http://labs.jboss.com/jbossas/downloads` and install JBoss server by extracting the ZIP file to a directory. In this chapter, you will learn how to do the following:

- Deploy a web application to JBoss Application Server from JDeveloper
    - JDBC 4.0 version of the web application deployed to JBoss server
- Configure JBoss server with Oracle database 10g with JDBC 4.0 Driver
- Configure JBoss server with MySQL Database with JDBC 4.0 Driver
- Configure JBoss server with PostgreSQL database server with JDBC 4.0 Driver
- Configure JBoss server with DB2 UDB database with JDBC 4.0 Driver
- Configure JBoss server with MS SQL Server with JDBC 4.0 Driver

Deploying a Web Application to JBoss from JDeveloper

In this section we will create a web application and deploy the web application to JBoss application server, all from JDeveloper IDE. JDeveloper has a built-in feature to configure a connection with JBoss application server, and deploy a web application to the server. First, create an application in JDeveloper by selecting **File | New**. In the **New Gallery** window select General in Categories and Application in Items and click on **OK**. In the **Create Application** window, specify an Application Name and click on the **OK** button. In the **Create Project** window, specify a project name and click **OK**. An application and a project get added to the Applications Navigator. Next, to add a JSP select the project node in the **Applications Navigator** and select **File | New**. In the **New Gallery** window select **Web Tier | JSP in Categories** and JSP in Items and click on **OK**. The **Create JSP Wizard** gets started. Now, click on **Next**. Select J2EE 1.4 in the **Web Application** window and click on **OK**. Specify a File Name in the **JSP File** window, and click on the **Next** button. Select the default setting in the **Error Page Options** window and click **Next**. Click on **Next** in the **Tag Libraries** window. Select the default settings in the **HTML Options** window, and click on **Next**. Click on **Finish** in the **Finish** window. Now, a JSP and **web.xml** gets added to **Applications Navigator**.

Next, create a database table in the MySQL database using the following SQL script:

```
CREATE TABLE Catalog( CatalogId VARCHAR(25)
PRIMARY KEY, Journal VARCHAR(25), Publisher VARCHAR(25),
 Edition VARCHAR(25), Title Varchar(45), Author Varchar(25));
INSERT INTO Catalog VALUES('catalog1', 'Oracle Magazine',
 'Oracle Publishing', 'Nov-Dec 2004', 'Database Resource Manager',
'Kimberly Floss');
INSERT INTO Catalog VALUES('catalog2', 'Oracle Magazine', 'Oracle
Publishing', 'Nov-Dec 2004', 'From ADF UIX to JSF', 'Jonas Jacobi');
```

Configure a connection with the MySQL database in JBoss application server as explained in the *Configuring JBoss Server with MySQL Database* section. We will obtain a connection with the MySQL database in catalog.jsp. Create an InitialContext object, and create a DataSource object using JNDI lookup on the MySQL data source, configured in JBoss application server.

```
InitialContext initialContext = new InitialContext();
DataSource ds = (DataSource)
initialContext.lookup("java:/MySqlDS");
```

Create a Connection object from the DataSource object using the getConnection() method and create a Statement object from the Connection object using the createStatement() method. Run an SQL query on the Catalog table using the executeQuery() method of the Statement interface. Iterate over the ResultSet and create an HTML table. The catalog.jsp file is listed below:

```
<%@ page contentType="text/html;charset=windows-1252"%>
<%@ page language="java" import="java.sql.*, javax.naming.*, javax.
sql.*" %>
<%
 InitialContext initialContext = new InitialContext();
 DataSource ds = (DataSource)
 initialContext.lookup("java:/MySqlDS");
 java.sql.Connection connection = ds.getConnection();
 Statement stmt=connection.createStatement();
 ResultSet resultSet=stmt.executeQuery("Select * from Catalog");
%>
<table border="1" cellspacing="0">
 <tr>
  <th>CatalogId</th>
  <th>Journal</th>
  <th>Publisher</th>
  <th>Edition</th>
  <th>Title</th>
  <th>Author</th>
 </tr>
 <%
 while (resultSet.next())
   {
%>
 <tr>
  <td><%out.println(resultSet.getString(1));%></td>
  <td><%out.println(resultSet.getString(2));%></td>
  <td><%out.println(resultSet.getString(3));%></td>
  <td><%out.println(resultSet.getString(4));%></td>
```

```
<td><%out.println(resultSet.getString(5));%></td>
<td><%out.println(resultSet.getString(6));%></td>
</tr>
<%
   }
%>
</table>
<%
resultSet.close();
stmt.close();
if(!connection.isClosed())
 connection.close();
%>
```

We will configure a connection with the JBoss application server in JDeveloper. Select the **Connections** tab, and in the Connections navigator, right-click on **Application Server** node and select the **New Application Server Connection**.

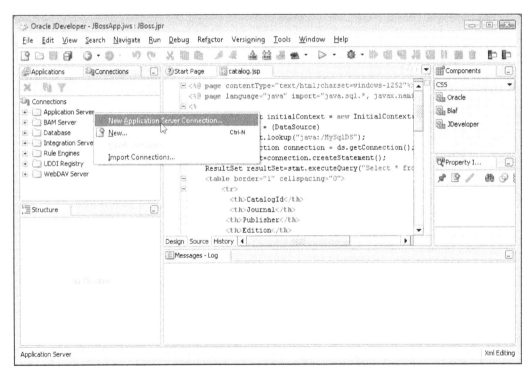

In the **Create Application Server Connection** Wizard, click the **Next** button. In the **Type** window specify a Connection Name, select Connection Type as JBoss 4.0.x, and click on **Next**.

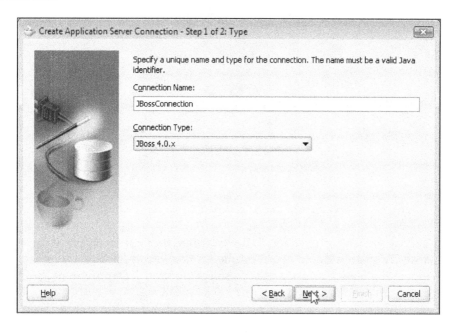

In the **JBoss Directory** window, specify the deploy directory of the JBoss application server and click on **Next**.

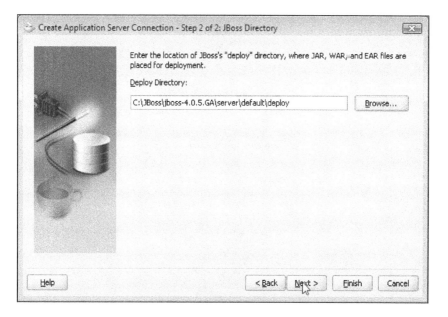

Click on **Finish** in the **Finish** window. A **JBossConnection** node gets added to the Application Server node in Connections navigator.

We will deploy the web application that we created to the JBoss application server. First, in order to create a deployment profile for the web application, select **File | New**. In the **New Gallery** window, select **General | Deployment Profiles** in Categories and WAR File in Items, and click on **OK**.

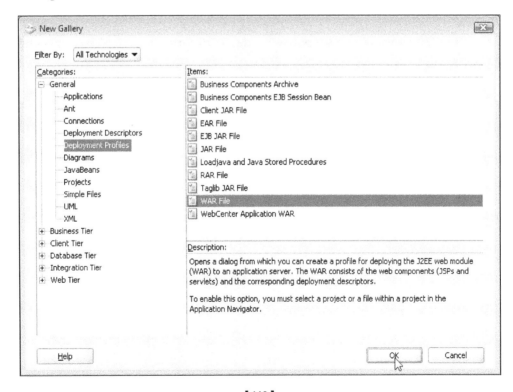

In the **Create Deployment Profile** window specify a Deployment Profile Name and click on **OK**. In the **WAR Deployment Profile Properties** window specify a J2EE Web Context Root and click **OK**.

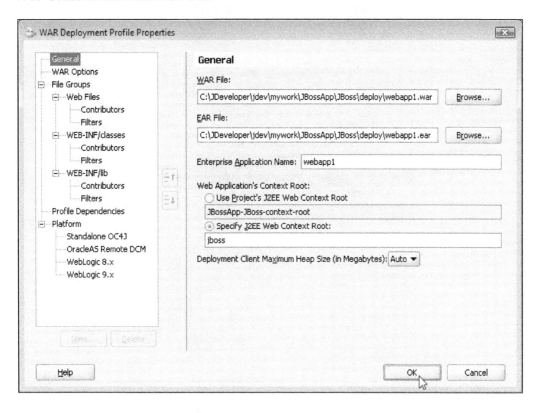

A deployment profile for the web application gets added to the **Applications Navigator**. We configured a connection with the JBoss application server earlier. So, next, deploy the deployment profile to the JBoss application server. Select **Deploy to | JBossConnection** by right-clicking on the deployment profile.

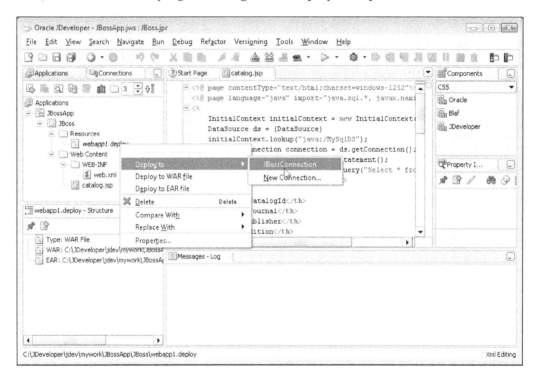

The web application gets deployed to the JBoss application server. Start the JBoss application server using the `C:\JBoss\jboss-4.0.5.GA\bin\run` batch script, if not done already. Run the `catalog.jsp` using URL `http://localhost:8080/jboss/catalog.jsp`. A connection gets established with MySQL database using the JNDI data source configured in the JBoss application server and an HTML table gets displayed for the `catalog.jsp`:

CatalogId	Journal	Publisher	Edition	Title	Author
catalog1	Oracle Magazine	Oracle Publishing	Nov-Dec 2004	Database Resource Manager	Kimberly Floss
catalog2	Oracle Magazine	Oracle Publishing	Nov-Dec 2004	From ADF UIX to JSF	Jonas Jacobi

JDBC 4.0 Version

JBoss application server 4 does not support JDBC 4.0. When support is added for JDBC 4.0, we will be able to use the new features in JDBC 4.0. JDBC 4.0 supports connection tracking to close unusable connections. Connection tracking is implemented by the connection pool manager using the `isValid()` method of the `Connection` interface. If the connection pool manager detects that a connection is not valid, it closes the connection thus reducing the accumulation of unusable connections, which hamper connection pool performance. For a `Connection` object `conn`, connection tracking is implemented as follows:

```
if(!connection.isValid())
  connection.close();
```

MySQL Connector/J 5.1 driver supports the wrapper pattern, which is implemented in the Wrapper interface. MySQL-specific extensions to the JDBC API contain vendor-specific methods, which may be accessed using the wrapper pattern. MySQL's extensions to the JDBC API are available in the `com.mysql.jdbc` package. It provides the `com.mysql.jdbc.Connection` interface as an extension to the `java.sql.Connection` interface. Check if the `java.sql.Connection` object is a wrapper for the `com.mysql.jdbc.Connection` interface using the `isWrapperFor()` method to unwrap the `com.mysql.jdbc.Connection` resource and obtain an object that implements the interface. If the `java.sql.Connection` object is a wrapper, then unwrap the MySQL extension to the `Connection` interface using the `unwrap()` method, and create an object of type `com.mysql.jdbc.Connection`.

```
Class class = Class.forName("com.mysql.jdbc.Connection");
if(connection.isWrapperFor(class)) {
com.mysql.jdbc.Connection conn= (com.mysql.jdbc.Connection)connection.
unwrap(class);
}
```

Another new feature available in JDBC 4.0 for connection management is the provision to set client info properties on a Connection object. Thus, if the connection pool has a reduced performance due to inordinate excessive use of CPU by some connections, the connection pool manager is able to identify which of the connections are causing the excessive use of CPU and is able to close those connections. To set and get client info properties, the `Connection` interface provides the `setClientInfo()` and the `getClientInfo()` methods. For example, set the `ApplicationName`, `ClientUser`, and `ClientHostname` client info properties:

```
conn.setClientInfo("ApplicationName","JBossApp");
conn.setClientInfo("ClientUser","JBossUser");
conn.setClientInfo("ClientHostname","JBossHost");
```

MySQL's extension to the `Connection` interface provides a method `clientPrepareStatement()`, which may be used to create a client-side prepared statement and run an SQL query.

```
String sql="SELECT CATALOGID, JOURNAL, PUBLISHER, EDITION, TITLE,
          AUTHOR from Catalog WHERE CATALOGID=?";
PreparedStatement pstmt=conn.clientPrepareStatement(sql);
```

Prepared statements are precompiled SQL statements that may run with different parameter values. Prepared statements reduce the risk of SQL injection due to separation of logic and data, and also improve performance. Prepared statements are either server-side prepared statements or client-side prepared statements. With server-side prepared statements, on receipt of a SQL statement, a database parses the statement, checks for syntax errors, prepares an execution plan for the statement, and runs the statement. When the database receives the same statement again, it uses the previously prepared statement with the same execution plan to run the statement. If a statement is to be run multiple times with different parameters, it is advantageous to use prepared statements. Prepared statements are compiled only once by the database server and run multiple times with different parameter values.

The advantage of prepared statements is better performance due to increased speed and reduced CPU load. Moreover, the same compiled statement and execution plan are used by the database server. If a database server does not support server-side prepared statements, which are the same as those of MySQL databases (versions before 4.1), the prepared statements may be emulated by the driver. These are called client-side prepared statements.

MySQL's Connector/J 5.1 driver provides support for enhanced chained exceptions. Exceptions chained to a `SQLException` and causes of the exceptions can be retrieved using the `For-Each` loop, introduced in J2SE 6.0. Specify an error page in catalog.jsp:

```
<%@ page errorPage="errorpage.jsp" %>
```

In the error page use the `For-Each` loop to output the chained exceptions and chained causes.

```
<%@ page isErrorPage="true" %>
<%
 for(Throwable e : exception )
  {
   out.println("Error encountered: " + e);
  }
%>
```

The JDBC 4.0 version of the `catalog.jsp` deployed to JBoss is listed below:

```
<%@ page contentType="text/html;charset=windows-1252"%>
<%@ page language="java" import="java.sql.*, javax.naming.*, javax.
sql.*,oracle.jdbc.*" %>
<%@ page errorPage="errorpage.jsp" %>
<%
 InitialContext initialContext = new InitialContext();
 DataSource ds = (DataSource)
 initialContext.lookup("java:/MySqlDS");
 java.sql.Connection connection = ds.getConnection();
connection.setClientInfo("ApplicationName","JBossApp");
connection.setClientInfo("ClientUser","JBossUser");
connection.setClientInfo("ClientHostname","JBossHost");
Class class = Class.forName("com.mysql.jdbc.Connection");
if(connection.isWrapperFor(class))
 {
  com.mysql.jdbc.Connection conn=
               (com.mysql.jdbc.Connection)connection.unwrap(class);
  conn.setClientInfo("ApplicationName","JBossApp");
  conn.setClientInfo("ClientUser","JBossUser");
  conn.setClientInfo("ClientHostname","JBossHost");
  String sql="SELECT CATALOGID, JOURNAL, PUBLISHER, EDITION, TITLE,
             AUTHOR from Catalog WHERE CATALOGID=?";
  PreparedStatement pstmt=conn.clientPrepareStatement(sql);
  pstmt.setString(1, "catalog1");
  ResultSet rs=pstmt.executeQuery();
%>
<table border="1" cellspacing="0">
 <tr>
  <th>Catalog Id</th>
  <th>Journal</th>
  <th>Publisher</th>
  <th>Edition</th>
  <th>Title</th>
  <th>Author</th>
 </tr>
 <%
  while (rs.next())
   {
%>
 <tr>
  <td><%out.println(resultSet.getString(1));%></td>
  <td><%out.println(resultSet.getString(2));%></td>
  <td><%out.println(resultSet.getString(3));%></td>
```

```
<td><%out.println(resultSet.getString(4));%></td>
<td><%out.println(resultSet.getString(5));%></td>
<td><%out.println(resultSet.getString(6));%></td>
</tr>
<%
    }
%>
</table>
<%
 rs.close();
 pstmt.close();
 if(!connection.isClosed())
  connection.close();
 }
%>
```

JBoss Deployment Descriptors for EJBs

We would need to configure some EJB configuration files to use a JBoss application server data source in an EJB. The `standardjaws.xml` configuration file represents the JBossCMP engine. It contains the JNDI name of the default data source, jdbc-sql mappings, and CMP entity bean settings. Instead use the `jaws.xml` file to use a custom configuration for mapping **Container-Managed-Persistence** (CMP) entity EJBs. In both cases, the file is copied to the META-INF directory of the EJB `.jar` file. The `standardjaws.xml` and `jaws.xml` configuration files do the following:

1. Specify a data source and a type mapping for the data source.

2. Specify how tables are built or used.

3. Define finder methods to access the entity beans.

4. Define type mappings.

A data source is a Java Naming and Directory Interface (JNDI) object used to obtain a connection from a connection pool to a database. Hypersonic Database is the default data source configured with JBoss 4.0. You need to modify `jaws.xml` or `standardjaws.xml` to use another database with CMP entity EJBs. The `standardjaws.xml` or `jaws.xml` is required to be modified only if using CMP 1.1 entity beans.

The `standardjbosscmp-jdbc.xml` configuration file is the standard deployment descriptor to configure the JBoss CMP container. It can be replaced with a custom configuration version called `jbosscmp-jdbc.xml` and goes in the META-INF directory of the EJB `.jar` file. JBoss 4.0 is set as a default to a Hypersonic Database. We need to edit this file to use another database. The file paths in the following sections would be relative to the JBoss installation directory, if they are relative paths.

Configuring JBoss Server with Oracle Database

Oracle is a leading enterprise database used for its performance and reliability. To configure JBoss 4.0 with Oracle, we need to put Oracle's driver classes in the runtime classpath of the JBoss application server. Copy Oracle database 11g JDBC 4.0 driver's JAR file, `ojdbc6.jar`, to the `C:\JBoss\jboss-4.0.5.GA\server\default\lib` directory. We also need to set the `JAVA_HOME` environment variable to JDK 6.0.

To use Oracle's transactional (XA) data source, copy `/docs/examples/jca/oracle-xa-ds.xml` to the `/server/default/deploy` directory. The directory paths are relative to the JBoss application server installation directory. To configure with the non-XA data source, copy `/docs/examples/jca/oracle-ds.xml` to the `/server/default/deploy` directory and modify the `oracle-ds.xml` configuration file. The `<driver-class/>` and `<connection-url/>` settings for Oracle would vary with the type of driver used. The `<driver-class/>` and `<connection-url/>` settings for Oracle are listed in the following table:

Driver Type	Driver Class	Connection URL
Oracle OCI Type 2 Driver	oracle.jdbc.OracleDriver	jdbc:oracle:oci:@<database>
Oracle Thin Type 4 Driver	oracle.jdbc.OracleDriver	jdbc:oracle:thin:@<host>:<port>:<database>
Oracle OCI XA Type 4 Driver	oracle.jdbc.xa.client.OracleXADataSource	jdbc:oracle:oci:@<database>
Oracle Thin XA Type 4 Driver	oracle.jdbc.xa.client.OracleXADataSource	jdbc:oracle:thin:@<host>:<port>:<database>

In the Connection URL setting, `<host>` is the HOST value specified in the `<Oracle10g>/network/ADMIN/tnsnames.ora` file, `<port>` is the PORT value specified in the `tnsnames.ora` file, and `<database>` is the database name. `<Oracle10g>` is the directory in which Oracle database is installed.

If you would rather encrypt database passwords instead of using text passwords in the datasource configuration file `oracle-ds.xml`, use the `org.jboss.resource.security.SecureIdentityLoginModule` module to encode the database password. Run the following command from the JBoss base directory to encrypt the database password:

```
C:\jboss> java -cp lib/jboss-common.jar;lib/jboss-jmx.jar;server/default/
lib/jbosssx.jar;server/default/lib/jboss-jca.jar org.jboss.resource.
security.SecureIdentityLoginModule password
```

The database password gets encoded/encrypted and the encoded password gets output. The encoded password corresponding to Oracle login password `password` is `5dfc52b51bd35553df8592078de921bc`. If using password encryption, remove the `user-name` and `password` settings from the `oracle-ds.xml` configuration file and specify the security-domain that maps to the `login-config.xml` security domain for the `org.jboss.resource.security.SecureIdentityLoginModule` login module for the Oracle database. The modified `oracle-ds.xml` is as follows:

```
<?xml version="1.0" encoding="UTF-8"?>
<datasources>
  <local-tx-datasource>
    <jndi-name>OracleDS</jndi-name>
    <connection-url>jdbc:oracle:thin:@localhost:1521:orcl
        </connection-url>
    <driver-class>oracle.jdbc.OracleDriver</driver-class>
    <!--   <user-name>OE</user-name>
    <password>pw</password>   -->
    <!-- Use the security domain defined in conf/login-config.xml -->
    <security-domain>OracleDBPassword</security-domain>
  </local-tx-datasource>
</datasources>
```

If using the encoded password modify the `login-config.xml` file in the `\server\default\conf` directory to add an application policy for the `OracleDBPassword` security domain. The security domain specifies the encoded/encrypted password, which we created earlier, for Oracle database. Add the following `<application-policy/>` element to the `<policy/>` element in the `login-config.xml` file.

```
<application-policy name="OracleDBPassword">
 <authentication>
 <login-module code="org.jboss.resource.security.
SecureIdentityLoginModule" flag="required">
   <module-option name="username">OE</module-option>
   <module-option name="password">5dfc52b51bd35553df8592078de921bc
   </module-option>
```

```
    <module-option name="managedConnectionFactoryName">
        jboss.jca:name=OraclelDS,service=LocalTxCM</module-option>
  </login-module>
  </authentication>
</application-policy>
```

This configures the JBoss application server with the Oracle database. To use CMP Entity EJBs with the Oracle data source, some additional modifications are required. Modify the `standardjbosscmp-jdbc.xml` or `jbosscmp-jdbc.xml` configuration file setting the `<datasource>` and `<datasource-mapping>` elements to use Oracle.

```
<jbosscmp-jdbc>
 <defaults>
  <datasource>java:/OracleDS</datasource>
   <datasource-mapping>Oracle9i</datasource-mapping>
 </defaults>
</jbosscmp-jdbc>
```

Modify the `standardjaws.xml` or `jaws.xml` configuration file setting the `<datasource>` and `<type-mapping>` elements, if using CMP 1.1 entity beans:

```
<jaws>
 <datasource>java:/OracleDS</datasource>
  <type-mapping>Oracle9i</type-mapping>
</jaws>
```

Modifying the `oracle-ds.xml`, `standardjaws.xml`, `standardjbosscmp-jdbc.xml`, and `login-config.xml` files configures the JBoss 4.0 server to be used with an Oracle database.

Configuring JBoss Server with MySQL Database

MySQL is an open-source database used by many open-source projects and small organizations. To use JBoss 4.0 with MySQL, we have to put the MySQL driver classes into the runtime classpath of JBoss application server and copy the MySQL Connector/J 5.1 driver JAR file to the `C:\JBoss\jboss-4.0.5.GA\server\default\lib` directory. MySQL Connector/J 5.1 driver supports JDBC 4.0 and can be obtained from `http://dev.mysql.com/downloads/connector/j/5.1.html`. We also need to set the `JAVA_HOME` environment variable to JDK 6.0.

To use the MySQL data source, copy `/docs/examples/jca/mysql-ds.xml` to the `/server/default/deploy` directory. Modify the `mysql-ds.xml` configuration file by setting `<driver-class/>` to `com.mysql.jdbc.Driver` and `<connection-url/>` to `jdbc:mysql://localhost:3306/test`.

By default a password is not required for the root user. Therefore, if a root user password is not set, the password element may be specified as an empty element (`<password></password>`). If you would rather encrypt database passwords instead of using text passwords in the datasource configuration file `mysql-ds.xml`, use the `org.jboss.resource.security.SecureIdentityLoginModule` module to encode the database password as discussed in the Oracle database section. If using password encryption, remove the `user-name` and `password` settings from the `mysql-ds.xml` configuration file and specify the security-domain that maps to the `login-config.xml` security domain for the `org.jboss.resource.security.SecureIdentityLoginModule` login module for the MySQL database. The modified `mysql-ds.xml` is as follows:

```
<?xml version="1.0" encoding="UTF-8"?>
<datasources>
  <local-tx-datasource>
    <jndi-name>MySqlDS</jndi-name>
    <connection-url>jdbc:mysql://localhost:3306/test</connection-url>
    <driver-class>com.mysql.jdbc.Driver</driver-class>
    <!--  <user-name>root</user-name>
    <password>pw</password>  -->
   <!-- Use the security domain defined in conf/login-config.xml -->
   <security-domain>MySQLDBPassword</security-domain>
  </local-tx-datasource>
</datasources>
```

If using the encoded password modify the `login-config.xml` file in the `\server\default\conf` directory to add an application policy for the `MySQLDBPassword` security domain. The security domain specifies the encoded/encrypted password, which we created earlier. Add the following `<application-policy/>` element to the `<policy/>` element in the `login-config.xml` file.

```
<application-policy name="MySQLDBPassword">
 <authentication>
 <login-module code="org.jboss.resource.security.
    SecureIdentityLoginModule" flag="required">
  <module-option name="username">root</module-option>
  <module-option name="password">5dfc52b51bd35553df8592078de921bc
  </module-option>
  <module-option name="managedConnectionFactoryName">jboss.jca:name=
    MySqlDS,service=LocalTxCM</module-option>
```

```
      </login-module>
      </authentication>
    </application-policy>
```

The following JBoss configuration with MySQL database is not required for the example application in this chapter. To use CMP entity EJBs with the MySQL data source some additional modifications are required. Set the `<datasource>` and `<datasource-mapping>` elements in the `standardjbosscmp-jdbc.xml` or `jbosscmp-jdbc.xml` file.

```
    <jbosscmp-jdbc>
     <defaults>
      <datasource>java:/MySqlDS</datasource>
       <datasource-mapping>mySQL</datasource-mapping>
     </defaults>
    </jbosscmp-jdbc>
```

We also have to set the `<datasource>` and `<type-mapping>` elements in the `standardjaws.xml` or `jaws.xml` file, if using CMP 1.1 entity beans.

```
    <jaws>
     <datasource>java:/MySqlDS</datasource>
      <type-mapping>mySQL</type-mapping>
    </jaws>
```

Modifying the `mysql-ds.xml`, `standardjaws.xml`, `standardjbosscmp-jdbc.xml`, and `login-config.xml` files configures the JBoss 4.0 server to be used with a MySQL database.

Configuring JBoss Server with PostgreSQL Database

PostgreSQL database is one of the most commonly used open-source relational databases. The first step is to get the database driver classes into the runtime classpath of JBoss application server. The JDBC 4.0 driver for PostgreSQL database may be obtained from `http://jdbc.postgresql.org/download.html`. Copy the PostgreSQL driver JAR file `postgresql-8.2-507.jdbc4.jar` to the JBoss installation's `/server/default/lib` directory. We also need to set the `JAVA_HOME` environment variable to JDK 6.0 and then use its data source by copying `/docs/examples/jca/postgres-ds.xml` to the `/server/default/deploy` directory.

Modify the `postgres-ds.xml` configuration file by setting `<driver-class/>` to `org.postgresql.Driver` and `<connection-url/>` to `jdbc:postgresql://localhost:5432/postgres`.

If you would rather encrypt database passwords instead of using text passwords in the datasource configuration file postgres-ds.xml, use the org.jboss.resource. security.SecureIdentityLoginModule module to encode the database password as discussed in the Oracle database section. If using password encryption, remove the user-name and password settings from the postgres-ds.xml configuration file and specify the security-domain that maps to the login-config.xml security domain for the org.jboss.resource.security.SecureIdentityLoginModule login module for the PosgreSQL database. The modified postgres-ds.xml is as follows:

```
<?xml version="1.0" encoding="UTF-8"?>
<datasources>
  <local-tx-datasource>
    <jndi-name>PosgreSQLDS</jndi-name>
    <connection-url>jdbc:postgresql://localhost:5432/postgres
    </connection-url>
    <driver-class>org.postgresql.Driver</driver-class>
    <!--  <user-name>postgresql</user-name>
    <password>pw</password>  -->
   <!-- Use the security domain defined in conf/login-config.xml -->
   <security-domain>PostgreSQLDBPassword</security-domain>
  </local-tx-datasource>
</datasources>
```

If using the encoded password, modify the login-config.xml file in the \server\ default\conf directory to add an application policy for the PostgreSQLDBPassword security domain. The security domain specifies the encoded/encrypted password, which we created earlier. Add the following <application-policy/> element to the <policy/> element in the login-config.xml file.

```
<application-policy name="PostgreSQLDBPassword">
 <authentication>
 <login-module code="org.jboss.resource.security.
    SecureIdentityLoginModule" flag="required">
  <module-option name="username">postgresql</module-option>
  <module-option name="password">5dfc52b51bd35553df8592078de921bc
  </module-option>
  <module-option name="managedConnectionFactoryName">jboss.jca:name=
    PostgreSQLDS,service=LocalTxCM</module-option>
 </login-module>
 </authentication>
</application-policy>
```

If a CMP entity EJB needs to access the `PostgreSQL` data source, some additional modifications would be required. Modify `standardjbosscmp-jdbc.xml` or `jbosscmp-jdbc.xml` to set the `<datasource>` and `<datasource-mapping>` elements.

```
<jbosscmp-jdbc>
 <defaults>
  <datasource>java:/PostgreSQLDS</datasource>
   <datasource-mapping>PostgreSQL</datasource-mapping>
 </defaults>
</jbosscmp-jdbc>
```

We also have to modify `standardjaws.xml` or `jaws.xml` to set the `<datasource>` and `<type-mapping>` elements, if using CMP 1.1 entity beans.

```
<jaws>
 <datasource>java:/PostgreSQLDS</datasource>
  <type-mapping>PostgreSQL</type-mapping>
</jaws>
```

By modifying the `postgres-ds.xml`, `standardjaws.xml`, `standardjbosscmp-jdbc.xml`, and `login-config.xml`, the JBoss 4.0 server is configured to be used with a PostgreSQL database.

Configuring JBoss Server with DB2 Database

IBM's DB2 Universal Database is a full-featured, robust, scalable, and easy-to-use database server, which may be used on Linux, UNIX, and Windows platforms. Begin by adding its driver to the runtime classpath of the JBoss application server. IBM Data Server Driver for JDBC and SQLJ Version 4.0 supports JDBC 4.0 and may be downloaded from `https://www14.software.ibm.com/webapp/iwm/web/reg/download.do?source=swg-informixfpd&S_PKG=dl&lang=en_US&cp=UTF-8#`. For JDBC 4.0 functionality add the `db2jcc4.jar` to the JBoss's installation `/server/default/lib` directory. To use the JDBC 4.0 features set the `JAVA_HOME` environment variable to JDK 6.0. Copy `/docs/examples/jca/db2-ds.xml` to the `/server/default/deploy` directory to configure the JBoss server with the DB2 data source.

Next, modify the `db2-ds.xml` configuration file by setting `<driver-class/>` to `com.ibm.db2.jcc.DB2Driver` and `<connection-url/>` to `jdbc:db2://localhost:50000/database` with DB2 being the database name.

For encrypting database passwords instead of using text passwords in the datasource configuration file db2-ds.xml, use the org.jboss.resource.security. SecureIdentityLoginModule module to encode the DB2 database password as discussed in the Oracle database section. If using password encryption, remove the user-name and password settings from the db2-ds.xml configuration file and specify the security-domain that maps to the login-config.xml security domain for the org.jboss.resource.security.SecureIdentityLoginModule login module for the DB2 database. The modified db2-ds.xml for DB2 database server called DB2 is as follows:

```
<?xml version="1.0" encoding="UTF-8"?>
<datasources>
  <local-tx-datasource>
    <jndi-name>DB2DS</jndi-name>
    <connection-url>jdbc:db2://localhost:50000/DB2</connection-url>
    <driver-class>com.ibm.db2.jcc.DB2Driver</driver-class>
    <!--  <user-name>db2</user-name>
    <password>pw</password>  -->
   <!-- Use the security domain defined in conf/login-config.xml -->
   <security-domain>DB2DBPassword</security-domain>
  </local-tx-datasource>
</datasources>
```

If using the encoded password, modify the login-config.xml file in the \server\ default\conf directory to add an application policy for the DB2DBPassword security domain. The security domain specifies the encoded/encrypted password, which we created earlier. Add the following <application-policy/> element to the <policy/> element in the login-config.xml file.

```
<application-policy name="DB2DBPassword">
 <authentication>
 <login-module code="org.jboss.resource.security.
    SecureIdentityLoginModule" flag="required">
  <module-option name="username">db2</module-option>
  <module-option name="password">5dfc52b51bd35553df8592078de921bc
  </module-option>
  <module-option name="managedConnectionFactoryName">jboss.jca:name=
    DB2DS,service=LocalTxCM</module-option>
 </login-module>
 </authentication>
</application-policy>
```

Additional modifications would be required, if the DB2 database is to be accessed from a CMP entity EJB. Modify the `standardjbosscmp-jdbc.xml` or `jbosscmp-jdbc.xml` as follows:

```
<jbosscmp-jdbc>
 <defaults>
  <datasource>java:/DB2DS</datasource>
    <datasource-mapping>DB2</datasource-mapping>
 </defaults>
</jbosscmp-jdbc>
```

We also have to modify `standardjaws.xml` or `jaws.xml` to set `<datasource>` and `<type-mapping>`, if using CMP 1.1 entity beans.

```
<jaws>
 <datasource>java:/DB2DS</datasource>
  <type-mapping>DB2</type-mapping>
</jaws>
```

The above configuration changes allow us to use DB2 with JBoss.

Configuring JBoss Server with SQL Server

SQL Server is a comprehensive data management and analysis solution to build, deploy, and manage enterprise applications. In this section, we will configure JBoss application server with SQL Server 2000 and SQL Server 2005. Copy the SQL Server JDBC 4.0 JAR file to JBoss server as we did with the other databases. I-net software's Merlia JDBC drivers support JDBC 4.0, where the Merlia driver ZIP file `Merlia_Trial_7.02.zip` may be obtained from `http://www.inetsoftware.de/products/jdbc/mssql/merlia/`. Extract the Merlia ZIP file to a directory, add `Merlia.jar` to the JBoss's installation `/server/default/lib` directory, and set the `JAVA_HOME` environment variable to JDK 6.0. We also have to copy the SQL Server data source file to the JBoss server deploy directory. Copy `docs\examples\jca\mssql-ds.xml` for non-transactional data source, or `\docs\examples\jca\mssql-xa-ds.xml` for transactional data source to the `\server\default\deploy` directory.

Modify the `mssql-ds.xml` configuration file to set the driver class and connection URL, and specify `<driver-class/>` as `com.inet.tds.TdsDriver`. For SQL Server 2000, specify `<connection-url/>` as `jdbc:inetdae7:localhost:1433`; for SQL Server 2005, specify `<connection-url/>` as `jdbc:inetdae7:localhost:port`. The variable `port` number for SQL Server 2005 is obtained from the SQL Server

Configuration Manager. Select the **SQL Server 2005 Network Configuration |
Protocols** for SQLEXPRESS node in **the SQL Server Configuration Manager**. Right-
click on the **TCP/IP** node, select Properties, and then select the **IP Addresses** tab.
In **IP ALL**, the TCP Dynamic Port specifies the port for SQL Server 2005. The port
number for SQL Server 2005 changes when the server is restarted.

For encrypting database passwords instead of using text passwords in the datasource
configuration file `mssql-ds.xml`, use the `org.jboss.resource.security.`
`SecureIdentityLoginModule` module to encode the SQL Server database password
as discussed in the Oracle database section. If using password encryption, remove
the `user-name` and `password` settings from the `mssql-ds.xml` configuration file and
specify the security-domain that maps to the `login-config.xml` security domain for
the `org.jboss.resource.security.SecureIdentityLoginModule` login module
for the SQL Server database. The modified `mssql-ds.xml` for SQL Server database
server is as follows:

```
<?xml version="1.0" encoding="UTF-8"?>
<datasources>
  <local-tx-datasource>
    <jndi-name>MSSQLDS</jndi-name>
    <connection-url>jdbc:inetdae7:localhost:1433</connection-url>
    <driver-class>com.inet.tds.TdsDriver</driver-class>
    <!--  <user-name>sqlserver</user-name>
    <password>pw</password>  -->
    <!-- Use the security domain defined in conf/login-config.xml -->
    <security-domain>MSSQLServerDBPassword</security-domain>
  </local-tx-datasource>
</datasources>
```

If using the encoded password, modify the `login-config.xml` file in the `\server\`
`default\conf` directory to add an application policy for the `MSSQLServerDBPassword`
security domain. The security domain specifies the encoded/encrypted password,
which we created earlier. Add the following `<application-policy/>` element to the
`<policy/>` element in the `login-config.xml` file.

```
<application-policy name="MSSQLServerDBPassword">
 <authentication>
 <login-module code="org.jboss.resource.security.
     SecureIdentityLoginModule" flag="required">
  <module-option name="username">sqlserver</module-option>
  <module-option name="password">5dfc52b51bd35553df8592078de921bc
  </module-option>
  <module-option name="managedConnectionFactoryName">jboss.jca:name=
     MSSQLDS,service=LocalTxCM</module-option>
 </login-module>
 </authentication>
 </application-policy>
```

If a CMP entity EJB is deployed to JBoss with SQL Server access, we have to modify the `standardjbosscmp-jdbc.xml`/`jbosscmp-jdbc.xml` and `standardjaws.xml`/ `jaws.xml` configuration files. Set the `<datasource>` and `<datasource-mapping>` elements of `standardjbosscmp-jdbc.xml` or `jbosscmp-jdbc.xml` as follows:

```
<jbosscmp-jdbc>
 <defaults>
  <datasource>java:/MSSQLDS</datasource>
   <datasource-mapping>MS SQLSERVER</datasource-mapping>
 </defaults>
</jbosscmp-jdbc>
```

Set the `<datasource>` and `<type-mapping>` elements in `standardjaws.xml` or `jaws.xml` as follows, if using CMP 1.1 entity beans:

```
<jaws>
 <datasource>java:/MSSQLDS</datasource>
  <type-mapping>MS SQLSERVER</type-mapping>
</jaws>
```

For SQL Server 2000, set the datasource-mapping or type-mapping to MS SQLSERVER2000. These configuration changes allow configuration of the JBoss with SQL Server database.

Summary

The JBoss 4.0 server is configured with the Hypersonic database by default. However, it is a simple matter of changing a few configuration files to use any one out of several popular databases. In this chapter, we have configured the JBoss application server with the Oracle database, MySQL database server, PostgreSQL database server, MS SQL Server database, and the DB2 UDB database.

5
Configuring JDBC in WebLogic Server

WebLogic Server provides database connectivity using data sources. A **data source** is a pool of database connections from which a connection can be obtained. A data source can be configured separately or combined with other data sources such as a multi data source. A **multi data source** is like a pool of data sources, configured to supply **failover** and **load balancing** across Database Management Systems. A data source is configured with a JNDI binding. A DataSource object represents a data source and is obtained using the JNDI lookup. A Connection object can be obtained from a DataSource object using the getConnection() method. WebLogic Server provides the Administration Console to configure a data source. WebLogic Server 9.x and 10.x includes Type 4 JDBC drivers, which are branded OEM versions of DataDirect drivers for DB2, Informix, MS SQL Server, Sybase, and Oracle databases. It also includes the DBMS vendor drivers from Sybase and Oracle. JDBC drivers for other databases may be incorporated in the server by including the JAR files in the server classpath.

New JDBC features in WebLogic Server 9.0 include support for JDBC 3.0, multiple JNDI names for a data source, and the **Logging Last Resource transaction** option. SQL Statement Timeout has been added to the connection pool configuration. SecondsToTrustAnIdlePoolConnection and PinnedToThread connection pool properties have been added to improve data source performance, which will be discussed later in this chapter. The multi data source failover feature has been improved. Statistics collection has been added to different connection parameters for their performance diagnostics. In WebLogic Server 9.1, new features have been added to WebLogic Type 4 JDBC drivers and Identity Based connection pooling has also been added. Transaction, Diagnostic, and Security tabs have been added to the Administration for configuring a data source. WebLogic Server 9.2 has added support for BEA WebLogic Type 4 JDBC MS SQL Server driver. WebLogic Server 10.3 supports JDBC 4.0, but is a Technology Preview edition, and does not support all the features of JDBC 4.0.

In this chapter, you will learn how to:

- Create a Data Source in WebLogic Server.
- Configure Connection Pool Properties for a Data Source.
- Create a multi data source in WebLogic Server.
- Performance Tune WebLogic Server Connections.
- Deploy a Web Application to WebLogic Server from JDeveloper.
- JDBC 4.0 version of the Web Application.

Setting the Environment

Install the database that requires a JDBC connection. The procedure to install the databases is discussed in Chapter 1. Download the JDBC driver for the database, if WebLogic does not have a driver for the DBMS. We will configure the JDBC connectivity with the Oracle database 10g. Copy the Oracle database JDBC driver JAR file `ojdbc14.jar` from `<Oracle>\jdbc\lib` directory to the `<weblogic91>\` `samples\domains\wl_server\lib` directory, `<Oracle>` being the Oracle database 10g installation directory and `<weblogic91>` being the WebLogic Server 9.1 installation directory. JAR files in the server `lib` directory get automatically added to the classpath, on server startup. If a later version is required, replace it in the `lib` directory. Alternatively, you can edit the `<weblogic91>\samples\domains\` `wl_server\bin\startWebLogic` script by adding a driver JAR file to the classpath argument constructed by the script. Put the JAR file ahead of `weblogic.jar` in the classpath. Double-click on the `<weblogic91>\samples\domains\wl_server\` `startWebLogicEx` command script to start the WebLogic examples server.

Creating a Data Source

A data source is a pool of JDBC connections from which a connection can be obtained using the `getConnection()` method of a `DataSource` object. In this section, we will create a data source in the WebLogic Server Administration Console. Access the Administration Console with the URL `http://localhost:7001/console`, and in the Administration Console, select the node **Services | JDBC | DataSources**.

Click on **Lock & Edit** to activate the Data Sources page buttons. To create a new JDBC data source, click on **New** in the Data Sources table.

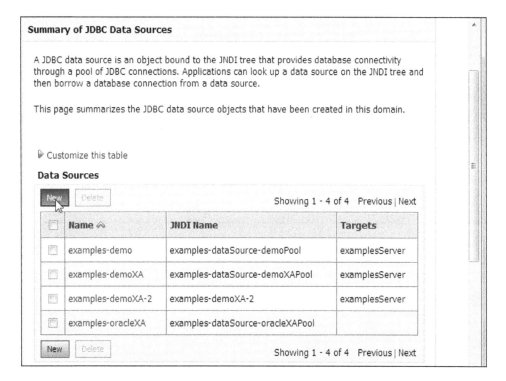

In the **Create a New JDBC Data Source** window, specify a data source name, and a **JNDI Name** for the data source. A data source is bound on a JNDI naming service with a JNDI name. Select a **Database Type**, and create a data source with the Oracle database. Select Oracle as the Database Type, and select Oracle's Driver (Thin) as the **Database Driver,** and click on next.

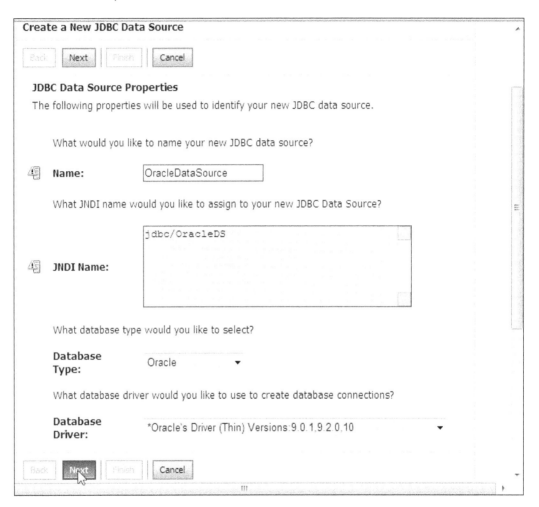

A data source may be configured with any of the commonly used databases. WebLogic Server provides Type 4 JDBC drivers from DataDirect for DB2, Informix, Oracle, SQL Server, and Sybase. BEA-branded DataDirect, Sybase jConnect, and Oracle thin drivers have been installed in the `<weblogic9.1>/server/lib` directory. The different JDBC Type 4 drivers provided by WebLogic Server are listed in the following table:

Database Versions Supported	Driver Classes	Connection URL
DB2 UDB 7.x, 8.1 and 8.2 on Linux, Unix, and Windows.	XA-weblogic.jdbcx. DB2DataSource. Non XA- weblogic.jdbc. db2. DB2Driver.	jdbc:bea:db2: //db2_server_name:port; DatabaseName= database
Informix 9.4 and later.	XA- weblogic.jdbcx. informix. InformixDataSource. Non XA- weblogic.jdbc. informix.InformixDriver.	jdbc:bea:informix: //dbserver1:1543; informixServer= dbserver1; databaseName= dbname
MS SQL Server 7.0, SQL Server 2000(SP1, SP2, and SP3a) and SQL Server 2005.	XA- weblogic. jdbcx.sqlserver. SQLServerDataSource. Non XA- weblogic.jdbc. sqlserver. SQLServerDriver.	jdbc:bea:sqlserver: //dbserver:port
Oracle 9i (R1 and R2) Oracle 10g.	XA- weblogic.jdbcx.oracle. OracleDataSource. Non XA- weblogic.jdbc. oracle.OracleDriver.	jdbc:bea:oracle: //dbserver:port
Sybase Adaptive Server 11.5, 11.9, 12.0, 12.5, 15.	XA- weblogic.jdbcx.sybase. SybaseDataSource. Non XA- weblogic.jdbc. Sybase.SybaseDriver.	jdbc:bea:sybase: //dbserver:port

Databases which do not include a JDBC driver can be selected. If one such driver is selected, add the driver zip or JAR file to the CLASSPATH variable in the startWebLogic script; else add the JAR or zip file to the server lib directory. A JDBC driver to a DBMS can be used, by specifying 'Other', and entering the driver class name manually to the console. Any Type 4 JDBC driver can be manually added to the classpath in the start-weblogic scripts, and need not to be put in the server or lib directory:

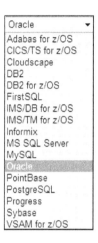

In the **Transaction Options** window, the transaction attributes of the data source are specified. If a XA driver is selected, global transactions would be automatically supported with Two-Phase commit transaction protocol. A global, distributed, or XA transaction is one that involves multiple DBMSes or resources, and which require a 2-Phase commit protocol to ensure an all-or-nothing resolution of the transaction. A global transaction is managed by a Transaction Manager using JTA. For a non-XA data source to support global transactions, check the **Global Transactions** checkbox. Select the protocol which supports global transactions. Different transaction protocols are listed in following table:

Transaction Protocol	Description
Logging Last Resource (LLR).	LLR optimization provides a better performance as compared to an XA JDBC driver, for insert, update, and delete operations. XA driver provides with a better performance for read operations. Recommended over a two-phase commit.
Two-Phase Commit.	Emulates participation in a global transaction using JTA.
One-Phase Commit.	This is the default setting. Only one resource may participate in the global transaction with one-phase commit.

In the Transaction Options page, click on **Next**. In the **Connection Properties** window, specify the **Database Name** as ORCL. **Host Name** as localhost, **Port** as 1521, and **User Name** as OE. Specify password for the OE username and click on the **Next button:**

In the **Test Database Connection** window, the driver class name, connection URL, and user name for the Oracle database are specified. Click on the **Test Database Configuration,** to test connection with the database:

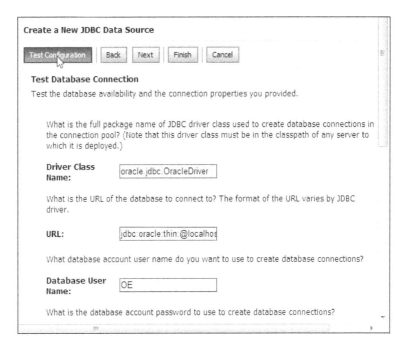

A message is displayed indicating that a connection has been established. If the database is not connected and an error message is displayed, then click on the **Next** button. In the **Select Targets** window, select the server to which the data source is to be deployed. To deploy to the examples server, select the `examplesServer`, and click on **Finish**.

A data source is configured and added to the **Data Sources** table. The data source is registered with the JNDI name, with the help of a naming service and a target server that are deployed by the data source and also listed in the data sources table:

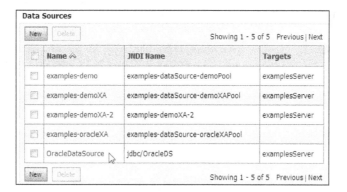

Make the data source available to the applications in the server, by clicking on the **Activate Changes** button. Until the **Activate Changes** or **Undo All Changes** button is selected, a web application is not deployed to the WebLogic server.

Configuring a Data Source

The data source created in the previous section will be configured. Select the data source to be configured in the Data Sources table, and also select the **Configuration** tab, which is the default setting. In the **Configuration** window, the data source JNDI name can be modified:

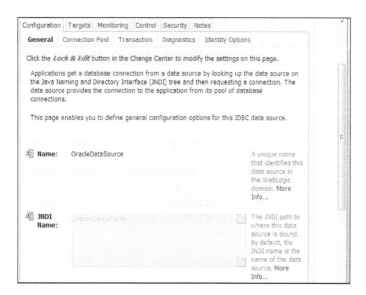

Other configuration options for a data source are listed in following table:

Data Source Setting	Description
Row Prefetch	Row Prefetch fetches multiple rows from the server to the client in a single server access, thus improving their performance.
Row Prefetch Size	If row prefetching is enabled, specify the number of rows to be fetched. Optimal size of the rows to be fetched depends on the query.
Stream Chunk Size	Specifies the data chunk size for streaming the data types.

Select the **Connection Pool** link to configure the connection pool associated with the data source. Initial capacity, maximum capacity, and capacity increment can be set in the connection pool configuration. The **Advanced** link is used to set the advanced connection pool properties. Some of the connection pool settings are listed in following table:

Connection Pool Setting	Description
Initial Capacity	Specifies the initial number of connections in the connection pool. It also specifies the minimum number of available connections in the connection pool.
Maximum Capacity	Specifies the maximum number of connections in the connection pool.
Capacity Increment	Specifies the number of connections added to the connection pool in a connection increment.
Statement Cache Type	Specifies the algorithm used for caching prepared statements. If the value is LRU, and a new statement is created, the **least recently used** statement in the cache is replaced. If the value is FIXED, the first statement that populates the cache stays indefinitely.
Test Connections on Reserve.	If Test Connections on Reserve checkbox is selected, then connections are tested before being given to the client. Test is required for connection pools in a multi data source created with the Failover algorithm. If Test Connections on Reserve is selected, then the Test Table Name should be specified.
Test Frequency	Specifies, in seconds, the interval to test unused connections in a connection pool. If test fails, the connection is closed and reopened. Again, if test fails, the connection is closed. If Test Frequency more than 0 is specified, then Test Table Name should be specified.

Connection Pool Setting	Description
Test Table Name	Specifies the database table used to test connections. To improve testing, specify a table without rows, or with just few rows. The SQL query to test connection can be specified with: SQL <query>. <query> is the query used to test the database connection.
Init SQL	Specifies the SQL statement used to initialize connection with a database. The SQL statement is specified with: SQL <sql statement>. <sql statement> is the SQL statement used to test connection. A database table can be specified without specifying 'SQL' at the start of the field. If a database table is specified, a database connection is tested with the SQL statement: "SELECT count(*) from InitSQL".
Shrink Frequency	Specifies the wait time for reducing the connection pool size with the pre-incremented value.
Connection Creation Retry Frequency.	Specifies the number of seconds between each attempt to establish a connection with a database.
Inactive Connection Timeout.	Specifies the number of seconds when an unused connection is returned to the connection pool.
Login Delay.	Specifies the number of seconds delayed for establishing a connection with a database. It is used for database servers that cannot handle successive connection requests.
Maximum Waiting for Connection	Specifies the maximum number of connection requests waiting to obtain a connection from the connection pool.
Connection Reserve Timeout	Specifies the number of seconds after which a connection request will be timed out.
Statement Timeout	Specifies the number of seconds after which a statement will be timed out.

The transaction protocol settings can be configured with the **Transaction** link. Monitoring statistics can be collected with the **Diagnostics** link. The profile information can be collected. Some of the data source profiles are listed in following table:

Profile	Description
Profile Connection Usage	Collects profile information about threads, which currently uses connections from the connection pool.
Profile Connection Reservation Wait	Collects profile information about threads, which is currently waiting to reserve a connection from the connection pool.
Profile Connection Leak	Collects profile information about threads, which reserved a connection from the connection pool and connection leak.

Profile	Description
Profile Connection Usage.	Collects profile information about threads, which currently uses connections from the connection pool.
Profile Connection Reservation Failed.	Collects profile information about threads, which failed to reserve a connection from the connection pool.
Profile Statement Cache Entry.	Collects profile information about callable and prepared statements, which is added to the statement cache and about threads that create the statements.
Profile Statement Usage	Collects profile information about threads, which currently executes statements from the statement cache.
Profile Connection Last Usage	Collects profile information about the previous thread that had ultimately used a connection from the connection pool.
Profile Connection Multithreaded Usage	Collects profile information about threads that erroneously uses a connection, which was earlier obtained by a different thread.
Profile Harvest Frequency	It is the interval, in seconds, between threads when the WebLogic Server harvests for profile data.

Select the **Monitoring** tab to monitor a data source. Select the **Control** tab to administer the WebLogic Server instances, which is deployed by the data source. In a deployed server instance, the statement cache can be cleared, and the server can be suspended or shutdown.

Creating a Multi Data Source

A multi data source is an abstract group of data sources, which provides failover and load balancing. A multi data source has a JNDI binding, similar to a data source. To create a multi data source, click on the **Services | JDBC | Multi Data Sources** link in the Administration Console:

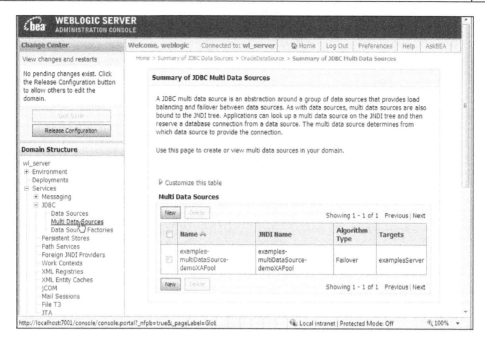

In the Multi Data Sources table, click on the **New** button to create a new multi data source. In the **Configure the Multi Data Source** window, specify a data source name, and a JNDI name. Select the algorithm type as **Failover** or **load-balancing, and** click on **Next**.

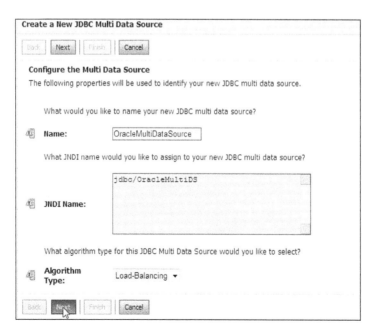

In the **Select Targets** window, select the **examplesServer** or any other server, by deploying the multi data source to it and click on next.

In the **Select Data Source Type** window, select XA Driver for an XA data source, or select Non-XA Driver for a non-XA data source, and click on **Next**. Because we created an Oracle data source using a non-XA JDBC driver select Non-XA Driver. In the **Add Data Sources** window, add data sources from the **Available** list to the **Chosen** list. If a new data source is required, click on the **Create a New Data Source** button, and then click on **Finish**.

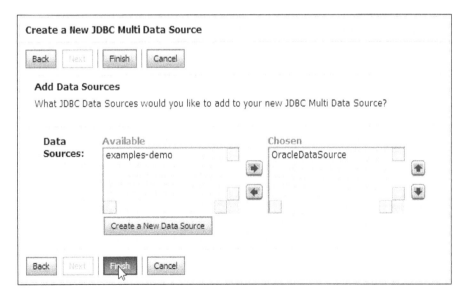

A new data source is configured and added to the **Multi Data Sources** table. Click on the **Activate Changes** button to make the data source available to the applications.

Multi Data Sources

	Name ⌃	JNDI Name	Algorithm Type	Targets
☐	examples-multiDataSource-demoXAPool	examples-multiDataSource-demoXAPool	Failover	examplesServer
☐	OracleMultiDataSource	jdbc/OracleMultiDS	Load-Balancing	examplesServer

New · Delete — Showing 1 - 2 of 2 Previous | Next

A multi data source can be configured by selecting the multi data source link. The targets to which the multi data source is deployed can be configured with the **Targets** tab. The data sources in the multi data source can be configured with the Data Sources link in the **Configuration** tab. The multi data source JNDI name can be modified in the **Configuration | General** window. The **Algorithm Type** specifies the algorithm used to select a data source from which a connection is obtained. If algorithm type is **Failover**, connection request is always sent to the first data source in the list. If the first data source has lost connectivity to the DBMS, connection request will be sent successively to the next data source of the list, until a connection is obtained or till it reaches to the end of the data source list. If the algorithm type is **Load Balancing,** connection request's load is distributed evenly over the data sources in the list. If load balancing is selected, connection failover is also provided with connection requests. These connection requests are being sent to different data sources in the list, until a connection gets established or till it reaches to the end of the data source list.

A multi data source also provides the **Failover Request If Busy**, **Failover Callback Handler**, and **Test Frequency** settings. For a multi data source with failover algorithm when **Failover Request If Busy** is selected, the connection request is sent to the next data source in the data source pool if all the connections in a data source are busy. The **Failover Callback Handler** specifies the application class to handle the callback, which is sent when a multi data source is ready to send a failover connection request to another data source. **Test Frequency** specifies the interval, in seconds, after which connections are tested. If a connection fails, the connection is closed and reopened. If the connection fails again, then it is closed.

WebLogic Server 9.x also supports Data Source Factories. Application scoped connection pools use JDBC Data Source factories to provide with default connection pool values. Configure a Data Source Factory by clicking on the **Services | JDBC | Data Source Factories** link. Click on new in the Data Source Factories table. In the **Create a New JDBC Data Source Factory** window, specify the data source factory name, user name, and password. These are specified to log in to the database, connection URL, driver class name, and factory name, and then click on **OK**. A data source factory is created, and can be deployed to a target server node. The data source factory name is used in the Administration Console, and in the configuration file, `config.xml`. The Factory Name is used in the deployment descriptors.

Performance Tuning JDBC

For best stability and performance, configure the pool to create all the connections it will need during startup, and retain them indefinitely. Hence, set the initial capacity to equal the maximum capacity, which would be identical for each execute-thread. Connection pooling provided by WebLogic Server data sources improves performance, by making a pool of connections available for JDBC applications. Connections do not have to be opened and closed for each client.

Test Connections on Reserve tests the connections before making a connection available to a client and can reduce the performance. To prevent frequent connection testing, set the connection pool attribute, **Seconds to Trust an Idle Pool Connection**. This attribute specifies the number of seconds for which a connection that is known to have been successfully used, is not tested with a SQL query. When JDBC is done in external client JVMs, using RMI to do JDBC through WebLogic to the DBMS, data source performance can be improved by selecting **Row Prefetch Enabled,** and an optimal prefetch size in configuring a data source. Row prefetching improves performance by prefetching multiple rows from the server to an external client. Row prefetch is not recommended for JDBC in external clients through WebLogic. It is much faster to produce JDBC in the WebLogic JVM, JSPs, servlet, EJBs, and so on. Caching statements improves the performance of the connection testing by reusing statements, rather than creating new statements. Statement caching is specified in the connection pool configuration.

Here is the ideal standard for riskless WebLogic JDBC coding style. Pooling is fast, it is best used in a quick per-invoke fashion:

/* This is how you should make any of your top-level methods that will produce JDBC, work for any of your applications.*/

```
public void myTopLevelJDBCMethod()
{
 Connection c = null;
```

/* All JDBC objects would be method level objects that ensure thread-safety and prevent connection leaking. Define the connection object before the JDBC 'try' block.*/

```
 try
 {
```

/* The above is the JDBC try block for the method. All the JDBCs' for this method in the block is connected directly from the DataSource in the try block. Do not connect it from any method that has kept a connection, and is sharing it for repeated use.*/

```
 c = myDataSource.getConnection();
```

/* You can pass the connection or sub-objects to sub-methods but none of these methods must expect to keep or use the objects they receive after their method call completes (eg).*/

```
 DoSomethingFancyWith(c);
```

/* Use Prepared or Callable Statements. They are usually faster, because we cache them transparently with the pool.*/

```
 PreparedStatement p = c.prepareStatement(...);
 ResultSet rs = p.executeQuery();
 ProcessResult(myrs);
```

/* Close JDBC objects in the proper order: first resultset,; then statement; and then connection.*/

```
 rs.close();
```

/* Always close result sets as soon as possible (**ASAP**) at the levels they were created*/

```
 p.close();
```

/* Always close statements ASAP at the levels they were created. When the JDBC is processed in the try-block, close the connection:*/

```
 c.close();
```

/* Always close connection-ASAP in the same method and the block that was used to create or obtain it.*/

```
 c = null;
```

```
/* Set the connection to null, so that the finally block below knows that it has been
taken care of.*/
}
catch (Exception e )
{

/* Do whatever, according to your needs. You would not have a catch block, if it is
not needed.*/
}
finally
{

/* Always have the above finally block. A finally block is crucial to ensure that the
connection is closed and returned to the pool, and is not leaked.*/

/* Failsafe: Do every individual thing you want to do in the finally block in it's own
try block-catch-ignore so everything is attempted.*/
  try
  {
  if (c != null) c.close();
  }
  catch (Exception ignore)
  {
  }
  }
}
```

Deploying a Web Application to WebLogic Server from JDeveloper

We will develop a web application to retrieve data from an Oracle database table with the data source configured in the Configuring a Data Source section. Create an example database table in the Oracle database. Create a table, `Catalog`, using a SQL Client tool such as SQL * Plus, or a command-line utility with the following QL script:

```
CREATE TABLE Catalog(CatalogId INTEGER
PRIMARY KEY, Journal VARCHAR(25), Publisher VARCHAR(25),
 Edition VARCHAR(25), Title Varchar(45), Author Varchar(25));
INSERT INTO Catalog VALUES('1', 'Oracle Magazine', 'Oracle Publishing',
'Nov-Dec 2004', 'Database Resource Manager', 'Kimberly Floss');
INSERT INTO Catalog VALUES('2', 'Oracle Magazine', 'Oracle Publishing',
'Nov-Dec 2004', 'From ADF UIX to JSF', 'Jonas Jacobi');
INSERT INTO Catalog VALUES('3', 'Oracle Magazine', 'Oracle Publishing',
'March-April 2005', 'Starting with Oracle ADF ', 'Steve Muench');
```

We will create a web application in JDeveloper to access the Oracle database. Before starting JDeveloper we need to copy the `<Weblogic91>\server\lib\weblogic.jar` to the `<JDeveloper>\jdev\lib\ext` directory. `<WebLogic91>` is the directory in which your WebLogic Server 9.1 is installed. `<JDeveloper>` is the directory in which JDeveloper is installed. Select **File | New** to create a new application and project. In the **New Gallery** window, select **General** in Categories and **Application** in Items, and click on **OK**. In the **Create Application** window, specify an application name and click on **OK**. In the **Create Project** window, specify a project name and click on **OK**. An application and a project are added to the **Applications Navigator** and create a JSP, `catalog.jsp`. Select **File | New**, and in the **New Gallery** window select **Web Tier | JSP** in **Categories**. Select **JSP** in **Items** and click **OK**. A JSP is added to the **Applications Navigator**.

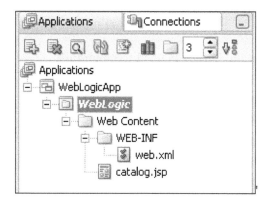

Import the `java.sql`, `javax.sql`, and `javax.naming` packages in the JSP. We have to create an `InitialContext` object, which is required for JNDI naming operations:

```
InitialContext ctx=new InitialContext();
```

Previously, we had created a data source with JNDI name, `jdbc/OracleDS`. Create a `DataSource` object from the JNDI name using the `lookup()` method:

```
DataSource ds=(DataSource)ctx.lookup("jdbc/OracleDS");
```

Obtain a JDBC connection from the `DataSource` object. Create a `Connection` object using the `getConnection()` method of the `DataSource` object:

```
Connection connection=ds.getConnection();
```

Create a `Statement` object from the `Connection` object using the `createStatement()` method:

```
Statement stmt=connection.createStatement();
```

Run a SQL query with the `executeQuery()` method to return a `ResultSet` object. Specify a SQL query, which selects all the columns of the example database table, `Catalog`:

```
ResultSet resultSet=stmt.executeQuery("Select * from Catalog");
```

Create a HTML table with a row that corresponds to each row in the result set, and a column that corresponds to each column in the result set. Add a header row to the html table. Iterate over the result set, and add row values to the html table:

```
while (resultSet.next())
{
 <tr>
  <td><%out.println(resultSet.getString(1));%></td>
 </tr>
}
```

The JSP page, `catalog.jsp`, which is used to generate a HTML table from the example database table with the data source configured in the WebLogic server, is listed below:

```
<%@ page contentType="text/html"%>
<%@ page import="java.sql.*,javax.sql.*,javax.naming.*"%>
<html>
<head>
<meta http-equiv="Content-Type" content="text/html">
 <title>WebLogic Application</title>
</head>
<body>
<%
 InitialContext ctx=new InitialContext();
 DataSource ds=(DataSource)ctx.lookup("jdbc/OracleDS");
 Connection connection=ds.getConnection();
 Statement stmt=connection.createStatement();
 ResultSet resultSet=stmt.executeQuery("Select * from Catalog");
%>
<table border="1" cellspacing="0">
 <tr>
  <th>CatalogId</th>
```

```
<th>Journal</th>
<th>Publisher</th>
<th>Edition</th>
<th>Title</th>
<th>Author</th>
</tr>
<%
while (resultSet.next())
{
%>
<tr>
<td><%out.println(resultSet.getString(1));%></td>
<td><%out.println(resultSet.getString(2));%></td>
<td><%out.println(resultSet.getString(3));%></td>
<td><%out.println(resultSet.getString(4));%></td>
<td><%out.println(resultSet.getString(5));%></td>
<td><%out.println(resultSet.getString(6));%></td>
</tr>
<%
}
resultSet.close();
stmt.close();
connection.close();
%>
</table>
</body>
</html>
```

We will deploy the web application to the WebLogic server. <JDeveloper> is the directory in which JDeveloper is installed. To deploy a web application to the WebLogic server, we have to perform the following operations:

1. Create a connection to the WebLogic Server.

2. Create a deployment profile for the web application.

3. Deploy the deployment profile to the WebLogic Server using the connection to the server.

We have to start the WebLogic server to establish a connection with the server. To create a connection to the WebLogic Server, right-click on the **Application Server** node in the **Connections** navigator, and select **New Application Server Connection**.

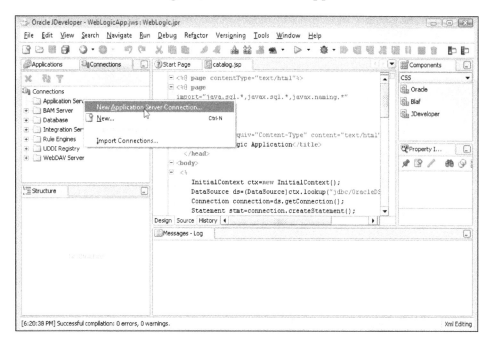

Click on **Next** in the **Create Application Server Connection Wizard**. In the **Type** window, specify a Connection Name and select Connection Type as WebLogic Server 9.x, and then click on **Next**.

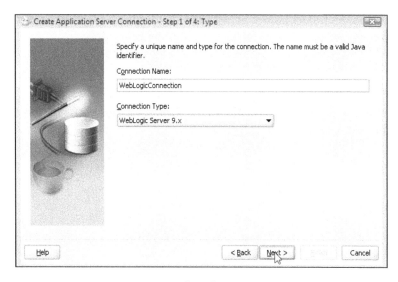

In the Authentication window specify the username (default is 'weblogic') and password (default is 'weblogic') which were specified when the WebLogic server was installed. In the **Connection** window, specify **Host Name** as localhost, **Port** as 1521, **Target Node** as examplesServer, and the **Path to weblogic.jar**.

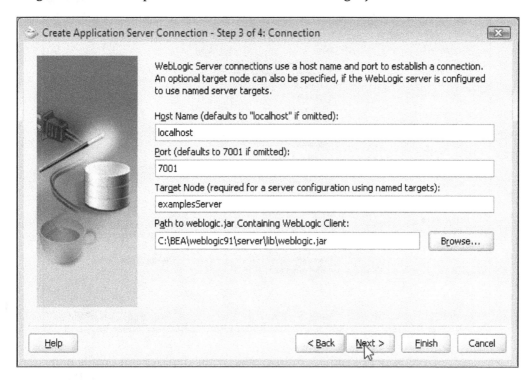

In the **Test** window, click the **Test Connection** button to test connection with the WebLogic server. A "Success" message is displayed, if a connection is established. If a connection is not established, an error message is generated. For example, an error is generated, if the WebLogic server have not been started prior to testing the connection with the server. An application server connection node is added to the **Connections** navigator.

We will create a deployment profile from the web application. Select **File | New** and in the **New Gallery** window, select **General | Deployment Profiles**. Select **WAR File** in **Items** and click on **OK**.

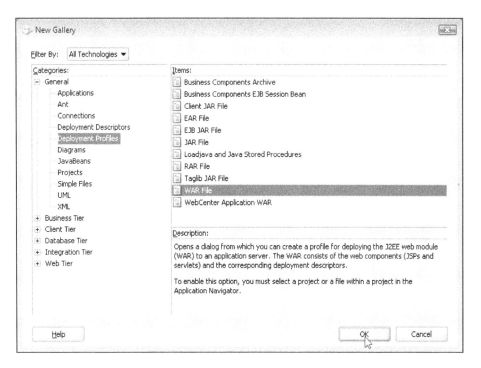

In the **Create Deployment Profile** window, specify the deployment profile name, webapp1, which is the default, and click on **OK**. In the WAR Deployment Profile Properties window specify J2EE web context root as 'weblogic'. The connection that we created with the WebLogic server is a t3 protocol connection. By default, a deployment profile uses the http protocol to deploy to the WebLogic server. Therefore, we have to modify the deployment profile protocol to t3. Select the **Platform | WebLogic 9.x** node, modify the **adminurl** option from http://${hostname}:${port} to t3://${hostname}:${port} and click on **OK**.

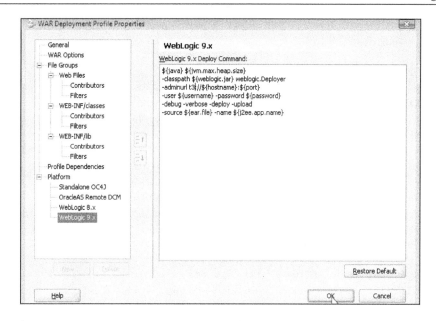

Before a J2EE application may be deployed to the WebLogic Server, the WebLogic Server is required not to be in the Lock & Edit mode. Deploy the deployment profile to the WebLogic Server, by right-clicking on the deployment profile and select the **Deploy to | WebLogicConnection** link.

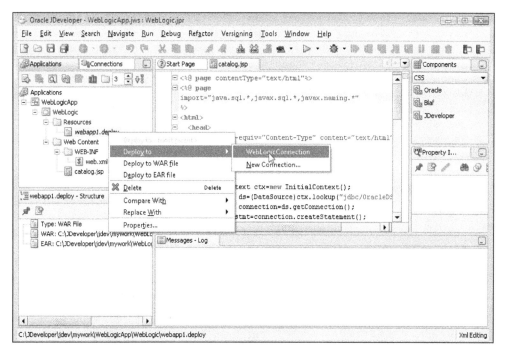

The web application is deployed to the WebLogic Server, and the output in
JDeveloper is shown below:

```
Deployment started.
Target platform is WebLogic Server 9.x (WebLogicConnection).
Checking weblogic.xml for completeness...
Wrote WAR file to C:\JDeveloper\jdev\mywork\WebLogicApp\WebLogic\
deploy\webapp1.war
Wrote EAR file to C:\JDeveloper\jdev\mywork\WebLogicApp\WebLogic\
deploy\webapp1.ear
C:\JDeveloper\jdk\jre\bin\javaw.exe -classpath
C:\wls\weblogic91\server\lib\weblogic.jar weblogic.Deployer -adminurl
t3://localhost:7001 -user weblogic -password **** -debug -verbose -
deploy -upload -source
C:\JDeveloper\jdev\mywork\WebLogicApp\WebLogic\deploy\webapp1.ear -
name webapp1
weblogic.Deployer invoked with options: -adminurl
t3://localhost:7001 -user weblogic -debug -verbose -deploy -upload -
source
C:\JDeveloper\jdev\mywork\WebLogicApp\WebLogic\deploy\webapp1.ear -
name webapp1
[WebLogicDeploymentManagerImpl.<init>():103] : Constructing
DeploymentManager for J2EE version V1_4 deployments
[WebLogicDeploymentManagerImpl.getNewConnection():146] : Connecting to
admin server at localhost:7001, as user weblogic
[ServerConnectionImpl.getEnvironment():282] : setting environment
[ServerConnectionImpl.getEnvironment():285] : getting context using
t3://localhost:7001
[ServerConnectionImpl.getMBeanServer():237] : Connecting to
MBeanServer at service:jmx:t3://localhost:7001/jndi/weblogic.
management.mbeanservers.domainruntime
[ServerConnectionImpl.getMBeanServer():237] : Connecting to
MBeanServer at service:jmx:t3://localhost:7001/jndi/weblogic.
management.mbeanservers.runtime
[DomainManager.resetDomain():36] : Getting new domain
[DomainManager.resetDomain():39] : Using pending domain: false
[MBeanCache.addNotificationListener():96] : Adding notification
listener for weblogic.deploy.api.spi.deploy.mbeans.TargetCache@1827d1
[MBeanCache.addNotificationListener():103] : Added notification
listener for weblogic.deploy.api.spi.deploy.mbeans.TargetCache@1827d1
[MBeanCache.addNotificationListener():96] : Adding notification
listener for weblogic.deploy.api.spi.deploy.mbeans.ModuleCache@8f9a32
[MBeanCache.addNotificationListener():103] : Added notification
listener for weblogic.deploy.api.spi.deploy.mbeans.ModuleCache@8f9a32
[ServerConnectionImpl.initialize():170] : Connected to WLS domain:
wl_server
```

```
[ServerConnectionImpl.setRemote():463] : Running in remote mode
[ServerConnectionImpl.init():160] : Initializing ServerConnection :
weblogic.deploy.api.spi.deploy.internal.ServerConnectionImpl@111bfbc
[BasicOperation.dumpTmids():744] : Incoming tmids:
[BasicOperation.deriveAppName():139] : appname established as: webapp1
<Info> <J2EE Deployment SPI> <BEA-260121> <Initiating deploy operation
for application, webapp1 [archive: C:\JDeveloper\jdev\mywork\
WebLogicApp\WebLogic\deploy\webapp1.ear], to configured targets.>
[ServerConnectionImpl.upload():639] : Uploaded app to C:\wls\
weblogic91\samples\domains\wl_server\.\servers\examplesServer\upload\
webapp1
[BasicOperation.hasJMSModules():489] : checking if jms: META-INF/
application.xml
[BasicOperation.hasJMSModules():489] :  checking if jms: webapp1.war
[BasicOperation.dumpTmids():744] : Incoming tmids:
[BasicOperation.dumpTmids():746] : {Target=examplesServer, WebLogicTar
getType=server, Name=webapp1}, targeted=true
[BasicOperation.loadGeneralOptions():661] : Delete Files:false
Timeout :3600000
Targets: examplesServer
ModuleTargets={}
SubModuleTargets={}
}
Files: null
Deployment Plan: null
App root: C:\wls\weblogic91\samples\domains\wl_server\.\servers\
examplesServer\upload\webapp1
App config: C:\wls\weblogic91\samples\domains\wl_server\.\servers\
examplesServer\upload\webapp1\plan
Deployment Options:
{isRetireGracefully=true,isGracefulProductionToAdmin=false,isGracefulI
gnoreSessions=false,retireTimeout
Secs= 1,undeployAllVersions=false,archiveVersion=null,planVersion=nul
l,isLibrary=false,libSpecVersion=null,libImplVersion=null,stageMode=n
ull,clusterTimeout=3600000,altDD=null,altWlsDD=null,name=webapp1,sec
urityModel=null,securityValidationEnabled=false,versionIdentifier=nul
l,isTestMode=false,forceUndeployTimeout=0,defaultSubmoduleTargets=tru
e,timeout=0}
[BasicOperation.execute():401] : Initiating deploy operation for app,
webapp1, on targets:
Task 1 initiated: [Deployer:149026]deploy application webapp1 on
examplesServer.
Task 1 completed: [Deployer:149026]deploy application webapp1 on
examplesServer.
Target state: deploy completed on Server examplesServer
[ServerConnectionImpl.close():328] : Closing DM connection
```

```
[ServerConnectionImpl.close():348] : Unregistered all listeners
[ServerConnectionImpl.closeJMX():368] : Closed JMX connection
[ServerConnectionImpl.closeJMX():380] : Closed Runtime JMX connection
Elapsed time for deployment: 2 minutes, 10 seconds
---- Deployment finished.
```

Invoke the JSP with the URL `http://localhost:7001/weblogic/catalog.jsp`. The JSP runs in the WebLogic server and generates an html table:

CatalogId	Journal	Publisher	Edition	Title	Author
1	Oracle Magazine	Oracle Publishing	Nov-Dec 2004	Database Resource Manager	Kimberly Floss
2	Oracle Magazine	Oracle Publishing	Nov-Dec 2004	From ADF UIX to JSF	Jonas Jacobi
3	Oracle Magazine	Oracle Publishing	March-April 2005	Starting with Oracle ADF	Steve Muench

JDBC 4.0 Version

Neither WebLogic Server 9.x nor 10.x supports JDBC 4.0. In a later version of WebLogic server, we can avail the new features in JDBC 4.0. To use the JDBC 4.0 driver, we will modify the `catalog.jsp` to get connected to the Oracle database from the WebLogic Server. Oracle database 11g JDBC drivers support JDBC 4.0, and can be downloaded from: `http://www.oracle.com/technology/software/tech/java/sqlj_jdbc/htdocs/jdbc_111060.html`. The JDBC 4.0 features can be used by adding the JDBC 4.0 JAR file, `ojdbc6.jar`, to the server `lib` directory, or to the `classpath` variable of the `startWebLogic` script. JDBC 4.0 has added support for setting client info properties on `Connection` objects to identify connections that could bog down an application. Standard client info properties are `ApplicationName`, `ClientUser`, and `ClientHostname`. In the JDBC 4.0 version of the web application, set the standard client info properties on the `Connection` object:

```
connection.setClientInfo("ApplicationName","OracleApp");
connection.setClientInfo("ClientUser","OracleUser");
connection.setClientInfo("ClientHostname","OracleHost");
```

Connection state tracking is a connection management feature added in JDBC 4.0. Connection state tracking is used to identify connections that are unusable, and close the connections. Connection state tracking is implemented by the WebLogic connection pool manager using the `isValid()` method of the `Connection` object:

```
if(!connection.isValid())
connection.close();
```

`PreparedStatements` are pooled by default in a connection pool, if the database supports statement pooling. Statement pooling reduces the overhead of opening, initializing, and closing the statements, which are frequently being used. JDBC 4.0 also has added support, for pooling of the `Statement` object. WebLogic server pools statements for all DBMSes or drivers, by default. In JDBC 4.0, the support for statement pooling is irrelevant to the WebLogic JDBC applications.

Oracle JDBC provides some extensions to the JDBC API with additional methods. JDBC 4.0 has added a new feature called **wrapper pattern**, which can be used to access the vendor-specific JDBC resources. The wrapper pattern is implemented in the `Wrapper` interface, which is extended by the following interfaces:

```
java.sql.Connection
java.sql.Statement
java.sql.DatabaseMetaData
java.sql.ParameterMetaData
java.sql.ResultSetMetaData
java.sql.ResultSet
javax.sql.Datasource
```

Oracle JDBC API provides the `oracle.jdbc.OracleStatement` interface as an extension to the `java.sql.Statement` interface. The `OracleStatement` interface can be unwrapped to create an object of its type. To create an `OracleStatement` object, test if a `Statement` object is a wrapper for the `OracleStatement` interface, using the `isWrapperFor()` method. If the `Statement` object is a wrapper, then unwrap the `OracleStatement` interface using the `unwrap()` method given below:

```
Class class = Class.forName("oracle.jdbc.OracleStatement");
if(stmt.isWrapperFor(class))
{
 OracleStatement oracleStmt = (OracleStatement)stmt.unwrap(class);
}
```

The `OracleStatement` object can be used to set the column type using the `defineColumnType()` method. Defining column type is used for performance optimization and data type conversion. If the same statement object is used to run different queries, then clear the previously defined column types using the `clearDefines()` method. Set the column type of the first column to `OracleTypes.Number`, and the second column to `OracleTypes.VARCHAR`:

```
oracleStmt.clearDefines();
oracleStmt.defineColumnType(1, OracleTypes.NUMBER);
oracleStmt.defineColumnType(2, OracleTypes.VARCHAR);
```

JDBC 4.0 also supports data types, such as ROWID, NCLOB, and NBLOB. Oracle database supports the ROWID data type. The ROWID psuedocolumn in an Oracle database table identifies a unique row in the table. Add the ROWID column to the SELECT query:

```
ResultSet resultSet=oracleStmt.executeQuery("Select ROWID, CATALOGID,
JOURNAL, PUBLISHER, EDITION, TITLE, AUTHOR from Catalog");
```

To the HTML table, add a column for the ROWID column, and add values to it using the getRowId() method in the ResultSet interface:

```
<td><%out.println(resultSet.getRowId("ROWID").toString());%></td>
```

JDBC 4.0 has added enhanced support for chained SQLExceptions. The chained exceptions and chained causes can be retrieved using the FOR-EACH loop introduced in JDK 6.0. In the error JSP page, the FOR-EACH loop is used to output the chained exceptions and chained causes. Previously, the getNextException() and getCause() methods were invoked iteratively to retrieve the chained exceptions and chained causes:

```
<%@ page isErrorPage="true" %>
<%
 for(Throwable e : exception )
 {
  out.println("Error encountered: " + e);
 }
%>
```

The JDBC 4.0 version of catalog.jsp is listed below:

```
<%@ page contentType="text/html"%>
<%@ page import="java.sql.*,javax.sql.*,java.util.*,javax.naming.*,
oracle.jdbc.OracleStatement"%>
<html>
<head>
<meta http-equiv="Content-Type" content="text/html">
 <title>WebLogic Application</title>
</head>
<body>
<%
 InitialContext ctx=new InitialContext();
 DataSource ds=(DataSource)ctx.lookup("jdbc/OracleDS");
 Connection connection=ds.getConnection();
 connection.setClientInfo("ApplicationName","OracleApp");
 connection.setClientInfo("ClientUser","OracleUser");
 connection.setClientInfo("ClientHostname","OracleHost");
 Statement stmt=connection.createStatement();
```

```
DatabaseMetaData metaData=connection.getMetaData();
if(metaData.supportsStatementPooling())
{
 if(stmt.isPoolable())
 stmt.setPoolable(true);
}
Class class = Class.forName("oracle.jdbc.OracleStatement");
if(stmt.isWrapperFor(class))
{
 OracleStatement oracleStmt = (OracleStatement)stmt.unwrap(class);
 oracleStmt.clearDefines();
 oracleStmt.defineColumnType(1, OracleTypes.NUMBER);
 oracleStmt.defineColumnType(2, OracleTypes.VARCHAR);
 oracleStmt.defineColumnType(3, OracleTypes.VARCHAR);
 oracleStmt.defineColumnType(4, OracleTypes.VARCHAR);
 oracleStmt.defineColumnType(5, OracleTypes.VARCHAR);
 oracleStmt.defineColumnType(6, OracleTypes.VARCHAR);
 oracleStmt.defineColumnType(7, OracleTypes.VARCHAR);
 ResultSet resultSet=oracleStmt.executeQuery("Select ROWID,
CATALOGID, JOURNAL, PUBLISHER, EDITION, TITLE, AUTHOR from Catalog");
%>
<table border="1" cellspacing="0">
 <tr>
  <th>CatalogId</th>
  <th>Journal</th>
  <th>Publisher</th>
  <th>Edition</th>
  <th>Title</th>
  <th>Author</th>
 </tr>
 <%
  while (resultSet.next())
  {
 %>
 <tr>
  <td><%out.println(resultSet.getRowId("ROWID").toString());%></td>
  <td><%out.println(resultSet.getString(1));%></td>
  <td><%out.println(resultSet.getString(2));%></td>
  <td><%out.println(resultSet.getString(3));%></td>
  <td><%out.println(resultSet.getString(4));%></td>
  <td><%out.println(resultSet.getString(5));%></td>
  <td><%out.println(resultSet.getString(6));%></td>
 </tr>
 <%
```

```
  }
  resultSet.close();
  stmt.close();
  connection.close();
  }
  %>
</table>
</body>
</html>
```

Summary

WebLogic Server 9.x has a new feature, multi data source, which is a group of data sources with a JNDI name binding. A multi data source facilitates the maximum data sources that are available. WebLogic Server 8.1 also had multi data sources called MultiPools. Any pool or multipool is accessed via a DataSource. For 9.0 and the later versions, the DataSource to access the notion of a pool or multipool have been combined. In WebLogic Server 9.x, a connection pool configuration used in WebLogic Server 8.1 has been removed. The data source configuration in WebLogic Server 9.x provides enhanced connection request failover and load balancing between data sources. In a WebLogic server version that supports JDBC 4.0, the new features of JDBC 4.0 such as connection state tracking, Java SE chained facility, and the wrapper pattern to access non-standard resources can be availed.

6
Configuring JDBC in WebSphere Application Server

WebSphere application server 6.1, is a J2EE and web services technology based application server for developing J2EE applications. The WebSphere application server is used to develop JDBC applications. The IBM DB2 9 offers some new features, which are suitable for developing a JDBC 4.0 application. DB2 9 has added support for the SQL XML data type, which can be used in conjunction with the SQLXML java data type. It is a new data type in JDBC 4.0 to store and retrieve XML documents. The DB2 database server provides access from WebSphere application server by configuring a **JDBC Provider**, which is a WebSphere proprietary term in the application server.

In this chapter, we will configure a data source in WebSphere application server 6.1 to connect to DB2 9 database. We will deploy a web application to the WebSphere application server that consists of a JSP to generate an HTML table using the data source configured in the server. We will use the DB2 JDBC Type 4 driver for creating JDBC connection to the DB2 9 database. The Type 4 driver has an advantage over the Type 2 driver: it provides direct access to the DB2 database. In this chapter, you'll learn about the following:

- Create a JDBC Provider with DB2 9 database in the WebSphere Application Server 6.1.
- Create a Data Source with DB2 9 database in the WebSphere Application Server 6.1.

- Deploy a Web Application from JDeveloper 10g to the WebSphere Application Server 6.1 to connect with the DB2 Database 9.

- JDBC 4.0 Version of the Web Application.

Setting the Environment

The following preliminary setup is required before configuring a JDBC connection with the DB2 9 database from the WebSphere application server 6.1:

1. Download and install the DB2 9 database from `http://www.ibm.com/developerworks/downloads/im/udb/?S_TACT=105AGX28&S_CMP=TRIALS`.

2. Create a sample database, SAMPLE, in the DB2 9 database server.

3. Create an example table comprising a catalog of journal articles in the database. The SQL script to create the example table is listed below:

```
CREATE TABLE DB2ADMIN.Catalog(CatalogId VARCHAR(25) PRIMARY KEY
NOT NULL, Journal VARCHAR(25), Section VARCHAR(25), Edition
VARCHAR(25), Title VARCHAR(75), Author VARCHAR(25))

INSERT INTO DB2ADMIN.Catalog VALUES('catalog1', 'developerWorks',
'Java Technology', 'Nov 2004', 'Getting started with enumerated
types', 'Brett McLaughlin');

INSERT INTO DB2ADMIN.Catalog VALUES('catalog2', 'developerWorks',
'XML', 'Apr 2005', 'Transform Eclipse navigation files to DITA
navigation files', 'Loretta Hicks');
```

4. Download the WebSphere application server 6.1 from `http://www14.software.ibm.com/webapp/download/preconfig.jsp?id=2005-01-19+10%3A47%3A53.647228R&S_TACT=104CBW71&S_CMP=` and install the WebSphere application server.

Configuring a JDBC Provider

In this section, we will configure a JDBC connection with the DB2 9 database from the WebSphere application server 6.1. Start the WebSphere application server from the **First steps** console. Access the WebSphere Administration console from the **First steps** console, or with the URL `https://localhost:9043/ibm/console/logon.jsp`.

In the login page, specify the **User ID** and **Password**, and click on **Login**. The administration console page is displayed. The administration console page has provision to configure JDBC, deploy applications, set environment variables, and define login configurations.

Select the **Resources | JDBC | JDBC Providers** node to configure a new JDBC provider. A JDBC provider is used to access a database. It consists of settings for the database, the JDBC driver type and the driver class.

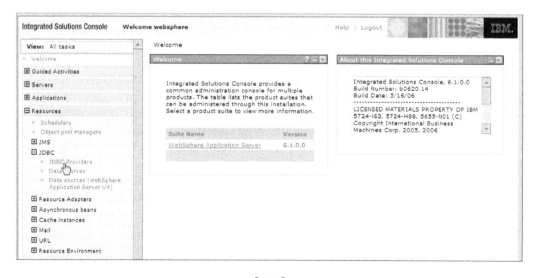

Select the **Scope**, **Server** for defining a new JDBC provider. Scope defines the level at which the JDBC providers are available. WebSphere architecture comprises of three levels: cells, nodes, and servers. A cell is an administrative domain that consists of a group of nodes. A node is a group of WebSphere Application Server that manages server processes. The application server is the primary runtime component in a WebSphere Application Server configuration. If the JDBC Provider is to be made available from all application servers in a node, select **Node** as the **Scope**. If the JDBC Provider is to be made available in all the nodes of a cell, select **Cell** as the **Scope**. Select **New** to configure a new JDBC provider.

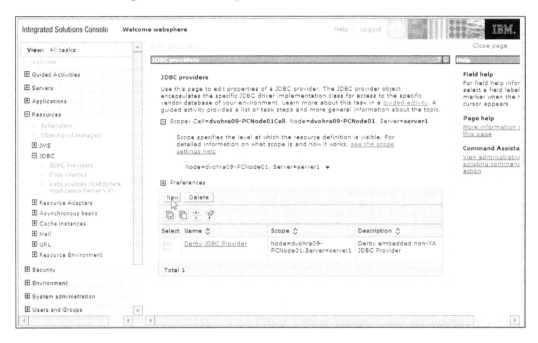

In the **Create a new JDBC provider** window, select DB2 as the database type. If the database with which a connection is to be configured is not listed, select **User-Defined** for the database type. Select the Provider type as **DB2 Universal JDBC Driver Provider**. For DB2 database type on Windows, the provider type **DB2 Universal JDBC Provider (XA)** is used for distributed transactions. If the database type selected is User-Defined, the provider type **User-Defined JDBC Provider** is specified. Select the implementation type, **Connection pool data source**. If the **User-Defined** database type is selected as the implementation type, **User-Defined** is also specified. If the provider type **DB2 Universal JDBC Provider (XA)** is selected, then select the implementation type, **XA DataSource** and click on next.

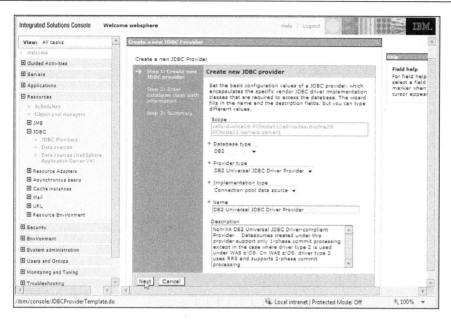

The **Class path** field specifies the JAR files in the Class path. The db2jcc.jar, which has the DB2 JDBC Type 4 driver, and the db2jcc_license_cu.jar, which is the license file for the DB2 database server are included in the Class path setting. The **Class path** field also includes some environment variables. Specify the directory location, which is saved as an environment variable DB2UNIVERSAL_JDBC_DRIVER_PATH, for the JDBC JAR files and click on **Next**.

In the **Summary** page, the summary of the JDBC Provider configuration is displayed. Now, click on the **Finish** button.

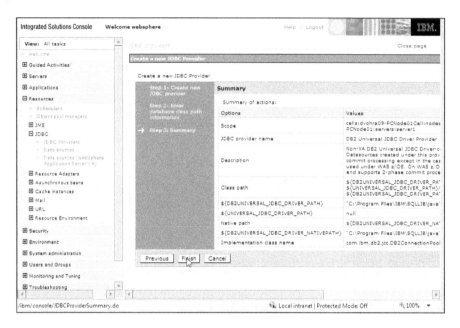

The settings specified are applied to the local configuration. On clicking the **Save** link in the **Messages** frame, the changes are applied to the master configuration.

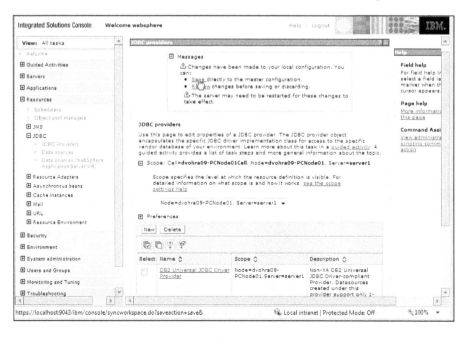

A **JDBC Provider** for the DB2 database is configured and added to the list of JDBC Providers.

Configuring a Data Source

We will configure a JDBC data source, to retrieve data from the DB2 database. The **JDBC Provider** that we have already configured, supplies the driver class for the data source. The default driver class name is `com.ibm.db2.jcc.DB2ConnectionPoolDataSource`. Another driver class can be specified instead of the default. To configure a new data source, select the JDBC provider, `DB2 Universal JDBC Driver Provider`.

Click on the **Datasources** link in the **Additional Properties** header.

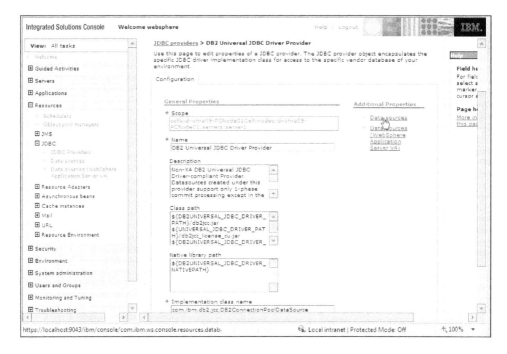

A table of data sources is displayed. Now, click on **New** to add a new data source.

In the **Create a data source** window, specify a data source name and a **JNDI name**. J2EE connector authentication data entries are used to login to a database, by a JDBC data source. Connector authentication data entries define the database access credentials. Click on **create a new J2C authentication alias** link to create a Component-managed authentication alias.

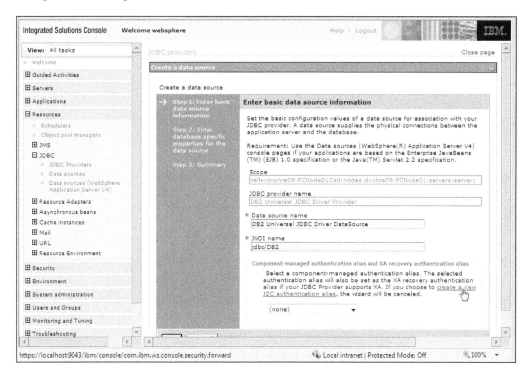

A table of J2C authentication data entries is displayed. Click on **New** to add a J2C authentication data entry.

In the J2C authentication data entry configuration frame, specify an alias for the data entry. Also specify the user id and password to login to the DB2 database, and click on **Apply**.

Click on **Save** to save the workspace changes to master configuration.

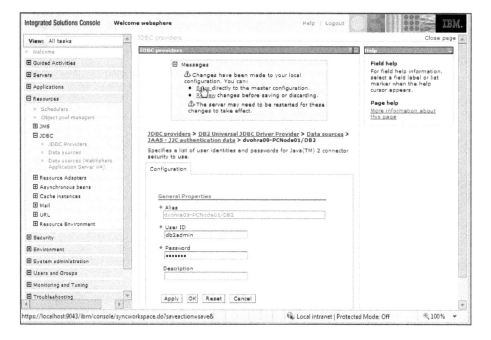

A new J2C authentication data entry is added. Click on the **Data sources** link to configure a new data source.

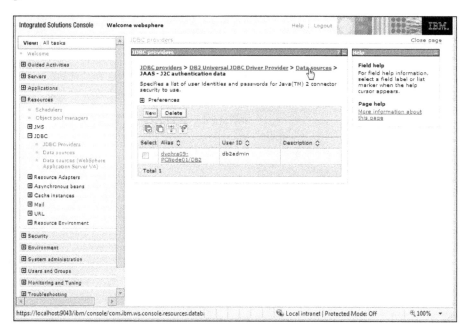

Click on **New** in the **Data sources** table to create a new data source.

Specify a JNDI name for the data source. In the **Component-managed authentication alias** field, select the J2C authentication alias that we have configured earlier, and click on **Next**.

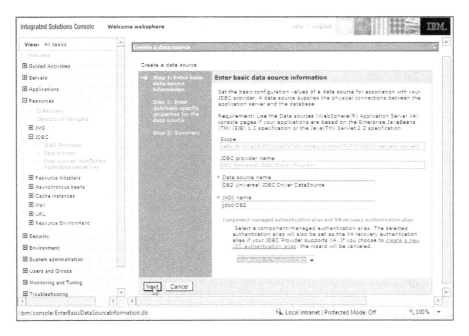

In the data source properties window, specify the database name (SAMPLE), driver type (type 4), server name (localhost), and port number (50000), and then click on **Next**.

In the **Summary** page, a summary of the data source configuration is displayed. Now, click on **Finish**.

A new data source is added to the data sources table. Click on **Save** to save the data source to the master configuration.

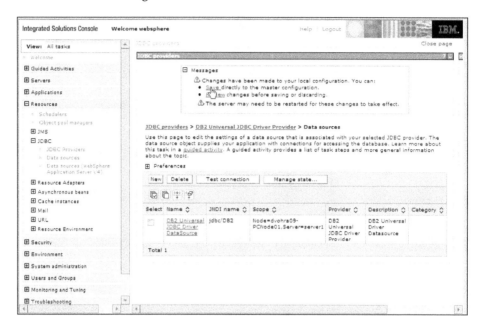

Select the data source checkbox, and click on **Test Connection** to test the JDBC connection with the DB2 database.

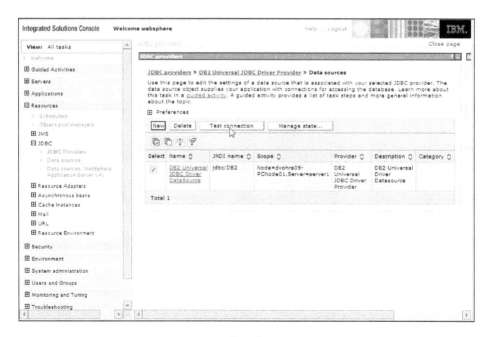

A message is displayed indicating that the JDBC connection with the DB2 database was successful.

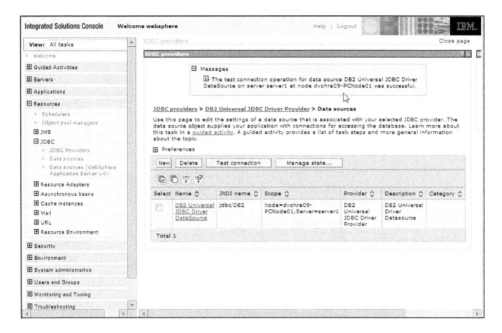

Configure additional connection pool properties by selecting the datasource link and the **Connection pool properties** link in the **Additional Properties** header.

Specify the connection pool properties. **Connection timeout** is the maximum number of seconds an application waits for a connection from the connection pool before timing out. **Maximum connections** is the maximum number of connections in the connection pool. **Minimum connections** is the minimum number of connections in the connection pool.

Deploying a Web Application to the WebSphere from JDeveloper

We will develop a JSP application to retrieve data from the DB2 database, and display the data in a browser. JDeveloper does not have the provision to connect to WebSphere application server, or deploy an application to WebSphere. JDeveloper can be used to create a JSP that can be deployed to WebSphere. Create an application by selecting **File | New**. In the **New Gallery** window, select **General** in **Categories** and **Application** in **Items**, and click on **OK**. In the **Create Application** window specify the application name, select application template as **no template** and click on **OK**. In the **Create Project** window, specify the project name and click on ok. An application and a project are added to JDeveloper. Add a JSP to the project. Select **File | New** and in the **New Gallery** window, select **Web Tier | JSP**. In the Items, select **JSP** and click on ok. Click on next in the **Create JSP Wizard**. Select J2EE 1.4

in the **Web Application** window, and click on next. Specify the File Name in the **JSP File** window, and click on next. As an error page is not being used, select the default settings in the **Error Page Options** and click on next. Click on next in the **Tag Libraries** window, as we will not be using any tag libraries. Click on next, in the **HTML Options** window. Click on finish, in the **Finish** window. A JSP and a `web.xml` is added to the WebSphere application.

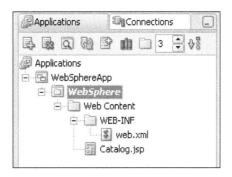

In the JSP, create an `InitialContext` object for JNDI naming operations. Create a `DataSource` object using the `lookup()` method on the data source JNDI name that we had created earlier, in this chapter. Create a `Connection` object from the `DataSource` object using the `getConnection()` method:

```
InitialContext initialContext = new InitialContext();
javax.sql.DataSource ds = (javax.sql.DataSource)initialContext.
lookup("jdbc/DB2");
java.sql.Connection conn = ds.getConnection();
```

Create a `Statement` object from the `Connection` object using the `createStatement()` method. Run a SQL query to retrieve data from the DB2 database, using the `executeQuery()` method of the `Statement` object. The query runs and generates a `ResultSet` object:

```
java.sql.Statement stmt = conn.createStatement();
ResultSet resultSet=stmt.executeQuery("Select * from Catalog");
```

Iterate over the result set using `next()` method, and display the data in a HTML table. The JSP page, `Catalog.jsp` is listed:

```
<%@ page contentType="text/html"%>
<%@ page import="java.sql.*,javax.naming.*" %>
<html>
<head>
<meta http-equiv="Content-Type" content="text/html">
<title>WebSphere JSP Application</title>
</head>
```

```
<body>
<%
 InitialContext initialContext = new InitialContext();
 javax.sql.DataSource ds = (javax.sql.DataSource)
 initialContext.lookup("jdbc/DB2");
 java.sql.Connection conn = ds.getConnection();
 java.sql.Statement stmt = conn.createStatement();
 ResultSet resultSet=stmt.executeQuery("Select * from Catalog");%>
 <table border="1" cellspacing="0">
  <tr>
   <th>CatalogId</th>
   <th>Journal</th>
   <th>Section</th>
   <th>Edition</th>
   <th>Title</th>
   <th>Author</th>
  </tr>
  <%
   while (resultSet.next())
   {
  %>
  <tr>
   <td><%out.println(resultSet.getString(1));%></td>
   <td><%out.println(resultSet.getString(2));%></td>
   <td><%out.println(resultSet.getString(3));%></td>
   <td><%out.println(resultSet.getString(4));%></td>
   <td><%out.println(resultSet.getString(5));%></td>
   <td><%out.println(resultSet.getString(6));%></td>
  </tr>
  <%
   }
  resultSet.close();stmt.close();conn.close();
  %>
 </table>
</body>
</html>
```

To create a web application deployment profile, select **File | New** and in the **New Gallery** window, select **General | Deployment Profiles** in Categories. In Items, select the **WAR File** and click on ok.

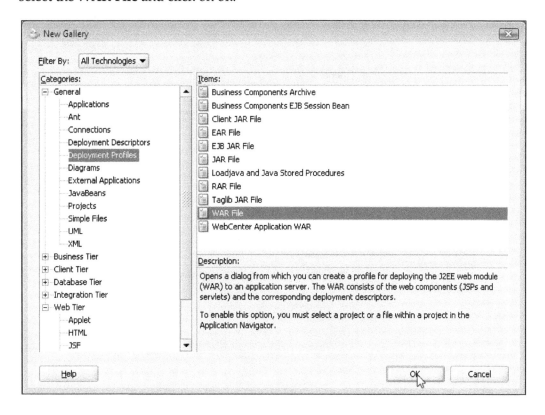

In the **Create Deployment Profile** window, specify a deployment profile name, webapp1, and click on ok. In the **WAR Deployment Profile Properties** window, select the **General** node. Specify a J2EE web context root, websphere (for example) and click on ok.

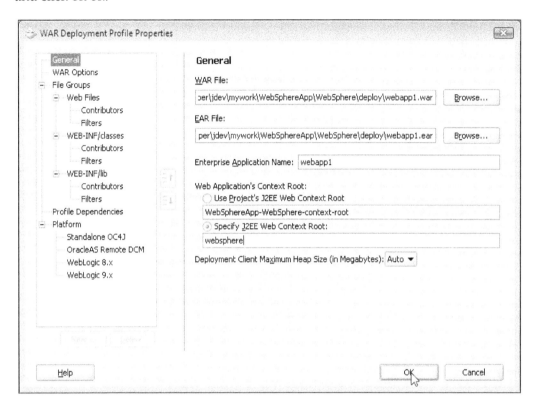

A web application deployment profile is created. Right-click on the deployment profile and select **Deploy to EAR file**.

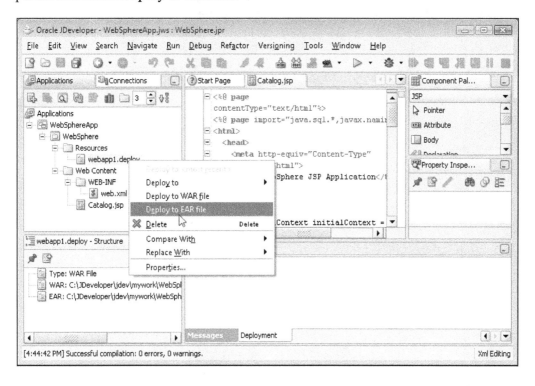

A `webapp1.ear` file is created in the project deploy directory. Copy the `webapp1.ear` file to the `C:\Program Files\IBM\WebSphere\AppServer\installableApps` directory. Install the `webapp1` web application to the WebSphere server. Select **Applications | Install New Application** node in the WebSphere administration console, and select the `webapp1.ear` file as the application to install. Click on the **Next** button.

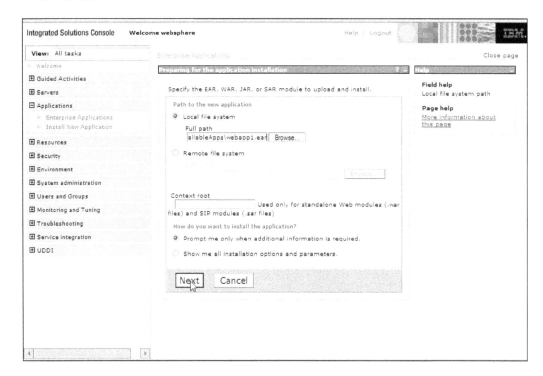

Select the default installation options, and click on **Next**. The webapp1 enterprise application has a web module, webapp1.war. In the **Map modules to servers** window, specify the server to which the web module is to be deployed. Select the webapp1.war module, select the WebSphere server node and click on **Apply** and then click on next.

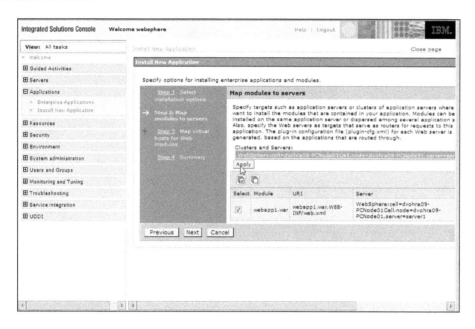

In the **Map virtual hosts for web modules** frame, select the checkbox adjacent to the webapp1.war file, and select default_host as the virtual host. Click on the **Next** button.

Click on finish in the **Summary** page to create the web application deployment configuration.

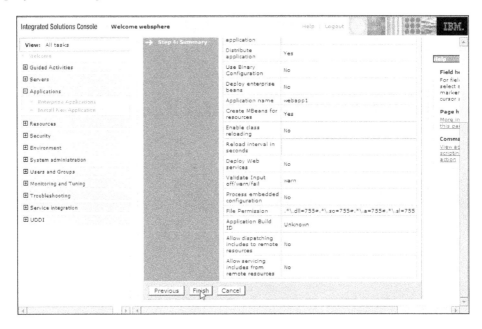

Web application is installed in the WebSphere application server and the deployment changes are saved in the local configuration. Click on **Save** to save the changes to the master configuration.

Select the **Applications | Enterprise Applications** link to display the installed applications. The webapp1 web application is listed in the table of installed enterprise applications. Select the checkbox adjacent to the webapp1 web application, and click on **Start**.

Web application, webapp1 is started on the WebSphere application server.

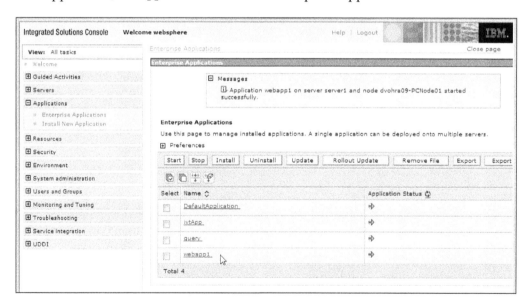

Run the `Catalog.jsp` in the server with the URL `http://localhost:9080/ websphere/Catalog.jsp`. The JSP application runs in the server and the data in DB2 database is displayed in the browser.

CatalogId	Journal	Section	Edition	Title	Author
catalog1	developerWorks	Java Technology	Nov 2004	Getting started with enumerated types	Brett McLaughlin
catalog2	developerWorks	XML	Apr 2005	Transform Eclipse navigation files to DITA navigation files	Loretta Hicks

JDBC 4.0 Version

WebSphere application server 6 does not support JDBC 4.0 specification, but IBM provides a JDBC driver that supports JDBC 4.0. IBM Data Server Driver and SQLJ Version 4.0 supports JDBC 4.0. They can be obtained from `https://www14. software.ibm.com/webapp/iwm/web/preLogin.do?lang=en_US&source=swg-idsjs11`. A WebSphere application server version that supports JDBC 4.0 adds `db2jcc4.jar from` the IBM Data Server Driver for JDBC and SQLJ, to the server class path. Also, the WebSphere server would have to be run on JDK 6.0 to use the JDBC 4.0 features.

JDBC 4.0 has added support for connection management, which includes the provision to track the state of connections and identify the connections based on client info properties. Connection state tracking has application in tracking the connections that are unusable, but they are still open and available in the connection pool. Unusable connections cause reduction in performance. Prior to the new feature in JDBC 4.0, a connection pool had to be reinitiated if unusable connections in the connection pool had been accummulated. With the connection state tracking feature implemented by the connection pool manager, a connection state can be obtained using the `isValid()` method of the `Connection` interface. If a `Connection` object is unusable, the `Connection` object would be closed.

```
if(!connection.isValid())
connection.close();
```

Another new connection management feature that has been added in JDBC 4.0 is connection tracking, which is different from connection state tracking. In connection tracking, some client info properties are set on a `Connection` object. If some connections reduces application performance those connections would be tracked using the client info properties. Client info properties are set on a `Connection` object using the `setClientInfo()` method and are retrieved using the `getClientInfo()` method. In the `catalog.jsp`, set the client info properties `ApplicationName`, `ClientUser`, and `ClientHostname` as follows:

```
connection.setClientInfo("ApplicationName","WebSphereApp");
connection.setClientInfo("ClientUser","WebSphereUser");
connection.setClientInfo("ClientHostname","WebSphereHost");
```

PreparedStatements are pooled by default and provide recycling of
PreparedStatement objects instead of creating new PreparedStatement objects.
PreparedStatement objects that are frequently used do not have to be opened,
initialized, and closed for each client request. JDBC 4.0 has also introduced
Statement pooling in which frequently used Statement objects are not closed, but
are returned to a statement pool from which other clients can use these objects.
To add statement pooling to a connection pool: First, test if the database supports
statement pooling using the supportsStatementPooling() method of the
DatabaseMetaData interface. Second, test if the Statement object is poolable using
the isPoolable() method. If it is poolable, the Statement object can be pooled
using the setPoolable(true) method:

```
java.sql.Statement stmt = conn.createStatement();
DatabaseMetaData metaData=connection.getMetaData();
if(metaData.supportsStatementPooling())
{
 if(stmt.isPoolable())
 stmt.setPoolable(true);
}
```

JDBC 4.0 has introduced support for the wrapper pattern using which nonstandard vendor-specific JDBC resources can be accessed. The wrapper pattern is
implemented in the Wrapper interface. JDBC interfaces that are to be made available
as extensions to the JDBC API should extend the Wrapper interface. In the IBM Data
Server Driver for JDBC and SQLJ, the Wrapper interface is extended by the following
interfaces in the com.ibm.db2.jcc package:

- DB2Connection.
- DB2BaseDataSource.
- DB2SimpleDataSource.
- DB2Statement.
- DB2ResultSet.
- DB2DatabaseMetaData.

Vendor-specific interfaces provide additional methods in the JDBC API. For example, create DB2Statement object using the wrapper pattern to use the setDB2ClientProgramId() method, which sets the program Id from a connection in the DB2Statement interface. Test if the Statement object is a wrapper for the DB2Statement interface using the isWrapperFor() method. If the Statement object is a wrapper, unwrap the DB2Statement interface using the unwrap() method to create a DB2Statement object. Also, invoke the setDB2ClientProgramId() method of the DB2Statement object:

```
Class class = Class.forName("com.ibm.db2.jcc.DB2Statement");
if(stmt.isWrapperFor(class))
{
  com.ibm.db2.jcc.DB2Statement  db2Stmt = (com.ibm.db2.jcc.
DB2Statement)stmt.unwrap(class);
  db2Stmt.setDB2ClientProgramId("WebSphereprogram");
}
```

JDBC 4.0 has introduced support for the SQL ROWID data type. ROWID type column values can be retrieved using the getRowId() method. ROWID identifies a row uniquely in a database table and is fastest method to access a row. As the DB2 database supports the ROWID data type, add a column for ROWID in the SELECT query:

```
ResultSet resultSet=db2Stmt.executeQuery("Select ROWID, CATALOGID,
JOURNAL, PUBLISHER, EDITION, TITLE, AUTHOR from Catalog");
```

Retrieve ROWID column values using the getRowId() method of the ResultSet interface:

```
<td><%out.println(resultSet.getRowId("ROWID").toString());%></td>
```

Prior to JDK 5.0, collections had to be iterated using the iterators and the index variables. JDK 5.0 introduced an enhanced FOR loop using which collections can be iterated without iterators and index variables. For example, if a java.util. Collection of String objects is to be iterated, then the String objects in the Collection are to be retrieved. An Iterator would be created using for loop. The String objects in the Collection are retrieved using the next() method:

```
for(Iterator i = c.iterator(); i.hasNext(); )
{
  String str = (String) i.next();
}
```

The String objects in a Collection of Strings are retrieved using the enhanced for loop, introduced in JDK 5.0:

```
for(String string : c)
{
  String str =string
}
```

SQLExceptions can have chained exceptions and cause of a SQLException can have chained causes. Using the enhanced for loop chained exceptions, the chained causes for a SQLException can be output as follows:

```
for(Throwable e : exception )
{
 out.println("Error encountered: " + e);
}
```

The JDBC 4.0 version of the web application JSP, catalog.jsp to retrieve DB2 UDB database data and to display it in a HTML table, is listed below:

```
<%@ page contentType="text/html"%>
<%@ page import="java.sql.*, javax.naming.*, com.ibm.db2.jcc.
DB2Statement " %>
<html>
<head>
<meta http-equiv="Content-Type" content="text/html">
<title>WebSphere JSP Application</title>
</head>
<body>
<%
 InitialContext initialContext = new InitialContext();
 javax.sql.DataSource ds = (javax.sql.DataSource)
 initialContext.lookup("jdbc/DB2DataSource");
 java.sql.Connection conn = ds.getConnection();
 connection.setClientInfo("ApplicationName","WebSphereApp");
 connection.setClientInfo("ClientUser","WebSphereUser");
 connection.setClientInfo("ClientHostname","WebSphereHost");
 java.sql.Statement stmt = conn.createStatement();
 DatabaseMetaData metaData=connection.getMetaData();
 if(metaData.supportsStatementPooling())
 {
  if(stmt.isPoolable())
  stmt.setPoolable(true);
 }
 Class class = Class.forName("com.ibm.db2.jcc.DB2Statement");
 if(stmt.isWrapperFor(class))
 {
  com.ibm.db2.jcc.DB2Statement db2Stmt = (com.ibm.db2.jcc.
DB2Statement)stmt.unwrap(class);
  db2Stmt.setDB2ClientProgramId("WebSphereprogram");
  ResultSet resultSet=db2Stmt.executeQuery("Select ROWID, CATALOGID,
JOURNAL, PUBLISHER, EDITION, TITLE, AUTHOR from Catalog");
%>
```

```
<table border="1" cellspacing="0">
 <tr>
  <th>RowId</th>
  <th>CatalogId</th>
  <th>Journal</th>
  <th>Section</th>
  <th>Edition</th>
  <th>Title</th>
  <th>Author</th>
 </tr>
 <%
 while (resultSet.next())
  {
%>
 <tr>
  <td><%out.println(resultSet.getRowId("ROWID").toString());%></td>
  <td><%out.println(resultSet.getString(1));%></td>
  <td><%out.println(resultSet.getString(2));%></td>
  <td><%out.println(resultSet.getString(3));%></td>
  <td><%out.println(resultSet.getString(4));%></td>
  <td><%out.println(resultSet.getString(5));%></td>
  <td><%out.println(resultSet.getString(6));%></td>
 </tr>
 <%
  }
 resultSet.close();
 stmt.close();
 connection.close();
 }
 %>
</table>
</body>
</html>
```

Summary

WebSphere 6.1 application server has the provision to create a JDBC Provider and a JDBC data source with a relational data source. In this chapter, we configured a JDBC connection in Web Sphere with DB2 9 database. The combination of the IBM's DB2 database and IBM's WebSphere application server is suitable for the development of JDBC applications. DB2 V9 supports the SQL XML data type that can be used with a new Java data type in JDBC 4.0, called SQLXML. IBM Data Server Driver for JDBC and SQLJ Version 4.0 supports JDBC 4.0 specification.

7
XML SQL Utility

Extensible Markup Language (XML) is the standard medium of data exchange on the Web. Examples of data exchange with XML are web feeds (RSS feeds and Atom feeds), and web services. Data exchanged using XML documents may be required to be stored in a relational database, or an XML document may require to be generated from a database table. An XML document is a hierarchical data structure where various elements may be mapped to columns in a database table. Therefore, by mapping various elements to a table, you can store XML in relational databases, and this mapping process is called XML-to-SQL mapping technology. Oracle created the **XML SQL Utility** (XSU) Java API to map XML to SQL and SQL to XML. The table to which an XML document is being mapped to must to be created prior to the mapping of the XML document to the database. With XSU, XML elements are mapped to database table columns. Mapping an XML document to a database table with XSU does not store the attributes of the document. The attributes may be stored by applying an **Extensible Stylesheet Language Transformation** (XSLT) to the XML document prior to storing it transforming the attributes you want to store into elements, which may be mapped to columns. With XSU, the data in the database may be updated, deleted, and retrieved. The XML document generated with XSU does not include attributes. Attributes may be added to the XML document by applying an XSLT to the document obtained with XSU.

JDBC 4.0 introduced the `SQLXML` Java data type, which we discussed in Chapter 1, to store and access XML documents in a column of SQL XML data type. But some database drivers such as the Oracle database 11g JDBC drivers do not support the `SQLXML` data type yet. Also, XSU has the advantage of the provision to apply an XSLT stylesheet to the data mapped from a database table to an XML document. We will use the Oracle database 11g JDBC 4.0 driver for the XML SQL Utility to take advantage of some of the JDBC 4.0 features such as automatic driver loading and support for enhanced chained exceptions.

JDeveloper 10.1.3 includes an XSU utility library to store an XML document in an SQL database, and to retrieve it from the database. Class `OracleXMLSave` is used to store an XML document in a database table, and the element tags are mapped to the database columns. Class `OracleXMLQuery` is used to generate an XML document from a database table. Database table columns are mapped to an XML document as element tags. Mapping of an XML document to a database table with the `OracleXMLSave` class does not include mapping of the XML document element attributes; we may store the element attributes by converting the attributes to elements. The procedure to map an XML document with elements and attributes to an Oracle database 10g table, and to map the database columns to an XML document with attributes; is discussed as an example in this chapter. You are not restricted to using Oracle to store XML documents with XSU. You can easily use another relational database such as MySQL. An XML document, `catalog.xml`, is used as an example to map to a database table and is listed below:

```xml
<?xml version="1.0" encoding="utf-8"?>
<catalog>
 <journal title="Oracle Magazine" publisher="Oracle Publishing"
edition="July-August 2005">
  <catalogId>catalog1</catalogId>
   <article section="Technology">
    <title> Tuning Undo Tablespace </title>
     <author> Kimberly Floss </author>
   </article>
 </journal>
 <journal title="Oracle Magazine" publisher="Oracle Publishing"
edition="Nov-Dec 2003">
  <catalogId>catalog2</catalogId>
   <article section="DEVELOPER">
    <title>Starting with Oracle ADF</title>
     <author>Steve Muench</author>
   </article>
 </journal>
</catalog>
```

In this chapter, you will learn how to:

- Map an XML Document to a Database Table with XSU
- Update a Database Table from an XML Document with XSU
- Delete a Database Table Row from an XML Document with XSU
- Map a Database Table to an XML Document with XSU

Setting the Environment

We need to create a JDeveloper project to store an XML document with XML SQL Utility. In the JDeveloper project, create an XML document `catalog.xml` by selecting **File | New**. In the **New Gallery** window, select **General | XML** in **Categories** and **XML Document** in **Items**. Also add XML files `catalog-update.xml` and `catalog-delete.xml`. Create XSL Stylesheets `input.xsl` and `output.xsl` in the JDeveloper project by selecting **File | New**. The chapter also lists the above-mentioned XML files and XSL stylesheets. XML documents `catalog-update.xml` and `catalog-delete.xml`, and XSLT stylesheets input.xsl and `output.xsl` are listed later in this chapter. Copy the catalog.xml, catalog-delete.xml, catalog-update.xml, input.xsl, and output.xsl listings to the JDeveloper XSU project. In the **New Gallery** window, select **General | XML** in **Categories** and **XSL Style Sheet** in **Items**. Create a Java application, `XMLToDatabase.java`, in the JDeveloper project by selecting **File | New**. In the **New Gallery** window, select **General** in **Categories** and **Java Class** in **Items**. The directory structure of the XSU application is shown below:

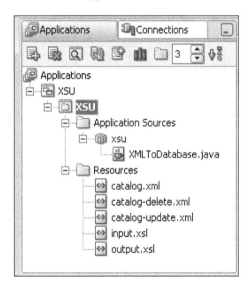

We need to add some libraries and JAR files to the project. As we are using the JDBC 4.0 driver, we need to add the JDBC 4.0 driver JAR file to the project libraries. Download the Oracle Database 11g JDBC driver's JAR file, `ojdbc6.jar` from `http://www.oracle.com/technology/software/tech/java/sqlj_jdbc/htdocs/ jdbc_111060.html`. **Select Tools | Project Properties**, and in the **Project Properties** window, select **Libraries**. Select the **Add Library** button to add Oracle XML SQL Utility and Oracle XML Parser v2 libraries. Select the **Add Jar/Directory** button to add `<JDeveloper>/rdbms/jlib/xdb.jar` and `ojdbc6.jar`, `<JDeveloper>` being the JDeveloper installation directory. The JAR files and libraries required for the XML SQL Utility are shown below:

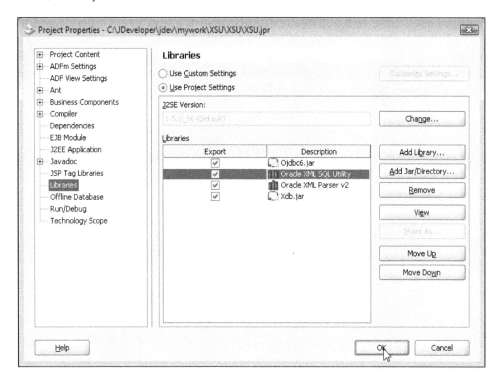

Oracle database 11g JDBC 4.0 drivers require JDK 6.0. We need to set the J2SE Version to JDK 6.0., then download and install JDK 6.0 from `http://java.sun. com/javase/downloads/index.jsp`. Select **Tools | Project Properties** to set the J2SE version to JDK 6.0 and in the **Project Properties** window, select **Libraries**. The **J2SE Version** field specifies the J2SE version used for Java applications in JDeveloper. Click on the **Change** button in J2SE Version, and click on **New** in the **Edit J2SE Definition** window to define a new J2SE version definition. Select the J2SE Executable for JDK 6.0 in the **Create J2SE** window and click on **OK**. A J2SE definition for JDK 6.0 gets added to **Edit J2SE Definition** window. Select the J2SE 6.0 definition and click on **OK** in the **Edit J2SE Definition** window.

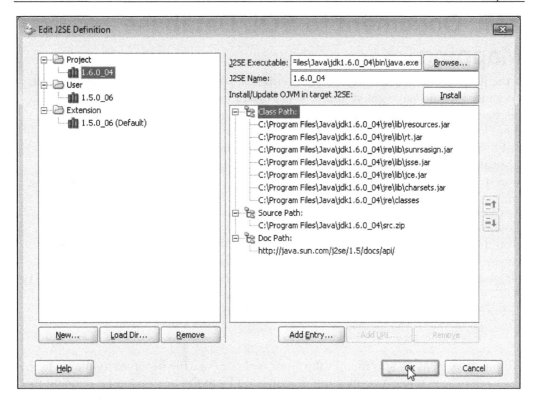

The JDK 6.0 J2SE definition gets added to the J2SE Version field in the **Project Properties** window. Now, click on **OK**.

Also install Oracle database 10g including sample schemas. Oracle database 11g JDBC drivers can be used with Oracle database 10g and all the JDBC 4.0 features can be advantageous if using an application server that supports JDBC 4.0. In the database create a database instance, and a database table, JOURNAL. The example XML document will be mapped to the database table. The SQL script used to create a database table in a sample schema, OE is illustrated below:

```
CREATE TABLE OE.JOURNAL (CATALOGID VARCHAR(255) PRIMARY KEY, JOURNAL_
TITLE VARCHAR(255), PUBLISHER VARCHAR(255), EDITION VARCHAR(255),
ARTICLE_SECTION VARCHAR(255), TITLE VARCHAR(255), AUTHOR VARCHAR(255));
```

XML Document to SQL Database Mapping

If the XML document had been stored with XSU, only the element tags in the XML document would have got stored. The attributes in the XML document would not have got stored. Attributes in an XML document can be stored by mapping them to elements. The attributes can be converted to elements by applying an XSLT stylesheet to the XML document. This section discusses the procedure to store an XML document with attributes in a database table. The XML document is stored in a database table using the `OracleXMLSave` class, which is imported in the `XMLToDatabase.java` application.

Create a connection with the database. If we were using a JDBC 3.0 driver, we would have registered the Oracle JDBC driver with `DriverManager` using the `registerDriver(Driver)` method. JDBC 4.0 adds support for automatic driver registration using the Java SE Service Provider mechanism. The Oracle database 11g JDBC 4.0 drivers JAR file, `ojdbc6.jar`, includes a `META-INF/services/java.sql.Driver` file. For the Oracle JDBC driver, this file includes:

```
oracle.jdbc.OracleDriver
```

All the driver classes specified in the `java.sql.Driver` file becomes available to the `DriverManager` when a connection is requested from the `DriverManager` using the `getConnection()` method. Therefore, we will not be registering the Oracle JDBC driver with the `DriverManager`. Obtain a connection from `DriverManager` using the `getConnection(String url, String user, String password)` method:

```
Connection conn =
DriverManager.getConnection("jdbc:oracle:thin:@<host>:<port>:<SID>",
"<user>","<password>");
```

<host> is the database host.

<port> is the database port.

<SID> is the database SID.

<user> is the username to log in to the database.

<password> is the password to log in to the database.

Values for <host>, <port>, and <SID> can be obtained from the <Oracle 10g>/NETWORK/ADMIN/tnsnames.ora file.

An `SQLException` can be generated while obtaining a connection to the Oracle database. The `SQLException` generated may contain chained exceptions and chained causes. JDBC 4.0 has added support for the Java SE chained exception facility, which is also called the cause facility. Prior to JDBC 4.0, the `getNextException()` and `getCause()` methods had to be called recursively to retrieve the chained exceptions and causes. JDBC 4.0 has enhanced support for these chained exceptions using the `for` loop introduced in J2SE 6.0. `SQLException` interface implements the `Iterable` interface. The chained exceptions may be output using the enhanced `for-each` loop as shown below:

```
catch(SQLException exception)
{
  for(Throwable e : exception )
   {
    System.out.println("Error encountered: " + e);
   }
}
```

We need to create an `OracleXMLSave` class object to save an XML document to a database table, JOURNAL.

```
OracleXMLSave oracleXMLSave =new OracleXMLSave(conn, "JOURNAL");
```

JOURNAL is the database table created in the *Setting the Environment* section. Convert the attributes to element tags in the given example XML document. The attributes are converted to element tags by applying an XSLT to the XML document. Set an XSLT on the `OracleXMLSave` object using the `setXSLT(Reader, String)` method. The `String` parameter specifies the URL to be used to include import and external entities.

```
Reader xsltReader=new FileReader(new File("input.xsl"));
oracleXMLSave.setXSLT(xsltReader, null);
```

The XSLT, `input.xslt`, is used to convert the attributes to elements in the given XML document, as an example:

```
<?xml version="1.0" encoding="UTF-8"?>
<xsl:stylesheet version="1.0" xmlns:xsl="http://www.w3.org/1999/XSL/
Transform">
<xsl:output method="xml/text" omit-xml-declaration="no"/>
<xsl:template match="/">
<xsl:element name="catalog">
<xsl:apply-templates select="catalog/journal"/>
</xsl:element>
</xsl:template>
<xsl:template match="journal">
```

```
<xsl:element name="journal">
<xsl:element name="journal_title">
<xsl:value-of select="@title"/>
</xsl:element>
<xsl:element name="catalogId">
<xsl:value-of select="catalogId"/>
</xsl:element>
<xsl:element name="publisher">
<xsl:value-of select="@publisher"/>
</xsl:element>
<xsl:element name="edition">
<xsl:value-of select="@edition"/>
</xsl:element>
<xsl:apply-templates select="article"/>
</xsl:element>
</xsl:template>
<xsl:template match="article">
<xsl:element name="article_section">
<xsl:value-of select="@section"/>
</xsl:element>
<xsl:copy-of select="title"/>
<xsl:copy-of select="author"/>
</xsl:template>
</xsl:stylesheet>
```

The `input.xslt` transformation converts attributes, `title` and `section` in the XML document, to elements, `journal_title` and `article_title`. Set the tag for the row enclosing element. Setting the row tag to `null` implies that a row tag is not defined and the top-level elements of the document correspond to the database table rows. The row tag is set to `journal`. Each `journal` tag in the example, XML document corresponds to a database table row. Each row in the table represents a journal entry; the journal entry is the row enclosing element.

```
oracleXMLSave.setRowTag("journal");
```

Set the columns containing the primary key in the database table using the `setKeyCo lumnList(String[]keyColNames)` method. Set CATALOGID as a primary key column:

```
String [] keyColNames = new String[1];
keyColNames[0] = "CATALOGID";
oracleXMLSave.setKeyColumnList(keyColNames);
```

XSU maps the XML document elements to database table columns, based on element tag names. To match element tags that are case-insensitive set ignore case to `true`.

```
oracleXMLSave.setIgnoreCase(true);
```

Create an `InputStream` from the XML document, `catalog.xml`.

```
InputStream input=new FileInputStream(new File("catalog.xml"));
```

Map the example XML document to a database table using the `insertXML(InputStream)` method. The `insertXML()` method is overloaded, and the input can be specified as a `Document` object, an `InputStream` object, a `Reader` object, a `String` object, or a `URL` object:

```
oracleXMLSave.insertXML(input);
```

The XSLT, `input.xslt`, gets applied to the XML document. The XML document, with the attributes converted to elements, gets stored in the database. Close the `OracleXMLSave` object using the `close()` method:

```
oracleXMLSave.close();
```

The `XMLToDatabase` application is listed completely, later in the chapter. Selected operations can be run by commenting out the methods that are not required. For example, to map an XML document to a database table, comment out invocations to all the methods except the `xmlToSQL()` method. To run an `XMLToDatabase.java` application, in JDeveloper right-click on the application node and select `Run`.

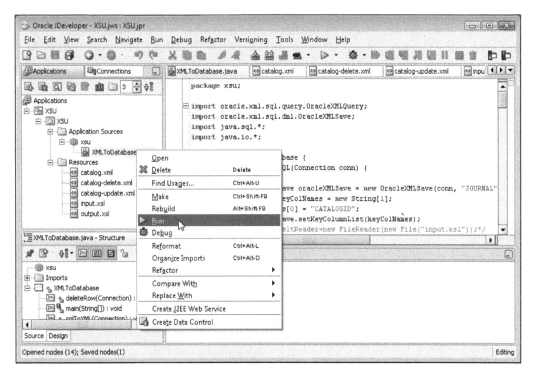

The XML document `input.xml` gets mapped to the Oracle database table JOURNAL.

Updating Database from XML Document

In this section, we will update a database table from an XML document, using the `OracleXMLSave` class, and create an `OracleXMLSave` object using a `Connection` object. JOURNAL is the database table that has to be modified.

```
OracleXMLSave oracleXMLSave =new OracleXMLSave(conn, "JOURNAL");
```

Set the row enclosing element tag using the `setRowTag(String)` method, and set the row tag to `journal`. Also set ignore case to `true`.

```
oracleXMLSave.setRowTag("journal");
oracleXMLSave.setIgnoreCase(true);
```

Set key columns using the `setKeyColumnList(String[])` method and set CATALOGID as a key column.

```
String [] keyColNames = new String[1];
keyColNames[0] = "CATALOGID";
oracleXMLSave.setKeyColumnList(keyColNames);
```

Specify an array of columns to be updated, and also specify the columns to be updated using the `setUpdateColumnList(String[])` method. We will modify the EDITION column and the TITLE column with an XML document.

```
String[] updateColNames = new String[2];
updateColNames[0] = "EDITION";
updateColNames[1] = "TITLE";
oracleXMLSave.setUpdateColumnList(updateColNames);
```

Data to be updated in the database table is specified in an XML document. The XML document, `catalog-update.xml`, specifies a `journal` element with `catalogId`, "catalog2". Only the EDITION and TITLE columns for table, JOURNAL with row `catalogId` containing `catalog2` will be modified. `Catalog-update.xml` is listed below:

```
<?xml version="1.0" encoding="utf-8"?>
<catalog>
<journal>
 <catalogId>catalog2</catalogId>
 <journal_title>Oracle Magazine</journal_title>
 <publisher>Oracle Publishing</publisher>
 <edition>September-October 2005</edition>
 <article_section>Developer</article_section>
```

```
  <title>Creating Search Pages</title>
  <author>Steve Muench</author>
 </journal>
 </catalog>
```

Create an `InputStream` object from `catalog-update.xml`.

```
InputStream input=new FileInputStream(new File("catalog-update.xml"));
```

Update database table `JOURNAL` using the `updateXML(InputStream)` method. The `updateXML()` method is overloaded and the database table row can be updated from one of the following: a `Document` object, an `InputStream` object, a `Reader` object, a `String` object, or a `URL` object. Close the `OracleXMLSave` object using `close()` method.

```
oracleXMLSave.updateXML(input);
oracleXMLSave.close();
```

To update the database table, `JOURNAL`, comment out all method invocations in the `XMLToDatabase.java` application, except the `updateDatabase()` method. As a result, database table `JOURNAL` gets updated.

Deleting a Row in a Database

We will delete a database table row using the XML SQL Utility. A database table row can be deleted by specifying element tags corresponding to key columns in an XML document. An example XML document, `catalog-delete.xml`, specifies the `catalogId`, "catalog2". We will delete from the table `JOURNAL` the row for which the primary key column, `CATALOGID`, that has the value "catalog2" as specified in `catalog-delete.xml` is listed below:

```
<?xml version="1.0" encoding="utf-8"?>
<catalog>
<journal>
 <catalogId>catalog2</catalogId>
</journal>
</catalog>
```

We have to create an `OracleXMLSave` object, setting the row enclosing tag and setting ignore case to `true`, as discussed in the previous section.

```
OracleXMLSave oracleXMLSave =new OracleXMLSave(conn, "JOURNAL");
oracleXMLSave.setRowTag("journal");
oracleXMLSave.setIgnoreCase(true);
```

Set key columns using the `setKeyColumnList(String[] keyColumns)` method and set `CATALOGID` as a key column.

```
String [] keyColNames = new String[1];
keyColNames[0] = "CATALOGID";
oracleXMLSave.setKeyColumnList(keyColNames);
```

Create an `InputStream` from the `catalog-delete.xml` document.

```
InputStream input=new FileInputStream(new File("catalog-delete.xml"));
```

Delete a database table row using the `deleteXML(InputStream)` method. The `deleteXML()` method is overloaded, and a database table row can be deleted using one of the following: a `Document` object, an `InputStream` object, a `Reader` object, a `String` object, or a `URL` object. Close the `OracleXMLSave` object using the `close()` method.

```
oracleXMLSave.deleteXML(input);
oracleXMLSave.close();
```

Comment out all the method invocations in the `XMLToDatabase.java` application, except the `deleteRow()` method, to delete a row from the `JOURNAL` table using `catalog-delete.xml`. As a result, a database table row specified in `catalog-delete.xml` gets deleted from the `JOURNAL` table.

SQL Database to XML Document Mapping

We will map the database table `JOURNAL` to an XML document, using the XML SQL Utility. The `OracleXMLQuery` class is used to convert a database table to an XML document. In the generated XML document, an XML element gets created corresponding to each of the database table columns. Element attributes do not get created, and to create them apply an XSLT to the XML document that was created from the database table with the `OracleXMLQuery` class.

The procedure to create an XML document with elements and element attributes is discussed in this section. Import the `OracleXMLQuery` class and create an `OracleXMLQuery` class object:

```
OracleXMLQuery query = new OracleXMLQuery(conn, "SELECT CATALOGID,
JOURNAL_TITLE, PUBLISHER, EDITION, ARTICLE_SECTION, TITLE,
AUTHOR FROM JOURNAL");
```

Variable `conn` is the JDBC connection used to query the database. The SELECT
SQL statement specifies the query to select data from the database table, JOURNAL.
Apply an XSLT to the `OracleXMLQuery` object to generate an XML document that
includes element attributes. An XSLT is set on an `OracleXMLQuery` object using the
`setXSLT(Reader, String)` method. The `String` parameter specifies the URL for
external entities.

```
Reader xsltReader=new FileReader(new File("output.xsl"));
query.setXSLT(xsltReader, null);
```

The XSLT, `output.xslt`, is listed below:

```
<?xml version="1.0" encoding="UTF-8"?>
 <xsl:stylesheet version="1.0"
                     xmlns:xsl="http://www.w3.org/1999/XSL/Transform">
 <xsl:output method="xml"/>
 <xsl:template match="/ROWSET">
  <xsl:element name="CATALOG">
   <xsl:apply-templates select="journal"/>
  </xsl:element>
 </xsl:template>
 <xsl:template match="journal">
  <xsl:element name="journal">
   <xsl:attribute name="title">
    <xsl:value-of select="JOURNAL_TITLE"/>
   </xsl:attribute>
   <xsl:attribute name="publisher">
    <xsl:value-of select="PUBLISHER"/>
   </xsl:attribute>
   <xsl:attribute name="edition">
    <xsl:value-of select="EDITION"/>
   </xsl:attribute>
   <xsl:element name="catalogId">
    <xsl:value-of select="CATALOGID"/>
   </xsl:element>
   <xsl:element name="article">
   <xsl:attribute name="section">
    <xsl:value-of select="ARTICLE_SECTION"/>
   </xsl:attribute>
    <xsl:copy-of select="TITLE"/>
    <xsl:copy-of select="AUTHOR"/>
   </xsl:element>
  </xsl:element>
 </xsl:template>
</xsl:stylesheet>
```

Set the row enclosing tag, the element tag in the XML document being generated corresponding to a database table row, as `journal`:

```
query.setRowTag("journal");
```

Generate an XML document from the database table, JOURNAL, using the `getXMLString()` method:

```
String xmlString=query.getXMLString();
```

Output the XML string to a `catalog-output.xml` file, using `PrintWriter`:

```
OutputStream output=new FileOutputStream(new File("catalog-output.
xml"));
PrintWriter printWriter=new PrintWriter(output);
printWriter.print(xmlString);
printWriter.flush();
```

The XSLT `output.xslt` is applied to the XML document generated with XSU. The XML document stored in the database is generated. In XSU version 2.1.0 (included in XDK 10g), a database column can be mapped to an attribute, by customizing the SQL SELECT statement. To map a column to an attribute, create an alias for the column and prepend the @ sign to the alias. To map the CATALOGID column to a `catalogId` attribute, the SELECT query would be as follows:

```
SELECT CATALOGID "@catalogId", JOURNAL_TITLE, PUBLISHER, EDITION,
ARTICLE_SECTION, TITLE, AUTHOR FROM JOURNAL;
```

`XMLToDatabase.java`, the Java program used to store an XML document in a database and to retrieve an XML document from a database, is listed below:

```
package xsu;
import oracle.xml.sql.query.OracleXMLQuery;
import oracle.xml.sql.dml.OracleXMLSave;
import java.sql.*;
import java.io.*;
public class XMLToDatabase
{
 public void xmlToSQL(Connection conn)
 {
  try
  {
   OracleXMLSave oracleXMLSave = new OracleXMLSave(conn, "JOURNAL");
   String[] keyColNames = new String[1];
   keyColNames[0] = "CATALOGID";
   oracleXMLSave.setKeyColumnList(keyColNames);
   /*Reader xsltReader=new FileReader(new File("input.xsl"));*/
   oracleXMLSave.setXSLT("input.xsl", null);
   oracleXMLSave.setIgnoreCase(true);
```

```
  oracleXMLSave.setRowTag("journal");
  InputStream input = new FileInputStream(new File("catalog.xml"));
  oracleXMLSave.insertXML(input);
  oracleXMLSave.close();
 }
 catch (IOException e)
 {
  System.out.println("IOException" + e.getMessage());
 }
}
public void updateDatabase(Connection conn)
{
 try
 {
  OracleXMLSave oracleXMLSave = new OracleXMLSave(conn, "JOURNAL");
  oracleXMLSave.setRowTag("journal");
  oracleXMLSave.setIgnoreCase(true);
  String[] keyColNames = new String[1];
  keyColNames[0] = "CATALOGID";
  oracleXMLSave.setKeyColumnList(keyColNames);
  String[] updateColNames = new String[2];
  updateColNames[0] = "EDITION";
  updateColNames[1] = "TITLE";
  oracleXMLSave.setUpdateColumnList(updateColNames);
  InputStream input = new FileInputStream(new File(
                          "catalog-update.xml"));
  oracleXMLSave.updateXML(input);
  oracleXMLSave.close();
 }
 catch (IOException e)
 {
  System.out.println("IOException" + e.getMessage());
 }
}
public void deleteRow(Connection conn)
{
 try
 {
  OracleXMLSave oracleXMLSave = new OracleXMLSave(conn, "JOURNAL");
  oracleXMLSave.setRowTag("journal");
  oracleXMLSave.setIgnoreCase(true);
  String[] keyColNames = new String[1];
  keyColNames[0] = "CATALOGID";
  oracleXMLSave.setKeyColumnList(keyColNames);
  InputStream input = new FileInputStream(
          new File("catalog-delete.xml"));
  oracleXMLSave.deleteXML(input);
  oracleXMLSave.close();
 }
 catch (IOException e)
```

```
    {
     System.out.println("IOException" + e.getMessage());
    }
   }
   public void sqlToXML(Connection conn)
   {
    try
    {
     OracleXMLQuery query = new OracleXMLQuery(conn, "SELECT CATALOGID,
         JOURNAL_TITLE, PUBLISHER, EDITION, ARTICLE_SECTION, TITLE,
         AUTHOR FROM JOURNAL");
     Reader xsltReader = new FileReader(new File("output.xsl"));
     query.setXSLT(xsltReader, null);
     query.setRowTag("journal");
     String xmlString = query.getXMLString();
     OutputStream output = new FileOutputStream(
               new File("catalog-output.xml"));
     PrintWriter printWriter = new PrintWriter(output);
     printWriter.print(xmlString);
     printWriter.flush();
    }
    catch (IOException e)
    {
     System.out.println("IOException" + e.getMessage());
    }
   }
   public static void main(String[] args)
   {
    try
    {
    Connection conn = DriverManager.getConnection(
            "jdbc:oracle:thin:@localhost:1521:ORCL", "OE", "calgary");
    XMLToDatabase xmlToDB = new XMLToDatabase();
    /* xmlToDB.xmlToSQL(conn);
    xmlToDB.updateDatabase(conn);
    xmlToDB.deleteRow(conn);*/
    xmlToDB.sqlToXML(conn);
    conn.close();
    }
    catch (SQLException exception)
    {
     for (Throwable e: exception)
     {
      System.out.println("Error encountered: " + e);
     }
    }
   }
}
```

The selected operations can be run by commenting out the methods that are not required. To map a database table, JOURNAL, to an XML document, comment out invocations to all the methods except the sqlToXML() method. To run an XMLToDatabase.java application, in JDeveloper right-click on the application node, and select **Run**.

The output from the application generates an XML document, catalog-output.xml, in which a journal element has been removed. To add the catalog-output.xml to XSU project, click on the project node and select **View | Refresh**.

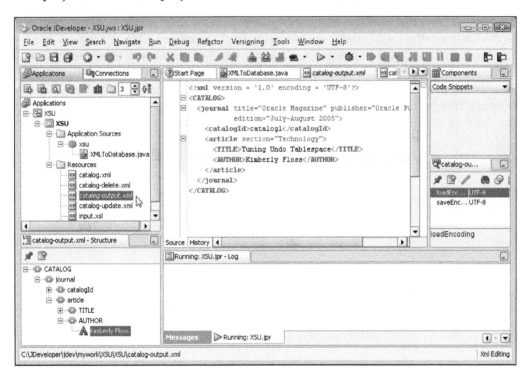

JDBC 4.0 has a new feature in SQLExceptions, categorization of SQLExceptions. SQLExceptions are categorized into SQLNonTransientException, SQLRecoverableException, and SQLTransientException. Stop the TNSListener for the Oracle database 10g, and run the XMLToDatabase.java application with all the commented method invocations, except the sqlToXML() method. The following exception is displayed:

```
Error encountered: java.sql.SQLRecoverableException: Io exception: The
Network Adapter could not establish the connection
```

The exception indicates that the SQLException is an SQLRecoverableException. This implies that a JDBC operation would succeed, if a recovery operation were performed. If the TNSListener is started, the SQLException is removed. In the exception message, the SQLException is not chained to another SQLException.

Summary

Oracle XML SQL Utility is used to map an XML document to a relational database and vice versa. The XML SQL Utility (XSU) does not store the attributes in an XML document. The attributes can be stored by applying an XSLT to the XML document. In this chapter, the Oracle database has been used to store an XML document. We can also use the open-source MySQL database to do the same. We used the Oracle database 11g JDBC 4.0 driver to map an XML document to an Oracle database table, and also to map an Oracle database table to an XML document. We used some of the new features in JDBC 4.0, such as automatic driver loading, and enhanced support for chained SQLExceptions.

8
XSQL

In Chapter 7, we discussed the mapping of XML to SQL and SQL to XML. XML SQL Utility is a Java API. However, SQL to XML mapping may also be done with XSQL using the JDBC driver without any Java code. The Oracle XSQL Pages Publishing Framework, which is included in Oracle JDeveloper 10g, supports the processing of SQL queries to generate XML. XSQL may also be used to run SQL DML (Data Manipulation Language) statements other than SQL SELECT such as INSERT, UPDATE, and DELETE. An XSQL page consists of the XSQL tags in the urn:oracle-xsql namespace. An XSQL page request is sent to the XSQL Servlet, which invokes the XSQL Page Processor.

The XSQL Pages Publishing Framework integrates XML, SQL, and XSLT. The XSQL Page Processor processes XSQL page templates. The XSQL Page Processor uses the Oracle XML Parser to parse XSQL Page templates and uses the XSLT Stylesheets to transform output from XSQL page processing. XSQL Pages Framework uses XML SQL Utility (XSU) to query the database and generate XML from an SQL query. A JDBC connection is used to access the database to process SQL queries. XML output generated with XSQL may be required in a different format or the output may need to be modified, for which XSQL Pages Framework supports XSLT transformations.

An XSQL application consists of a client XSQL page, an XSQLConfig.xml configuration file, a server-side XSQL Servlet, and a database. An XSQL page (.xsql file) consists of SQL query statements defined in <xsql:query></xsql:query> tags. XSQL may also be used to create and update a database table with data from an XML document with <xsql:dml></xsql:dml> tags. XSQL supports XSLT transformation of XML data retrieved using an XSQL query. The XSLT Stylesheet with which XML data is to be transformed is specified in the XSQL page. When an XSQL page is run in JDeveloper the following procedure is followed to process the XSQL page:

1. The XSQL page request is sent from a browser to the XSQL Servlet.
2. The XSQL Servlet forwards the request to the XSQL Page Processor to process the .xsql page.

3.   The XSQL Page Processor parses the XSQL page with Oracle XML Parser and caches the page.

4.   The XSQL Page processor connects to the database using the `connection` attribute in the XSQL page.

5.   The XSQL Page Processor uses XML SQL Utility (XSU) to generate XML from SQL queries.

6.   The XSQL Page Processor generates an XML datagram by replacing each XSQL action element, such as `xsql:query`, with the XML results returned by its action handler.

7.   If an XSLT Stylesheet is specified, the XSQL Page Processor parses the stylesheet and caches it.

8.   The XSQL Page Processor transforms the XML datagram by applying the XSLT stylesheet using the Oracle XSLT Processor.

9.   The XSQL Page Processor returns the XML/HTML output from the XSLT transformation to the XSQL Servlet to be displayed in a browser.

In this chapter, we will query an example database table containing a catalog with XSQL. Subsequently, we will display the XML output as an HTML table via XSLT transformation. In this chapter you will learn the following:

- Creating an XSQL page to run an SQL query and generating XML
- Using bind parameters in the SQL query
- Applying XSQL query attributes to customize XML output
- Applying XSLT transformation to XML output

Overview of XSQL Tags

In this section, we will discuss the different XSQL tags that may be specified in an XSQL page. The root element in an XSQL page is `<page>`. Some of the XSQL tags are discussed in following table. XSQL tag attributes are optional unless specified to be required in the table.

XSQL Tag	Description	Attributes
xsql:query	Runs an SQL query and includes result set as XML.	Refer to the second Table
xsql:dml	Runs a DML SQL statement or a PL/SQL anonymous block.	name (required): Name of page level parameter.
		ignore-empty-value: Specifies if empty value ("") should be ignored. Default is 'no'.
		value:Param value.
xsql:set-page-param	Sets a page-level parameter.	name (required): Name of page level parameter.
		ignore-empty-value: Specifies if empty value ("") should be ignored. Default is 'no'.
		value:Param value.
xsql:set-session-param	Sets a session level param.	Same as xsql:set-page-param.
xsql:set-stylesheet-param	Sets XSLT stylesheet param.	Same as xsql:set-page-param.
xsql:include-param	Includes XML representing name and value of a page param. For example, If page param is defined as: <xsql:set-page-param name="param1" value="paramValue"/> An include-param defined as <xsql:include-param name="param1"/> includes following XML in XML output: <param1>paramValue</param1>	Name (required): Name of param to include.
xsql:query	Runs an SQL query and includes result set as XML	Refer to the second Table

XSQL Tag	Description	Attributes
xsql:include-request-params	Includes an XML fragment representing the names and values of all HTTP parameters, cookies, and session variables. For example, if <xsql:include-request-params/> is specified, the following XML fragment gets included: <request><parameters><param1>value1 </param1></parameters><session><var1> value1</var1></session><cookies> <cookiename1>cookieValue </cookiename1></cookies> </request>	
xsql:include-xml	Includes external XML content from an absolute, relative, or parameterized URL.	href (required): Absolute, relative or parameterized URL that may be a static file or a dynamic source.
xsql:include-xsql	Includes XML output of another XSQL page.	href (required): Absolute, relative, or parameterized URL of an XSQL resource. reparse: Specifies if the included XSQL page should be reparsed. Default value is 'no'.

XSQL Tag	Description	Attributes
xsql:insert-request	Inserts XML document or HTML Form that has been posted in the request to a database table or view. The XML document may be transformed with an XSLT. If an HTML Form is posted, an XML document containing request parameters, session variables, and cookies. Example XML document: <request><parameters><param1>value1 </param1></parameters><session><var1> varValue</var1></session><cookies> <cookiename1>cookieValue</cookiename1> </cookies></request>	table (required): Name of table view or synonym. transform: Relative or absolute URL of XSLT to transform the XML document. columns: Space or comma separated list of columns date-format: Date format for data field values.
xsql:update-request	Updates the rows represented in the XML document posted.	In addition to attributes of xsql: insert-request: key-columns: Space or comma-separated listed of columns whose values are used to identify a table row.
xsql:delete-request	Deletes the rows represented in the XML document posted.	Same as xsql:update-request except columns is not an attribute.
xsql:insert-param	Inserts the value of a parameter into a database table or view.	name (required): Param name. table (required): Table name. date-format: Date format for date field values. transform: Relative, absolute or parameterized URL of XSLT.

XSQL Tag	Description	Attributes
xsql:set-cookie	Sets the value of an HTTP cookie.	name (required):
		Name of HTTP cookie.
		domain: Domain in which cookie is valid and readable. Default value is complete domain of document creating the cookie.
		ignore-empty-value: Specifies if empty value is to be ignored. Default value is 'no'.
		max-age: Maximum age of cookie in seconds. Default age is the user current browser session.
		only-if-unset: Specifies if cookies should be set only if cookie is currently not defined. Default value is 'no'.
		path: Relative URL within the domain in which cookie is valid and readable. Default value is the URL path of the document creating the cookie.
		value: Cookie value.

Setting the Environment

In this section, we will discuss the preliminary setup required to create an XSQL application, which is not much, as the XSQLServlet is specified in web.xml and the XSQL libraries are added to the project when an XSQL page is created. Oracle database 11g JDBC drivers may be used with any Oracle database version 9i and later. We will use Oracle database 10g. We need to install Oracle database 10g including sample schemas. We need to create and start an instance of the Oracle Database. Connect to the database with the Order Entry (OE) sample schema (username).

```
CONNECT OE/<password>
```

Run the following SQL script to create a database table that consists of an example catalog:

```
CREATE TABLE Catalog(Journal VARCHAR(25), Publisher
  Varchar(25),Edition VARCHAR(25), Title Varchar(45), Author
  Varchar(25));
INSERT INTO Catalog VALUES('Oracle Magazine',  'Oracle
  Publishing','July-August 2005', 'Tuning Undo Tablespace', 'Kimberly
  Floss');
INSERT INTO Catalog VALUES('Oracle Magazine',   'Oracle
  Publishing','September-October 2005', 'Creating Search Pages',
  'Steve Muench');
```

We need to create a JDeveloper project for an XSQL application:

Configuring a Connection

We also need to create a database connection to run an XSQL query. By default Oracle XSQL Pages use Oracle JDBC data sources configured in the J2EE web application environment. The `factory` element in the `connection-manager` element in `XSQLConfig.xml` sets the XSQL Pages to use the JDBC data sources.

```
<connection-manager>
...
<factory>
  oracle.xml.xsql.XSQLOracleDatasourceConnectionManager
</factory>
</connection-manager>
```

XSQL pages also have the provision to use `XSQLConfig.xml`-based named connections by setting the `connection-manager factory` class in `XSQLConfig.xml` as follows:

```
<factory>oracle.xml.xsql.XSQLConnectionManagerFactoryImpl</factory>
```

If third-party JDBC data sources are to be used in an XSQL page set the
`connection-manager factory` class in `XSQLConfig.xml` as follows:

```
<factory> oracle.xml.xsql.XSQLDatasourceConnectionManager</factory>
```

JDeveloper 10.1.3.3 provides three different methods to create a database connection
from an XSQL page:

- A JDBC Connection in **Connections Navigator**. A **Connections Navigator**
  connection has a corresponding data source with a JNDI name
  binding available.

- A data source configured in the **Embedded OC4J Preferences** Window or the
  `data-sources.xml`.

- A connection specified in `XSQLConfig.xml` file.

To create a database connection in **Connections Navigator**, select the **Database
| New Database Connection** node in the **Connections Navigator**. A Create
Connection Wizard starts. Click on **Next**. In the **Type** frame, specify a **Connection
Name** and select **Connection Type** as Oracle (JDBC). In the **Authentication** frame,
specify a **Username** and **Password** and click **Next**. In the **Connection** frame specify a
JDBC Driver, Host Name, JDBC Port, and database **SID** and click **Next**.

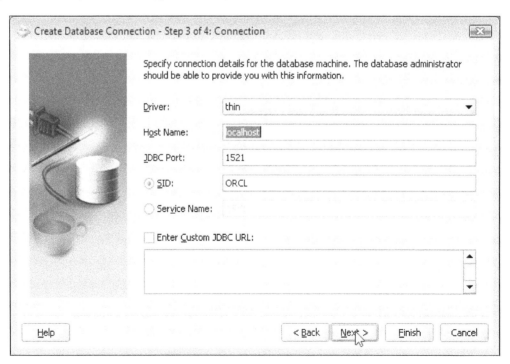

In the **Test** frame, click the **Test Connection** button to test the JDBC connection. Click the **Finish** button to configure the database connection. A connection node is added to the **Connections | Database** node in the **Applications Navigator**. The xsqlConnection is available as a jdbc/xsqlConnectionDS JNDI resource.

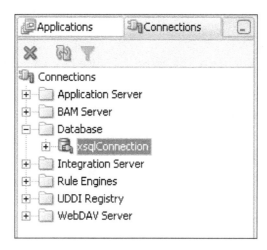

A connection may also be configured in embedded OC4J server data-sources.xml configuration file, <JDeveloper10.1.3>\jdev\system\oracle. j2ee.10.1.3.34.12\embedded-oc4j\config\data-sources.xml, declaratively or using the **Tools | Embedded OC4J Preferences | Global | Data Sources** as explained in Chapter 2. <JDeveloper10.1.3> is the directory in which JDeveloper is installed. Add a managed-data-source element to the data-sources.xml file, specifying the connection configuration for a data source. The managed-data-source element includes the data source class used to obtain a data source object. The managed-data-source element is listed below:

```
<managed-data-source name='XSQLDataSource'    connection-pool-
name='Oracle Connection Pool'     jndi-name='jdbc/XSQLDataSource'/>
<connection-pool name='Oracle Connection Pool'>    <connection-factory
factory-class='oracle.jdbc.pool.OracleDataSource'       user='OE'
password='pw'        url="jdbc:oracle:thin:@<host>:<port>:<SID>">    </
connection-factory>   </connection-pool>
```

<host> is the database host, localhost by default.

<port> is the port number, 1521 by default.

<SID> is the database SID, ORCL by default.

<host>, <port>, and <SID> values may be obtained from the tnsnames.ora file.

To connect to a database in an XSQL page using a JDBC data source, specify the JDBC data source JNDI name in the `connection` attribute of the `page` element. For example, if the JDBC data source JNDI name is `jdbc/XSQLDataSource`, specify the `connection` attribute as follows.

```
<page xmlns:xsql="urn:oracle-xsql" connection="jdbc/XSQLDataSource">
</page>
```

An XSQL page connection with a database may also be created by modifying the `XSQLConfig.xml` file. An `XSQLConfig.xml` file is added to the `src` folder of a project when an XSQL file is created. First specify the `connection-manager factory` class in `XSQLConfig.xml` as follows:

```
<factory>oracle.xml.xsql.XSQLConnectionManagerFactoryImpl</factory>
```

In the `<connectiondefs>` element, in `XSQLConfig.xml`, add a `<connection>` element specifying the connection to be created. Create a connection with the OE schema:

```
<connection name="dbConnection">
        <username>OE</username>
        <password>pw</password>
        <dburl>jdbc:oracle:thin:@<HOST>:<PORT>:<SID></dburl>
        <driver>oracle.jdbc.OracleDriver</driver>
</connection>
```

Attribute `name` is the connection name.

`<username>` is the username used to log in to the database.

`<password>` is the password used to log in to the database.

`<dburl>` is the URL of the database.

`<driver>` is the JDBC driver used to connect to the database.

`<HOST>` is the Oracle 10g Production database host.

`<PORT>` is the database port.

`<SID>` is the database SID.

To use a named connection configured in the `XSQLConfig.xml` file in an XSQL page, specify the value of the `connection` attribute in the `<page>` tag of an XSQL page as `dbConnection`.

Creating XSQL Queries

In this section, we will create an XSQL page (`queryDb.xsql`) in JDeveloper. To create an XSQL file, select the project node in the **Applications Navigator** frame and select **File | New**. In the **New Gallery** window, select **General | XML** in **Categories**. In **Items**, select the **XSQL File** and click on **OK**.

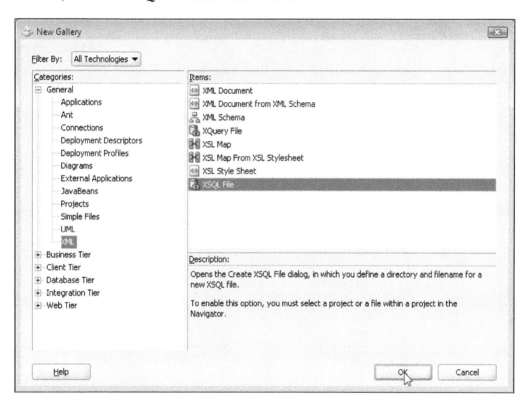

In the **Create XSQL File** frame, specify a **File Name** and click on **OK**. An XSQL page is added to the JDeveloper project including an XSQLConfig.xml configuration file.

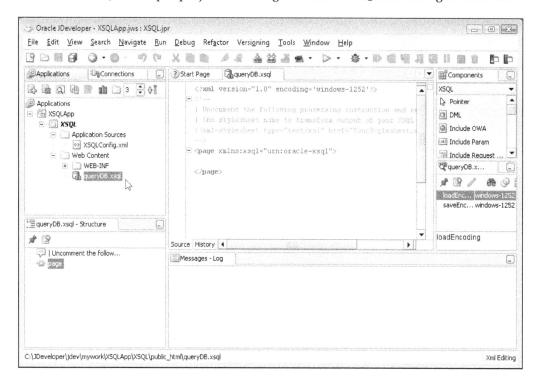

The libraries required for an XSQL application are added to the project libraries.

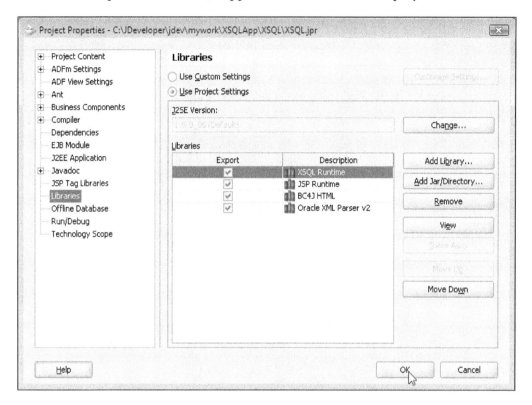

We will construct an XSQL page to query the example database table `Catalog` and generate an XML document. The XSQL Component Palette provides different XSQL components that were discussed in the first table in this chapter. Next we'll add `<xsql:query></xsql:query>` tags to the XSQL page to process XSQL queries. The application of XSQL queries may require the use of bind variables, the variables in a SQL statement.

Bind variables can be set using the values of URL parameters, session variables, cookie values, or page parameters. In our example, we'll set XSQL query bind variables with page parameters. Bind variables, specified with the `bind-params` attribute in the `<xsql:query>` tag, are used in the SQL statement within the `<xsql:query>` tag. The bind variables are represented with '?' in a SQL statement. The value of the bind parameters is specified with the `<xsql:set-page-params/>` tag. Position the cursor in the XSQL page and select **Set Page Param** component in the Component Palette.

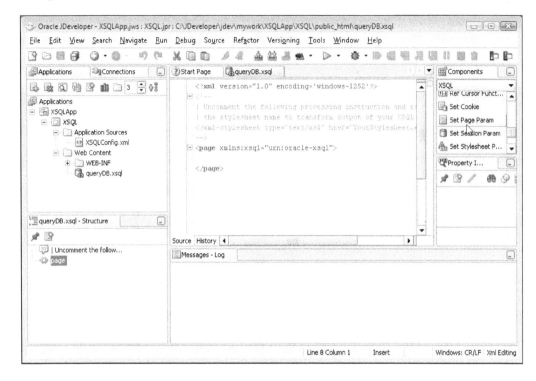

In the **Set Page Param** frame, specify the **name** property value as **JOURNAL**, and click on **Next**. Specify value of a page param as SQL or a String. Select **Specify Param Value As String** and specify **param** value as **"Oracle Magazine"**, and click on **Next**. Select a database connection to be used by the XSQL page and select **Finish**.

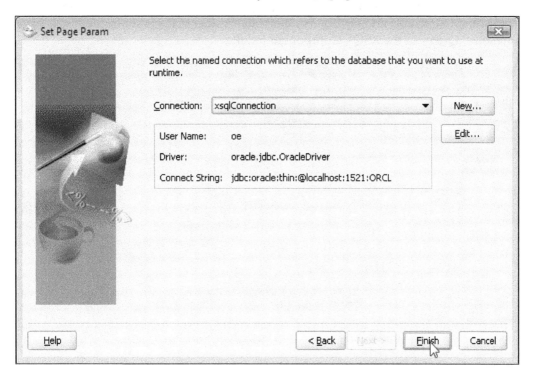

In an XSQL page, a database connection may be specified as a global connection using the connection attribute in the page tag. If some of the XSQL page elements use a different connection specify the connection using the connection attribute in the individual elements. The connection attribute in an element overrides the global connection. Similarly add another page param, PUBLISHER with value "Oracle Publishing" Next, add an xsql:Query element. Position the cursor in the XSQL page and select **Query** in the XSQL Component Palette.

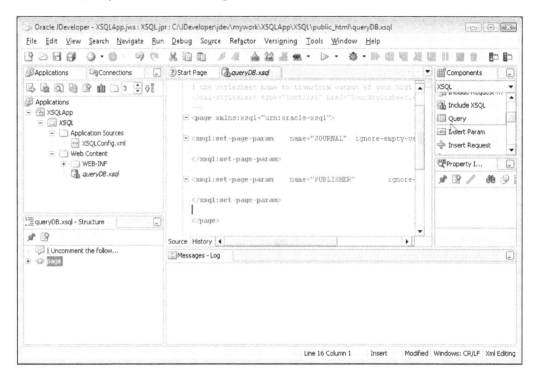

Specify any `xsql:query` element properties if required and click on **Next**.

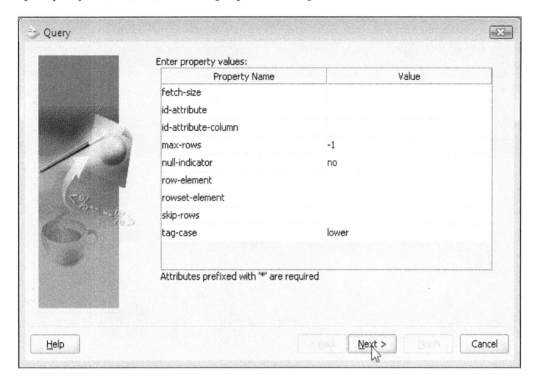

Select the database connection to be used by the XSQL query and click on **Next**. In the **Query** window, specify an SQL statement that defines an SQL query and click on **Finish**. Use the following SQL statement to retrieve data from the `Catalog` database:

```
SELECT JOURNAL, PUBLISHER, EDITION, TITLE, AUTHOR FROM CATALOG WHERE
                              JOURNAL=? AND PUBLISHER=?
```

An `xsql:query` tag is added to the XSQL page. A `connection` attribute specifying the JDBC data source is added to the `page` tag. Next we will add bind params to the `xsql:query` element. Position the cursor in `xsl:query` tag and select `bind-params` from the list displayed.

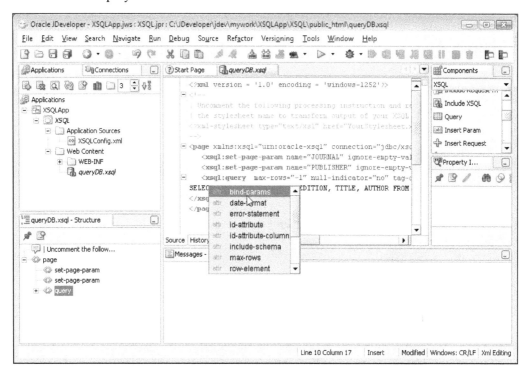

A `bind-params` attribute is added to the `xsql:query` element. Add to the `bind-params` attribute `"JOURNAL PUBLISHER"`. The `bind-params` attribute value is a string list and the values for the parameters are obtained from the `set-page-param` tag. The `queryDb.xsql` page is listed below:

```
<page xmlns:xsql="urn:oracle-xsql"
  connection="jdbc/xsqlConnectionDS">
  <xsql:set-page-param name="JOURNAL" ignore-empty-value="no"
    value="Oracle Magazine"/>
  <xsql:set-page-param name="PUBLISHER" ignore-empty-value="no"
     value="Oracle Publishing"/>
  <xsql:query bind-params="JOURNAL PUBLISHER"  max-rows="-1" null-
    indicator="no" tag-case="lower">
SELECT  JOURNAL, PUBLISHER, EDITION, TITLE, AUTHOR from
  OE.Catalog WHERE JOURNAL=? AND PUBLISHER=?
</xsql:query>
</page>
```

Some of the other attributes that may be specified in the `xsql-query` tag are discussed in the following table:

Attribute	Description	Type
bind-params	Ordered, space-delimited list of query parameters including array valued parameters, whose values are used in the JDBC bind variable.	String
date-format	Date Format for data column. Valid values are of the type java.text.SimpleDateFormat.	String
id-attribute	Attribute to identify each row in the result set. The default is 'num'.	String
error-statement	If set to true (default), generates an xsql-error element for an SQL statement with an error.	boolean
id-attribute-column	Specifies name of column in result set whose value is to be used in each row as the row ID attribute value. Default is to use the row count value.	String
include-schema	If yes, includes an inline XML schema for the structure of the result set. Default value is no.	boolean
max-rows	Maximum number of rows to fetch after skipping the rows specified in the skip-rows attribute. Default is to fetch all rows.	boolean
null-indicator	Specifies if null column values are to be included in the output XML with NULL="Y" for the element. Default is to omit elements with null values.	boolean
row-element	Specifies the row element to be used instead of the default ROW.	String
rowset-element	Specifies the row set element to use instead of the default ROWSET element.	String
skip-rows	Number of rows to skip before fetching from the result set.	integer
tag-case	Case of the element names. Valid values are lower and upper. Default is to use the name of the column as specified in the query statement.	String

To run the XSQL page, right-click on the `queryDb.xsql` node and select **Run**. The XSQL query runs and an XML document that represents the result set of the XSQL query is generated.

```xml
<?xml version="1.0" encoding="windows-1252" ?>
<!--
    | Uncomment the following processing instruction and replace
    | the stylesheet name to transform output of your XSQL Page using XSLT
    <?xml-stylesheet type="text/xsl" href="YourStylesheet.xsl" ?>
-->
<page>
  <rowset>
    <row num="1">
        <journal>Oracle Magazine</journal>
        <publisher>Oracle Publishing</publisher>
        <edition>July-August 2005</edition>
        <title>Tuning Undo Tablespace</title>
        <author>Kimberly Floss</author>
    </row>
    <row num="2">
        <journal>Oracle Magazine</journal>
        <publisher>Oracle Publishing</publisher>
        <edition>September-October 2005</edition>
        <title>Creating Search Pages</title>
        <author>Steve Muench</author>
    </row>
  </rowset>
</page>
```

In the next section, we'll use some of the `<xsql:query>` tag attributes in an XSQL query.

Applying XSQL Query Attributes

The `<xsql:query>` tag provides XSQL attributes to modify the data retrieved with the XSQL query and to modify the XML document produced with the XSQL query. The different XSQL attributes and their applications were discussed in the second table in this chapter. Some of the `xsql-query` attributes, such as `page-params`, are only available in the XSQL page.

To demonstrate XSQL query attributes, delete `queryDB.xsql` and create an XSQL page similar to the previous section, except when an XSQL Query is added from Component Palette, specify query attributes, and click on **Next**.

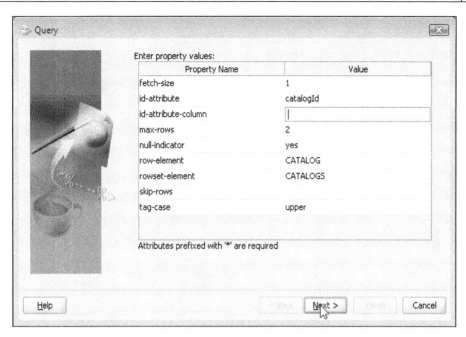

Select a database connection and click on **Next**. In the **Query** window, specify an SQL statement and click on **Finish**. Specify parameter markers in the SQL statement as we will be using bind parameters.

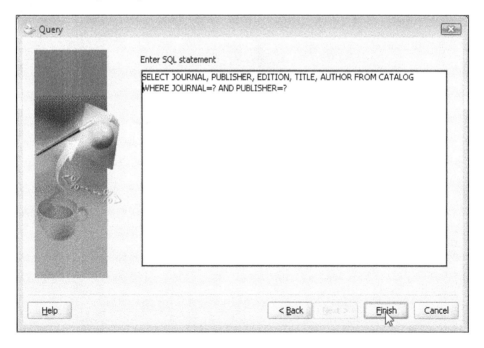

The `queryDB.xsql` page is listed below:

```
<?xml version = '1.0' encoding = 'windows-1252'?><page xmlns:
xsql="urn:oracle-xsql" connection="jdbc/xsqlConnectionDS">
<xsql:set-page-param name="JOURNAL" ignore-empty-value="no"
  value="Oracle Magazine"/>
<xsql:set-page-param name="PUBLISHER" ignore-empty-value="no"
  value="Oracle Publishing"/>
<xsql:query bind-params="JOURNAL PUBLISHER" fetch-size="1" id-
  attribute="catalogId" max-rows="2" null-indicator="yes" row-
  element="CATALOG" rowset-element="CATALOGS" tag-case="upper">
SELECT  JOURNAL, PUBLISHER, EDITION, TITLE, AUTHOR from
  OE.Catalog WHERE JOURNAL=? AND PUBLISHER=?
</xsql:query>
</page>
```

Right-click on `queryDb.xsql` XSQL page and select **Run**. The XSQL query runs and an XML document is displayed.

```
<?xml version="1.0" encoding="windows-1252" ?>
- <page>
  - <CATALOGS>
    - <CATALOG catalogId="1">
        <JOURNAL>Oracle Magazine</JOURNAL>
        <PUBLISHER>Oracle Publishing</PUBLISHER>
        <EDITION>July-August 2005</EDITION>
        <TITLE>Tuning Undo Tablespace</TITLE>
        <AUTHOR>Kimberly Floss</AUTHOR>
      </CATALOG>
    - <CATALOG catalogId="2">
        <JOURNAL>Oracle Magazine</JOURNAL>
        <PUBLISHER>Oracle Publishing</PUBLISHER>
        <EDITION>September-October 2005</EDITION>
        <TITLE>Creating Search Pages</TITLE>
        <AUTHOR>Steve Muench</AUTHOR>
      </CATALOG>
    </CATALOGS>
  </page>
```

In the following section, we'll discuss XSLT transformation of the output from an XSQL query.

Transforming XSQL Output

An XSQL page supports the transformation of query output using an XSLT. In this section, we will add XSLT transformation to the XML document generated with an XSQL query. Add an XSLT file with **File | New**. In the **New Gallery** window select **General | XML** in **Categories** and **XSL Style Sheet** in **Items**, and click on **OK**. In the **Create XSL File** frame, specify a file name and click on **OK**. An XSL stylesheet is added to XSQL project.

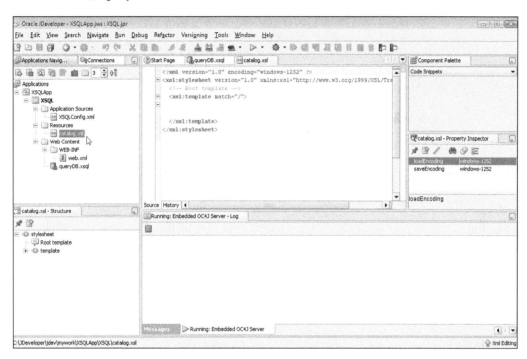

The XSLT, `catalog.xsl`, used to generate an HTML table from an XSQL query XML output is listed below:

```xml
<?xml version="1.0" encoding="UTF-8"?>
<xsl:stylesheet version="1.0" xmlns:xsl="http://www.w3.org/1999/XSL/
Transform">
<xsl:output encoding="ISO-8859-1"  method="text/html" />
<xsl:template match="//page">
<html>
  <head>
    <title>Oracle Catalog</title>
  </head>
  <body>
    <table border="1" cellspacing="0">
```

```
        <tr>
         <th>Journal</th>
         <th>Publisher</th>
         <th>Edition</th>
         <th>Title</th>
         <th>Author</th>
        </tr>
       <xsl:for-each select="ROWSET/ROW">
        <tr>
         <td><xsl:value-of select="JOURNAL"/></td>
         <td><xsl:value-of select="PUBLISHER"/></td>
         <td><xsl:value-of select="EDITION"/></td>
         <td><xsl:value-of select="TITLE"/></td>
         <td><xsl:value-of select="AUTHOR"/></td>
        </tr>
       </xsl:for-each>
      </table>
    </body>
  </html>
 </xsl:template>
 </xsl:stylesheet>
```

Save the `catalog.xls` stylesheet to the same directory as the `queryDB.xsql`, the `public_html` directory, using **File | Save**. The XSL Stylesheet to transform XSQL output is specified in an XSQL page with `xml-stylesheet` element:

```
<?xml-stylesheet type="text/xsl" href="catalog.xsl"?>
```

The XSQL page, `queryDb.xsql`, with an `xml-stylesheet` element is listed below:

```
<?xml version = '1.0' encoding = 'windows-1252'?>
<?xml-stylesheet type="text/xsl" href="catalog.xsl"?>
<page xmlns:xsql="urn:oracle-xsql" connection="jdbc/xsqlConnectionDS">
    <xsql:set-page-param name="JOURNAL"  value="Oracle Magazine"/>
    <xsql:set-page-param name="PUBLISHER"  value="Oracle Publishing"/>
    <xsql:query bind-params="JOURNAL PUBLISHER">
SELECT  JOURNAL, PUBLISHER, EDITION, TITLE, AUTHOR from
  OE.Catalog WHERE JOURNAL=? AND PUBLISHER=?
</xsql:query>
</page>
```

To run XSQL page, right-click on `queryDb.xsql` node and select **Run**.

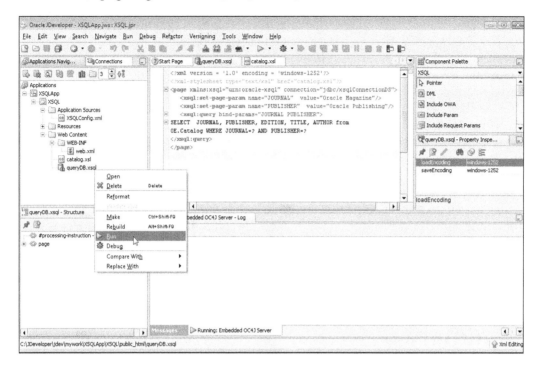

The XSQL query runs and the XML output is transformed with an XSLT.

Journal	Publisher	Edition	Title	Author
Oracle Magazine	Oracle Publishing	July-August 2005	Tuning Undo Tablespace	Kimberly Floss
Oracle Magazine	Oracle Publishing	September-October 2005	Creating Search Pages	Steve Muench

JDBC 4.0 Version

OC4J server embedded in JDeveloper 10g or JDeveloper 11g does not support the JDBC 4.0 specification. In a later version of JDeveloper that supports JDBC 4.0 specification, the new features in JDBC 4.0 may be used with an XSQL application. To use the JDBC 4.0 features we would need to configure the JDBC connection with Oracle database using the Oracle database 11g JDBC 4.0 drivers JAR file, `ojdbc6.jar`. As JDBC 4.0 drivers required JDK 6.0, set the J2SE Version to JDK 6.0 by selecting **Tools | Project Properties** and subsequently selecting **Libraries**. The JDK version may be set in the **J2SE Version** field. With the JDBC 4.0 driver we may use the connection management features such as connection state tracking. Connection state tracking is implemented by the connection pool manager using the `isValid()` method of the `Connection` interface. The connection pool manager determines if a connection in a connection pool is unusable by invoking the `isvalid()` method on the connection. If the connection is not valid the connection pool manager closes the connection using the `close()` method.

```
if(!connection.isValid())
    connection.close();
```

Summary

Oracle XSQL Pages Publishing Framework is used to generate an XML document using an SQL query. XSLT may be applied to the XML generated with XSQL to transform the XML output. A JDBC connection is used to connect to a database to run the SQL query statements. Oracle JDeveloper supports the XSQL framework. The XML document generated with XSQL may be customized by specifying the row element, the row set element, and other attributes of the XSQL query. In a JDeveloper version that supports JDBC 4.0 in the embedded OC4J, JDBC 4.0 features such as connection state tracking may be used in an XSQL application.

Oracle Web RowSet

9

In the previous two chapters we mapped an XML document to a relational database using XSU and a relational database table to an XML document using XSU and XSQL. In this chapter we will use the XML document representation of a result set generated with an SQL query to modify a relational database table.

The ResultSet interface requires a persistent connection with a database to invoke the insert, update, and delete row operations on the database table data. The RowSet interface extends the ResultSet interface and is a container for tabular data that may operate without being connected to the data source. Thus, the RowSet interface reduces the overhead of a persistent connection with the database.

In J2SE 5.0, five new implementations of RowSet—JdbcRowSet, CachedRowSet, WebRowSet, FilteredRowSet, and JoinRowSet—were introduced. The WebRowSet interface extends the RowSet interface and is the XML document representation of a RowSet object. A WebRowSet object represents a set of fetched database table rows, which may be modified without being connected to the database.

Support for Oracle Web RowSet is a new feature in Oracle Database 10g driver. Oracle Web RowSet precludes the requirement for a persistent connection with the database. A connection is required only for retrieving data from the database with a SELECT query and for updating data in the database after all the required row operations on the retrieved data have been performed. Oracle Web RowSet is used for queries and modifications on the data retrieved from the database. Oracle Web RowSet, as an XML document representation of a RowSet facilitates the transfer of data.

In Oracle Database 10g and 11g JDBC drivers, Oracle Web RowSet is implemented in the oracle.jdbc.rowset package. The OracleWebRowSet class represents a Oracle Web RowSet. The data in the Web RowSet may be modified without connecting to the database. The database table may be updated with the OracleWebRowSet class after the modifications to the Web RowSet have been made. A database JDBC connection is required only for retrieving data from the database and for updating the database. An XML document representation of the data in a Web RowSet may be obtained for data exchange. In this chapter the Web RowSet feature in Oracle 10g database JDBC driver is implemented in JDeveloper 10g. An example Web RowSet will be created from a database. The Web RowSet will be modified and stored in the database table.

In this chapter we will learn the following:

- Creating a Oracle Web RowSet object
- Adding a row to Oracle Web RowSet
- Reading a row from Oracle Web RowSet
- Updating a row in Oracle Web RowSet
- Deleting a row from Oracle Web RowSet
- Updating Database Table with modified Oracle Web RowSet

Setting the Environment

We will use Oracle database to generate an updatable `OracleWebRowSet` object. Therefore, install Oracle database 10g including the sample schemas. Connect to the database with the OE schema:

```
SQL> CONNECT OE/<password>
```

Create an example database table, `Catalog`, with the following SQL script:

```
CREATE TABLE OE.Catalog(Journal VARCHAR(25), Publisher Varchar(25),
  Edition VARCHAR(25), Title Varchar(45), Author Varchar(25));
INSERT INTO OE.Catalog VALUES('Oracle Magazine',  'Oracle
  Publishing', 'July-August 2005', 'Tuning Undo Tablespace',
  'Kimberly Floss');
INSERT INTO OE.Catalog VALUES('Oracle Magazine',   'Oracle
  Publishing', 'March-April 2005', 'Starting with Oracle ADF', 'Steve
  Muench');
```

Configure JDeveloper 10g for Web RowSet implementation. Create a project in JDeveloper. Select **File | New | General | Application**. In the **Create Application** window specify an **Application Name** and click on **Next**. In the **Create Project** window specify a **Project Name** and click on **Next**. A project is added in the **Applications Navigator**.

Next, we will set the project libraries. Select **Tools | Project Properties** and in the **Project Properties** window select **Libraries | Add Library** to add a library. Add the **Oracle JDBC** library to project libraries. If the Oracle JDBC drivers version prior to the Oracle database 10g (R2) JDBC drivers version is used, create a library from the Oracle Web RowSet implementation classes JAR file, `C:\JDeveloper10.1.3\jdbc\lib\ocrs12.jar`. The `ocrs12.jar` is required only for JDBC drivers prior to Oracle database 10g (R2) JDBC drivers. In Oracle database 10g (R2) JDBC drivers Oracle RowSet implementation classes are packaged in the `ojdbc14.jar`. In Oracle database 11g JDBC drivers Oracle RowSet implementation classes are packaged in `ojdbc5.jar` and `ojdbc6.jar`.

In the **Add Library** window select the **User** node and click on **New**. In the **Create Library** window specify a **Library Name**, select the **Class Path** node and click on **Add Entry**. Add an entry for `ocrs12.jar`. As Web RowSet was introduced in J2SE 5.0, if J2SE 1.4 is being used we also need to add an entry for the RowSet implementations JAR file, `rowset.jar`. Download the JDBC RowSet Implementations 1.0.1 zip file, `jdbc_rowset_tiger-1_0_1-mrel-ri.zip`, from `http://java.sun.com/products/jdbc/download.html#rowset1_0_1` and extract the JDBC RowSet zip file to a directory. Click on **OK** in the **Create Library** window. Click on **OK** in the **Add Library** window. A library for the Web RowSet application is added.

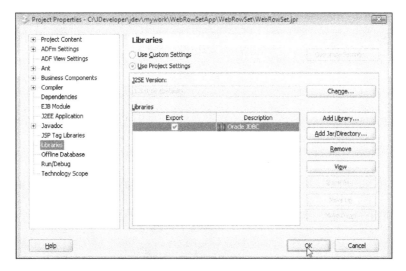

Now configure an OC4J data source. Select **Tools | Embedded OC4J Server Preferences**. A data source may be configured globally or for the current workspace. If a global data source is created using **Global | Data Sources,** the data source is configured in the `C:\JDeveloper10.1.3\jdev\system\oracle.j2ee.10.1.3.36.73\embedded-oc4j\config \data-sources.xml` file. If a data source is configured for the current workspace using **Current Workspace | Data Sources**, the data source is configured in the `data-sources.xml` file. For example, the data source file for the `WebRowSetApp` application is `WebRowSetApp-data-sources.xml`. In the **Embedded OC4J Server Preferences** window configure either a global data source or a data source in the current workspace with the procedure discussed in Chapter 2. A global data source definition is available to all applications deployed in the OC4J server instance. A `managed-data-source` element is added to the `data-sources.xml` file.

```
<managed-data-source name='OracleDataSource' connection-pool-
  name='Oracle Connection Pool' jndi-name='jdbc/OracleDataSource'/>
<connection-pool name='Oracle Connection Pool'>
 <connection-factory factory-
    class='oracle.jdbc.pool.OracleDataSource' user='OE' password='pw'
    url="jdbc:oracle:thin:@localhost:1521:ORCL">
 </connection-factory>
</connection-pool>
```

Add a JSP, `GenerateWebRowSet.jsp`, to the `WebRowSet` project. Select **File | New | Web Tier | JSP | JSP**. Click on **OK**. Select `J2EE 1.3` or `J2EE 1.4` in the Web Application window and click on **Next**. In the **JSP File** window specify a **File Name** and click on **Next**. Select the default settings in the **Error Page Options** page and click on **Next**. Select the default settings in the **Tag Libraries** window and click on **Next**. Select the default options in the **HTML Options** window and click on **Next**. Click on **Finish** in the **Finish** window. Next, configure the `web.xml` deployment descriptor to include a reference to the data source resource configured in the `data-sources.xml` file as shown in following listing:

```
<resource-ref>
 <res-ref-name>jdbc/OracleDataSource</res-ref-name>
 <res-type>javax.sql.DataSource</res-type>
 <res-auth>Container</res-auth>
</resource-ref>
```

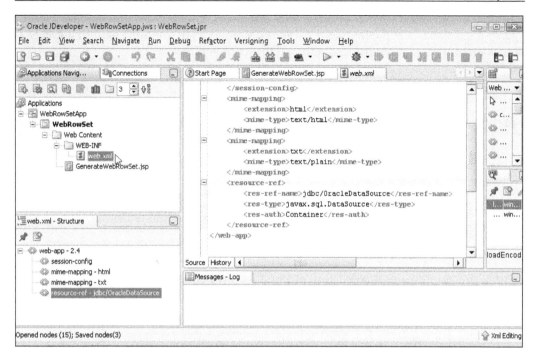

Creating a Web RowSet

In this section we will create a Web RowSet from a database table and an XML document representation of the Web RowSet is generated. Create a Java class in JDeveloper with **File | New | General | Java Class**. In the **Create Java Class** window specify the class name, `WebRowSetQuery`, and package name and click on **OK**. A Java class, `WebRowSetQuery.java` gets added to the `WebRowSet` project. In the Java application first import the `oracle.jdbc.rowset` package classes. Create an `OracleWebRowSet` class object:

```
OracleWebRowSet webRowSet=new OracleWebRowSet();
```

Set the data source name to obtain a JDBC connection with the database. The data source name is configured in the `data-sources.xml` file:

```
webRowSet.setDataSourceName("jdbc/OracleDataSource");
```

Set the SQL query command for the `OracleWebRowSet` class object:

```
webRowSet.setCommand(selectQuery);
```

Variable `selectQuery` is the `String` value for the SQL statement that is to be used to query the database. SQL statement value is obtained from an input field in a JSP. Set the username and password to obtain a JDBC connection:

```
webRowSet.setUsername("OE");
webRowSet.setPassword("<password>");
```

Set the read only, fetch size, and max rows attributes of the `OracleWebRowSet` object:

```
webRowSet.setReadOnly(false);
webRowSet.setFetchSize(5);
webRowSet.setMaxRows(3);
```

Run the SQL command specified in the `setCommand()` method with the `execute()` method:

```
webRowSet.execute();
```

A Web RowSet is created consisting of the data retrieved from the database table with the SQL query. Generate an XML document from the Web RowSet using the `writeXml()` method;

```
OutputStreamWriter output=new OutputStreamWriter( new
FileOutputStream(new File("c:/output/output.xml")));
webRowSet.writeXml(output);
```

Oracle Web RowSet also provides `readXml()` methods to read an Oracle Web RowSet object in XML format using a Reader object or an InputStream object. If the `readXml()` methods are to be used set one of the following JAXP system properties:

- `javax.xml.parsers.SAXParserFactory`
- `javax.xml.parsers.DocumentBuilderFactory`

For example, set the `SAXParserFactory` property as follows:

```
System.setProperty("javax.xml.parsers.SAXParserFactory",
        "oracle.xml.jaxp.JXSAXParserFactory");
```

`WebRowSetQuery.java` also has methods to read, update, delete, and insert a row in the database table, which will be discussed in the subsequent sections. `WebRowSetQuery.java` application is listed below:

```
package webrowset;
import oracle.jdbc.rowset.*;
import java.io.*;
import java.sql.SQLException;
public class WebRowSetQuery
{
```

```
public OracleWebRowSet webRowSet;
public String selectQuery;
public WebRowSetQuery()
{
}
public WebRowSetQuery(OracleWebRowSet webRowSet)
{
 this.webRowSet = webRowSet;
}
public void generateWebRowSet(String selectQuery)
{
 try
 {
  webRowSet = new OracleWebRowSet();
  webRowSet.setDataSourceName("jdbc/OracleDataSource");
  webRowSet.setCommand(selectQuery);
  webRowSet.setUsername("oe");
  webRowSet.setPassword("pw");
  webRowSet.setReadOnly(false);
  webRowSet.setFetchSize(5);
  webRowSet.setMaxRows(3);
  webRowSet.execute();
 }
 catch (SQLException e)
 {
  System.out.println(e.getMessage());
 }
}
public void generateXMLDocument()
{
 try
 {
  OutputStreamWriter output = new OutputStreamWriter(
           new FileOutputStream(new File("c:/output/output.xml")));
  webRowSet.writeXml(output);
 }
 catch (SQLException e)
 {
  System.out.println(e.getMessage());
 }
 catch (IOException e)
 {
 }
}
public void deleteRow(int row)
{
 try
 {
  webRowSet.absolute(row);
  webRowSet.deleteRow();
```

```
  }
  catch (SQLException e)
  {
   System.out.println(e.getMessage());
  }
 }
 public void insertRow(String journal, String publisher,
           String edition, String title, String author)
 {
  try
  {
   webRowSet.moveToInsertRow();
   webRowSet.updateString(1, journal);
   webRowSet.updateString(2, publisher);
   webRowSet.updateString(3, edition);
   webRowSet.updateString(4, title);
   webRowSet.updateString(5, author);
   webRowSet.insertRow();
  }
  catch (SQLException e)
  {
   System.out.println(e.getMessage());
  }
 }
 public void updateRow(int rowUpdate, String journal,
      String publisher, String edition, String title, String author)
 {
  try
  {
   webRowSet.absolute(rowUpdate);
   webRowSet.updateString(1, journal);
   webRowSet.updateString(2, publisher);
   webRowSet.updateString(3, edition);
   webRowSet.updateString(4, title);
   webRowSet.updateString(5, author);
   webRowSet.updateRow();
  }
  catch (SQLException e)
  {
   System.out.println(e.getMessage());
  }
 }
 public String[] readRow(int rowRead)
 {
  String[] resultSet = null;
  try
  {
   resultSet = new String[5];
   webRowSet.absolute(rowRead);
   resultSet[0] = webRowSet.getString(1);
```

```
   resultSet[1] = webRowSet.getString(2);
   resultSet[2] = webRowSet.getString(3);
   resultSet[3] = webRowSet.getString(4);
   resultSet[4] = webRowSet.getString(5);
  }
 catch (SQLException e)
 {
  System.out.println(e.getMessage());
 }
 return resultSet;
 }
 public void updateDatabase()
 {
  try
  {
   webRowSet.acceptChanges();
  }
  catch (java.sql.SQLException e)
  {
   System.out.println(e.getMessage());
  }
 }
}
}
```

The SELECT query with which the Web RowSet is created is input from the
GenerateWebRowSet.jsp JSP, which was added in the *Setting the Environment*
section, and is listed below:

```
<%@ page contentType="text/html;charset=windows-1252"%>
<html>
 <head>
  <meta http-equiv="Content-Type" content="text/html;
charset=windows-1252">
  <title>Generate WebRowSet</title>
 </head>
 <body>
  <form>
  </form>
  <%
  String selectQuery=request.getParameter("selectQuery");
  webrowset.WebRowSetQuery query=new webrowset.WebRowSetQuery();
  if(selectQuery!=null)
  {
   query.generateWebRowSet(selectQuery);
   query.generateXMLDocument();
  }
  %>
    <form name="query" action="GenerateWebRowSet.jsp" method="post">
      <table>
        <tr>
```

```
        <td>Select Query:</td>
    </tr><tr><td>
        <textarea name="selectQuery" rows="5"
            cols="50"></textarea>
    </td>
    </tr><tr><td>
        <input class="Submit" type="submit" value="Apply"/>
    </td>
    </tr>
    </table>
  </form>
 </body>
</html>
```

Right-click on the `GenerateWebRowSet.jsp` and select **Run** to run the JSP.

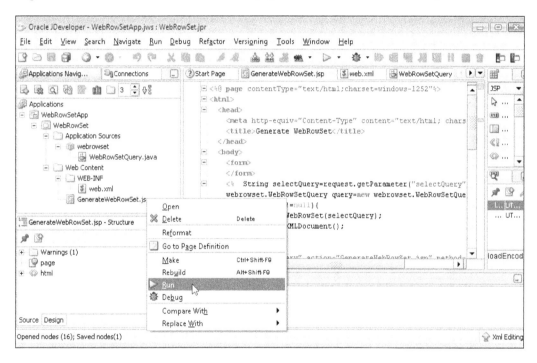

In the JSP page displayed, specify the SQL query from which a Web RowSet is to be generated. For example, specify SQL Query:

```
SELECT JOURNAL, PUBLISHER, EDITION, TITLE, AUTHOR FROM OE.Catalog
```

Click on **Apply**.

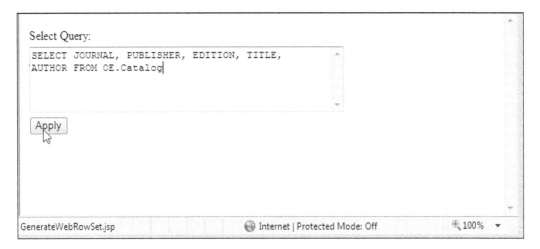

A Web RowSet is generated and an XML document is generated from the Web RowSet. The XML document output from the Web RowSet includes the metadata information for the JDBC data source, the database table, and the data in the table; the data element tag represents the data in the database table. An XML document generated from a Web RowSet is based on the DTD (`http://java.sun.com/j2ee/dtds/RowSet.dtd`). The XML document generated from the example database table `Catalog` as follows:

```
<?xml version="1.0" encoding="UTF-8"?>
<!DOCTYPE RowSet PUBLIC '-//Sun Microsystems, Inc.//DTD RowSet//EN'
    'http://java.sun.com/j2ee/dtds/RowSet.dtd'>
<RowSet>
  <properties>
    <command>SELECT JOURNAL, PUBLISHER, EDITION, TITLE, AUTHOR FROM
        OE.Catalog</command>
    <concurrency>1007</concurrency>
    <datasource>jdbc/OracleDataSource</datasource>
    <escape-processing>true</escape-processing>
    <fetch-direction>1002</fetch-direction>
    <fetch-size>10</fetch-size>
    <isolation-level>2</isolation-level>
    <key-columns>
    </key-columns>
    <map></map>
    <max-field-size>0</max-field-size>
    <max-rows>3</max-rows>
    <query-timeout>0</query-timeout>
```

```xml
      <read-only>false</read-only>
      <rowset-type>1005</rowset-type>
      <show-deleted>false</show-deleted>
      <url>jdbc:oracle:thin:@localhost:1521:ORCL</url>
  </properties>
  <metadata>
    <column-count>5</column-count>
    <column-definition>
      <column-index>1</column-index>
      <auto-increment>false</auto-increment>
      <case-sensitive>true</case-sensitive>
      <currency>false</currency>
      <nullable>1</nullable>
      <signed>true</signed>
      <searchable>true</searchable>
      <column-display-size>25</column-display-size>
      <column-label>JOURNAL</column-label>
      <column-name>JOURNAL</column-name>
      <schema-name></schema-name>
      <column-precision>0</column-precision>
      <column-scale>0</column-scale>
      <table-name></table-name>
      <catalog-name></catalog-name>
      <column-type>12</column-type>
      <column-type-name>VARCHAR2</column-type-name>
    </column-definition>
    <column-definition>
      <column-index>2</column-index>
      <auto-increment>false</auto-increment>
      <case-sensitive>true</case-sensitive>
      <currency>false</currency>
      <nullable>1</nullable>
      <signed>true</signed>
      <searchable>true</searchable>
      <column-display-size>25</column-display-size>
      <column-label>PUBLISHER</column-label>
      <column-name>PUBLISHER</column-name>
      <schema-name></schema-name>
      <column-precision>0</column-precision>
      <column-scale>0</column-scale>
      <table-name></table-name>
      <catalog-name></catalog-name>
      <column-type>12</column-type>
      <column-type-name>VARCHAR2</column-type-name>
```

```
    </column-definition>
    <column-definition>
      <column-index>3</column-index>
      <auto-increment>false</auto-increment>
      <case-sensitive>true</case-sensitive>
      <currency>false</currency>
      <nullable>1</nullable>
      <signed>true</signed>
      <searchable>true</searchable>
      <column-display-size>25</column-display-size>
      <column-label>EDITION</column-label>
      <column-name>EDITION</column-name>
      <schema-name></schema-name>
      <column-precision>0</column-precision>
      <column-scale>0</column-scale>
      <table-name></table-name>
      <catalog-name></catalog-name>
      <column-type>12</column-type>
      <column-type-name>VARCHAR2</column-type-name>
    </column-definition>
    <column-definition>
      <column-index>4</column-index>
      <auto-increment>false</auto-increment>
      <case-sensitive>true</case-sensitive>
      <currency>false</currency>
      <nullable>1</nullable>
      <signed>true</signed>
      <searchable>true</searchable>
      <column-display-size>45</column-display-size>
      <column-label>TITLE</column-label>
      <column-name>TITLE</column-name>
      <schema-name></schema-name>
      <column-precision>0</column-precision>
      <column-scale>0</column-scale>
      <table-name></table-name>
      <catalog-name></catalog-name>
      <column-type>12</column-type>
      <column-type-name>VARCHAR2</column-type-name>
    </column-definition>
    <column-definition>
      <column-index>5</column-index>
      <auto-increment>false</auto-increment>
      <case-sensitive>true</case-sensitive>
      <currency>false</currency>
```

```
      <nullable>1</nullable>
      <signed>true</signed>
      <searchable>true</searchable>
      <column-display-size>25</column-display-size>
      <column-label>AUTHOR</column-label>
      <column-name>AUTHOR</column-name>
      <schema-name></schema-name>
      <column-precision>0</column-precision>
      <column-scale>0</column-scale>
      <table-name></table-name>
      <catalog-name></catalog-name>
      <column-type>12</column-type>
      <column-type-name>VARCHAR2</column-type-name>
    </column-definition>
  </metadata>
  <data>
    <row>
      <col>Oracle Magazine</col>
      <col>Oracle Publishing</col>
      <col>July-August 2005</col>
      <col>Tuning Undo Tablespace</col>
      <col>Kimberly Floss</col>
    </row>
    <row>
      <col>Oracle Magazine</col>
      <col>Oracle Publishing</col>
      <col>March-April 2005</col>
      <col>Starting with Oracle ADF</col>
      <col>Steve Muench</col>
    </row>
  </data>
</RowSet>
```

In this section, the procedure to generate a Web RowSet from a database table was explained. In the following section the Web RowSet is modified and the modified data stored in the database table.

Modifying a Database Table with Web RowSet

With `ResultSet` interface, to modify the data in the database, a JDBC connection with the database is required to insert, delete, or update a database table row. With a Web RowSet, the data may be modified in the `OracleWebRowSet` object, and a connection is required only to update the database table with the data in the Web RowSet after all the modifications have been made to the Web RowSet. In this section, the data in the Web RowSet is modified and the database table is updated with the modified Web RowSet. A JDBC connection is not required to modify the data in the example Web RowSet. An `OracleWebRowSet` object is generated as in the previous section.

Create a JSP, ModifyWebRowSet.jsp, to create and modify a Web RowSet from an SQL query. Also add JSPs `CreateRow.jsp`, `ReadRow.jsp`, `UpdateRow.jsp`, `DeleteRow.jsp`, and `UpdateDatabase.jsp`, which are listed later in this chapter. `ModifyWebRowSet.jsp`, the JSP used to create and modify a Web RowSet is listed as follows:

```
<!DOCTYPE HTML PUBLIC "-//W3C//DTD HTML 4.01 Transitional//EN"
"http://www.w3.org/TR/html4/loose.dtd">
<%@ page contentType="text/html;charset=windows-1252"%>
<%@ page session="true"%>
<html>
  <head>
    <title>Modify Database Table with Web RowSet</title>
  </head>
  <body>
    <h3>Modify Database Table with Web RowSet</h3>
      <%webrowset.WebRowSetQuery query=null;%>
    <%String selectQuery=request.getParameter("selectQuery");
    if(selectQuery!=null){
    query=new webrowset.WebRowSetQuery();
    query.generateWebRowSet(selectQuery);
    session.setAttribute("query", query);
    }
%>
    <form name="query" action="ModifyWebRowSet.jsp" method="post">
      <table>
       <tr>
         <td>Select Query:</td>
       </tr><tr><td>
           <textarea name="selectQuery" rows="5"
                cols="50"></textarea>
```

```
      </td></tr><tr><td>
        <input class="Submit" type="submit" value="Apply Query"/>
      </td></tr>
   <tr><td><a href="CreateRow.jsp">Create Row</a></td></tr>
   <tr><td><a href="ReadRow.jsp">Read Row</a></td></tr>
   <tr><td><a href="UpdateRow.jsp">Update Row</a></td></tr>
    <tr><td><a href="DeleteRow.jsp">Delete Row</a></td></tr>
    <tr><td><a href="UpdateDatabase.jsp">Update
        Database</a></td></tr>
   </table>
 </form>
 </body>
</html>
```

The directory structure of the Web RowSet application is shown in the **Applications Navigator**. Run the `ModifyWebRowSet.jsp` JSP in JDeveloper. The JSP is displayed in a browser. Specify a SQL query to generate a Web RowSet. Click on **Apply Query** Subsequently we will modify the Web RowSet and update the database.

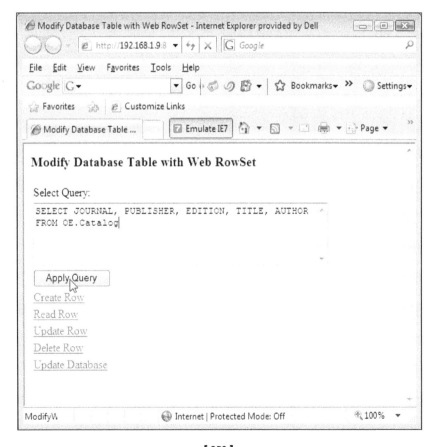

A Web RowSet is generated. We will use the Web RowSet object to create, read, update, and delete the result set obtained with the SQL query. In the `ModifyWebRowSet.jsp`, set the `WebRowSetQuery` object as a `session` object attribute:

```
session.setAttribute("query", query);
```

The `OracleWebRowSet` object of the `ModifyWebRowSet` object will be used in the Create, Read, Update, and Delete JSPs.

Creating a New Row

Next, create a new row in the Web RowSet. Click on the **Create Row** link in the `ModifyWebRowSet.jsp` JSP.

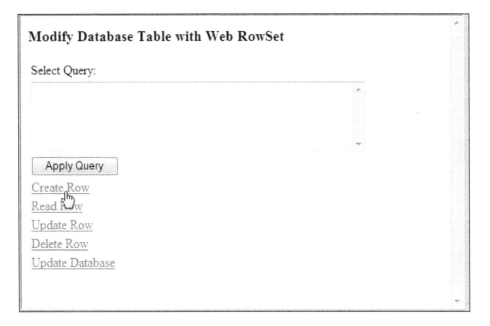

The CreateRow.jsp is displayed. Specify the row values to add and click on **Apply**.

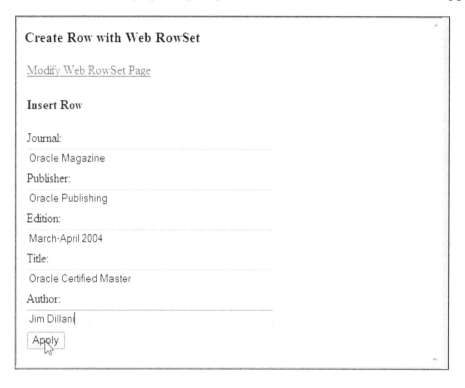

In the CreateRow.jsp, the input values are retrieved from the JSP and the insertRow() method of the WebRowSetQuery class is invoked. The WebRowSetQuery object is retrieved from the session object:

```
WebRowSetQuery query=( webrowset.WebRowSetQuery)
              session.getAttribute("query");
```

In the insertRow() method OracleWebRowSet object cursor is moved to the insert row:

```
webRowSet.moveToInsertRow();
```

Set the row values with the updateString() method:

```
webRowSet.updateString(1, journal);
webRowSet.updateString(2, publisher);
webRowSet.updateString(3, edition);
webRowSet.updateString(4, title);
webRowSet.updateString(5, author);
```

Add the row to the `OracleWebRowSet`:

```
webRowSet.insertRow();
```

A new row is added in the `OracleWebRowSet` object. A new row is not yet added to the database. `CreateRow.jsp` is listed as follows:

```
<%@ page contentType="text/html;charset=windows-1252"%>
<%@ page session="true"%>
<html>
  <head>
    <meta http-equiv="Content-Type" content="text/html;
          charset=windows-1252">
    <title>Create Row  with Web RowSet</title>
  </head>
  <body>
    <form><h3>Create Row with Web RowSet</h3>
      <table>
       <tr><td><a href="ModifyWebRowSet.jsp">Modify Web RowSet
            Page</a></td></tr>
      </table>
    </form>
    <%
        webrowset.WebRowSetQuery query=null;
        query=(webrowset.WebRowSetQuery)
            session.getAttribute("query");
    String journal=request.getParameter("journal");
    String publisher=request.getParameter("publisher");
    String edition=request.getParameter("edition");
    String title=request.getParameter("title");
    String author=request.getParameter("author");
    if(journal!=null||publisher!=null||edition!=null||title!=null
                                              ||author!=null){
    query.insertRow(journal, publisher, edition, title, author);

    }
    %>
    <form name="query" action="CreateRow.jsp" method="post">
      <table>
        <tr>
         <td>
           <h4>Insert Row</h4>
         </td>
        </tr>
```

```
<tr>
  <td>Journal:</td>
</tr>
<tr>
  <td>
    <input name="journal" type="text" size="50"
      maxlength="250"/>
  </td>
</tr>
<tr>
  <td>Publisher:</td>
</tr>
<tr>
  <td>
    <input name="publisher" type="text" size="50"
      maxlength="250"/>
  </td>
</tr>
<tr>
  <td>Edition:</td>
</tr>
<tr>
  <td>
    <input name="edition" type="text" size="50"
      maxlength="250"/>
  </td>
</tr>
<tr>
  <td>Title:</td>
</tr>
<tr>
  <td>
    <input name="title" type="text" size="50"
      maxlength="250"/>
  </td>
</tr>
<tr>
  <td>Author:</td>
</tr>
<tr>
  <td>
    <input name="author" type="text" size="50"
      maxlength="250"/>
  </td>
```

```
      </tr>
      <tr>
        <td>
          <input class="Submit" type="submit" value="Apply"/>
        </td>
      </tr>
    </table></form></body></html>
```

Reading a Row

Next, we will read a row from the `OracleWebRowSet` object. Click on **Modify Web RowSet** link in the `CreateRow.jsp`. In the `ModifyWebRowSet` JSP click on the **Read Row** link. The `ReadRow.jsp` JSP is displayed. In the `ReadRow` JSP specify the **Database Row to Read** and click on **Apply**.

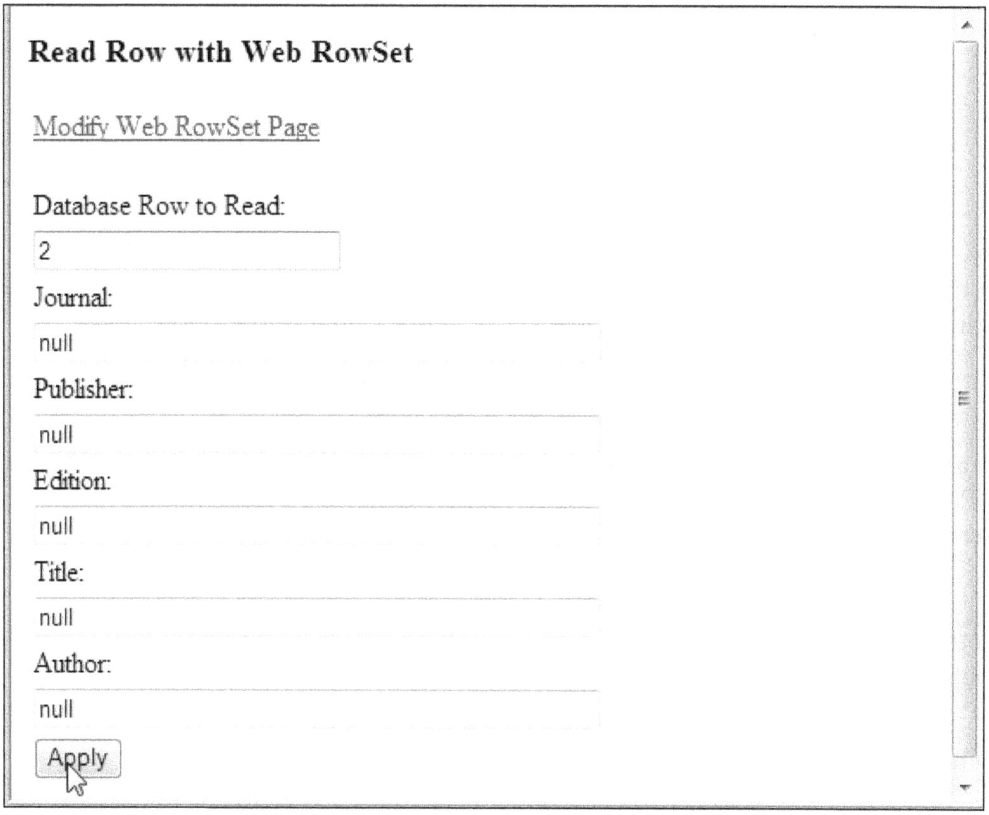

Read Row with Web RowSet

Modify Web RowSet Page

Database Row to Read:

2

Journal:

null

Publisher:

null

Edition:

null

Title:

null

Author:

null

Apply

The second row values are retrieved from the Web RowSet:

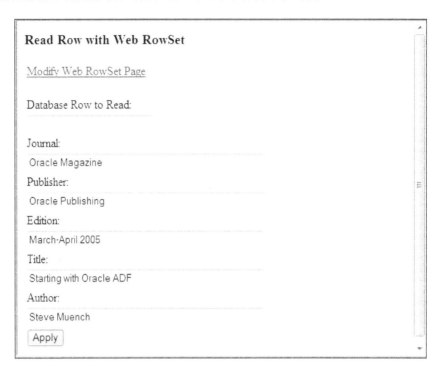

In the ReadRow JSP the readRow() method of the WebRowSetQuery.java application is invoked. The WebRowSetQuery object is retrieved from the session object.

```
WebRowSetQuery query=( webrowset.WebRowSetQuery)
               session.getAttribute("query");
```

The String[] values returned by the readRow() method are added to the ReadRow JSP fields. In the readRow() method the OracleWebRowSet object cursor is moved to the row to be read.

```
webRowSet.absolute(rowRead);
```

Retrieve the row values with the getString() method and add to String[]. Return the String[] object.

```
String[] resultSet=new String[5];
resultSet[0]=webRowSet.getString(1);
resultSet[1]=webRowSet.getString(2);
resultSet[2]=webRowSet.getString(3);
resultSet[3]=webRowSet.getString(4);
resultSet[4]=webRowSet.getString(5);
return resultSet;
```

ReadRow.jsp JSP is listed as follows:

```
<!DOCTYPE HTML PUBLIC "-//W3C//DTD HTML 4.01 Transitional//EN"
"http://www.w3.org/TR/html4/loose.dtd">
<%@ page contentType="text/html;charset=windows-1252"%>
<%@ page session="true"%>
<html>
  <head>
    <meta http-equiv="Content-Type" content="text/html;
        charset=windows-1252">
    <title>Read Row with Web RowSet</title>
  </head>
  <body>
    <form><h3>Read Row  with Web RowSet</h3>
<table>
    <tr>
        <td><a href="ModifyWebRowSet.jsp">Modify Web RowSet
        Page</a></td>
    </tr>
</table>
    </form>
    <%
        webrowset.WebRowSetQuery query=null;
        query=( webrowset.WebRowSetQuery)
          session.getAttribute("query");
    String rowRead=request.getParameter("rowRead");
    String journalUpdate=request.getParameter("journalUpdate");
    String publisherUpdate=request.getParameter("publisherUpdate");
    String editionUpdate=request.getParameter("editionUpdate");
    String titleUpdate=request.getParameter("titleUpdate");
    String authorUpdate=request.getParameter("authorUpdate");
        if((rowRead!=null))
{
    int row_Read=Integer.parseInt(rowRead);
    String[] resultSet=query.readRow(row_Read);
journalUpdate=resultSet[0];
publisherUpdate=resultSet[1];
  editionUpdate=resultSet[2];
titleUpdate=resultSet[3];
authorUpdate=resultSet[4];
    }
    %>
    <form name="query" action="ReadRow.jsp" method="post">
      <table>
        <tr>
          <td>Database Row to Read:</td>
        </tr>
        <tr>
          <td>
            <input name="rowRead"  type="text" size="25"
```

```
        maxlength="50"/>
   </td>
</tr>
<tr>
   <td>Journal:</td>
</tr>
<tr>
   <td>
     <input name="journalUpdate" value='<%=journalUpdate%>'
        type="text" size="50" maxlength="250"/>
   </td>
</tr>
<tr>
   <td>Publisher:</td>
</tr>
<tr>
   <td>
     <input name="publisherUpdate"
        value='<%=publisherUpdate%>' type="text" size="50"
        maxlength="250"/>
   </td>
</tr>
<tr>
   <td>Edition:</td>
</tr>
<tr>
   <td>
     <input name="editionUpdate" value='<%=editionUpdate%>'
        type="text" size="50" maxlength="250"/>
   </td>
</tr>
<tr>
   <td>Title:</td>
</tr>
<tr>
   <td>
     <input name="titleUpdate" value='<%=titleUpdate%>'
        type="text" size="50" maxlength="250"/>
   </td>
</tr>
<tr>
   <td>Author:</td>
</tr>
<tr>
   <td>
     <input name="authorUpdate" value='<%=authorUpdate%>'
        type="text" size="50" maxlength="250"/>
   </td>
</tr><tr>
   <td>
```

```
            <input class="Submit" type="submit" value="Apply"/>
          </td>
        </tr>
      </table>
    </form>
  </body></html>
```

Updating a Row

Next, we will update a row in the OracleWebRowSet object. Click on the **Modify Web RowSet Page** link in the ReadRow JSP. In the ModifyWebRowSet JSP click on the **Update Row** link. In the UpdateRow JSP specify the row to be updated and specify the modified values. For example, update the second row. Click on **Apply**.

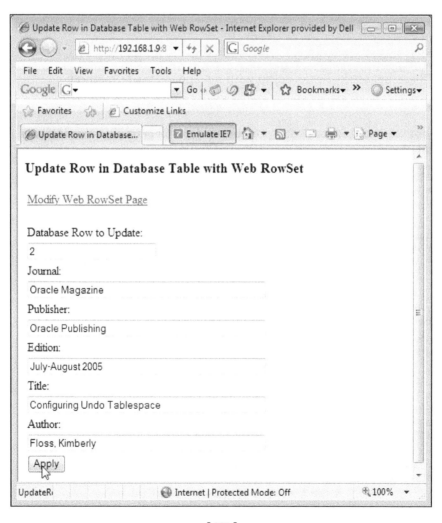

The `UpdateRow` JSP invokes the `updateRow()` method of the `WebRowSetQuery` Java class. The `WebRowSetQuery` object is retrieved from the `session` object:

```
WebRowSetQuery query=( webrowset.WebRowSetQuery)
              session.getAttribute("query");
```

In the `updateRow()` method the `OracleWebRowSet` object cursor is moved to the row to be updated:

```
webRowSet.absolute(rowUpdate);
```

The row values are updated with the `updateString()` method of the `OracleWebRowSet` object:

```
webRowSet.updateString(1, journal);
webRowSet.updateString(2, publisher);
webRowSet.updateString(3, edition);
webRowSet.updateString(4, title);
webRowSet.updateString(5, author);
```

Update the `OracleWebRowSet` object with the `updateRow()` method:

```
webRowSet.updateRow();
```

The row in the `OracleWebRowSet` object is updated. The row in the database table is not updated yet. `UpdateRow.jsp` is listed as follows:

```
<!DOCTYPE HTML PUBLIC "-//W3C//DTD HTML 4.01 Transitional//EN"
"http://www.w3.org/TR/html4/loose.dtd">
<%@ page contentType="text/html;charset=windows-1252"%>
<%@ page session="true"%>
<html>
  <head>
    <meta http-equiv="Content-Type" content="text/html;
        charset=windows-1252">
    <title>Update Row in Database Table with Web RowSet</title>
  </head>
  <body>
    <form><h3>Update Row in Database Table with Web RowSet</h3>
      <table>
      <tr>
         <td><a href="ModifyWebRowSet.jsp">Modify Web RowSet
         Page</a></td>
      </tr>
</table>
    </form>
    <%
webrowset.WebRowSetQuery query=null;
      query=( webrowset.WebRowSetQuery)
        session.getAttribute("query");
```

```
    String rowUpdate=request.getParameter("rowUpdate");
    String journalUpdate=request.getParameter("journalUpdate");
    String publisherUpdate=request.getParameter("publisherUpdate");
    String editionUpdate=request.getParameter("editionUpdate");
    String titleUpdate=request.getParameter("titleUpdate");
    String authorUpdate=request.getParameter("authorUpdate");
        if((rowUpdate!=null))
{
        System.out.println(rowUpdate +"Row to Update");
    int row_Update=Integer.parseInt(rowUpdate);
    query.updateRow(row_Update, journalUpdate, publisherUpdate,
        editionUpdate, titleUpdate, authorUpdate);
}
%>
<form name="query" action="UpdateRow.jsp" method="post">
  <table>
    <tr>
      <td>Database Row to Update:</td>
    </tr>
    <tr>
      <td>
        <input name="rowUpdate" type="text" size="25"
            maxlength="50"/>
      </td>
    </tr>
    <tr>
      <td>Journal:</td>
    </tr>
    <tr>
      <td>
        <input name="journalUpdate" type="text" size="50"
            maxlength="250"/>
      </td>
    </tr>
    <tr>
      <td>Publisher:</td>
    </tr>
    <tr>
      <td>
        <input name="publisherUpdate" type="text" size="50"
            maxlength="250"/>
      </td>
    </tr>
    <tr>
      <td>Edition:</td>
    </tr>
    <tr>
      <td>
        <input name="editionUpdate" type="text" size="50"
```

```
          maxlength="250"/>
     </td>
   </tr>
   <tr>
     <td>Title:</td>
   </tr>
   <tr>
     <td>
       <input name="titleUpdate" type="text" size="50"
           maxlength="250"/>
     </td>
   </tr>
   <tr>
     <td>Author:</td>
   </tr>
   <tr>
     <td>
       <input name="authorUpdate" type="text" size="50"
           maxlength="250"/>
     </td>
   </tr>
   <tr>
     <td>
       <input class="Submit" type="submit" value="Apply"/>
     </td>
   </tr>
 </table>
</form>
</body>
</html>
```

Deleting a Row

Next, we will delete a row from the `OracleWebRowSet` object. Click on the **Modify Web RowSet** link in the `UpdateRow` JSP. In the `ModifyWebRowSet` JSP click on the **Delete Row** link. In the **Delete Row** JSP specify the row to delete and click on **Apply**. For example, delete the third row.

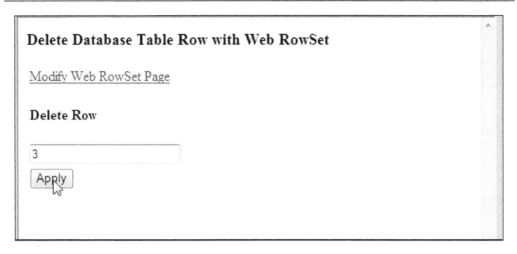

In the `DeleteRow` JSP the `deleteRow()` method of the `WebRowSetQuery` Java class is invoked. The `WebRowSetQuery` object is retrieved from the `session` object:

```
WebRowSetQuery query=( webrowset.WebRowSetQuery)
                session.getAttribute("query");
```

In the `deleteRow()` method the `OracleWebRowSet` object cursor is moved to the row to be deleted:

```
webRowSet.absolute(row);
```

Delete the row with the `deleteRow()` method of the `OracleWebRowSet` object. The create, update, and delete operations are performed on the `OracleWebRowSet` object, not on the database table. The `DeleteRow.jsp` is as follows:

```
<!DOCTYPE HTML PUBLIC "-//W3C//DTD HTML 4.01 Transitional//EN"
"http://www.w3.org/TR/html4/loose.dtd">
<%@ page contentType="text/html;charset=windows-1252"%>
<%@ page session="true"%>
<html>
  <head>
    <meta http-equiv="Content-Type" content="text/html;
        charset=windows-1252">
    <title>Delete Database Table Row with Web RowSet</title>
  </head>
  <body>
    <form><h3>Delete Database Table Row with Web RowSet</h3>
      <table>
      <tr>
          <td><a href="ModifyWebRowSet.jsp">Modify Web RowSet
```

```
                Page</a></td>
        </tr>
    </table>
        </form>
        <%
            webrowset.WebRowSetQuery query=null;
            query=(
                webrowset.WebRowSetQuery)session.getAttribute("query");
            String deleteRow=request.getParameter("deleteRow");
        if((deleteRow!=null)){
        int delete_Row=Integer.parseInt(deleteRow);
        query.deleteRow(delete_Row);
        }
        %>
        <form name="query" action="DeleteRow.jsp" method="post">
            <table>
                <tr>
                    <td><h4>Delete Row</h4></td>
                </tr>
                <tr>
                    <td>
                        <input name="deleteRow" type="text" size="25"
                            maxlength="50"/>
                    </td>
                </tr>
                <tr>
                    <td>
                        <input class="Submit" type="submit" value="Apply"/>
                    </td>
                </tr>
            </table>
        </form>
    </body>
</html>
```

Updating Database Table

Next, we will update the database table with the modified OracleWebRowSet object. Click on the **Modify Web RowSet** link in the DeleteRow JSP. In the ModifyWebRowSet JSP, click on the **Update Database** link. In the UpdateDatabase. jsp, click on **Apply**.

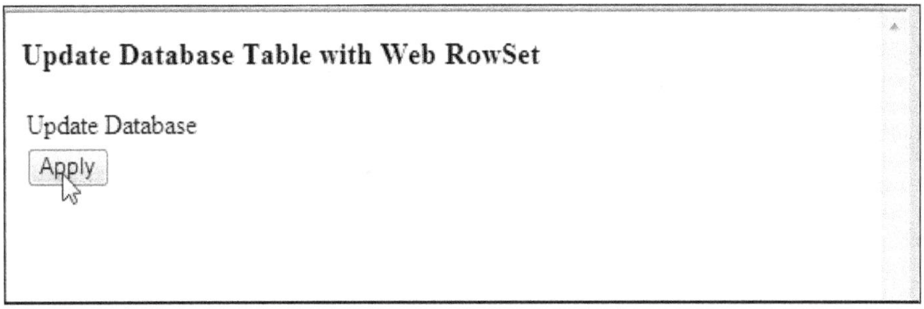

Update Database Table with Web RowSet

Update Database

[Apply]

In the `UpdateDatabase.jsp`, the `WebRowSetQuery` object is retrieved from the `session` object:

```
WebRowSetQuery query=(WebRowSet.WebRowSetQuery)
                session.getAttribute("query");
```

If the `WebRowSetQuery` object is not `null`, invoke the `updateDatabase()` method of the `WebRowSetQuery.java` class. Also output the XML document which represents the modifications made to the Web RowSet:

```
if(query!=null){
        query.updateDatabase();
    query.generateXMLDocument();
}
```

In the `updateDatabase()` method the database table is updated using the `acceptChanges()` method:

```
webRowSet.acceptChanges();
```

The database table, `Catalog`, is updated with the modifications made in the `OracleWebRowSet`. The `UpdateDatabase.jsp` JSP is listed below:

```
<!DOCTYPE HTML PUBLIC "-//W3C//DTD HTML 4.01 Transitional//EN"
"http://www.w3.org/TR/html4/loose.dtd">
<%@ page contentType="text/html;charset=windows-1252"%>
<%@ page session="true"%>
<html>
  <head>
    <meta http-equiv="Content-Type" content="text/html;
charset=windows-1252">
    <title>Update Database Table with Web RowSet</title>
  </head>
  <body>
    <h3>Update Database Table with Web RowSet</h3>
      <% webrowset.WebRowSetQuery query=null;%>
```

```
    <%
        String
updateDatabase=request.getParameter("updateDatabase");
        if(updateDatabase!=null)
        query
=( webrowset.WebRowSetQuery)session.getAttribute("query");
        if(query!=null)
{
        query.updateDatabase();
    query.generateXMLDocument();}
%>
    <form name="query" action="UpdateDatabase.jsp" method="post">
    <input type="hidden" name="updateDatabase" value=
                                "Update Database"/>
        <table>
         <tr>
            <td>Update Database
            </td>
        </tr>
        <tr>
            <td>
                <input class="Submit" type="submit" value="Apply"/>
            </td>
        </tr>
        </table>
    </form>
    </body>
</html>
```

The XML document corresponding to the `OracleWebRowSet` object after the modifications are made is listed below. The modified XML document, as compared to the XML document before modifications has a row added, a row modified, and a row deleted.

```
<?xml version="1.0" encoding="UTF-8"?>
<!DOCTYPE RowSet PUBLIC '-//Sun Microsystems, Inc.//DTD RowSet//EN'
        'http://java.sun.com/j2ee/dtds/RowSet.dtd'>
<RowSet>
  <properties>
    <command>SELECT JOURNAL, PUBLISHER, EDITION, TITLE, AUTHOR FROM
        OE.Catalog</command>
    <concurrency>1007</concurrency>
    <datasource>jdbc/OracleDataSource</datasource>
```

```
    <escape-processing>true</escape-processing>
    <fetch-direction>1002</fetch-direction>
    <fetch-size>10</fetch-size>
    <isolation-level>2</isolation-level>
    <key-columns>
    </key-columns>
    <map></map>
    <max-field-size>0</max-field-size>
    <max-rows>3</max-rows>
    <query-timeout>0</query-timeout>
    <read-only>false</read-only>
    <rowset-type>1005</rowset-type>
    <show-deleted>false</show-deleted>
    <url>jdbc:oracle:thin:@localhost:1521:ORCL</url>
</properties>
<metadata>
  <column-count>5</column-count>
  <column-definition>
    <column-index>1</column-index>
    <auto-increment>false</auto-increment>
    <case-sensitive>true</case-sensitive>
    <currency>false</currency>
    <nullable>1</nullable>
    <signed>true</signed>
    <searchable>true</searchable>
    <column-display-size>25</column-display-size>
    <column-label>JOURNAL</column-label>
    <column-name>JOURNAL</column-name>
    <schema-name></schema-name>
    <column-precision>0</column-precision>
    <column-scale>0</column-scale>
    <table-name></table-name>
    <catalog-name></catalog-name>
    <column-type>12</column-type>
    <column-type-name>VARCHAR2</column-type-name>
  </column-definition>
  <column-definition>
    <column-index>2</column-index>
    <auto-increment>false</auto-increment>
    <case-sensitive>true</case-sensitive>
    <currency>false</currency>
    <nullable>1</nullable>
    <signed>true</signed>
    <searchable>true</searchable>
```

```
      <column-display-size>25</column-display-size>
      <column-label>PUBLISHER</column-label>
      <column-name>PUBLISHER</column-name>
      <schema-name></schema-name>
      <column-precision>0</column-precision>
      <column-scale>0</column-scale>
      <table-name></table-name>
      <catalog-name></catalog-name>
      <column-type>12</column-type>
      <column-type-name>VARCHAR2</column-type-name>
    </column-definition>
    <column-definition>
      <column-index>3</column-index>
      <auto-increment>false</auto-increment>
      <case-sensitive>true</case-sensitive>
      <currency>false</currency>
      <nullable>1</nullable>
      <signed>true</signed>
      <searchable>true</searchable>
      <column-display-size>25</column-display-size>
      <column-label>EDITION</column-label>
      <column-name>EDITION</column-name>
      <schema-name></schema-name>
      <column-precision>0</column-precision>
      <column-scale>0</column-scale>
      <table-name></table-name>
      <catalog-name></catalog-name>
      <column-type>12</column-type>
      <column-type-name>VARCHAR2</column-type-name>
    </column-definition>
    <column-definition>
      <column-index>4</column-index>
      <auto-increment>false</auto-increment>
      <case-sensitive>true</case-sensitive>
      <currency>false</currency>
      <nullable>1</nullable>
      <signed>true</signed>
      <searchable>true</searchable>
      <column-display-size>45</column-display-size>
      <column-label>TITLE</column-label>
      <column-name>TITLE</column-name>
      <schema-name></schema-name>
      <column-precision>0</column-precision>
      <column-scale>0</column-scale>
```

```xml
      <table-name></table-name>
      <catalog-name></catalog-name>
      <column-type>12</column-type>
      <column-type-name>VARCHAR2</column-type-name>
    </column-definition>
    <column-definition>
      <column-index>5</column-index>
      <auto-increment>false</auto-increment>
      <case-sensitive>true</case-sensitive>
      <currency>false</currency>
      <nullable>1</nullable>
      <signed>true</signed>
      <searchable>true</searchable>
      <column-display-size>25</column-display-size>
      <column-label>AUTHOR</column-label>
      <column-name>AUTHOR</column-name>
      <schema-name></schema-name>
      <column-precision>0</column-precision>
      <column-scale>0</column-scale>
      <table-name></table-name>
      <catalog-name></catalog-name>
      <column-type>12</column-type>
      <column-type-name>VARCHAR2</column-type-name>
    </column-definition>
  </metadata>
  <data>
    <row>
      <col>Oracle Magazine</col>
      <col>Oracle Publishing</col>
      <col>July-August 2005</col>
      <col>Configuring Undo Tablespace</col>
      <col>Floss, Kimberly</col>
    </row>
    <row>
      <col>Oracle Magazine</col>
      <col>Oracle Publishing</col>
      <col>March-April 2004</col>
      <col>Oracle Certified Master</col>
      <col>Jim Dillani</col>
    </row>
  </data>
</RowSet>
```

Query the database table `Catalog`, the output produced. A new row has been added, a row modified, and a row deleted.

```
SQL> SELECT * FROM OE.CATALOG;

JOURNAL                     PUBLISHER               EDITION
--------------------------- ----------------------- ---------------------------
TITLE                                               AUTHOR
--------------------------------------------------- ---------------------------
Oracle Magazine             Oracle Publishing           July-August 2005
Configuring Undo Tablespace                         Floss, Kimberly

Oracle Magazine             Oracle Publishing           March-April 2004
Oracle Certified Master                             Jim Dillani


SQL> |
```

In this section a Web RowSet was generated from a database table, the WebRowSet was modified, and the database table updated with the modified Web RowSet.

JDBC 4.0 Version

The OC4J embedded in JDeveloper 10g or JDeveloper 11g does not implement JDBC 4.0 specification. The new features in JDBC 4.0 may be availed of in a later version of JDeveloper that supports JDBC 4.0 specification.

In the JDBC 4.0 version of the web application, add the Oracle database 11g JDBC 4.0 drivers JAR file, `ojdbc6.jar`, to the `j2ee/home/applib` directory, which is in the runtime class path of a web applications running in OC4J server. Also add `ojdbc6.jar` to the project libraries by selecting **Tools | Project Properties** and subsequently selecting **Libraries | Add Jar/Directory**. For the JDBC 4.0 drivers we need to set the JDK version to JDK 6.0. Select the project node in **Applications-Navigator** and select **Tools | Project Properties**. Select the **Libraries** node in the **Project Properties** window and click on **J2SE Version** field's **Change** button to set the JDK version. In the **Edit J2SE Definition** window, click on **New**. In the **Create J2SE** window, select a JDK 6.0 **J2SE Executable** and click on **OK**.

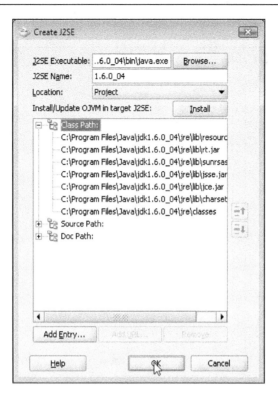

In the **Edit J2SE Definition** window, select the JDK 6.0 **J2SE Definition** and click **OK**.

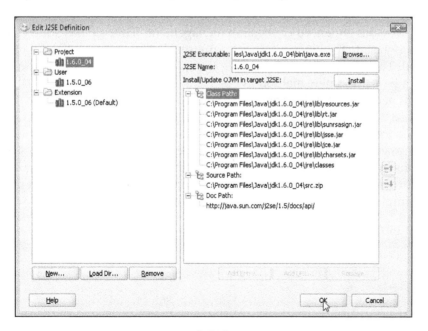

In the **Project Properties** window the **J2SE Version** gets set to JDK 6.0.

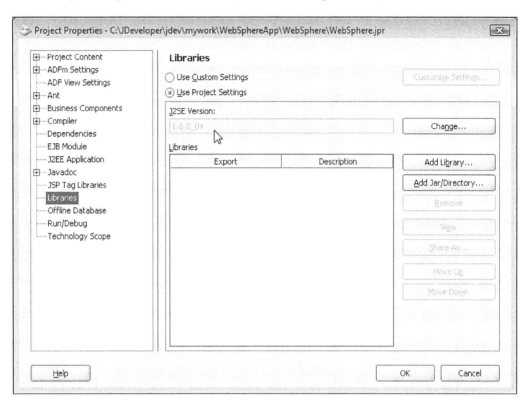

JDBC 4.0 provides enhanced connection management. JDBC 4.0 has added support for connection state tracking using which unusable connections can be identified and closed. The connection state tracking is implemented by the connection pool manager using a new method in the `Connection` interface, `isValid()`. The connection pool manager determines if a `Connection` object is valid by invoking the `isValid()` method on the `Connection` object. If the `Connection` object is not valid the connection pool manager closes the connection. Prior to the new feature, to track connection state the connection pool manager typically had to close all the connections in a connection pool and reinitiate the connection pool if the connection pool performance got reduced due to unusable connections. A connection pool manager implements the connection state tracking as follows:

```
if(!connection.isValid())
connection.close();
```

An SQLException in a JDBC application might be chained to other SQLExceptions and a developer would be interested in retrieving the chained exceptions. In JDBC 3.0 the chained exceptions and the chained causes of the exceptions had to be retrieved by invoking the getNextException() and getCause() methods recursively.

```
catch(SQLException e)
  {
while(e != null)
  {
System.out.println("SQLException Message:" + e.getMessage());
Throwable t = e.getCause();
while(t != null)
  {
System.out.println("SQLException Cause:" + t);
t = t.getCause();
}
e = e.getNextException();
}
}
```

JDBC 4.0 has added support for the Java SE chained exception facility also called the **cause facility**. The support for the Java SE chained exception facility is implemented with following new features.

- Four new constructors in the SQLException class that have the Throwable cause as one of the parameters.

- SQLException class supports the enhanced for-each loop introduced in J2SE 5.0 to retrieve the chained exceptions and chained causes without invoking the getNextException() and getCause() methods recursively.

- The getCause() method supports non-SQLExceptions.

Chained exceptions and chained causes may be retrieved using the enhanced for-each loop as follows:

```
catch(SQLException sqlException)
  {
for(Throwable e : sqlException )
  {
System.out.println("Error encountered: " + e);
}
}
```

JDBC 4.0 drivers have also added support for SQL data types ROWID and National Character Set data types NCHAR, NVARCHAR, LONGNVARCHAR, and NCLOB in the RowSet interface.

The `WebRowSetQuery` class used in this chapter with the chained exceptions retrieved using the enhanced `for-each` loop is listed below:

```java
package webrowset;
import oracle.jdbc.rowset.*;
import java.io.*;
import java.sql.SQLException;
public class WebRowSetQuery
  {
     public OracleWebRowSet webRowSet;
     public String selectQuery;
     public WebRowSetQuery() {
     }
     public WebRowSetQuery(OracleWebRowSet webRowSet)
  {
         this.webRowSet = webRowSet;
     }
     public void generateWebRowSet(String selectQuery)
  {
         try
  {
             webRowSet = new OracleWebRowSet();
             webRowSet.setDataSourceName("jdbc/OracleDataSource");
             webRowSet.setCommand(selectQuery);
             webRowSet.setUsername("oe");
             webRowSet.setPassword("pw");
             webRowSet.setReadOnly(false);
             webRowSet.setFetchSize(5);
             webRowSet.setMaxRows(3);
             webRowSet.execute();

         }
  catch (SQLException sqlException)
  {
             for (Throwable e: sqlException)
  {
                 System.out.println("Error encountered: " + e);
             }
         }
     }
     public void generateXMLDocument()
```

```
{
        try
    {

            OutputStreamWriter output =
                new OutputStreamWriter(new FileOutputStream(new
                    File("c:/output/output.xml")));
            webRowSet.writeXml(output);
        } catch (SQLException sqlException)
    {

            for (Throwable e: sqlException)
    {

                System.out.println("Error encountered: " + e);
            }
        }
        catch (IOException e)
    {

        }
    }
    public void deleteRow(int row)
    {

        try
    {

            webRowSet.absolute(row);
            webRowSet.deleteRow();
        } catch (SQLException sqlException)
    {

            for (Throwable e: sqlException)
    {

                System.out.println("Error encountered: " + e);
            }
        }
    }
public void insertRow(String journal, String publisher, String
                edition,
                    String title, String author)
    {

        try
    {

            webRowSet.moveToInsertRow();
            webRowSet.updateString(1, journal);
            webRowSet.updateString(2, publisher);
            webRowSet.updateString(3, edition);
            webRowSet.updateString(4, title);
            webRowSet.updateString(5, author);
```

```
                webRowSet.insertRow();
        } catch (SQLException sqlException)
    {
            for (Throwable e: sqlException)
    {
                System.out.println("Error encountered: " + e);
        }
        }
    }
    public void updateRow(int rowUpdate, String journal, String
                publisher,
                        String edition, String title, String author)
    {
        try
    {
            webRowSet.absolute(rowUpdate);
            webRowSet.updateString(1, journal);
            webRowSet.updateString(2, publisher);
            webRowSet.updateString(3, edition);
            webRowSet.updateString(4, title);
            webRowSet.updateString(5, author);
            webRowSet.updateRow();
        } catch (SQLException sqlException)
    {
            for (Throwable e: sqlException)
    {
                System.out.println("Error encountered: " + e);
        }
        }
    }
    public String[] readRow(int rowRead)
    {
        String[] resultSet = null;
        try
    {
            resultSet = new String[5];
            webRowSet.absolute(rowRead);
            resultSet[0] = webRowSet.getString(1);
            resultSet[1] = webRowSet.getString(2);
            resultSet[2] = webRowSet.getString(3);
            resultSet[3] = webRowSet.getString(4);
            resultSet[4] = webRowSet.getString(5);
        } catch (SQLException sqlException)
    {
```

```
                for (Throwable e: sqlException)
    {
                        System.out.println("Error encountered: " + e);
                }
        }
        return resultSet;
    }
    public void updateDatabase()
    {
            try {
                webRowSet.acceptChanges();
            } catch (SQLException sqlException)
    {
                for (Throwable e: sqlException)
    {
                        System.out.println("Error encountered: " + e);
                }
        }
        }
    }
}
```

Summary

A persistent connection with a database is required to make updates to the database with the ResultSet interface. The RowSet extends the ResultSet interface. RowSet has the advantage of not requiring a persistent JDBC database connection for the modification of data. WebRowSet interface further extends the RowSet interface and represents a RowSet object as an XML document, thus facilitating the transfer of data for query and modification by remote clients who are not connected to the database. JDBC 4.0 features such as connection state tracking and Java SE chained exceptions facility may be availed of in a Web RowSet application in a server that supports JDBC 4.0.

10

Creating a JSF Data Table

JavaServer Faces (JSF) provides a set of **User Interface (UI)** components that may be used to display database data in conjunction with the JDBC API. JDeveloper 10.1.3 edition supports the reference implementation of JSF 1.1_02. The JSF HTML tag library provides different User Interface components in the Component Palette for developing a web application. Data Table is a UI component, which represents a data collection in a table, in the JSF HTML component palette. The Data Table component may be used to display database data with a static or dynamically generated SQL query.

JDeveloper 10.1.3 provides a Create Data Table Wizard to create a JSF Data Table. In this chapter we will create a Data Table by binding the Data Table to a managed bean (MBean) in the Create Data Table Wizard and by binding the Data Table to a specified number of columns in the Create Data Table Wizard, and by subsequently creating a Data Table with the JSF API. The JSF class `javax.faces.component.html.HtmlDataTable` represents a Data Table. The columns in a Data Table are represented by the `javax.faces.component.UIColumn` class. Managed beans are Java objects that represent some resources, and that are managed by the JSF framework and that may be used as a component model. In this chapter we will learn about:

- Creating a Data Table using an MBean with the Create Data Table Wizard
- Creating a Data Table using the JSF API with the Create Data Table Wizard

Setting the Environment

Install the Oracle database 10g, including the sample schemas, and create a database instance. The Data Table is created from an example database table, `OE.Catalog`. Create the example table, `OE.Catalog`, using the following SQL script:

```
CREATE TABLE OE.Catalog(CatalogId INTEGER PRIMARY KEY, Journal
  VARCHAR(25), Publisher VARCHAR(25), Edition VARCHAR(25), Title
  Varchar(45), Author Varchar(25));
```

```
INSERT INTO OE.Catalog VALUES('1', 'Oracle Magazine', 'Oracle
    Publishing', 'Nov-Dec 2004', 'Database Resource Manager',
    'Kimberly Floss');
INSERT INTO OE.Catalog VALUES('2', 'Oracle Magazine', 'Oracle
    Publishing', 'Nov-Dec 2004', 'From ADF UIX to JSF','Jonas Jacobi');
INSERT INTO OE.Catalog VALUES('3', 'Oracle Magazine', 'Oracle
    Publishing', 'March-April 2005', 'Starting with Oracle ADF ',
    'Steve Muench');
```

Creating a Data Table by Binding a MBean

In this section we will create a Data Table with the Create Data Table Wizard by binding the Data Table with a managed bean that represents the data source for the Data Table . The procedure to create a Data Table using an MBean is as follows:

1. Create a JavaBean class for a Web Service.

2. Create a **Service Endpoint Interface (SEI)** for the Web Service.

3. Generate a Web Service from the Javabean class and the SEI.

4. Create a client class for Web Service. In the client class, connect to Oracle database using JDBC and run an SQL query to create a `ResultSet`, which represents the collection of data objects that we will bind to the Data Table.

5. Create an MBean from the Web Service client class.

6. In a JSF page bind a Data Table to the MBean.

First, create an application and a project in JDeveloper 10.1.3 as shown.

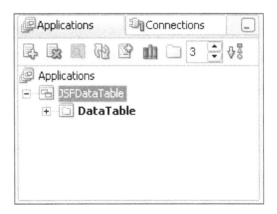

The Data Table JSF application consists of three tiers: the database, the middle-tier MBean, and the JSF user interface. Add a JavaBean class to the project for the middle tier. The Bean class consists of getter and setter values for the different columns of the Data Table. The JavaBean class is added with **File | New**. In the **New Gallery** window select **General | Java Class** in **Categories** and click on **OK**. JavaBean class `DataTable.java` is listed below.

```
package datatable;
public class DataTable
{
  private int catalogId;
  private String journal;
  private String publisher;
  private String edition;
  private String title;
  private String author;
  public DataTable()
  {}
  public int getCatalogId(){
    return this.catalogId;}
  public void setCatalogId(int catalogId){
    this.catalogId=catalogId;}
  public String getJournal(){
    return this.journal;}
  public void setJournal(String journal){
    this.journal=journal;}
  public String getPublisher(){
    return this.publisher;}
  public void setPublisher(String publisher){
    this.publisher=publisher;}
  public String getEdition(){
    return this.edition;}
  public void setEdition(String edition){
    this.edition=edition;}
  public String getTitle(){
    return this.title;}
  public void setTitle(String title){
    this.title=title;}
  public String getAuthor(){
    return this.author;}
  public void setAuthor(String author){
    this.author=author;}
  public static void main(String[] args){
    DataTable dataTable = new DataTable();
  }
}
```

Add a `MyWebService1SEI.java` SEI for the Bean class with **File | New**. In the **New Gallery** window select **General** in **Categories** and **Java Interface** in **Items**. `MyWebService1SEI.java` is listed below.

```java
package datatable;
import java.rmi.RemoteException;
public interface MyWebService1SEI extends java.rmi.Remote
{   public java.lang.String getTitle() throws RemoteException;
    public void setTitle(java.lang.String param0) throws
RemoteException;
    public int getCatalogId() throws RemoteException;
    public void setCatalogId(int param0) throws RemoteException;
    public java.lang.String getJournal() throws RemoteException;
    public void setJournal(java.lang.String param0) throws
RemoteException;
    public java.lang.String getPublisher() throws RemoteException;
    public void setPublisher(java.lang.String param0) throws
RemoteException;
    public java.lang.String getEdition() throws RemoteException;
    public void setEdition(java.lang.String param0) throws
RemoteException;
    public java.lang.String getAuthor() throws RemoteException;
    public void setAuthor(java.lang.String param0) throws
RemoteException;
}
```

Next, generate a web service from the middle-tier JavaBean class and SEI. Right-click on the `DataTable.java` Bean class and select **Create J2EE Web Service**.

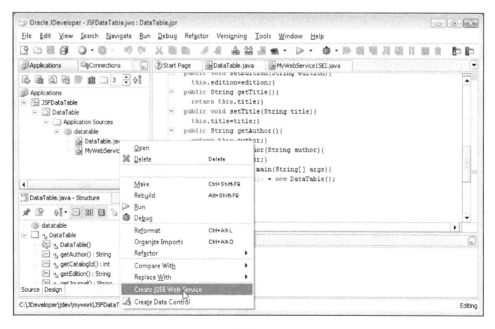

In the **Select J2EE Version** window, select J2EE 1.4 (JAX-RPC) web services. In the **Class** window select the default **Web Service Name** and select the default settings for **Service Endpoint Interface** and click on **Next**. In the **Message Format** window select the **SOAP Message Format**, which may be set to **Wrapped** or **Unwrapped**. The **SOAP Message Format** specifies the SOAP binding document style. In the **Wrapped** style the **wsdl:operation** name is specified as the same as the root element of an XML document. Select the **SOAP Message Format** as **Document/Wrapped**. The **Generate Schema with Qualified Elements** checkbox is selected by default, which implies that schema elements are namespace prefixed. Web service attachments are processed using **MIME** encoding.

Multipurpose Internet Mail Extensions (**MIME**) format is used to transmit messages and is a basic component of the HTTP communication protocol. MIME supports text and header information in non-ASCII character sets, and non-text attachments. To use **MIME** encoding, select the **Use MIME Encoding** checkbox. Click on **Next**. In **Specify Custom DataType Serializers**, specify mapping between the XML types and their corresponding Java types. Select the default settings and click on **Next**. In the **Mapping** window optionally specify the mapping between **Java Web Service** and the corresponding WSDL elements. Select the default settings and click on **Next**. The **Methods** window displays the Web Service methods. Click on **Next**. In the **Handler Details** window, select the default settings and click on **Next**. In the **State** window, select the default settings and click on **Next**. In the **Additional Classes** window, click on **Next**. A web service for the middle-tier gets added to the project.

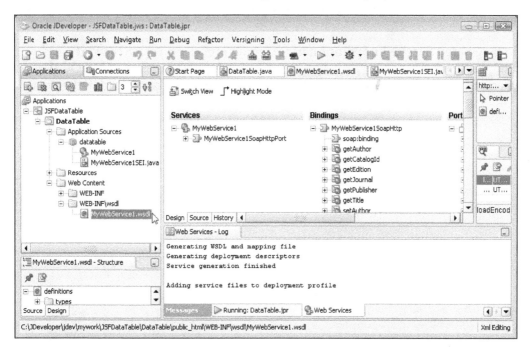

Next, generate a client class for the web service. Right-click on the web service node and select **Generate Web Service Proxy**.

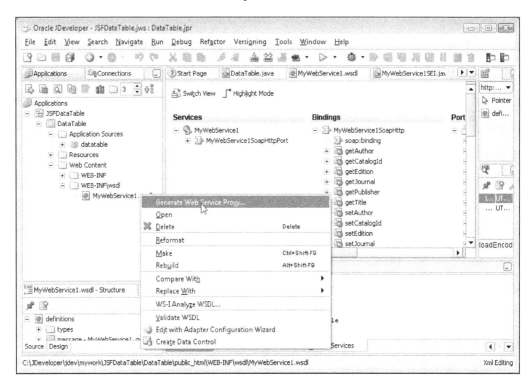

In the **Shared Service Endpoint Interface** window, click on **Yes**. In the **Port Endpoints** window, select **Run Against a service deployed to Embedded OC4J** checkbox and click on **OK**. A client class for the web service gets added to the project.

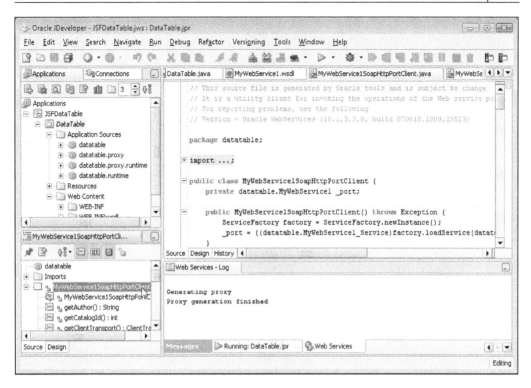

In the client class we will access Oracle database and run an SQL query to create a `ResultSet` from the `Catalog` table, which we created earlier. To the client class, add an import statement for the `java.sql.*` package and a `getDataResultSet` method, which returns a `ResultSet` of data retrieved from a database table. In the `getDatResultSet` method, load the Oracle JDBC driver class `oracle.jdbc.OracleDriver` and create a connection with Oracle database using `getConnection` method of the `DriverManager` class. Create a `Statement` object from the `Connection` object using the `createStatement` method of `Connection` object. By default you may iterate through a `ResultSet` only once and from the first row to the last row. To create a scrollable result, specify result set type as `ResultSet.TYPE_SCROLL_INSENSITIVE`. For a read-only result set specify result set concurrency as `ResultSet.CONCUR_READ_ONLY`. Run an SQL query using `executeQuery` method of `Statement` object.

The `getDataResultSet` method is listed as follows:

```
public ResultSet getDataResultSet(){
      ResultSet rs=null;
   try{
   Class.forName("oracle.jdbc.OracleDriver");
   String url="jdbc:oracle:thin:@localhost:1521:ORCL";
   Connection connection = DriverManager.getConnection(url,
                     "OE", "pw");
   Statement stmt=connection.createStatement(ResultSet.
            TYPE_SCROLL_INSENSITIVE, ResultSet.CONCUR_READ_ONLY);
    rs=stmt.executeQuery("SELECT * FROM OE.CATALOG");
   }catch(SQLException e){}
    catch(ClassNotFoundException e){}
   return rs;
   }
```

Next, we will create a Data Table in a JSF page. Add a JSF page to the
Applications-Navigator project with **File | New**. In the **New Gallery** window
select **Web Tier | JSF** in **Categories** and **JSF JSP** in **Items**.

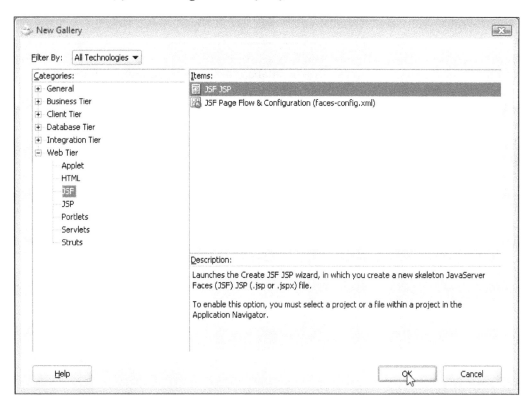

In the **JSP File** window specify a **File Name**, `catalog.jsp`, and click on **Next**. In the **Component Binding** window select **Automatically Expose UI Components in a New Managed Bean**.

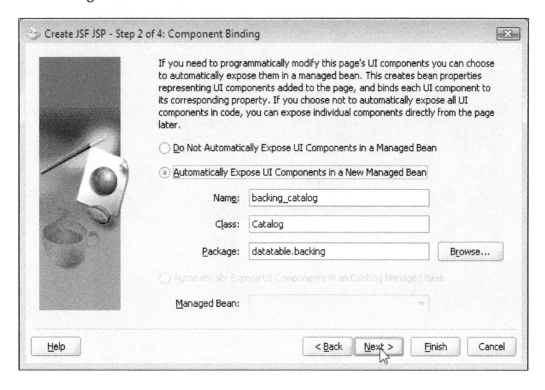

In the **Error Page Options** window, select the default setting, which is to not use an error page, and click on **Next**. In the **Tag Libraries** window, the **JSF HTML** and **JSF Core** tag libraries are pre-selected. Data Table is a JSF HTML tag library component. JSF Core tag library implements the standard JSF core tags. Click on **Next**.

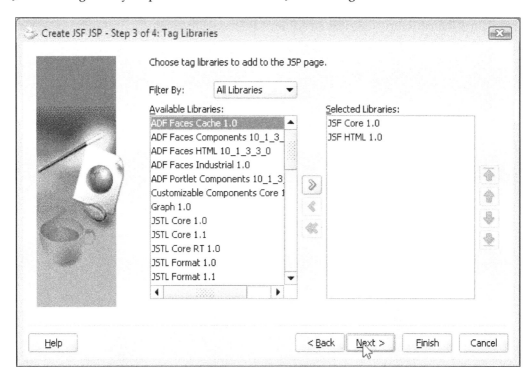

In the **HTML Options** window, select the default settings and click on **Next**. In the **Finish** window, click on **Finish**. A JSF page including the `faces-config.xml` configuration file and a backing bean for the JSF page are added to the **Applications-Navigator** project node. Next we will add an MBean, which encapsulates the client class of the middle-tier Web Service. Open the `faces-config.xml` configuration file, select the **Overview** tab and click on **New**.

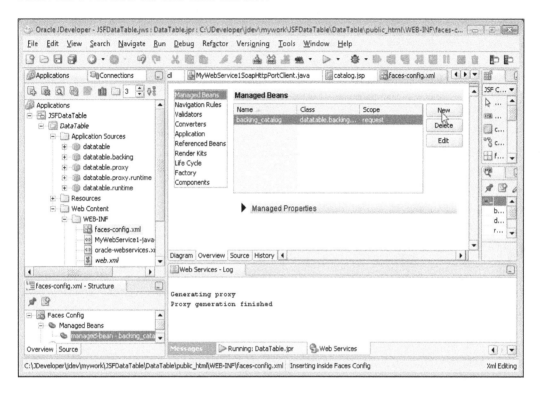

In the **Create Managed Bean** window, specify managed bean name, **CatalogBean**, and specify the Web Service client class, which was generated earlier, in the **Class** field and select **request** as the **Scope**. Click on **OK**.

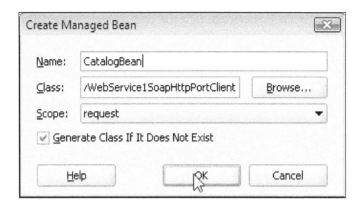

A managed bean for the Web service client class gets added.

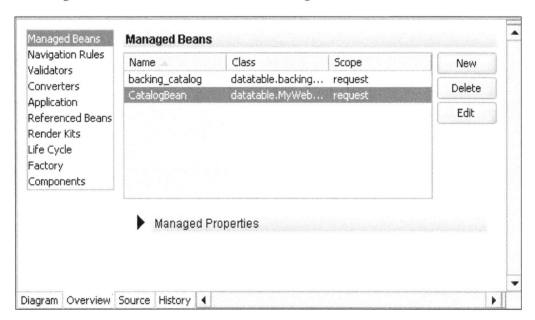

Next, we will add a Data Table to the JSF page. Select the **JSF HTML Component Palette**. Select the JSF page node in the **Applications Navigator**, position the cursor in the JSF page, and select **Data Table** in the **JSF HTML Component Palette**.

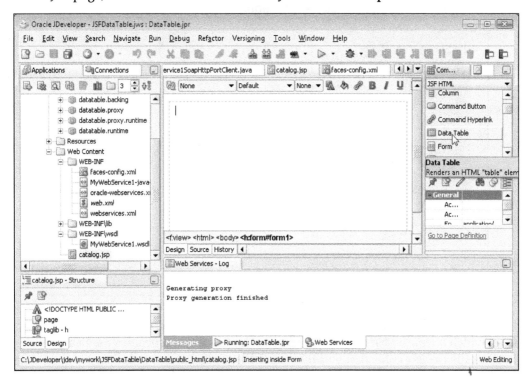

The **Create Data Table Wizard** starts. Click on **Next** in the introduction window. In the **Binding** window, select the **Bind the Data Table Now** radio button and click on **Next**. The **Number of Columns** option is for binding the Data Table using the JSF API, which we will discuss in the next section.

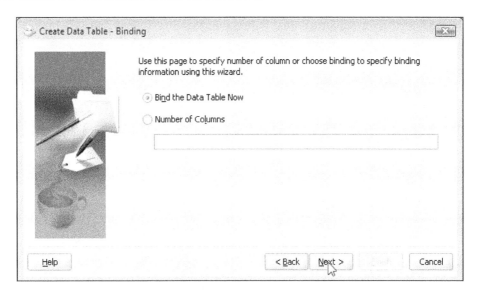

In the **Bind Data Table** window, the **Value** field specifies the data objects collection from which a Data Table is to be generated. The **Class** field specifies the Bean class for the data objects collection and the **Var** field specifies the variable for a row of data in the data objects collection. Click on **Bind** to bind a data objects collection to the Data Table.

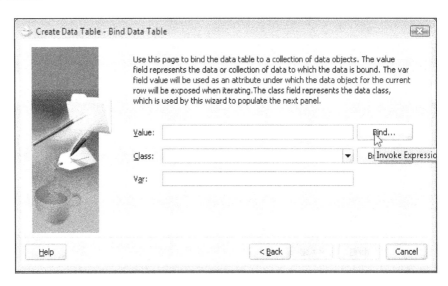

Select **All Types** in the **Filter By** selection. Select the `dataResultSet` variable from the `CatalogBean` MBean that we generated earlier. Add the selected variable to the **Expression** window with the **>** button. Click on **OK**. The **Expression** represents an EL expression for the data objects collection returned by the `dataResultSet` method of the Web Service client class, which was encapsulated in the `CatalogBean` MBean.

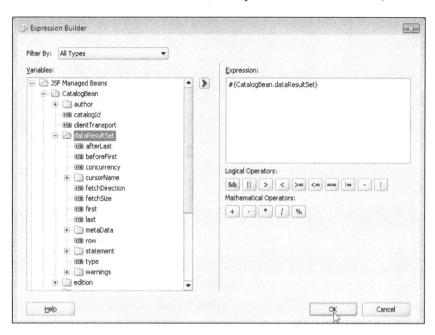

In the **Bind Data Table** window, specify the bean class `DataTable` from which the Web service was created in the **Class** field. In the **Var** field, specify a variable for a row of data in the data objects collection. Click on **Next**.

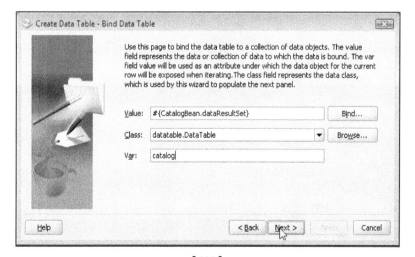

In the **Header and Row Data** window, the column headers in the Data Table and EL expressions for the column values in the Data Table are specified. Modify the order of columns to match the columns in the database table from which Data Table is to be generated and click on **Next**.

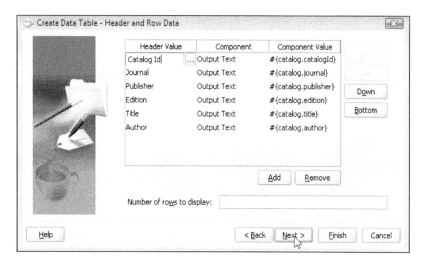

In the **Finish** window, click on the **Finish** button. The Data Table headers and EL expressions for column values are added to the JSF page. Right-click on the catalog.jsp node and select **Run** to generate a Data Table.

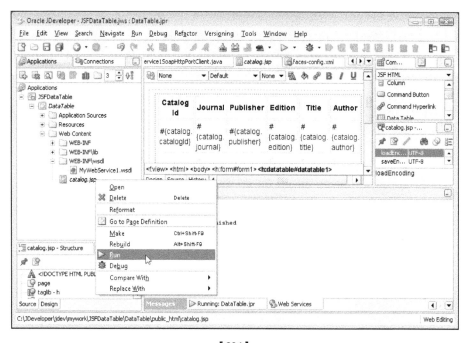

A Data Table gets generated and gets displayed in the default browser.

Catalog Id	Journal	Publisher	Edition	Title	Author
1	Oracle Magazine	Oracle Publishing	Nov-Dec 2004	Database Resource Manager	Kimberly Floss
2	Oracle Magazine	Oracle Publishing	Nov-Dec 2004	From ADF UIX to JSF	Jonas Jacobi
3	Oracle Magazine	Oracle Publishing	March-April 2005	Starting with Oracle ADF	Steve Muench

Creating a Data Table with the JSF API

In the previous section, we generated a Data Table from a static query in a Web service client class. In this section we will generate a Data Table from a dynamic query specified in the JSF page. We will use the **Create Data Table Wizard** to bind the Data Table to a specified number of columns and in the backing bean generate the Data Table with the JSF API. The procedure to create a Data Table from a database table with the JSF API is as follows:

1. Create a JSF Page.

2. Add an **Input Text** JSF component to the JSF page. We will use the Input Text to specify an SQL query from which the Data Table will be generated.

3. Add a **Command Button** from the Component Palette to submit the SQL query. We will bind the command button to a backing bean method with which we will create the Data Table.

4. Add a **Data Table** from the Component Palette. In the Create Data Table Wizard specify the number of columns to match the number of columns in the database table from which the Data Table is to be created.

5. In the backing bean retrieve the SQL query specified in the Input Text and create a Data Table using the JSF API.

Delete the JSFDataTable application, including the application contents, created in the previous section. As in the previous section, create an application and a project. Add a JSF page with **File | New**. In the **New Gallery** window, select **Web Tier | JSF** in **Categories** and **JSF JSP** in **Items**. Click on **OK**. To the JSF page add the **JDeveloper** CSS style from the **CSS** Component Palette. To the JSF page add a **Heading 2**. Specify heading as 'JSF Data Table'.

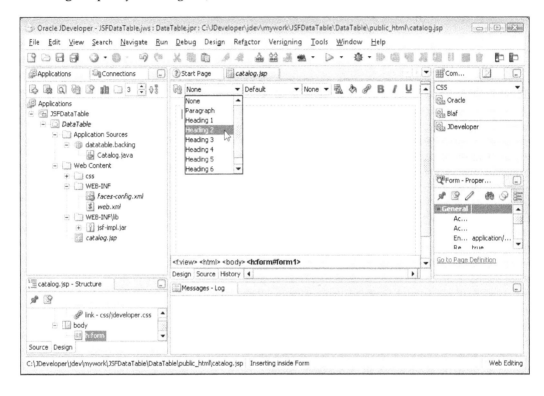

Next, position the cursor below the heading in the JSF page Design view and add an **Input Text** UI component from the **JSF HTML Component Palette**. To add a UI component from the JSF HTML Component Palette, click on the component in the Component Palette. We will specify the SQL query for generating a Data Table in the Input Text.

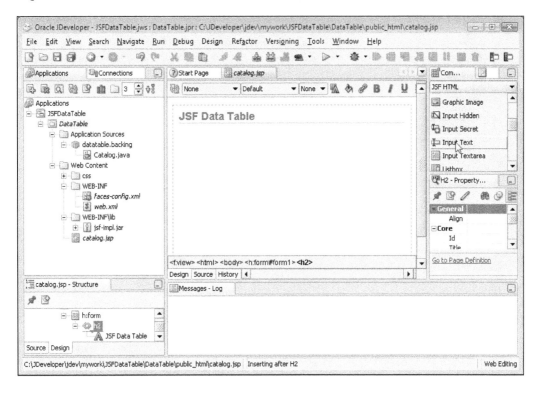

Position the cursor in the JSF page below the input text and add a **Command Button** component from the JSF HTML Component Palette. We will submit the SQL query with the command button. Set the text on the Command Button in the **Property Inspector**.

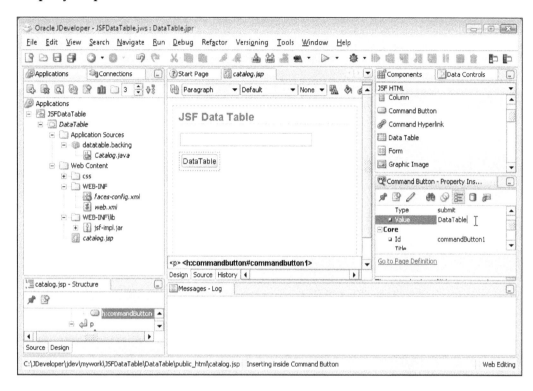

Next, position the cursor in the JSF page below the command button and add a **Data Table** from the Component Palette.

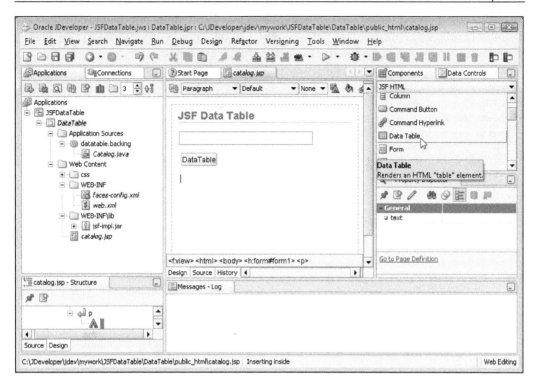

The **Create Data Table Wizard** gets started. Click on **Next**. In the **Binding** window, select **Number of Columns** and specify a value, the number of columns in the database table from which the Data Table is generated as 6. Click on **Finish**.

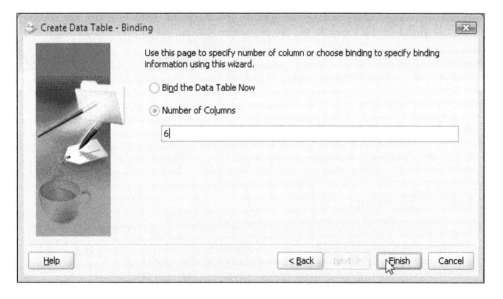

A Data Table gets added to the JSF page. The Data Table does not contain any column headers or column data yet. We will add backing bean binding for the Data Table columns and column headers to generate a Data Table.

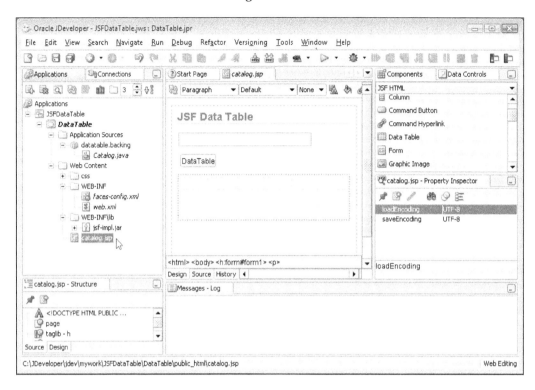

Modify the `catalog.jsp` JSF page to specify the backing bean binding for the different columns in the Data Table. Replace the following listing:

```
<h:dataTable binding="#{backing_catalog.dataTable1}" id="dataTable1">
        <h:column/>
        <h:column/>
        <h:column/>
        <h:column/>
        <h:column/>
        <h:column/>
    </h:dataTable>
```

with the following listing:

```
<h:dataTable rows="5" binding="#{backing_catalog.dataTable1}">
    <h:column binding="#{backing_catalog.column1}"/>
    <h:column binding="#{backing_catalog.column2}"/>
    <h:column binding="#{backing_catalog.column3}"/>
```

```
<h:column binding="#{backing_catalog.column4}"/>
<h:column binding="#{backing_catalog.column5}"/>
<h:column binding="#{backing_catalog.column6}"/>
</h:dataTable>
```

Next, bind the command button to a backing bean method in which the Data Table will be generated. Double-click on the command button. In the **Bind Action Property** window, select the default action method in the backing bean for the command button and click on **OK**. The backing bean class for the JSF page, `Catalog.java` gets displayed. Add `UIColumn` component variables for the Data Table columns and add getter/setter methods for the `UIColumn` components. Modify the `commandButton1_action` method, which is called when the Data Table button is clicked. In the `commandButton1_action` method, obtain a JDBC connection with the database. Load the driver class `oracle.jdbc.OracleDriver` using the `Class.forName` method. Create a `Connection` object using the `getConnection` method of the `DriverManager` class:

```
Class.forName("oracle.jdbc.driver.OracleDriver");
String url="jdbc:oracle:thin:@<host>:1521:<database>";
Connection connection = DriverManager.getConnection(url,
                "OE", "<password>");
```

 In the connection URL `<host>` is the database Host and `<database>` is the database instance.

Create a `Statement` object using `createStatement` method. Specify result set type as scrollable and result set concurrency as read-only.

```
Statement
  stmt=connection.createStatement(ResultSet.TYPE_SCROLL_INSENSITIVE,
  ResultSet.CONCUR_READ_ONLY);
```

Query the database with the SQL Select statement specified in the **Input Text** field of the JSF page. The Input Text value is retrieved by invoking the `getValue` method of the backing bean property for the Input Text. The SQL query is run using the `executeQuery` method of `Statement` object. The `executeQuery` method generates a `ResultSet` object.

```
ResultSet rs=stmt.executeQuery((String)inputText1.getValue());
```

Using the backing bean property for the Data Table, set the border and cell padding on the Data Table. The border is set using the `setBorder` method and the cell padding is set using the `setCellPadding` method:

```
dataTable1.setBorder(5);
dataTable1.setCellpadding("1");
```

Set the variable for a row of data in the `ResultSet` retrieved from the database with the `setVar` method:

```
dataTable1.setVar("catalog");
```

Set the header values for the columns in the Data Table. The Data Table has columns for each of the columns in the database table. Column headers are added by creating `HtmlOutputText` header components and setting the headers on the `UIColumn` components with the `setHeader` method. `HtmlOutputText` value is setting using the `setValue` method. For example, the column header for the `CatalogId` column is added as follows:

```
HtmlOutputText headerComponent = new HtmlOutputText();
headerComponent.setValue("CatalogId");
column1.setHeader(headerComponent);
```

For each of the columns in the Data Table, specify a value binding for an `HtmlOutputText` component and add the component to the column. Value binding for an `HtmlOutputText` component is set using the `setValueBinding` method. An `HtmlOutputText` component is added to a `UIColumn` component by invoking the `getChildren` method and subsequently invoking the `add` method. For example, for the `CatalogId` column an `HtmlOutputText` component is added as follows:

```
HtmlOutputText column1Text=new HtmlOutputText();
ValueBinding vb =
FacesContext.getCurrentInstance().getApplication().createValueBinding(
"#{catalog.catalogid}");
column1Text.setValueBinding("value", vb);
column1.getChildren().add(column1Text);
```

Create a `ResultSetDataModel` object. A `ResultSetDatModel` object is used to wrap a `ResultSet` object, which is required to be scrollable. Set the `ResultSet` retrieved with the SQL query as the data for the `ResultSetDataModel` using the `setWrappedData` method:

```
ResultSetDataModel dataModel=new ResultSetDataModel();
dataModel.setWrappedData(rs);
```

Bind the Data Table with the `ResultSetDataModel` object using the `setValue` method.

```
dataTable1.setValue(dataModel);
```

The modified backing bean class `Catalog.java` is listed below:

```
package datatable.backing;
import javax.faces.component.html.HtmlCommandButton;
import javax.faces.component.html.HtmlDataTable;
```

```java
import javax.faces.component.html.HtmlForm;
import javax.faces.component.html.HtmlInputText;
import javax.faces.component.UIColumn;
import javax.faces.component.html.HtmlOutputText;
import javax.faces.context.FacesContext;
import javax.faces.el.ValueBinding;
import javax.faces.model.ResultSetDataModel;
import java.sql.*;
public class Catalog {
    private HtmlForm form1;
    private HtmlInputText inputText1;
    private HtmlCommandButton commandButton1;
    private HtmlDataTable dataTable1;
    private UIColumn column1;
    private UIColumn column2;
    private UIColumn column3;
    private UIColumn column4;
    private UIColumn column5;
    private UIColumn column6;
    public void setForm1(HtmlForm form1) {
        this.form1 = form1;
    }
    public HtmlForm getForm1() {
        return form1;
    }
    public void setInputText1(HtmlInputText inputText1) {
        this.inputText1 = inputText1;
    }
    public HtmlInputText getInputText1() {
        return inputText1;
    }
    public void setCommandButton1(HtmlCommandButton commandButton1) {
        this.commandButton1 = commandButton1;
    }
    public HtmlCommandButton getCommandButton1() {
        return commandButton1;
    }
    public void setDataTable1(HtmlDataTable dataTable1) {
        this.dataTable1 = dataTable1;
    }
    public HtmlDataTable getDataTable1() {
        return dataTable1;
    }
    public void setColumn1(UIColumn column1) {
        this.column1 = column1;
    }
    public UIColumn getColumn1() {
```

```
            return column1;
        }
        public void setColumn2(UIColumn column2) {
            this.column2 = column2;
        }
        public UIColumn getColumn2() {
            return column2;
        }
        public void setColumn3(UIColumn column3) {
            this.column3 = column3;
        }
        public UIColumn getColumn3() {
            return column3;
        }
        public void setColumn4(UIColumn column4) {
            this.column4 = column4;
        }
        public UIColumn getColumn4() {
            return column4;
        }
        public void setColumn5(UIColumn column5) {
            this.column5 = column5;
        }
        public UIColumn getColumn5() {
            return column5;
        }
        public void setColumn6(UIColumn column6) {
            this.column6 = column6;
        }
        public UIColumn getColumn6() {
            return column6;
        }
        public String commandButton1_action()
          {
            // Add event code here...
            ResultSet rs=null;
            try{
            Class.forName("oracle.jdbc.OracleDriver");
        String url="jdbc:oracle:thin:@localhost:1521:ORCL";
        Connection connection = DriverManager.getConnection(url,
                        "OE", "pw");
        Statement stmt=connection.createStatement(ResultSet.
                    TYPE_SCROLL_INSENSITIVE, ResultSet.CONCUR_READ_ONLY);
         rs=stmt.executeQuery((String)inputText1.getValue());
         dataTable1.setBorder(5);
         dataTable1.setCellpadding("1");
         dataTable1.setVar("catalog");
```

```
HtmlOutputText headerComponent = new HtmlOutputText();
    headerComponent.setValue("CatalogId");
    column1.setHeader(headerComponent);
 headerComponent = new HtmlOutputText();
    headerComponent.setValue("Journal");
    column2.setHeader(headerComponent);
 headerComponent = new HtmlOutputText();
    headerComponent.setValue("Publisher");
    column3.setHeader(headerComponent);
 headerComponent = new HtmlOutputText();
    headerComponent.setValue("Edition");
    column4.setHeader(headerComponent);
 headerComponent = new HtmlOutputText();
    headerComponent.setValue("Title");
    column5.setHeader(headerComponent);
 headerComponent = new HtmlOutputText();
    headerComponent.setValue("Author");
    column6.setHeader(headerComponent);
HtmlOutputText column1Text=new HtmlOutputText();
ValueBinding vb =
FacesContext.getCurrentInstance().getApplication().createValueBinding(
"#{catalog.catalogid}");
    column1Text.setValueBinding("value", vb);
    column1.getChildren().add(column1Text);
    HtmlOutputText column2Text=new HtmlOutputText();
     vb =
FacesContext.getCurrentInstance().getApplication().createValueBinding(
"#{catalog.journal}");
    column2Text.setValueBinding("value", vb);
    column2.getChildren().add(column2Text);
    HtmlOutputText column3Text=new HtmlOutputText();
     vb =
FacesContext.getCurrentInstance().getApplication().createValueBinding(
"#{catalog.publisher}");
    column3Text.setValueBinding("value", vb);
    column3.getChildren().add(column3Text);
    HtmlOutputText column4Text=new HtmlOutputText();
     vb =
FacesContext.getCurrentInstance().getApplication().createValueBinding(
"#{catalog.edition}");
    column4Text.setValueBinding("value", vb);
    column4.getChildren().add(column4Text);
    HtmlOutputText column5Text=new HtmlOutputText();
     vb = FacesContext.getCurrentInstance().getApplication().createVal
ueBinding("#{catalog.title}");
    column5Text.setValueBinding("value", vb);
    column5.getChildren().add(column5Text);
```

```
HtmlOutputText column6Text=new HtmlOutputText();
 vb = FacesContext.getCurrentInstance().getApplication().
                createValueBinding("#{catalog.author}");
column6Text.setValueBinding("value", vb);
column6.getChildren().add(column6Text);
ResultSetDataModel dataModel=new ResultSetDataModel();
dataModel.setWrappedData(rs);
dataTable1.setValue(dataModel);
rs.close();
stmt.close();
connection.close();
}
 catch(SQLException e){System.out.println(e.getMessage());}
 catch(ClassNotFoundException e){ System.out.println(e.
getMessage());}
     return null;
   }}
```

Right-click on the JSF JSP page node and select **Run**. The JSF page gets displayed. Specify a SQL query in the input field (for example, `SELECT * FROM OE.CATALOG`) and select the **Data Table** button.

The Data Table for the specified `SELECT` SQL query is generated.

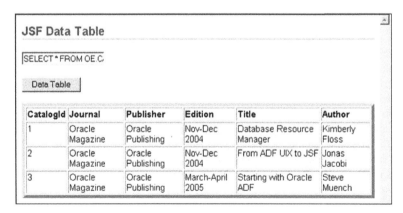

JDBC 4.0 Version

The OC4J server embedded in JDeveloper 10g or 11g does not support JDBC 4.0 specification; but in a later version of JDeveloper that supports JDBC 4.0, the JDBC 4.0 features may be added to the JSF application used to create a Data Table. JDBC 4.0 provides new features such as enhanced connection management, automatic driver loading, support for wrapper pattern, statement pooling, categorization of SQLExceptions and enhanced support for the Java SE chained exceptions facility. To use the JDBC 4.0 features you would need to download the Oracle database 11g JDBC 4.0 drivers JAR file, ojdbc6.jar from http://www.oracle.com/technology/ software/tech/java/sqlj_jdbc/htdocs/jdbc_111060.html. Copy ojdbc6. jar to the j2ee/home/lib directory, which is in the runtime class path of web applications running in OC4J server. As JDBC 4.0 drivers require JDK 6.0, we would also need to set J2SE version to JDK 6.0. To set the JDK version select **Tools | Project Properties** and select **Libraries** in **Project Properties** window. Select the **Change** button for the **J2SE Version** field to set the JDK to 6.0.

You don't have to modify the JSF application to add connection state tracking to the application. Connection state tracking is implemented by the connection pool manager and is used to track unusable connections in the connection pool. Unusable connections could hamper connection pool performance. Prior to the new feature in JDBC 4.0, a connection pool manager had to close all the connections and reinitiate the connection pool if some of the connections in the connection pool became unusable The Connection interface in JDBC 4.0 provides a new method isValid() using which a connection pool manager tests if a connection is still valid and closes the connection if the connection has become unusable.

```
if(!connection.isValid())
connection.close();
```

We used two different methods to create a Data Table. In each of the methods we obtained a connection with the database using the Class.forName method to load the Oracle JDBC driver. JDBC 4.0 provides automatic driver loading using the Java SE Service Provider mechanism. To use the Java SE Service Provider mechanism, create a java.sql.Driver file in the META-INF/services directory and specify the different JDBC drivers that are to be available for automatic loading. The Oracle database 11g drivers JAR file ojdbc 6.jar contains a META-INF/services/java.sql.Driver file with the oracle.jdbc.OracleDriver class specified in it. With the automatic driver loading feature, we won't need to invoke the Class.forName method.

Unlike connection state tracking, you have to modify the JSF application if you want to avail of the connection identification feature in JDBC 4.0. The `Connection` interface in JDBC 4.0 has two new methods `setClientInfo` and `getClientInfo` to set and get client info properties. Sometimes one or more connections bog down the whole application by using excessive CPU. Using the client info properties the JDBC driver is able to identify the connection clients that could be causing the reduction in performance. The standard client info properties that are supported in JDBC 4.0 are `ApplicationName`, `ClientUser`, and `ClientHostname`. In the `getDataResultSet` method in the Web Service client class, which was used to create an MBean and subsequently a Data Table, set the client info properties as follows:

```
connection.setClientInfo("ApplicationName","OracleApp");
connection.setClientInfo("ClientUser","OracleUser");
connection.setClientInfo("ClientHostname","OracleHost");
```

Similarly, set the client info properties in the backing bean method `commandButton1_action`, which was used to create a Data Table with an SQL query specified in the Input Text field. A `ResultSet` of client info properties supported by a database may be obtained using the `getClientInfoProperties()` method of `DatabaseMetaData` interface:

```
DatabaseMetaData metaData=connection.getMetaData();
ResultSet clientInfo=metaData.getClientInfoProperties();
```

`PreparedStatements` are pooled by default if the database supports statement pooling. For efficient use of `Statement` objects JDBC 4.0 provides `Statement` object pooling. Frequently used `Statement` objects may be pooled using the `setPoolable` method. First, test if the `Statement` object is poolable using the `isPoolable` method and subsequently set the `Statement` object to be poolable.

```
if(stmt.isPoolable())
stmt.setPoolable(true);
```

JDBC 4.0 supports the wrapper pattern for accessing nonstandard methods in vendor specific extensions to the JDBC API. For example, the `oracle.jdbc.OracleStatement` interface, which extends the `Statement` interface provides some methods not in the `Statement` interface. The `Statement` interface extends the `Wrapper` interface in JDK 6.0. To use the wrapper pattern to access the `OracleStatement`, interface test if the `Statement` object is a wrapper for the `OracleStatement` interface using the `isWrapperFor` method. If a wrapper, create an object of type `OracleStatement` using the `unwrap` method. Subsequently the `defineColumnType` method of `OracleStatement` interface may be invoked to specify the column SQL type for a column. Database table data is fetched into a `ResultSet` in the specified column type. Pre-defining column types saves the JDBC driver a round trip to the database to find out what the column type for a column is. If column types are to be specified using `defineColumnType` column types of all the columns has to be set. If only a few of the columns are set or more columns than columns in a SQL query are set a `SQLException` gets generated. For example, the column types for the different columns in the SQL query with which a Data Table is created is set as follows:

```
Class class = Class.forName("oracle.jdbc.OracleStatement");
if(stmt.isWrapperFor(class)) {
OracleStatement oracleStmt = (OracleStatement)stmt.unwrap(class);
oracleStmt.defineColumnType(1, OracleTypes.VARCHAR);
oracleStmt.defineColumnType(2, OracleTypes.VARCHAR);
oracleStmt.defineColumnType(3, OracleTypes.VARCHAR);
oracleStmt.defineColumnType(4, OracleTypes.VARCHAR);
oracleStmt.defineColumnType(5, OracleTypes.VARCHAR);
oracleStmt.defineColumnType(6, OracleTypes.VARCHAR);
oracleStmt.defineColumnType(7, OracleTypes.VARCHAR);
}
```

Another new feature JDBC 4.0 provides is support for the `for-each` loop to iterate over chained exceptions and chained causes. Chained exceptions are exceptions that are linked to an exception. In JDBC 3.0, chained exceptions could only be retrieved by invoking the `getNextException` method recursively. Using the Java SE chained exception facility in JDBC 4.0 chained exceptions and chained causes may be retrieved as follows:

```
catch(SQLException e){
for(Throwable e : exception ) {
out.println("Error encountered: " + e);
}
}
```

The `getDataResultSet` method with the JDBC 4.0 features added is listed as follows:

```
public ResultSet getDataResultSet(){
        ResultSet rs=null;
    try{
    String url="jdbc:oracle:thin:@localhost:1521:ORCL";
    Connection connection = DriverManager.getConnection(url,
                    "OE", "pw");
connection.setClientInfo("ApplicationName","OracleApp");
connection.setClientInfo("ClientUser","OracleUser");
connection.setClientInfo("ClientHostname","OracleHost");

    Statement stmt=connection.createStatement(ResultSet.TYPE_SCROLL_
INSENSITIVE, ResultSet.CONCUR_READ_ONLY);
DatabaseMetaData metaData=connection.getMetaData();
if(metaData.supportsStatementPooling()){
if(stmt.isPoolable())
stmt.setPoolable(true);
}
```

```
Class class = Class.forName("oracle.jdbc.OracleStatement");
if(stmt.isWrapperFor(class)) {
OracleStatement oracleStmt = (OracleStatement)stmt.unwrap(class);
oracleStmt.defineColumnType(1, OracleTypes.VARCHAR);
oracleStmt.defineColumnType(2, OracleTypes.VARCHAR);
oracleStmt.defineColumnType(3, OracleTypes.VARCHAR);
oracleStmt.defineColumnType(4, OracleTypes.VARCHAR);
oracleStmt.defineColumnType(5, OracleTypes.VARCHAR);
oracleStmt.defineColumnType(6, OracleTypes.VARCHAR);
oracleStmt.defineColumnType(7, OracleTypes.VARCHAR);

rs=stmt.executeQuery("SELECT * FROM OE.CATALOG");
}

    }catch(SQLException e){for(Throwable e : exception ) {
out.println("Error encountered: " + e);
}
        return rs;
    }
```

Similarly, modify the `commandButton1_action` method in the JSF backing bean.

Summary

JSF UI Component Data Table may be used to display database data retrieved with a static SQL query or a dynamically generated SQL query. JDeveloper provides the Create Data Table Wizard to create a Data Table. A Data Table may be generated by either binding the Data Table to an MBean or with the JSF API. In a JDeveloper version that supports JDBC 4.0 the new features in JDBC 4.0 such as connection state tracking, statement pooling, connection identification, support for wrapper pattern, and Java SE chained exception facility may be availed of.

11
Creating a JSF Panel Grid

In the previous chapter, we displayed database data using the JSF Data Table component. In this chapter, we will discuss JSF Panel Grid to add and retrieve data from a database with the JDBC API. We will also validate data as data is added to the database. A panel grid is a `UIPanel` component represented by the `javax.faces.HtmlPanelGrid` class and the `h:panelGrid` tag. JDeveloper provides the Create PanelGrid Wizard to create a panel grid.

A panel grid displays a set of components in a specified number of columns. Only the number of columns needs to be specified in generating a panel grid; the number of rows is not required. The number of rows is based on the number of components in the grid and the number of columns in the grid. The components in a panel grid are added to the specified number of columns. A new panel grid row is started after the specified number of columns in a row have been allocated. For example, if the specified number of columns in a panel grid is three and the number of components to be added to the panel grid is ten. The first three components are added to the first row, the next three to the second row. Another three components are added to the third row and one to the fourth row.

In this chapter, a panel grid will be generated from a database table with the Create PanelGrid Wizard. The Create PanelGrid Wizard provides two methods to create a panel grid. A panel grid may be created either by first creating an empty panel grid and subsequently adding components to the panel grid, or by binding a managed bean to the panel grid. We will discuss both these methods to create a panel grid. The data for the panel grid will be retrieved/added using JDBC in the JSF backing bean. In this chapter, we will learn the following:

- Creating an empty panel grid with Create JSF Panel Grid Wizard and adding JSF UI Components to the panel grid.
- Creating a panel grid with Create JSF Panel Grid Wizard by binding a managed bean to the panel grid.
- Adding a JSF Validator to a panel grid.
- Adding a JSF Converter to a panel grid.

Setting the Environment

Install the JDeveloper 10.1.3 IDE. Install the Oracle 10g database including the sample schemas. In SQL Plus, create an example database table from which a panel grid will be generated. The SQL script to generate the example database table is as follows:

```
CREATE TABLE OE.Catalog(CatalogId INTEGER PRIMARY KEY, Journal
   VARCHAR(25), Publisher VARCHAR(25), Edition VARCHAR(25), Title
   Varchar(45), Author Varchar(25), HREF VARCHAR(125));
INSERT INTO OE.Catalog VALUES('1', 'Oracle Magazine', 'Oracle
   Publishing', 'Nov-Dec 2004', 'Database Resource Manager', 'Kimberly
   Floss', 'http://www.oracle.com/technology/oramag/oracle/04-
   nov/o64tuning.html');
INSERT INTO OE.Catalog VALUES('2', 'Oracle Magazine', 'Oracle
   Publishing', 'Nov-Dec 2004', 'From ADF UIX to JSF', 'Jonas
   Jacobi','http://www.oracle.com/technology/oramag/oracle/04-
   nov/o64jsf.html');
INSERT INTO OE.Catalog VALUES('3', 'Oracle Magazine', 'Oracle
   Publishing', 'March-April 2005', 'Starting with Oracle ADF ',
   'Steve Muench', 'http://www.oracle.com/technology/oramag/oracle/05-
   mar/o25window.html');
```

Creating a Panel Grid by Binding Rows

In this section we will create a panel grid by binding rows to the panel grid. First, we will create an empty panel grid by specifying the number of columns in the panel grid. Subsequently, we will add JSF UI components to the empty panel grid from the JSF HTML Component Palette. The components added to an empty panel grid automatically get added in the specified number of columns. To create a JSF panel grid, only the number of columns needs to be specified.

In this section, we will generate a panel grid of output labels, an input text field, output text fields, and command buttons. We will add a panel grid to a JSF page and add UI components from the Component Palette to the panel grid. We will create a panel grid from the fields of a journal catalog. The example journal catalog in the `Catalog` table has catalog id, journal, publisher, edition, title, author and url href fields. In the JSF application, the values for the various output text fields are retrieved from the Oracle database for a specified input catalog id. First, create a project for creating a panel grid.

Next, add a JSF page to the project with **File | New**. In the **New Gallery** window, select **Web Tier | JSF** in **Categories** and **JSF JSP** in **Items**. In the Create JSF JSP wizard select **J2EE 1.4** in the **Web Application** window and click on **Next**. In the **JSP File** window specify a **File Name** and click on **Next**. In the **Component Binding** window select the **Automatically Expose UI Components in a New Managed Bean**. The backing bean name, class and package are pre-specified. Click on **Next**.

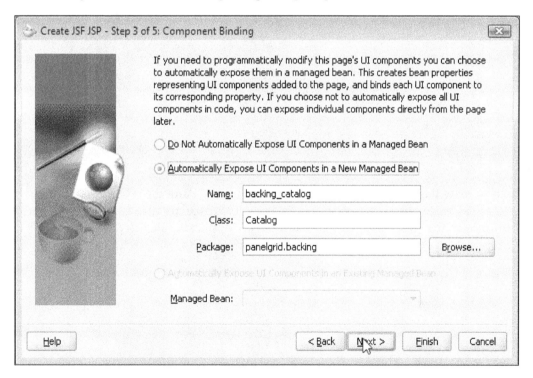

In the **Error Page Options** window, select the default settings, which are to not use an error page, and click **Next**. In the **Tag Libraries** window, the default libraries (JSF Core 1.0 and JSF HTML 1.0) are selected by default. Click **Next**. In the **HTML Options** window, select the default settings and click on **Next**. In the **Finish** window, click on **Finish**. A JSF page gets added to the project. Add the **JDeveloper** CSS stylesheet to the JSF JSP page. Add a **Heading 2** header **JSF Panel Grid**. Next, add a Panel Grid to the JSF page. Position the cursor below the heading in the JSF page and select Panel Grid in the JSF HTML Component Palette.

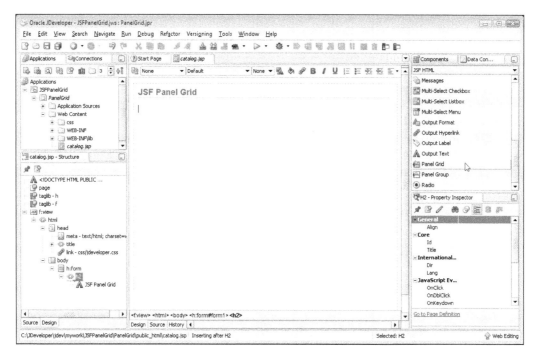

In the **Create PanelGrid Wizard,** click on **Next**. In the **PanelGrid Options** window select the **Create empty panel grid** radio button and specify the **Number of Columns** in the panel grid, **2** in the example JSF application. Click on **Finish**.

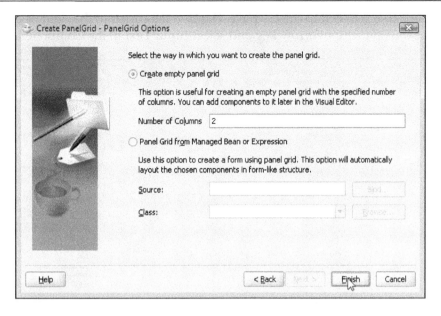

An empty JSF Panel Grid is added to the JSF page. Next, we will add components from the Component Palette to the panel grid. The components added to the empty panel grid are arranged in two columns. Position the cursor in the panel grid and select **Output Label** in the Component Palette.

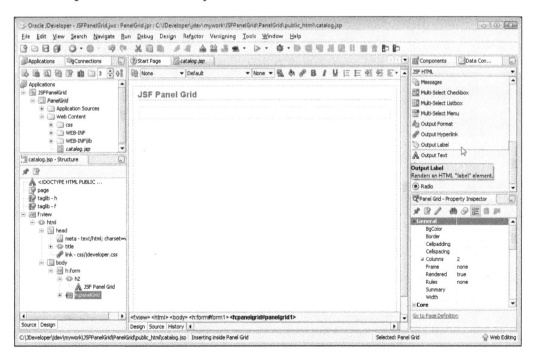

An Output Label is added to the JSF page. Position the cursor to the right of the output label with the right arrow key and select **Input Text** in the Component Palette.

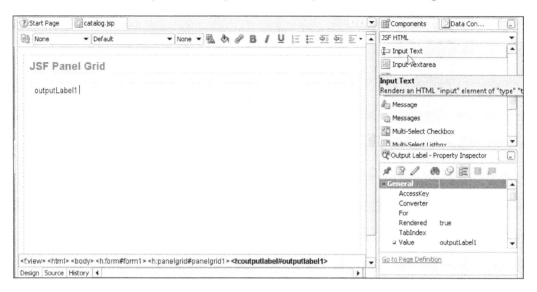

An input text field gets added to the JSF page. To add another component to the JSF page, position the cursor to the right of the previous component with the right arrow key. Next, add an **Output Label**. The output label gets added in a new row as the panel grid has only two columns.

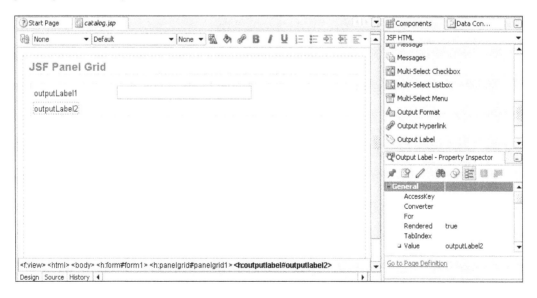

Add **Output Text** fields and **Output Label**s to the panel grid to four rows. In the fifth row add a **Output Label** and a **Output Hyperlink.**

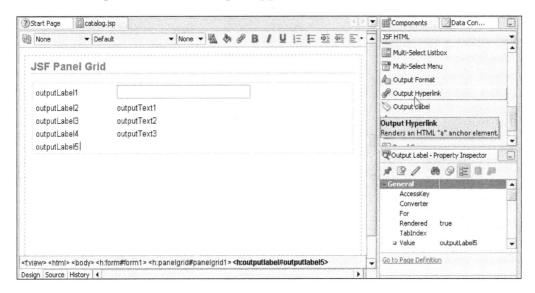

Next, we will add an **Output Text** component to the **Output Hyperlink** component. Select the **Output Hyperlink** component in the JSF page and select **Output Text** in the Component Palette. An output text field gets added to the output hyperlink component. An output hyperlink is a UI component that is similar to a `<a/>` component in a HTML page. The output text in the output link is text that gets displayed in the hyperlink.

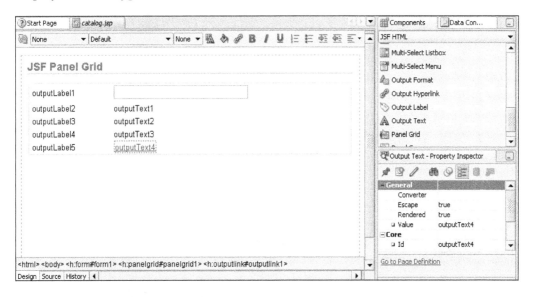

Add another row of **Output Label** and **Output Text** components. Next, add a row of command buttons to the panel grid.

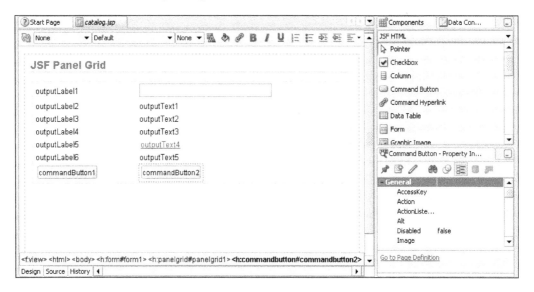

In the **Property Inspector**, set the text on the **Output Labels** and the command buttons. To specify the text value for a component, click on the component and specify the text value in the **Value** property in the **Property Inspector**.

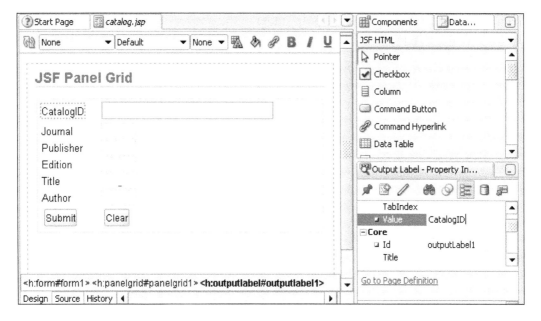

The example JSF application also demonstrates the data conversion and validation provided by the JSF specification. By specifying a **Validator** for a component the component value may be validated to be within a specified range, and by specifying a **Converter** for a component, the component value may be converted to the specified converter type. Specify the `validateLongRange` validator for the `Catalog ID` input text field:

```
<f:validateLongRange minimum="1" maximum="3"/>
```

If the value in the Catalog ID input field is not within the specified range of 1 and 3 a validation error gets generated. The different types of validators provided by the JSF are listed in the following table:

Validator	Description
validateLongRange	Validates a long value to be within a specified range.
validateLength	Validates the length of a String value to be within a specified range.
validateDoubleRange	Validates a double value to be within the specified range.

Register an `Integer` data type converter with the Catalog ID input text field:

```
<f:converter converterId="javax.faces.Integer" />
```

The value specified in the input text field gets converted to `java.lang.Integer` type. Next, add a message component to display an error message by the Catalog ID input text field. Add the input text and message components to a panel group component. Select the `catalog.jsp` node in the **Applications Navigator** and select the **Source** tab in the editor window. Replace the `<h:inputText binding="#{backing_catalog.inputText1}" id="inputText1"/>` component with the following `h:panelGroup` component.

```
<h:panelGroup>
    <h:inputText binding="#{backing_catalog.inputText1}"
                                   id="inputText1">
     <f:converter converterId="javax.faces.Integer" />
     <f:validateLongRange minimum="1" maximum="3"/>
    </h:inputText>
    <h:message for="inputText1"/>
</h:panelGroup>
```

We have added the h:panelGroup component declaratively. JDeveloper also has the provision to add the panelGroup component when adding the inputText component using the **surround with** option. Next, add a action method for the command buttons. Select the catalog.jsp node in **Applications Navigator** and select the **Design** tab. Double click on the **Submit** command button. In the **Bind Action Property** window, select the managed Bean backing_catalog and backing bean method as commandButton1_action. Add an import statement for the java.sql package to the backing bean class panelgrid.backing.Catalog.java.

In the command button action method query the example database table OE.CATALOG with the Catalog ID specified in the input field. Load the Oracle JDBC driver oracle.jdbc.OracleDriver using the Class.forName method. Create a Connection object using the getConnection method of the DriverManager class. Create a Statement object from the Connection object using the createStatement method. Specify the result set type as scrollable and result set concurrency as read-only. Retrieve the Catalog ID input in the JSF page in the **Input Text** field by invoking the getValue method on the backing bean attribute for the **Input Text**. Run an SQL query using the executeQuery method to generate a ResultSet. Set the values retrieved in the result set in the output text fields and the output hyperlink using the setValue method. The following listing shows the commandButton1_action method:

```
public String commandButton1_action() {
            // Add event code here...
  ResultSet rs=null;
        try{
            Class.forName("oracle.jdbc.OracleDriver");
            String url="jdbc:oracle:thin:@localhost:1521:ORCL";
            Connection connection =
            DriverManager.getConnection(url,"OE", "pw");
    Statement stmt=connection.createStatement(ResultSet.
                TYPE_SCROLL_INSENSITIVE, ResultSet.CONCUR_READ_ONLY);
    String query="SELECT * FROM OE.CATALOG WHERE CATALOGID=
                            "+inputText1.getValue();
            rs=stmt.executeQuery(query);
            rs.next();
            outputText1.setValue(rs.getString("Journal"));
            outputText2.setValue(rs.getString("Publisher"));
            outputText3.setValue(rs.getString("Edition"));
            outputLink1.setValue(rs.getString("HRef"));
            outputText4.setValue(rs.getString("Title"));
            outputText5.setValue(rs.getString("Author"));
              rs.close();
              stmt.close();
              connection.close();
              }catch(SQLException e){
              }catch(ClassNotFoundException e){
```

```
                }
        return null;
    }
```

The SQL query handling may also be specified in a server-side helper class instead of directly in the managed bean. The **Clear** button clears the fields in the JSF page. Double click on the **Clear** command button in the **Design** mode. In the **Bind Action Property** window, select the `backing_catalog` managed bean and the `commandButton2_action` method. Modify the `commandButton2_action` method to set the output text field values to an empty string. The `commandButton2_action` method is listed below:

```
public String commandButton2_action() {
            // Add event code here...
        outputText1.setValue("");
        outputText2.setValue("");
        outputText3.setValue("");
        outputText4.setValue("");
        outputLink1.setValue("");
        outputText5.setValue("");
        return null;
    }
```

Right-click on the JSF JSP page `catalog.jsp` in the **Applications Navigator** and select **Run**. The JSF Panel Grid gets displayed. The output labels and input text field/output text fields are displayed in two columns.

Specify a Catalog ID in the input field and select the **Submit** button. The database table column values corresponding to the specified catalog id are displayed in the panel grid. The title is displayed as a hyperlink, which may be selected to display the referred document.

The output text fields may be reset to empty text fields by selecting the **Clear** button. Next, we will demonstrate the validation of the input text value. Specify a Catalog Id input text value that is not within the validator range of 1 and 3 and click on the **Submit** button:

A validation error is generated to indicate that the specified Catalog ID is not in the range specified in the validator.

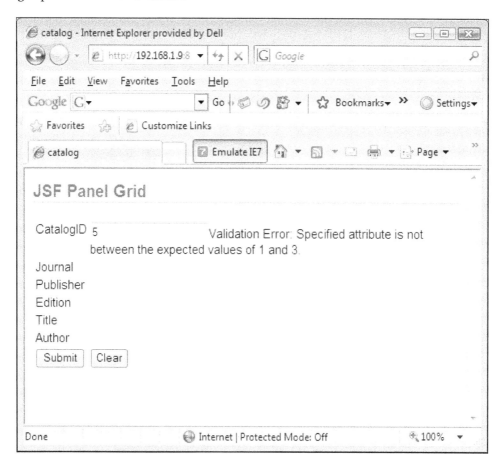

In this section, we created a JSF panel grid by binding two columns to the panel grid and subsequently adding JSF components to the empty panel grid from the Component Palette.

Creating a Panel Grid by Binding a Managed Bean

In this section, we will create a panel grid by binding a managed bean to the panel grid in the **Create PanelGrid Wizard**. We had used a similar managed bean binding to create a Data Table in the previous chapter. A managed bean is a Java object that represents a resource. The example panel grid is an input form to update a journal catalog in Oracle database. The procedure to create a panel grid by binding a managed bean is as follows.

1. Create a Java Bean class to represent the different fields in a journal catalog.
2. Create a managed bean from the Java Bean class.
3. Bind the managed bean to a panel grid in a JSF page.

Delete the JSFPanelGrid application created in the pevious section and create a similar application and a project in **Applications-Navigator** for the panel grid. Generate a managed bean from a JavaBean class. A managed bean implements a resource, a JavaBean class in the example application. The JavaBean class has properties and getter/setter methods for the properties corresponding to the different columns in the example database table. Add a Java class to the project with **File | New**. In the **New Gallery** window select **General** in **Categories** and **Java Class** in **Items**. In the **Create Java Class** window specify the class name, **PanelGridBean**, and the package name, **example.panelgrid**. To the **PanelGridBean** copy the following listing.

```java
package example.panelgrid;
public class PanelGridBean
{
   private int catalogId;
   private String journal;
   private String publisher;
   private String edition;
   private String title;
   private String author;
   private String href;
   public PanelGridBean(){
   }
   public int getCatalogId(){
       return this.catalogId;
   }
   public void setCatalogId(int catalogId){
       this.catalogId=catalogId;
   }
   public String getJournal(){
       return this.journal;
   }
   public void setJournal(String journal){
       this.journal=journal;
   }
   public String getPublisher(){
       return this.publisher;
   }
   public void setPublisher(String publisher){
       this.publisher=publisher;
   }
   public String getEdition(){
```

```
            return this.edition;
      }
      public void setEdition(String edition){
            this.edition=edition;
      }
      public String getTitle(){
            return this.title;
      }
      public void setTitle(String title){
            this.title=title;
      }
      public String getAuthor(){
            return this.author;
      }
      public void setAuthor(String author){
             this.author=author;
      }
      public String getHref(){
            return this.href;
      }
      public void setHref(String href){
            this.href=href;
      }
}
```

Next, add a JSF JSP page, catalog.jsp, to the project with **File | New**. In the **New Gallery** window select **Web Tier | JSF** in **Categories** and select **JSF JSP** in **Items**. Click on **OK**. Next, we will create a managed bean from the Java Bean class. Open the **faces-config.xml** configuration file node in the **Applications Navigator** and select the **Overview** tab in the editor window. Select the **Managed Beans** node (if not already selected). Click on **New** to add a new managed bean.

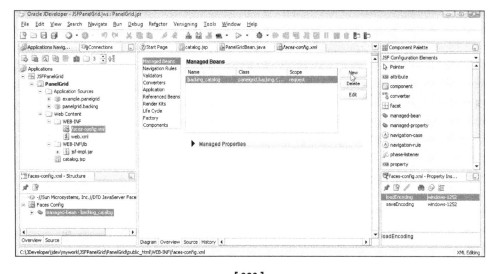

In the **Create Managed Bean** window, specify the managed bean name,
PanelGridMBean, and select the Javabean class, **PanelGridBean,** as the **Class** for
the managed bean. Select **request** as the **Scope** and click on **OK**. A managed bean,
`PanelGridMBean` gets created.

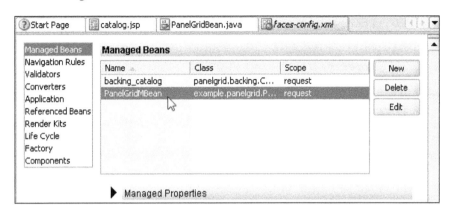

The JSF panel grid may also be used to specify initial values for the input text fields
in an input form. Specify the initial values of managed bean properties in the
`faces-config.xml` file. Select the **faces-config.xml** file node and the **Source** tab. To
the `PanelGridMBean`, add the initial values of the managed bean properties with the
`<managed-property/>` element. The `managed-bean` element in `faces-config.xml`
with the managed bean properties specified is listed:

```
<managed-bean>
    <managed-bean-name>backing_catalog</managed-bean-name>
    <managed-bean-class>panelgrid.backing.Catalog</managed-bean-class>
    <managed-bean-scope>request</managed-bean-scope>
    <!--oracle-jdev-comment:managed-bean-jsp-link:1catalog.jsp-->
  </managed-bean>
  <managed-bean>
    <managed-bean-name>PanelGridMBean</managed-bean-name>
    <managed-bean-class>example.panelgrid.PanelGridBean</managed-
        bean-class>
    <managed-bean-scope>request</managed-bean-scope>
<managed-property>
<property-name>catalogId</property-name>
<value>1</value>
</managed-property>
<managed-property>
<property-name>journal</property-name>
<value>Oracle Magazine</value>
</managed-property>
<managed-property>
<property-name>publisher</property-name>
```

```
<value>Oracle Publishing</value>
</managed-property>
<managed-property>
<property-name>edition</property-name>
<value>Nov-Dec 2004</value>
</managed-property>
<managed-property>
<property-name>title</property-name>
<value>Database Resource Manager</value>
</managed-property>
<managed-property>
<property-name>author</property-name>
<value>Kimberly Floss</value>
</managed-property>
<managed-property>
<property-name>href</property-name>
<value>http://www.oracle.com/technology/oramag/oracle/04-
    nov/o64tuning.html</value>
</managed-property>
 </managed-bean>
```

Add a panel grid to the JSF page, `catalog.jsp`. Position the cursor in the JSF page and select **Panel Grid** in the **Component Palette**.

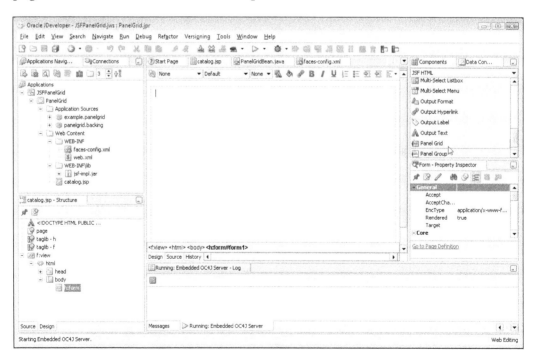

The **Create PanelGrid Wizard** gets started. Click on **Next**. In the **PanelGrid Options** window select the **Panel Grid from Managed Bean or Expression** radio button. Click on **Bind** to bind the panel grid with a managed bean.

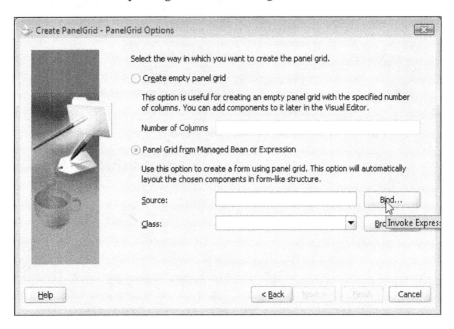

In the **Expression Builder** window, select the **JSF Managed Beans | PanelGridMBean** node and add the **PanelGridMBean** to the **Expression** field with the **>** button.

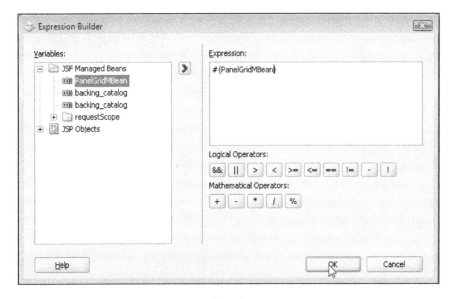

In the **PanelGrid Options** window, select the Javabean class, **PanelGridBean** in the **Class** field and click on **Next**.

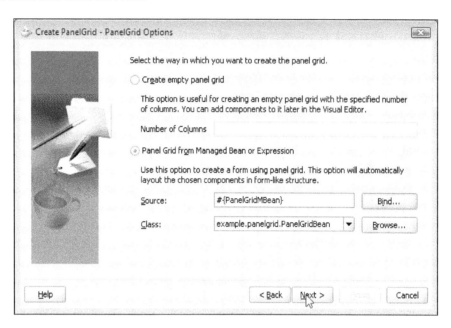

In the **Fields Selection** window sort the order of the selected fields to correspond to the OE.CATALOG database table columns. Click on **Next**.

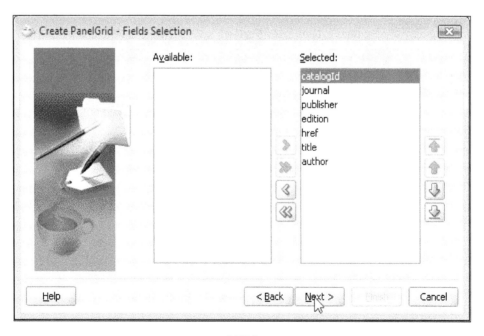

In the **Components Detail** select the **<header>** row and specify a header in the **Label** field. Select the `Catalog Id` row and select the **Type** as **Input Text**. Specify the `Catalog Id` field as a required field by selecting the **Required** checkbox. Select the **Associate Message** checkbox to add a message component column to the panel grid. The error messages get displayed in the message component. Click on the **Advanced** button to register a validator and a converter with the Catalog Id input text field. A JSF validator is used to validate input fields values and a JSF converter is used to convert input field values.

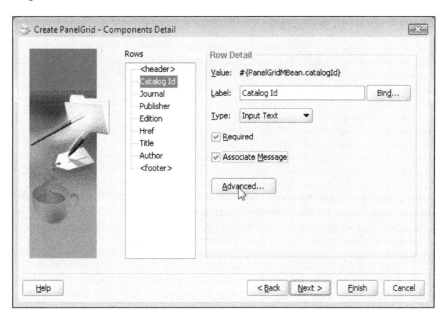

In the **Advanced Properties** window, select the **Integer** converter. The Catalog Id input text field value gets converted to `Integer` type with the converter.

Next, select the **Validator** tab and select the **Validate Long Range** validator. Specify the **Minimum** and **Maximum** values for the validator. The validator validates the Catalog Id input field value to be within the specified range.

In the **Components Detail** window, specify the **Type** as **Input Text** for the other fields and click on **Next**. In the **Finish** window click on **Finish**. A JSF Panel grid is added to the JSF page `catalog.jsp`. Add a command button **Submit** to the JSF page.

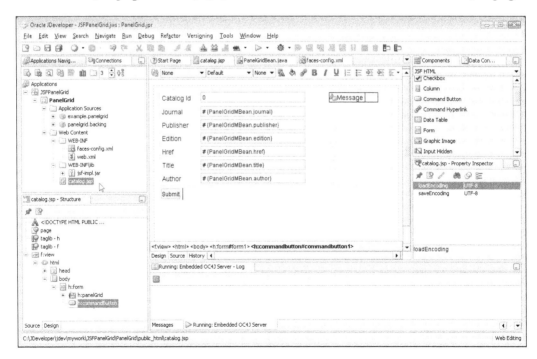

Next, we will modify the command button action method in the backing bean. Double-click on the command button in the **Design** tab. In the **Bind Action property** window select the default settings for **Managed Bean** and **Method** and click on **OK**. In the command button action method retrieve the input field values and update the database table for the specified catalog id. Add an import statement to the backing bean class for the java.sql package. In the commandButton1_action method load the Oracle JDBC driver oracle.jdbc.OracleDriver using the Class.forName method.

Create a Connection object using the getConnection method of DriverManager class. Create a Statement object from the Connection object using createStatement method. Specify the result set type as scrollable and result set concurrency as read-only. Retrieve the Input Text field values using getValue method. Update database table Catalog by running an UPDATE SQL statement using the executeQuery method. The commandButton1_action method is listed below.

```
public String commandButton1_action() {
        // Add event code here...
    ResultSet rs=null;
        try{Class.forName("oracle.jdbc.OracleDriver");
            String url="jdbc:oracle:thin:@localhost:1521:ORCL";
            Connection connection =
            DriverManager.getConnection(url,"OE", "pw");
Statement
  stmt=connection.createStatement(ResultSet.TYPE_SCROLL_INSENSITIVE,
  ResultSet.CONCUR_READ_ONLY);
            int catalogId=((Integer)(inputText0.getValue())).
intValue();
            String journal=(String)inputText1.getValue();
            String publisher=(String)inputText2.getValue();
            String edition=(String)inputText3.getValue();
            String title=(String)inputText4.getValue();
            String author=(String)inputText5.getValue();
            String href=(String)inputText6.getValue();
String query="UPDATE OE.CATALOG SET
  JOURNAL="+"'"+journal+"'"+","+"PUBLISHER="+"'"+publisher+ "'"+
  ","+"EDITION="+"'"+edition+"'"+","+ "TITLE=" +"'"+title+"'"+","+"
  AUTHOR="+"'"+author+"'"+", " +" HREF="+"'"+href+"'"+"WHERE
  CATALOGID="+"'"+catalogId+"'";
stmt.executeUpdate(query);stmt.close();connection.close();}
  catch(SQLException e){System.out.println(e.getMessage());}
  catch(ClassNotFoundException e)
  {System.out.println(e.getMessage());}return null;}
```

Right-click on the **catalog.jsp** node and select **Run**. The panel grid with the initial values specified in the input fields is displayed:

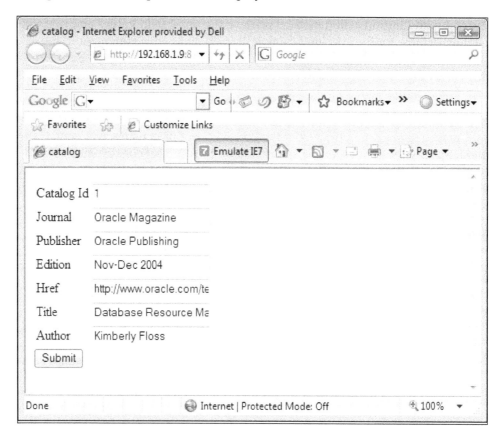

To update a database table row specify the Catalog Id for the row and the input field values, and click on the **Submit** button. The input field **Catalog Id** is specified as a **Required** field. If an input value is not specified in the **Catalog Id** field a validation error is generated. The validation error gets displayed in the message component column.

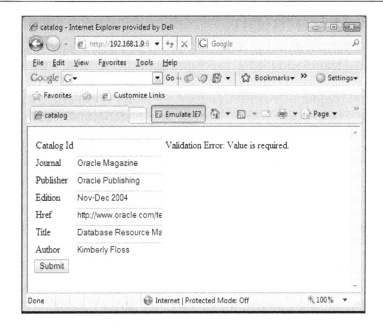

Next, we will demonstrate the validator registered with the **Catalog Id** input field. Specify a Catalog Id input value not within the range of 1 and 3 and click on the **Submit** button. A validation error is generated in the message column.

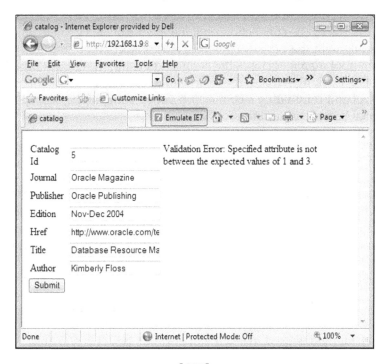

JDBC 4.0 Version

In a JDeveloper version that supports JDBC 4.0 in its embedded OC4J server, we may add the JDBC 4.0 features to the JSF panel grid application. JDBC 4.0 provides new features such as enhanced connection management, automatic driver loading using Java SE Service Provider mechanism, support for wrapper pattern to access vendor-specific extensions to JDBC API, statement pooling, and support for Java SE chained exceptions facility and categorization of exceptions.

For the JDBC 4.0 version of the JSF panel grid application, we need to download the Oracle database 11g JDBC 4.0 drivers JAR file, `ojdbc6.jar`, from `http://www.oracle.com/technology/software/tech/java/sqlj_jdbc/htdocs/jdbc_111060.html`. The JDBC 4.0 driver requires JDK 6.0. Therefore, we need to set the J2SE version to JDK 6.0 in JDeveloper. To set the JDK version select **Tools | Project Properties**. In the **Project Properties** window select **Libraries** and in the **J2SE Version** field specify the JDK 6.0 version.

The JDBC 4.0 drivers JAR file, `ojdbc6.jar`, contains a `META-INF/services/java.sq.Driver` file that specifies the Oracle JDBC driver class `oracle.jdbc.OracleDriver`. The `java.sql.Driver` field is included in `ojdbc6.jar` for the Java SE Service Provider mechanism to load JDBC drivers. In the JDBC 4.0 version of `commandButton1_action()` method in the backing bean class, remove the line in which the Oracle JDBC driver is loaded using the `Class.forName()` method.

JDBC 4.0 provides connection state tracking using the `isValid()` method in the `Connection` interface. The connection pool manager tests if a connection has become unusable with the `isValid` method. If a connection has become unusable, the connection pool manager closes the connection using the `close()` method. Connection state tracking reduces the overhead of closing all the connections in a connection pool and reinitiating a connection pool if some of the connections in the connection pool become unusable.

Another connection management feature JDBC 4.0 provides is connection client identification. Sometimes some of the client connections bog down the application by consuming excessive CPU. Earlier versions of JDBC did not have the provision to identify such client connections. The Connection interface in JDBC 4.0 has two new methods `setClientInfo` and `getClientInfo` to set and get client info properties. Thus, a `Connection` object is identified by its client info properties. The different client info properties supported by a database may be obtained using the `getClientInfoProperties` method of the `DatabaseMetaData` interface. The standard client info properties are `ApplicationName`, `ClientUser`, and `Hostname`.

In addition to `PreparedStatements` pooling JDBC 4.0 provides `Statement` pooling. Frequently used `Statements` may be pooled using the `setPoolable()` method. The `isPoolable()` method is used to test if a `Statement` object is poolable.

JDBC 4.0 supports the wrapper pattern in the Wrapper interface to access vendor-specific extensions to JDBC API. Oracle JDBC extensions are available in the oracle.jdbc. package. For example, to access the nonstandard methods in the OracleStatement interface, which extends the Statement interface, test if a Statement object is a wrapper for the OracleStatement interface using the isWrapperFor method. If the Statement object is a wrapper, unwrap the OracleStatement interface using the unwrap() method to create a OracleStatement object. Subsequently, the defineColumnType method of the OracleStatement object may be invoked to define column types. Defining column types saves the JDBC driver a roundtrip to the database to find the column types. When an SQL query is run the database table data is fetched into the defined column types in the ResultSet.

JDBC 4.0 provides support for the Java SE chained exceptions facility, also called the cause facility, to retrieve chained exceptions. JDBC 4.0 also retrieves non-SQLException chained exceptions. In the JDBC 4.0 version of the panel grid application, the chained exceptions and chained causes are retrieved using the enhanced for-each loop introduced in J2SE 5.0.

The JDBC 4.0 version of the commandButton1_action() method to retrieve the field values for a specified Catalog ID is listed as follows:

```
public String commandButton1_action() {
            // Add event code here...
  ResultSet rs=null;
        try{

                String url="jdbc:oracle:thin:@localhost:1521:ORCL";
                Connection connection =
                DriverManager.getConnection(url,"OE", "pw");
connection.setClientInfo("ApplicationName","OracleApp");
connection.setClientInfo("ClientUser","OracleUser");
connection.setClientInfo("ClientHostname","OracleHost");

Statement stmt=connection.createStatement(ResultSet.TYPE_SCROLL_
INSENSITIVE, ResultSet.CONCUR_READ_ONLY);

DatabaseMetaData metaData=connection.getMetaData();
if(metaData.supportsStatementPooling()){
if(stmt.isPoolable())
stmt.setPoolable(true);
}

Class class = Class.forName("oracle.jdbc.OracleStatement");
if(stmt.isWrapperFor(class)) {
OracleStatement oracleStmt = (OracleStatement)stmt.unwrap(class);
oracleStmt.defineColumnType(1, OracleTypes.VARCHAR);
```

```
oracleStmt.defineColumnType(2, OracleTypes.VARCHAR);
oracleStmt.defineColumnType(3, OracleTypes.VARCHAR);
oracleStmt.defineColumnType(4, OracleTypes.VARCHAR);
oracleStmt.defineColumnType(5, OracleTypes.VARCHAR);
oracleStmt.defineColumnType(6, OracleTypes.VARCHAR);
oracleStmt.defineColumnType(7, OracleTypes.VARCHAR);
String query="SELECT * FROM OE.CATALOG WHERE CATALOGID="+inputText1.
getValue();
                rs=stmt.executeQuery(query);
rs=stmt.executeQuery("SELECT * FROM OE.CATALOG");

outputText1.setValue(rs.getString("Journal"));
        outputText2.setValue(rs.getString("Publisher"));
        outputText3.setValue(rs.getString("Edition"));
        outputLink1.setValue(rs.getString("HRef"));
        outputText4.setValue(rs.getString("Title"));
        outputText5.setValue(rs.getString("Author"));
} rs.close();
stmt.close();
connection.close();
                }catch(SQLException e){for(Throwable e : exception ) {
out.println("Error encountered: " + e);
}
        return null;
    }
```

Summary

JSF panel grid is a UI component used to display a set of UI components in a specified number of columns in a grid layout. In this chapter, the panel grid is used to display catalog data retrieved from a database. Panel grid is also used to convert and validate input field values. A panel grid may be created in Create PanelGrid Wizard either by binding rows or by binding a managed bean. In the JDBC 4.0 version of the panel grid application, we added JDBC 4.0 features automatic driver loading, client info properties, statement pooling, and wrapper pattern.

12
Creating a Report with JasperReports

JasperReports is a Java reporting tool to prepare reports for presentation. A JasperReports report is an HTML, PDF, Excel XLS, CSV, or a XML report. The data for a JasperReports report is static data or is data retrieved from a database table with an SQL query. JasperReports is designed to be included in Java/J2EE applications to generate dynamic presentation reports.

In this chapter, we will create JasperReports reports in JDeveloper. JasperReports uses JDBC to connect to database and retrieve data for a JasperReports report. A JDBC connection with the Oracle database 10g is established in the JasperReports configuration file (`.xml` file). We will create a PDF report and an Excel spreadsheet report using JasperReports. In this chapter we will learn the following:

- Create a PDF Report with JasperReports
- Create a Excel Spreadsheet with JasperReports

Setting the Environment

Download the open-source JasperReports tool JAR file `jasperreports-2.0.5.jar`. Download the iText Java-PDF library `itext-2.1.0.jar`. Download the Jakarta-POI ZIP file `poi-bin-3.0.2-FINAL-20080204.zip`. Download `Commons Digester 1.8` and extract the ZIP file to a directory. Install the JDeveloper 10g IDE Studio Edition Complete Install. Download and install the Oracle database from: `http://www.oracle.com/database/index.html` 10g.

Create an example database table, `Catalog` from which a JasperReports PDF report and Excel report will be generated. Create the database table in Oracle SQL *Plus. The SQL script to create the example table is listed below.

```
CREATE TABLE OE.Catalog(CatalogId VARCHAR(25), Journal VARCHAR(25),
   Publisher Varchar(25),Edition VARCHAR(25), Title Varchar(45),
   Author Varchar(25));
INSERT INTO OE.Catalog VALUES('catalog1', 'Oracle Magazine', 'Oracle
   Publishing', 'July-August 2005', 'Tuning Undo Tablespace',
   'Kimberly Floss');
INSERT INTO OE.Catalog VALUES('catalog2', 'Oracle Magazine', 'Oracle
   Publishing','March-April 2005', 'Starting with Oracle ADF ', 'Steve
   Muench');
```

Create a JDBC connection to the Oracle database from the JDeveloper IDE. To create a connection select the **Connections** tab, select the **Database** node in the **Connections Navigator**, right-click on the **Database** node, and select **New Database Connection**. In the Create Database Connection (**Type**) window displayed, specify a **Connection Name** and set **Connection Type** to **Oracle(JDBC)**.

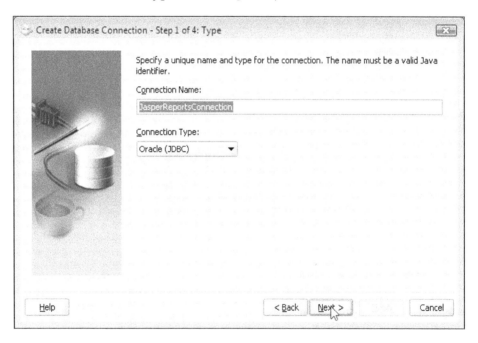

Click on **Next**. In the **Authentication** window, specify the **Username** and **Password** and click on **Next**. In the **Connection** window, specify the **Driver type, Host Name, JDBC Port, SID** and click on **Next**.

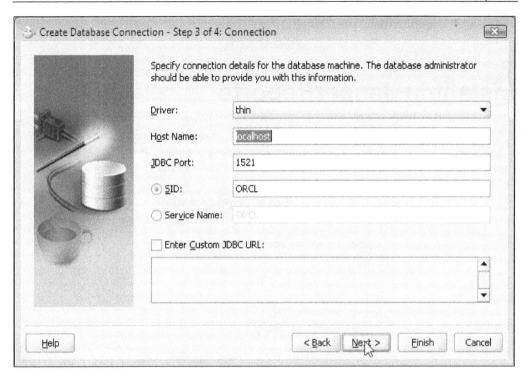

In the **Test** window, click on **Test Connection**. If a connection with the database is established, a success message is displayed. Click on **Finish** to complete the connection configuration. A connection node gets added to the **Connections Navigator**. The JDBC connection `JasperReportsConnection` is available as a JNDI resource `jdbc/JasperReportsConnectionDS`. The data source will be used to retrieve data from the database to generate a JasperReports report.

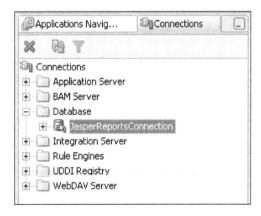

We also need to download and install Adobe Acrobat Reader for the PDF report and MS Excel for the Excel report.

Installing JasperReports

In this section, a JasperReports project is created in JDeveloper IDE and the libraries required for the JasperReports report are created. First, select **File | New** in the JDeveloper IDE. In the **New Gallery** window, select **General** in the **Categories** listed and select **Application** in the **Items** listed. Click on the **OK** button. Specify an **Application Name** in the **Create Application** window. Click on the **OK** button. Specify a **Project Name** in the **Create Project** window and click on the **OK** button. A JasperReports application and project is added to the **Applications-Navigator**.

Next, add libraries required to generate a JasperReports report to the project. Select the JasperReports project node in the **Applications-Navigator** and select **Tools | Project Properties**. In the **Project Properties** window, select the **Libraries** node. Add a library with the **Add Library** button and add a JAR/Directory with the **Add Jar/Directory** button. Add the libraries/JAR files listed in the following table.

Library/Jar/Zip	Description
`jasperreports-2.0.5.jar`	JasperReports API.
`Commons BeanUtils`	JavaBeans utility classes
`Commons Collections`	Collections framework extension classes
`Commons Digester 1.8 jar`	Classes for processing XML documents
`Commons Logging`	Logging classes
`poi-bin-3.0.2-FINAL-20080204.jar`	Jakarta POI API to generate an Excel document
`itext-2.1.0`	PDF library
`Oracle XML Parser v2`	XML parser API

The libraries created are listed in the **Libraries** window. Click on the **OK** button in the **Project Properties** window.

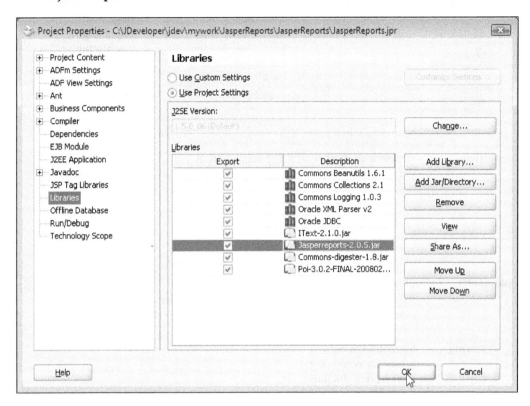

Configuring the JasperReports Configuration File

A JasperReports report design is specified in a XML configuration file. In this section, the XML configuration file, `catalog.xml`, is configured for a PDF report. A JasperReports configuration file is an XML file based on the `jasperreport.dtd` DTD. The root element of the configuration file is `jasperReport`. Some of the other elements (with commonly used sub elements and attributes) in a JasperReports XML file are listed in following table:

XML Element	Description	Sub Elements	Attributes
jasperReport	Root Element	reportFont, parameter, queryString, field, variable, group, title, pageHeader, columnHeader, detail, columnFooter, pageFooter.	name, columnCount, pageWidth, pageHeight, orientation, columnWidth, columnSpacing, leftMargin, rightMargin, topMargin, bottomMargin.
reportFont	Report level font definitions.	Report level font definitions.	name, isDefault, fontName,size, isBold, isItalic, isUnderline, isStrikeThrough, pdfFontName, pdfEncoding, isPdfEmbedded
parameter	Object references used in generating a report. Referenced with P${name}	parameterDescription, defaultValueExpression.	name,class
queryString	Specifies the SQL query for retrieving data from a database.	-	-
field	Database table columns included in report. Referenced With F${name}	fieldDescription	name,class
variable	Variable used in the report XML file. Referenced with V${name}	variableExpression, initialValueExpression	name,class
title	Report title.	band	-
pageHeader	Page Header	band	-
columnHeader	Specifies the different columns in the report.	band	-
detail	Specifies the column values.	band	-
columnFooter	Column footer	band	-
pageFooter	Page footer.	band	-

A band in a report represents a report section. A `band` element includes `staticText` and `textElement` elements. A `staticText` element is used to add static text to a report, for example column headers. A `textElement` element is used to add dynamically generated text to a report, for example column values retrieved from a database table. In the *Generating a PDF Report* section, a JasperReports PDF report is generated from the example `Catalog` table. The `queryString` of the example JasperReports configuration XML file, `catalog.xml`, specifies the SQL query to retrieve the data for the report.

```
<queryString><![CDATA[SELECT CatalogId, Journal, Publisher, Edition,
   Title, Author FROM OE.Catalog]]></queryString>
```

The `reportElement` elements specify the `ARIAL_NORMAL`, `ARIAL_BOLD`, and `ARIAL_ITALIC` fonts used in the report. The PDF report has the columns `CatalogId`, `Journal`, `Publisher`, `Edition`, `Title`, `Author`. The JasperReports configuration file, `catalog.xml`, is listed below.

```xml
<?xml version='1.0' encoding='utf-8'?>
<!DOCTYPE jasperReport PUBLIC "-//JasperReports//DTD Report Design//
EN"
"http://jasperreports.sourceforge.net/dtds/jasperreport.dtd">
<jasperReport name="PDFReport" pageWidth="1250">
<!-- Specify report fonts. -->
<reportFont name="Arial_Normal" isDefault="true" fontName="Arial"
   size="15" isBold="false" isItalic="false"
isUnderline="false" isStrikeThrough="false" pdfFontName="Helvetica"
   pdfEncoding="Cp1252" isPdfEmbedded="false"/>
<reportFont name="Arial_Bold" isDefault="false" fontName="Arial"
   size="15" isBold="true" isItalic="false" isUnderline="false"
isStrikeThrough="false" pdfFontName="Helvetica-Bold"
   pdfEncoding="Cp1252" isPdfEmbedded="false"/>
   <reportFont name="Arial_Italic" isDefault="false" fontName="Arial"
      size="12" isBold="false" isItalic="true"
isUnderline="false" isStrikeThrough="false" pdfFontName="Helvetica-
   Oblique" pdfEncoding="Cp1252" isPdfEmbedded="false"/>
<!-- Specify report parameters. -->
<parameter name="ReportTitle" class="java.lang.String"/>
<!-- Specify SQL Query -->
<queryString><![CDATA[SELECT CatalogId, Journal, Publisher, Edition,
   Title, Author FROM Catalog]]></queryString>
<field name="CatalogId" class="java.lang.String"/>
<field name="Journal" class="java.lang.String"/>
<field name="Publisher" class="java.lang.String"/>
<field name="Edition" class="java.lang.String"/>
<field name="Title" class="java.lang.String"/>
```

```
<field name="Author" class="java.lang.String"/>
<!-- Specify report title.-->
<title>
    <band height="50">
      <textField>
        <reportElement x="350" y="0" width="200" height="50" />
        <textFieldExpression
            class="java.lang.String">$P{ReportTitle}
        </textFieldExpression>
      </textField>
    </band>
</title>
<!-- Specify page header.-->
 <pageHeader>
    <band>
    </band>
  </pageHeader>
<!-- Specify column headers.-->
 <columnHeader>
    <band height="20">
      <staticText>
        <reportElement x="0" y="0" width="100" height="20"/>
        <textElement>
          <font isUnderline="false" reportFont="Arial_Bold"/>
        </textElement>
        <text><![CDATA[CATALOG ID]]></text>
      </staticText>
     <staticText>
        <reportElement x="125" y="0" width="150" height="20"/>
        <textElement>
          <font isUnderline="false" reportFont="Arial_Bold"/>
        </textElement>
        <text><![CDATA[JOURNAL]]></text>
      </staticText>
      <staticText>
        <reportElement x="300" y="0" width="150" height="20"/>
        <textElement>
          <font isUnderline="false" reportFont="Arial_Bold"/>
        </textElement>
        <text><![CDATA[PUBLISHER]]></text>
      </staticText>
      <staticText>
        <reportElement x="475" y="0" width="150" height="20"/>
        <textElement>
```

```
              <font isUnderline="false" reportFont="Arial_Bold"/>
          </textElement>
          <text><![CDATA[EDITION]]></text>
      </staticText>
<staticText>
          <reportElement x="650" y="0" width="250" height="20"/>
          <textElement>
             <font isUnderline="false" reportFont="Arial_Bold"/>
          </textElement>
          <text><![CDATA[TITLE]]></text>
      </staticText>
      <staticText>
          <reportElement x="925" y="0" width="200" height="20"/>
          <textElement>
             <font isUnderline="false" reportFont="Arial_Bold"/>
          </textElement>
          <text><![CDATA[AUTHOR]]></text>
      </staticText>
    </band>
  </columnHeader>
<!-- Specify column data binding.-->
<detail>
    <band height="20">
      <textField>
         <reportElement x="0" y="0" width="100" height="20"/>
         <textFieldExpression
            class="java.lang.String"><![CDATA[$F{CatalogId}]]>
         </textFieldExpression>
      </textField>
      <textField pattern="0.00">
         <reportElement x="125" y="0" width="150" height="20"/>
         <textFieldExpression
            class="java.lang.String"><![CDATA[$F{Journal}]]>
         </textFieldExpression>
      </textField>
      <textField pattern="0.00">
         <reportElement x="300" y="0" width="150" height="20"/>
         <textFieldExpression
            class="java.lang.String"><![CDATA[$F{Publisher}]]>
         </textFieldExpression>
      </textField>
  <textField>
         <reportElement x="475" y="0" width="150" height="20"/>
         <textFieldExpression
```

```
                        class="java.lang.String"><![CDATA[$F{Edition}]]>
                  </textFieldExpression>
               </textField>
             <textField pattern="0.00">
                  <reportElement x="650" y="0" width="250" height="20"/>
                  <textFieldExpression
                     class="java.lang.String"><![CDATA[$F{Title}]]>
                  </textFieldExpression>
               </textField>
         <textField>
                  <reportElement x="925" y="0" width="200" height="20"/>
                  <textFieldExpression
                     class="java.lang.String"><![CDATA[$F{Author}]]>
                  </textFieldExpression>
               </textField>
            </band>
         </detail>
      <columnFooter>
         <band>
         </band>
      </columnFooter>
      <pageFooter>
         <band height="15">
            <staticText>
               <reportElement x="0" y="0" width="40" height="15"/>
                <textElement>
                 <font isUnderline="false" reportFont="Arial_Italic"/>
               </textElement>
               <text><![CDATA[Page #]]></text>
            </staticText>
            <textField>
               <reportElement x="40" y="0" width="100" height="15"/>
               <textElement>
                  <font isUnderline="false" reportFont="Arial_Italic"/>
               </textElement>
               <textFieldExpression
                  class="java.lang.Integer"><![CDATA[$V{PAGE_NUMBER}]]>
               </textFieldExpression>
            </textField>
         </band>
      </pageFooter>
      <summary>
         <band>
         </band>
      </summary>
   </jasperReport>
```

Generating a PDF Report

We will use the JasperReports classes and interfaces to generate a PDF file from the
`catalog.xml` file. Add an XML file to the JasperReports project with **File | New**.
In the **New Gallery** window, select **General | XML** in the **Categories** listed and
XML Document in the **Items** listed. Click on the **OK** button. Specify a **File Name**,
`catalog.xml`, in the **Create XML File** window and click on the **OK** button.

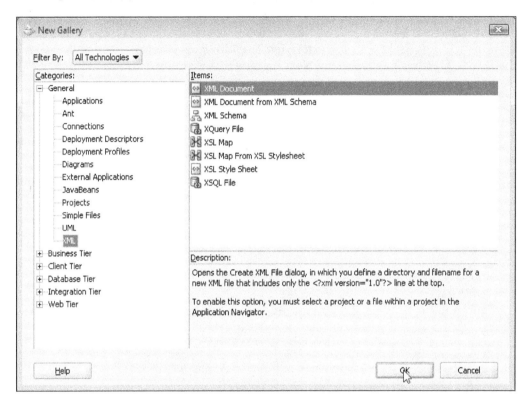

An XML document is added to the JasperReports project. Copy catalog.xml listing from the previous section to the XML document, catalog.xml. Save catalog.xml to the C:/JasperReports directory with **File | Save As**. Create a JSP to generate a JasperReports report. Right-click on the JasperReports project node and select **New**. In the **New Gallery** window, select **Web Tier | JSP** in the **Categories** listed and select JSP in the **Items** listed. Click on the **OK** button. In the **Create JSP Wizard**, click on **Next**. In the **Web Application** window, select **Servlet 2.4/JSP 2.0** and click on **Next**. In the **JSP File** window, specify catalog.jsp as the **File Name** and select the default **Directory Name**. Click on **Next**. Select the default selection in the **Error Page Options** window and click on **Next**. In the **Tag Libraries** window, click on **Next**. In the **HTML Options** page, click on **Next**. In the **Finish** window, click on **Finish**. JSP catalog.jsp is added to the JasperReports project.

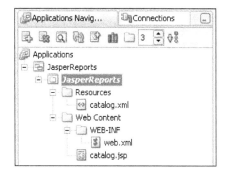

The JDBC data source, jdbc/JasperReportsConnectionDS, is required to be configured in the JSP web.xml configuration file. Add the following resource-ref element to the web.xml file:

```
<resource-ref>
<res-ref-name>jdbc/JasperReportsConnectionDS</res-ref-name>
<res-type>javax.sql.DataSource</res-type>
<res-auth>Container</res-auth>
</resource-ref>
```

In the catalog.jsp, first, import the JasperReports classes and interfaces:

```
<%@ page import="java.io.*, java.util.*, java.sql.Connection,javax.
sql.DataSource, javax.naming.InitialContext, net.sf.jasperreports.
engine.*, net.sf.jasperreports.engine.design.JasperDesign,net.
sf.jasperreports.engine.xml.JRXmlLoader" %>
```

Next, create a InputStream for the JasperReports configuration file, catalog.xml. Next, load the XML file with JRXmlLoader class static method load(). The load() method is overloaded and a XML configuration file may be loaded from a File object, an InputStream object, or a String object. The load() method returns a JasperDesign object.

```
InputStream input=new FileInputStream(new File("c:/JasperReports/
catalog.xml"));
JasperDesign design = JRXmlLoader.load(input);
```

A `JasperDesign` object represents the report design. Compile the report design file with the `JasperCompileManager` method `compileReport()`. The compilation of the report design file validates the JasperReports XML file (`catalog.xml`) with the `jaspereports.dtd` DTD and converts the report expressions in a ready-to-evaluate form. The `compileReport()` method returns a `JasperReport` object, which represents the compiled report.

```
JasperReport report = JasperCompileManager.compileReport(design);
```

Create a `Connection` object to retrieve data from the database to create a PDF file. Create a `InitialContext` object to lookup the data source JNDI with the `lookup()` method. Obtain a JDBC connection from the data source using the `getConnection()` method.

```
InitialContext initialContext = new InitialContext();
DataSource ds = (DataSource)initialContext.lookup
  ("java:comp/env/jdbc/JasperReportsConnectionDS");
Connection conn = ds.getConnection();
```

Generate a JasperReports report from the compiled report. Fill the compiled report with data from the database using the `fillReport()` method of the `JasperFillManager` class. The `fillReport()` method returns a `JasperPrint` object, which represents the report document that may be viewed, printed, or exported to other formats:

```
JasperPrint print =JasperFillManager.fillReport(report,parameters,
        conn);
```

The parameters in the `fillReport()` method consist of the parameter values specified in the `<parameter/>` elements of the XML configuration file. `Catalog.xml` has the parameter `ReportTile`, therefore specify a value for the `ReportTitle` parameter.

```
Map parameters = new HashMap();
parameters.put("ReportTitle", "PDF JasperReport");
```

A JasperReports report may be exported to a XML file, a PDF file, an HTML file, a CSV file, or a Excel XLS file. Export the generated JasperReports to a PDF file using the `exportReportToPdfStream()` method of the `JasperExportManager` class:

```
OutputStream output=new FileOutputStream(new File("c:/JasperReports/
catalog.pdf"));
JasperExportManager.exportReportToPdfStream(print, output);
```

The JSP file, `catalog.jsp`, is listed below:

```jsp
<%@ page contentType="text/html;charset=windows-1252"%>
<%@ page import="java.io.*, java.util.*, java.sql.Connection,javax.
sql.DataSource, javax.naming.InitialContext,
net.sf.jasperreports.engine.*, net.sf.jasperreports.engine.design.
JasperDesign,net.sf.jasperreports.engine.xml.JRXmlLoader" %>
<%InputStream input=new FileInputStream(new
  File("c:/JasperReports/catalog.xml"));
  JasperDesign design = JRXmlLoader.load(input);
  JasperReport report = JasperCompileManager.compileReport(design);
  Map parameters = new HashMap();
  parameters.put("ReportTitle", "PDF JasperReport");
    InitialContext initialContext = new InitialContext();
    DataSource ds = (DataSource)initialContext.lookup
        ("java:comp/env/jdbc/JasperReportsConnectionDS");
    Connection conn = ds.getConnection();
    JasperPrint print = JasperFillManager.fillReport(report,
     parameters, conn);
    OutputStream output=new FileOutputStream
        (new File("c:/JasperReports/catalog.pdf"));
    JasperExportManager.exportReportToPdfStream(print, output);%>
```

Copy code from the `catalog.jsp` listing to `catalog.jsp` in the JasperReports application. To run the `catalog.jsp` JSP, right-click on the `catalog.jsp` node and select **Run**.

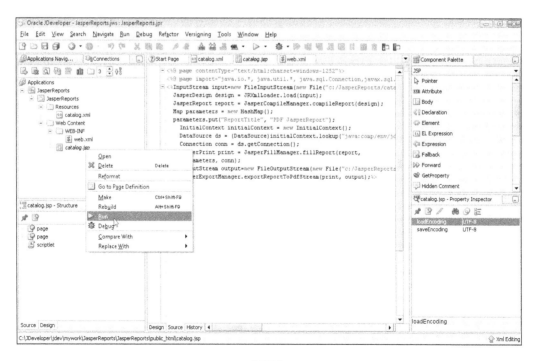

A `catalog.pdf` PDF file is generated. The PDF file can be opened in an Adobe Acrobat Reader.

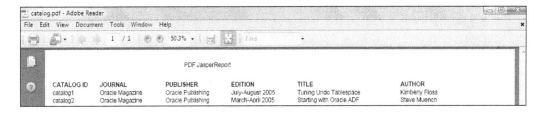

Creating an Excel Spreadsheet

Create a `catalog-excel.jsp` in the JasperReports project in JDeveloper for creating a Excel spreadsheet. If an Excel report is required, use a `JRXlsExporter` object to export the JasperReports document to an Excel spreadsheet. Specify an `OutputStream` to output the Excel spreadsheet. Specify a `ByteArrayOutputStream` for the output from the `JRXlsExporter` object:

```
OutputStream ouputStream=new FileOutputStream
  (new File("c:/JasperReports/catalog.xls"));
ByteArrayOutputStream byteArrayOutputStream = new
  ByteArrayOutputStream();
```

Create a `JRXlsExporter` object and set the `JasperPrint` object from which the report is to be generated and the `OutputStream` to output the report.

```
JRXlsExporter exporterXLS = new JRXlsExporter();
exporterXLS.setParameter(JRXlsExporterParameter.JASPER_PRINT, print);
exporterXLS.setParameter
(JRXlsExporterParameter.OUTPUT_STREAM,byteArrayOutputStream);
```

Export the JasperReport document using the `exportReport()` method:

```
exporterXLS.exportReport();
```

Output the JasperReports excel report to `catalog.xls` file:

```
ouputStream.write(byteArrayOutputStream.toByteArray());
ouputStream.flush();
ouputStream.close();
```

The `catalog-excel.jsp` is listed as follows:

```
<%@ page contentType="text/html;charset=windows-1252"%>
<%@ page import="java.io.*, java.util.*, java.sql.Connection,javax.
sql.DataSource, javax.naming.InitialContext,
net.sf.jasperreports.engine.*, net.sf.jasperreports.engine.design.
JasperDesign,net.sf.jasperreports.engine.xml.JRXmlLoader,
```

```
net.sf.jasperreports.engine.export.*"
%>
<%
  InputStream input=new FileInputStream
    (new File("c:/JasperReports/catalog.xml"));
  JasperDesign design = JRXmlLoader.load(input);
  JasperReport report = JasperCompileManager.compileReport(design);
  Map parameters = new HashMap();
  parameters.put("ReportTitle", "Excel JasperReport");
    InitialContext initialContext = new InitialContext();
    DataSource ds = (DataSource)initialContext.lookup
      ("java:comp/env/jdbc/JasperReportsConnectionDS");
    Connection conn = ds.getConnection();
    JasperPrint print = JasperFillManager.fillReport
      (report, parameters, conn);
        OutputStream ouputStream=new FileOutputStream
          (new File("c:/JasperReports/catalog.xls"));
        ByteArrayOutputStream byteArrayOutputStream = new
          ByteArrayOutputStream();
        JRXlsExporter exporterXLS = new JRXlsExporter();
        exporterXLS.setParameter(
                        JRXlsExporterParameter.JASPER_PRINT, print);
        exporterXLS.setParameter(JRXlsExporterParameter.
                OUTPUT_STREAM, byteArrayOutputStream);
        exporterXLS.exportReport();
        ouputStream.write(byteArrayOutputStream.toByteArray());
        ouputStream.flush();
        ouputStream.close();
%>
```

To generate an Excel report right-click on the `catalog-excel.jsp` and select **Run**. The Excel spreadsheet may be opened in MS Excel or Excel Viewer.

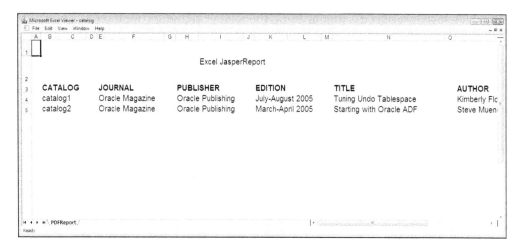

JDBC 4.0 Version

In the JDBC 4.0 version of the JasperReports application, to generate a PDF report, use the Oracle database 11g JDBC 4.0 drivers JAR file, `ojdbc6.jar`, instead of the **Oracle JDBC** library. JDBC 4.0 drivers require JDK 6.0. Therefore, set the J2SE Version to JDK 6.0 in the **Project Properties** window. To modify the **J2SE Version**, select the **Libraries** node in **Project Properties** window. Click on the **Change** button for the **J2SE Version** field. In the **Edit J2SE Definition** window, click on **New** to create a J2SE definition for JDK 6.0. In the **Create J2SE** window, select a JDK 6.0 Java Executable and click on **OK**. Select the JDK 6.0 definition in **Edit J2SE Definition** window and click on **OK**. The J2SE Version gets set to JDK 6.0 in **Project Properties** window. Click on **OK** in **Project Properties**.

The JDBC 4.0 features can be availed in a JDeveloper version that supports JDBC 4.0 in the embedded OC4J. JDBC 4.0 provides enhanced connection management with connection state tracking and connection client identification. Connection state tracking is implemented by the connection pool manager. If some of the connections in a connection pool become unusable, the connection pool manager closes those connections. Prior to the connection state tracking feature, the connection pool manager typically closed all connections and reinitiated the connection pool if some of the connections became unusable. Closing connections and opening new connections incurs an overhead. The `Connection` interface in JDK 6.0, which supports JDBC 4.0, has a `isValid()` method to test the validity of a connection. The connection pool manager invokes the `isValid` method on connections and if a connection returns false the connection pool manager closes the connection using `close()` method as follows:

```
if(!connection.isValid())
connection.close();
```

The connection client identification is implemented by the JDBC driver. Connection client identification is used to identify connections that might be bogging down an application due to excessive usage of CPU. The JDK 6.0 Connection interface provides two new methods for connection client identification; `setClientInfo()` and `getClientInfo()`. A `Connection` object is identifiable by the client info properties set on the `Connection` using `setClientInfo()`. The different client info properties supported by a database may be obtained from the database metadata using `getClientInfoProperties` method of the `DatabaseMetaData` interface.

```
DatabaseMetaData metaData=connection.getMetaData();
ResultSet clientInfo=metaData.getClientInfoProperties();
```

The standard client info properties are `ApplicationName`, `ClientUser,` and `ClientHostname`. In the JDBC 4.0 version of the JasperReports application, set the standard client info properties as follows:

```
connection.setClientInfo("ApplicationName","OracleApp");
connection.setClientInfo("ClientUser","OracleUser");
connection.setClientInfo("ClientHostname","OracleHost");
```

In JDBC 4.0 version of the JasperReports application we may also avail the support for Java SE chained exceptions facility. Specify an error page in the JasperReports JSP and in the error page, retrieve the chained exceptions and chained causes using the enhanced `for-each` loop introduced in J2SE 5.0 as follows:

```
for(Throwable e : exception ) {
out.println("Error encountered: " + e);
}
```

The JDBC 4.0 version of the JasperReports application to generate a PDF report is listed below.

```
<%@ page contentType="text/html;charset=windows-1252"%>
<%@ page import="java.io.*, java.util.*, java.sql.Connection,javax.
sql.DataSource, javax.naming.InitialContext,
net.sf.jasperreports.engine.*, net.sf.jasperreports.engine.design.
JasperDesign,net.sf.jasperreports.engine.xml.JRXmlLoader"
%>
<%
  InputStream input=new FileInputStream
    (new File("c:/JasperReports/catalog.xml"));
  JasperDesign design = JRXmlLoader.load(input);
  JasperReport report = JasperCompileManager.compileReport(design);
  Map parameters = new HashMap();
  parameters.put("ReportTitle", "PDF JasperReport");
    InitialContext initialContext = new InitialContext();
    DataSource ds = (DataSource)initialContext.lookup
      ("java:comp/env/jdbc/JasperReportsConnectionDS");
    Connection conn = ds.getConnection();
connection.setClientInfo("ApplicationName","OracleApp");
connection.setClientInfo("ClientUser","OracleUser");
connection.setClientInfo("ClientHostname","OracleHost");

  JasperPrint print = JasperFillManager.fillReport(report,
   parameters, conn);
  OutputStream output=new FileOutputStream(new File("c:/
JasperReports/catalog.pdf"));
    JasperExportManager.exportReportToPdfStream(print, output);
%>
```

The same modifications apply to the JasperReports application to generate an Excel spreadsheet.

Summary

JasperReports is a Java reporting tool to generate HTML, XML, PDF, CSV, or XLS reports. In this chapter we learned how to create a PDF and an Excel spreadsheet report from a database table using JDBC to connect to the database and run an SQL query. We added JDBC 4.0 features connection state tracking and connection client identification in the JDBC 4.0 version of the JasperReports application.

13
Creating a Spreadsheet with Apache POI

Database table data is often required to be presented as an Excel spreadsheet. The Apache POI project provides Java APIs for processing Microsoft OLE 2 Compound Document Format Files, which include XLS and DOC files. The **Apache POI HSSF** component of the Apache POI project is a Java API to access and generate Excel Workbooks and Excel spreadsheets. Apache POI HSSF does not support the new Excel 2007 `.xlsx` OOXML file format, which is not OLE2 based. An Excel workbook consists of spreadsheets and an Excel spreadsheet consists of rows and cells. The layout and fonts of a spreadsheet are also set with the Apache POI HSSF Java API.

The Apache POI HSSF project is a Java API to create an Excel workbook and an Excel spreadsheet. The implementation of the Apache POI HSSF project is provided in the `org.apache.poi.hssf.usermodel` package. The data in the Excel spreadsheet generated with the POI HSSF project may be static data, or dynamically retrieved data from a database. In this chapter we will discuss the procedure to create an Excel spreadsheet from an Oracle database table. The Excel spreadsheet is generated in the JDeveloper IDE.

Setting the Environment

The `org.apache.poi.hssf.usermodel` package classes are required to generate an Excel spreadsheet. Download the Apache POI library's `poi-bin-3.0.2-FINAL-20080204.zip` file from `http://www.apache.org/dyn/closer.cgi/poi/` and extract the ZIP file to an installation directory. Install JDeveloper 10g (10.1.3). Install the Oracle database 10g including sample schemas. Create a database instance. Create an example database table from which an Excel spreadsheet will be generated. The SQL script to create example table `Catalog` is listed as follows:

```
CREATE TABLE OE.Catalog(CatalogId VARCHAR(25), Journal VARCHAR(25),
    Publisher Varchar(25),Edition VARCHAR(25), Title Varchar(255),
    Author Varchar(25));
INSERT INTO OE.Catalog VALUES('catalog1', 'Oracle Magazine',
    'Oracle Publishing', 'March-April 2005', 'Starting with Oracle ADF
    ', 'Steve Muench');
INSERT INTO OE.Catalog VALUES('catalog2', 'Oracle Magazine',
    'Oracle Publishing','Jan-Feb 2005', 'Understanding Optimization',
    'Kimberly Floss');
```

Next, we will create a JDeveloper project for generating an Excel spreadsheet and add a library for the Apache POI JAR file to the project. Also, we will create a JDBC connection with the Oracle database for retrieving the data for the Excel spreadsheet.

First, create a JDBC connection to the Oracle database from the JDeveloper IDE. To create a connection select the **Connections** tab, select the **Database** node in the **Connections Navigator**, right click on the **Database** node, and select **New Database Connection**. In the **Create Database Connection (Type)** window displayed, specify a **Connection Name** and set **Connection Type** to **Oracle(JDBC)**.

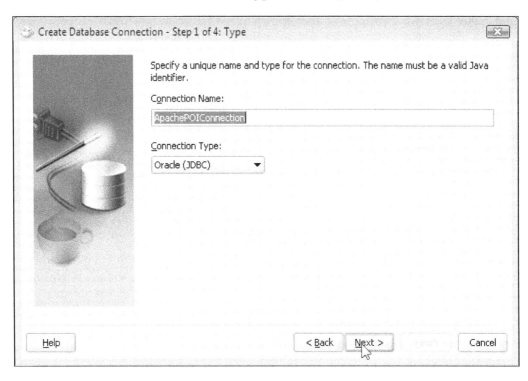

Click on **Next**. In the **Authentication** window, specify the **Username** and **Password** and click on **Next**. In the **Connection** window, specify the **Driver type**, **Host Name**, **JDBC Port**, **SID** and click on **Next**.

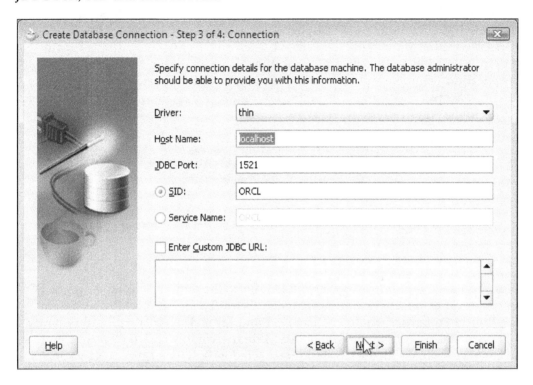

In the **Test** window, click on **Test Connection**. If a connection with the database is established a success message is displayed. Click on **Finish** to complete the connection configuration. A connection node is added to the **Connections Navigator**.

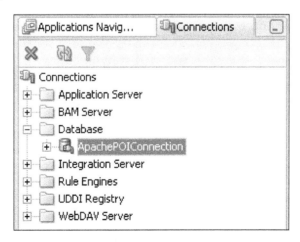

The JDBC connection `ApachePOIConnection` is available as a data source `jdbc/ApachePOIConnectionDS`. The data source is used to retrieve data from the database to generate an Excel spreadsheet. Next, create a JDeveloper project for generating an Excel spreadsheet. Select **File | New** in the JDeveloper IDE. In the **New Gallery** window, select **General|Applications** in the **Categories** listed and select **Application** in the **Items** listed. Click on the **OK** button. In the **Create Application** window, specify an **Application Name**, select the **No Template Application Template** and click on the **OK** button. In the **Create Project** window, specify a **Project Name** and click on the **OK** button. An application and a project is added to the **Applications-Navigator**.

Next, add a library for the Apache POI JAR file to the project. Select the Apache POI project node in the **Applications-Navigator**. Select **Tools | Project Properties**. In the **Project Properties** window, select the **Libraries** node. Click on the **Add Library** button to create a new library. In the **Add Library** window click on the **New** button to add a new library. In the **Create Library** window specify a **Library Name** and click on the **Add Entry** button.

In the **Select Path Entry** window select the `poi-3.0.2-FINAL-20080204.jar` file and click on the **Select** button. The selected JAR file is added to the **Class Path** node in the **Create Library** window. Click on the **OK** button in the **Create Library** window. The Apache POI library is added to the **Add Library** window. Click on the **OK** button in the **Add Library** window. The Apache POI library is created and added to the **Libraries**. The `poi-3.0.2-FINAL-20080204.jar` file can also be added to the ApachePOI project using the **Add Jar/Directory** button.

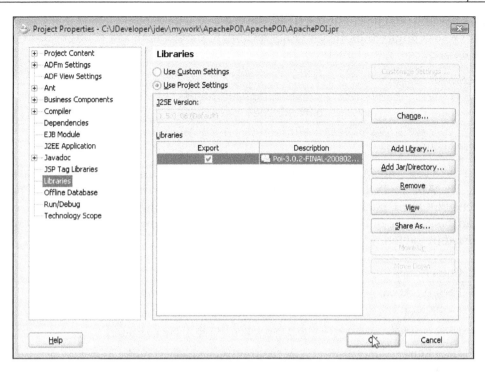

Creating an Excel Spreadsheet

In this section an Excel spreadsheet will be generated from the example database table. First, create a JSP application to generate an Excel spreadsheet. Right-click on the ApachePOI project node in the **Applications Navigator** and select **New**. In the **New Gallery** window select **Web Tier | Java Server Pages**. In the **Items** listed, select **JSP Page** and click on the **OK** button. In the **Create JSP Wizard** select a **Web Application** version and click on the **Next** button. In the **JSP File** window specify a file name and click on **Next**. Click on the **Next** window in the **Tag Libraries** window. Select the default options in the **HTML Options** page and click on the **Next** button. In the **Finish** window, click on **Finish**. A JSP gets added to the Apache POI project in the **Applications-Navigator**.

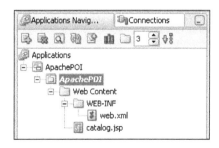

Add a resource reference for the JDBC data source `jdbc/ApachePOIConnectionDS`, which was configured in the previous section, to the JSP `web.xml` configuration file. Add a `resource-ref` element to the `web.xml` file.

```
<resource-ref>
  <res-ref-name>jdbc/ApachePOIConnectionDS</res-ref-name>
  <res-type>javax.sql.DataSource</res-type>
  <res-auth>Container</res-auth>
</resource-ref>
```

In the `catalog.jsp` an Excel spreadsheet will be created from an Oracle database table. The Apache POI HSSF project is used to generate an Excel spreadsheet. The Apache POI HSSF package has classes for the different components of an Excel spreadsheet. Some of the commonly used classes of the Apache POI HSSF package are listed in the following table.

Class Name	Description
HSSFWorkbook	Represents an Excel Spreadsheet Workbook.
HSSFSheet	Represents an Excel Spreadsheet.
HSSFHeader	Specifies a Spreadsheet Header.
HSSFRow	Specifies a Spreadsheet Row.
HSSFCell	Specifies a Spreadsheet Cell.
HSSFCellStyle	Specifies the Cell style
HSSFFont	Specifies the font for the spreadsheet
HSSFChart	Represents a Chart
HSSFDateUtil	Specifies Excel dates
HSSFPrintSetup	Specifies the print setup for an Excel document

In the JSP application, first, import the Apache POI HSSF package:

```
<%@ page import="org.apache.poi.hssf.usermodel.*, java.sql.*,
  java.io.*,javax.naming.InitialContext"%>
```

Create an Excel stylesheet workbook using the `HSSFWorkbook` class:

```
HSSFWorkbook wb=new HSSFWorkbook();
```

Next, create an Excel spreadsheet from the `HSSFWorkbook` object using the `createSheet()` method:

```
HSSFSheet sheet1=wb.createSheet("sheet1");
```

The data for the stylesheet is retrieved from an Oracle database table. Obtain a JDBC connection from the database. First, create an `InitialContext` object. Subsequently, create a `DataSource` object using the `lookup()` method of the `InitialContext` class to lookup the data source JNDI. Obtain a connection from the `DataSource` object using the `getConnection()` method:

```
InitialContext initialContext = new InitialContext();
javax.sql.DataSource ds = (javax.sql.DataSource)
initialContext.lookup("java:comp/env/jdbc/ApachePOIConnectionDS");
java.sql.Connection conn = ds.getConnection();
```

Create a `Statement` object using the `createStatement()` method of the `Connection` interface. Run an SQL query on the `Catalog` table using the `executeQuery()` method of the `Statement` interface to generate a `ResultSet` object.

```
Statement stmt=conn.createStatement();
ResultSet resultSet=stmt.executeQuery("Select * from Catalog");
```

Create a header row for the Excel spreadsheet using the `createRow()` method of the `HSSFRow` class. The rows in an Excel spreadsheet are '0' based.

```
HSSFRow row=sheet1.createRow(0);
```

Set the header row cell values corresponding to the table columns. Create a cell with the `createCell()` method of the `HSSFRow` class and set the cell value using the `setCellValue()` method. For example, the value for the first cell in the row is set to `CatalogId` as follows:

```
row.createCell((short)0).setCellValue("CatalogId");
```

To add rows to the spreadsheet, iterate over the result set and add a row for each of the table rows. Retrieve the column values from the `ResultSet` and set the values in the row cells:

```
for (int i=1;resultSet.next(); i++){
    row=sheet1.createRow(i);
    row.createCell((short)0).setCellValue(resultSet.getString(1));
    row.createCell((short)1).setCellValue(resultSet.getString(2));
    row.createCell((short)2).setCellValue(resultSet.getString(3));
    row.createCell((short)3).setCellValue(resultSet.getString(4));
    row.createCell((short)4).setCellValue(resultSet.getString(5));
    }
```

Create a directory `C:/excel`. Create a `FileOutputStream` to output the Excel spreadsheet to an XLS file. An XLS file represents an excel spreadsheet.

```
FileOutputStream output=new FileOutputStream(new File("c:/excel/
catalog.xls"));
```

Output the Excel spreadsheet to a XLS file using the `write()` method of the `HSSFWorkbook` class.

```
wb.write(output);
```

The `catalog.jsp` used to generate an Excel spreadsheet is listed below.

```
<%@ page contentType="text/html;charset=windows-1252"%>
<%@ page import="org.apache.poi.hssf.usermodel.*, java.sql.*, java.
io.*,javax.naming.InitialContext"%>
<html>
  <head>
    <meta http-equiv="Content-Type" content="text/html;
charset=windows-1252">
    <title>untitled</title>
  </head>
  <body><%HSSFWorkbook wb=new HSSFWorkbook();
HSSFSheet sheet1=wb.createSheet("sheet1");
InitialContext initialContext = new InitialContext();
    javax.sql.DataSource ds = (javax.sql.DataSource)
    initialContext.lookup("java:comp/env/jdbc/ApachePOIConnectionDS");
  java.sql.Connection conn = ds.getConnection();
Statement stmt=conn.createStatement();
ResultSet resultSet=stmt.executeQuery("Select * from Catalog");
HSSFRow row=sheet1.createRow(0);
row.createCell((short)0).setCellValue("CatalogId");
row.createCell((short)1).setCellValue("Journal");
row.createCell((short)2).setCellValue("Publisher");
row.createCell((short)3).setCellValue("Edition");
row.createCell((short)4).setCellValue("Title");
row.createCell((short)5).setCellValue("Author");
    for (int i=1;resultSet.next(); i++)
        {
 row=sheet1.createRow(i);
row.createCell((short)0).setCellValue(resultSet.getString(1));
row.createCell((short)1).setCellValue(resultSet.getString(2));
row.createCell((short)2).setCellValue(resultSet.getString(3));
row.createCell((short)3).setCellValue(resultSet.getString(4));
row.createCell((short)4).setCellValue(resultSet.getString(5));
row.createCell((short)5).setCellValue(resultSet.getString(6));
}
```

```
FileOutputStream output=new FileOutputStream(new File("c:/excel/
catalog.xls"));
wb.write(output);
output.close();
resultSet.close();
stmt.close();
conn.close();
%>
   </body>
</html>
```

To run the `catalog.jsp` JSP in the JDeveloper embedded OC4J server, right-click on the JSP node in the **Applications-Navigator** and select **Run**.

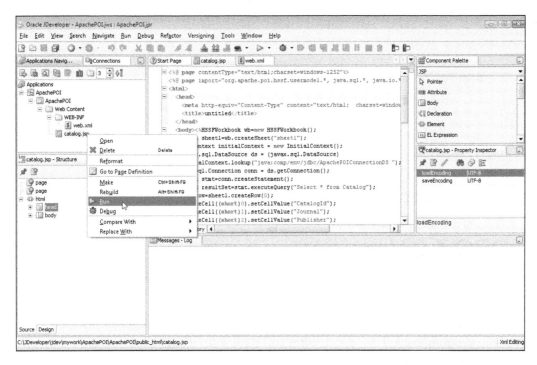

An Excel spreadsheet which may be opened in MS Excel or the Excel Viewer tool is generated:

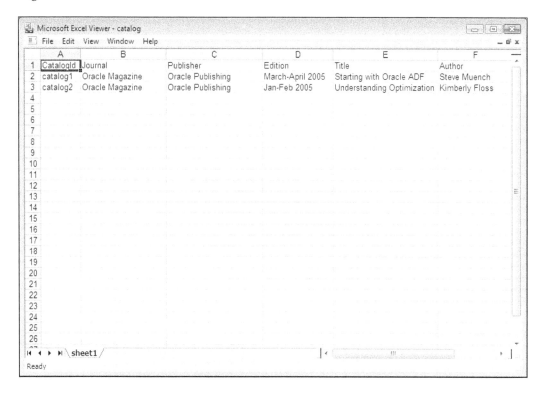

JDBC 4.0 Version

In the JDBC 4.0 version of the Apache POI application, we need to create a JDBC connection with Oracle database using the Oracle database 11g JDBC 4.0 drivers, which may be obtained from: `http://www.oracle.com/technology/software/ tech/java/sqlj_jdbc/htdocs/jdbc_111060.html`. Use the `ojdbc6.jar` JDBC JAR file to configure a JDBC connection and data source with Oracle data source. As JDBC 4.0 drivers required JDK 6.0, set the J2SE Version to JDK 6.0 by selecting **Tools | Project Properties**. In the **Project Properties** window, select the **Libraries** node and select a JDK 6.0 Java executable in the **J2SE Version** field.

We will add the following JDBC 4.0 features to the Apache POI application:

- Connection state tracking
- Connection client identification using client info properties
- Statement pooling

- Wrapper pattern
- Java SE chained exception facility

Connection state tracking is implemented by the connection pool manager and is used to identify connections that have become unusable in the connection pool. JDBC 4.0 provides the isValid() method in the Connection interface for connection state tracking. If the isValid() method returns false the connection pool manager closes the connection.

```
if(!connection.isValid())
connection.close();
```

Connection client identification is used to identify connections that might cause reduced performance due to excessive CPU usage. Connections are associated with application clients using client info properties. The Connection interface in JDBC 4.0 includes two new method setClientInfo() and getClientInfo() to set and get client info properties. Client info properties supported by a database may be retrieved using the getClientInfoProperties() method of the DatabaseMetaData interface as follows:

```
DatabaseMetaData metaData=connection.getMetaData();
ResultSet rsClientInfo=metadata.getClientInfoProperties();
```

The standard client info properties ApplicationName, ClientUser, and ClientHostname may be set on the Connection object as follows:

```
conn.setClientInfo("ApplicationName","OracleApp");
conn.setClientInfo("ClientUser","OracleUser");
conn.setClientInfo("ClientHostname","OracleHost");
```

PreparedStatement objects are pooled by default if the database supports statement pooling. JDBC 4.0 has also added the provision to pool Statement objects. Frequently used Statement objects are recommended to be pooled to avoid the overhead of closing and opening new Statement objects. Statement pooling is implemented using the isPoolable() and setPoolable() methods of the Statement object as follows:

```
if(stmt.isPoolable())
stmt.setPoolable(true);
```

The Wrapper interface in JDBC 4.0 provides access to nonstandard JDBC methods in vendor-specific extensions to JDBC API using the wrapper pattern. The Wrapper interface is extended by the following JDBC interfaces:

- CachedRowSet
- CallableStatement

- Connection
- DatabaseMetaData
- DataSource
- FilteredRowSet
- JdbcRowSet
- JoinRowSet
- ParameterMetaData
- PreparedStatement
- ResultSet
- ResultSetMetaData
- RowSet
- RowSetMetaData
- Statement
- WebRowSet

Any vendor-specific interface extending these interfaces implement the wrapper pattern as it also extends the Wrapper interface. For example, the OracleStatement interface in Oracle's extension to the JDBC API extends the Statement interface and thus extends the Wrapper interface. The OracleStatement interface provides methods that are not defined in the Statement interface. We will use the OracleStatement interface instead of the Statement interface to run SQL queries. To create an OracleStatement object, first determine if the Statement object is a wrapper for the OracleStatement interface using the isWrapperFor() method. If a wrapper, unwrap the OracleStatement interface to create an OracleStatement object using unwrap() method in the Wrapper interface. Subsequently invoke the defineColumnType() method of OracleStatement object to set column types.

JDBC 4.0 supports the Java SE chained exceptions facility to retrieve chained exceptions and chained causes. Chained exceptions are exceptions that are linked to an exception. JDBC 4.0 supports the enhanced for loop introduced in J2SE 5.0 to iterate over chained exceptions as follows:

```
for(Throwable e : exception ) {
out.println("Error encountered: " + e);
}
```

The JDBC 4.0 version of the Apache POI application is listed as follows.

```
<%@ page contentType="text/html;charset=windows-1252"%>
<%@ page import="org.apache.poi.hssf.usermodel.*, java.sql.*, java.
io.*,javax.naming.InitialContext, oracle.jdbc.OracleStatement"%>
```

```
<html>
  <head>
    <meta http-equiv="Content-Type" content="text/html;
charset=windows-1252">
    <title>untitled</title>
  </head>
  <body><%
ResultSet resultSet;
HSSFWorkbook wb=new HSSFWorkbook();
HSSFSheet sheet1=wb.createSheet("sheet1");
InitialContext initialContext = new InitialContext();
    javax.sql.DataSource ds = (javax.sql.DataSource)
    initialContext.lookup("java:comp/env/jdbc/ApachePOIConnectionDS
");
    java.sql.Connection conn = ds.getConnection();

conn.setClientInfo("ApplicationName","OracleApp");
conn.setClientInfo("ClientUser","OracleUser");
conn.setClientInfo("ClientHostname","OracleHost");

Statement stmt=conn.createStatement();
DatabaseMetaData metaData=connection.getMetaData();
if(metaData.supportsStatementPooling()){
if(stmt.isPoolable())
stmt.setPoolable(true);
}

Class class = Class.forName("oracle.jdbc.OracleStatement");
if(stmt.isWrapperFor(class)) {
OracleStatement oracleStmt = (OracleStatement)stmt.unwrap(class);
oracleStmt.defineColumnType(1, OracleTypes.VARCHAR);
oracleStmt.defineColumnType(2, OracleTypes.VARCHAR);
oracleStmt.defineColumnType(3, OracleTypes.VARCHAR);
oracleStmt.defineColumnType(4, OracleTypes.VARCHAR);
oracleStmt.defineColumnType(5, OracleTypes.VARCHAR);
oracleStmt.defineColumnType(6, OracleTypes.VARCHAR);


resultSet=oracleStmt.executeQuery("SELECT * FROM OE.CATALOG");
}
HSSFRow row=sheet1.createRow(0);
row.createCell((short)0).setCellValue("CatalogId");
row.createCell((short)1).setCellValue("Journal");
row.createCell((short)2).setCellValue("Publisher");
```

```
row.createCell((short)3).setCellValue("Edition");
row.createCell((short)4).setCellValue("Title");
row.createCell((short)5).setCellValue("Author");
    for (int i=1;resultSet.next(); i++)
        {
 row=sheet1.createRow(i);
row.createCell((short)0).setCellValue(resultSet.getString(1));
row.createCell((short)1).setCellValue(resultSet.getString(2));
row.createCell((short)2).setCellValue(resultSet.getString(3));
row.createCell((short)3).setCellValue(resultSet.getString(4));
row.createCell((short)4).setCellValue(resultSet.getString(5));
row.createCell((short)5).setCellValue(resultSet.getString(6));
}
FileOutputStream output=new FileOutputStream(new File("c:/excel/
catalog.xls"));
wb.write(output);
output.close();
resultSet.close();
stmt.close();
conn.close();
%>
   </body>
</html>
```

Summary

In this chapter, an Excel spreadsheet was generated from an Oracle database table using the Apache POI HSSF API. The Apache POI HSSF API may also be used to parse an Excel spreadsheet and subsequently store the spreadsheet in a database. In the JDBC 4.0 version of the Apache POI application we added JDBC 4.0 features connection state tracking, setting of client info properties, statement caching, access of nonstandard JDBC methods using the Wrapper interface, and the Java SE chained exceptions facility.

14
Creating Oracle ADF Business Components

Oracle **Application Development Framework (ADF)** is a J2EE framework that simplifies J2EE development and Oracle JDeveloper provides a declarative development environment for it. The **Business Components for Java (BC4J)** layer of the ADF is a JDBC-based programming framework for developing database-centric business services in Java. ADF Business Components use JDBC to query the database. A Business Components application consists of entity objects, view objects, and application module and additionally associations and view links. ADF Business Components may be used with different view layers like JavaServer pages, UIX, and Swing.

The Entity Object in ADF Business Components performs all the database interaction and validation and is also where the business logic gets defined. Entity Objects are based on database tables and map table columns to attributes in Java. Entity Objects encapsulate business logic, define validation rules, and also cache data. Typically, View Objects consist of SQL queries to present a subset of the business data (view) modeled by the entity objects. View Objects may or may not be based on Entity Objects.

View Objects provide a client with row sets of data, which may be modified, by the client; View Objects are basically row set iterators that allow programs to navigate over a collection of data. One Entity Object can be accessed from different View Objects. Multiple instances of a View Object can be used in an application. The ADF Business Components View Objects are exposed to the view layer through an Application Module, which represents the logical data model and manages data transactions. The business components associations represent the associations between entity objects, and the view links represent the links between the queries in different view objects. Associations and view links are not required features of a business components applications.

The BC4J layer of ADF is used to develop view objects and entity objects for a database table. An application module, which consists of the view objects, connects to the database and retrieves the data to create view objects. An application module may be used to connect to a database in the **Connections Navigator** or may be integrated with a Client/View web application using the business components Java API. A Client/View web application, which may be a Java/JSP application, has the `oracle.jbo` package classes and interfaces available to connect an application module to a database and create view objects. In this chapter, business components are created from an Oracle database table. Subsequently, a web application is created to connect the business components application module to the database and create view objects.

Setting the Environment

Business components are developed in JDeveloper 10g. Install the JDeveloper 10g IDE. Install the Oracle 10g database. Create an instance of the database. Create an example table in the database from which business components will be generated. The SQL script to create the example table `Catalog` is listed below.

```
CREATE TABLE  OE.Catalog(CatlogId VARCHAR(25) PRIMARY KEY, Journal
   VARCHAR(25), Publisher Varchar(25),Edition VARCHAR(25), Section
   VARCHAR(25), Title Varchar(75), Author Varchar(25));
INSERT INTO OE.Catalog VALUES('catalog1', 'Oracle Magazine', 'Oracle
   Publishing', 'Nov-Dec 2004','ORACLE DEVELOPER', 'From ADF UIX to
   JSF', 'Jonas Jacobi');
INSERT INTO OE.Catalog VALUES('catalog2', 'Oracle Magazine', 'Oracle
   Publishing', 'Nov-Dec 2004', 'TECHNOLOGY', 'Database Resource
   Manager', 'Kimberly Floss');
INSERT INTO OE.Catalog VALUES('catalog3', 'Oracle Magazine','Oracle
   Publishing','March-April 2005','ORACLE DEVELOPER','Starting with
   Oracle ADF', 'Steve Muench');
```

Next, create a JDBC connection with the Oracle 10g database. In the **Connections Navigator**, right-click on the **Database** node and select **New Database Connection**. In the **Create Database Connection Type** window, specify a connection name and select **Oracle JDBC** as the **Connection Type**. In the **Authentication** window, specify a **Username** and **Password** and click on **Next**. In the **Connection** window, select **thin** or **oci** as the Driver. In the **Host Name** field, specify the Oracle database host name. The Host is specified in the `tnsnames.ora` file of the database. Specify the **JDBC Port** and **SID**, which are also specified in the `tnsnames.ora` file. Click on **Next** to display the **Test** window. In the **Test** window click, on the **Test Connection** button to test the JDBC connection. A Success message is displayed if the connection with the database is established. Click on **Finish** to complete the connection configuration.

A connection node is added to the **Connections Navigator**. The OE schema of the connection node displays the **Catalog** table, which was created in the database.

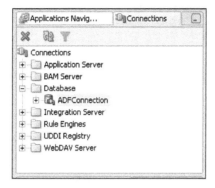

Configuring a BC4J Project

In this section, a business components workspace and project are created, business components are created from an Oracle database table, and the business components project is tested in JDeveloper. First, create an application workspace. Select **File | New** in JDeveloper. In the **New Gallery** window, select **General** and **Application** in the **Items** listed. In the **Create Application** window specify the **Application Name**, a **Directory Name** for the application, and select an **Application Template**. Select the **Web Application [JSP, Struts ADF BC]** template.

An application workspace, **BC4JApp** gets added to the **Applications-Navigator**. The application has a **Model** node and a **ViewController** node.

Creating Business Components

In this section, business components are created from the Oracle database table Catalog, which was created in the previous section. The default business components created from the table will be modified in JDeveloper. Right-click on the **Model** node and select **New**.

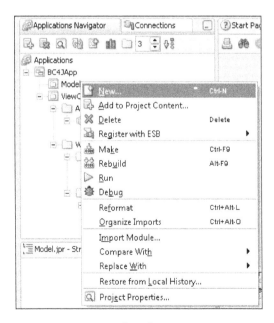

In the **New Gallery** window select **Project Technologies** in the **Filter By**. Select **Business Tier | ADF Business Components** in **Categories,** and select **Business Components from Tables** in the **Items** listed.

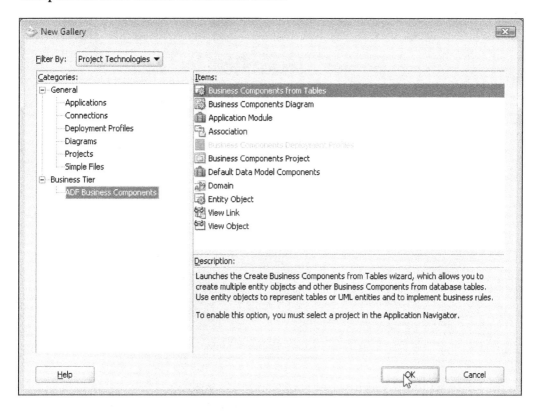

In the **Initialize Business Components Project** window, select the database connection in the **Connection** list to create business components from database tables.

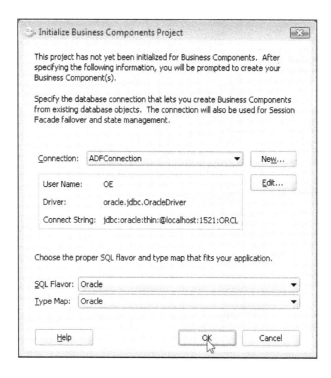

In the **Login** window, specify **User Name** and **Password** and click on **OK**. The **Create Business Components from Tables** wizard starts. Click on **Next**.

The **Entity Objects** window is displayed. Specify the entity objects that are to be created from the database tables. First, select the schema in the **Schema** list that has the database tables from which the business components are created. The catalog table is in the OE schema, thus select the OE schema. Click on the **Query** button. The database tables in the OE schema are listed in the **Available** display section. Select OE.CATALOG table in the **Available** list and with the **Copy (>)** button or with *Alt+C* transfer the selected table to the **Selected** section. Entity Object catalog gets specified. Click on **Next**.

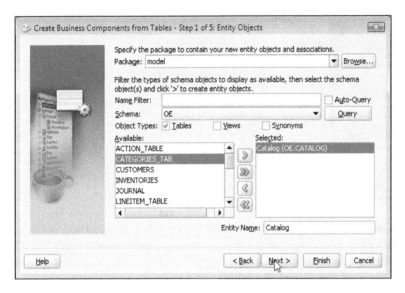

The **View Objects** window is displayed. The entity objects that are available to generate the default updatable view objects are listed in the **Available** section. Select entity objects from the **Available** section and transfer them to the **Selected** section with the **Copy (>)** button or with *Alt+C*. Select the Catalog entity object in the **Available** list and copy the entity object to the **Selected** list. View Object, **CatalogView**, is specified. **CatalogView** is the default view object for the selected entity object.

The default view object has all of the attributes in the entity object, and the SELECT query selects all of the database columns. Click on **Next**.

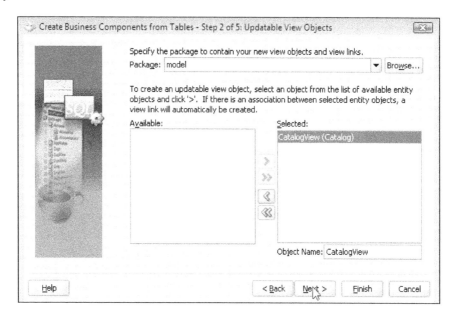

The **Read-Only View Objects** window is displayed. The database Schema for which the tables for view objects are available is listed in the **Schema** field. The **Object Types** checkbox **Tables** is checked by default. The available tables are listed in the **Available** selection list. Select the tables for which read-only view objects are to be generated and shift the tables to the **Selected** list. As an example select the Catalog table for read-only view objects and click on **Next**.

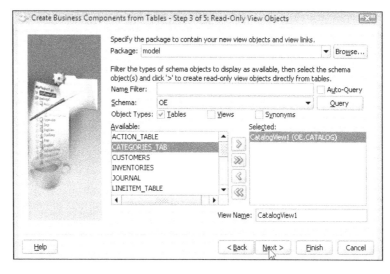

The **Application Module** window is displayed. Specify an application module name and click on **Next**.

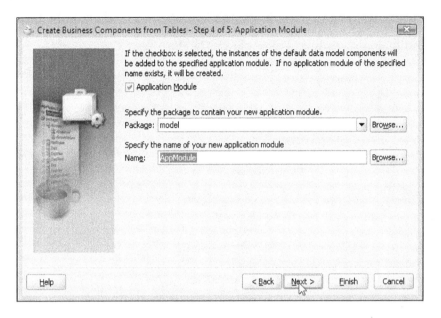

In the **Diagram** window, select the **Business Components Diagram** checkbox if a diagram is required to created and click on **Next**. In the **Finish** window, the business components are listed. For the Oracle database table `Catalog`, the business components are entity object `Catalog`, updatable view object `CatalogView`, read-only view object `CatalogView1`, and application module `AppModule`. If the selected entity objects have an association, a view link is also generated. Click on **Finish** to generate the business components.

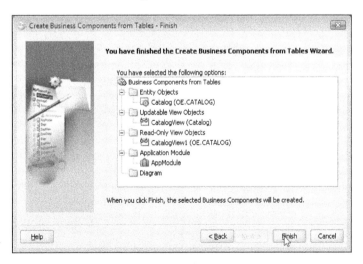

The business components for the Catalog table are generated and added to the **Applications-Navigator**. View Object instances **CatalogView1** and **CatalogView1_1** are generated. **CatalogView1** is the view object instance corresponding to the updatable view object **CatalogView**. **CatalogView1_1** is the view object instance corresponding to the read-only view object, **CatalogView1**.

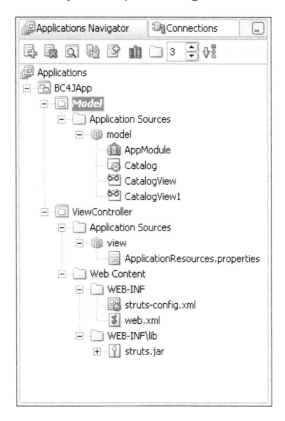

The business components created from the database table Catalog are the default business components. The entity object, the view objects, and the application module may be modified in JDeveloper. To modify the entity object, Catalog, right-click on the Catalog entity object node and select **Edit Catalog**.

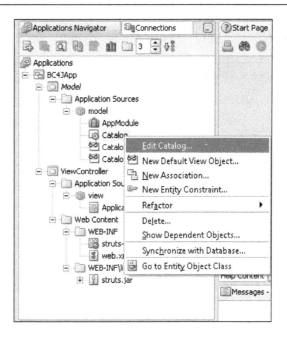

In the **Entity Object Editor**, click on the **Attributes** node. The attributes of the entity object are listed. The entity object attributes correspond to the database columns in the Catalog table. To remove an attribute select the attribute in the **Entity Attributes** list and click on the **Remove** button. To add an attribute from an unmapped table column click on the **New from Table** button. To add an attribute, which does not have a corresponding table column click on the **New** button. As an example, add a new attribute, which does not have a corresponding table column.

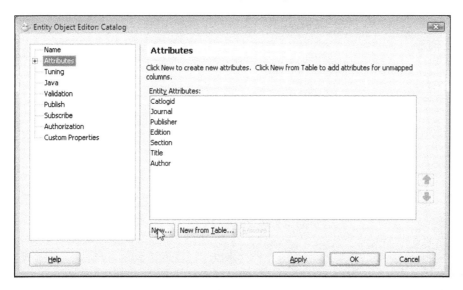

In the **New Entity Attribute** window specify the attribute **Name**, **Type** and **Default** value. Select the **Persistent** checkbox for a persistent field and click on **OK**.

The new attribute `ArticleAbstract` is added to the entity object `Catalog`. To remove an attribute from an entity object, first remove the attribute from the view objects. Click on the **Apply** button to apply the attribute additions/removals. Click on the **OK** button.

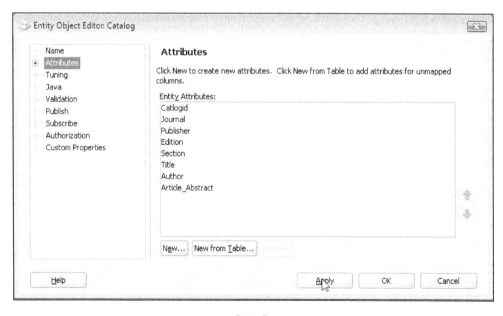

To synchronize the attribute additions made to the Catalog entity object with the Oracle database table, right-click on the entity object node and select **Synchronize with Database**. The **Synchronize with Database** window displays the modifications required to synchronize the database with the entity object. If a new `persistent` attribute is added to an entity object, a new table column is also required in the table prior to creating the `persistent` attribute. If a new table column is not added, a `persistent` entity object is modified to a `transient` attribute. Select **Entity: Catalog** and click on the **Synchronize** button to synchronize the entity object with the database. A window displays the message, **The following Synchronization Actions were performed successfully**. As a database table column was not created for the `ArticleAbstract` column, the `ArticleAbstract` attribute is set as a `transient` attribute.

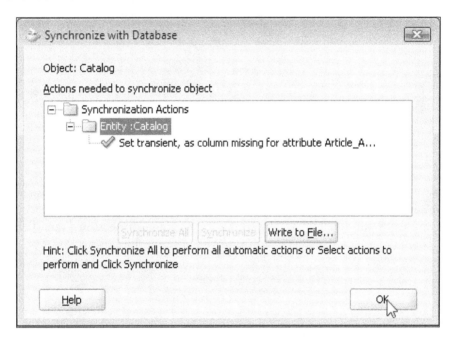

To modify the updatable view object, `CatalogView`, right-click on the view object node and select **Edit CatalogView**. The **View Object Editor** displays the attributes and SQL query of the view object. Select the **Attributes** node to edit the view object attributes. Select the **SQL Statement** node to edit the view object `SELECT` query.

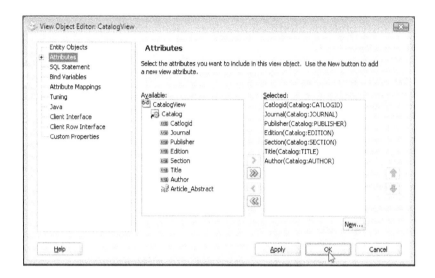

Next, we will test the business components application. To test the business components application, right-click on the application module node and select **Test**. The **Connect** window is displayed. In the **Connect** window, the JDBC connection used to connect with the database is selected. Select the **Connection Type** (JDBC URL or Datasource) and **Connection Name** and click on the **Connect** button.

The business components application is connected to the database and the **Local** window is displayed. The **Local** window has an application module node and a view objects instance results nodes. **CatalogView1** is the view object instance for the updatable view object **CatalogView** and **CatalogView1_1** is the view object instance for the read-only view object **CatalogView1**. Double-click on the updatable view object instance **CatalogView1** node to display the results of the view object query.

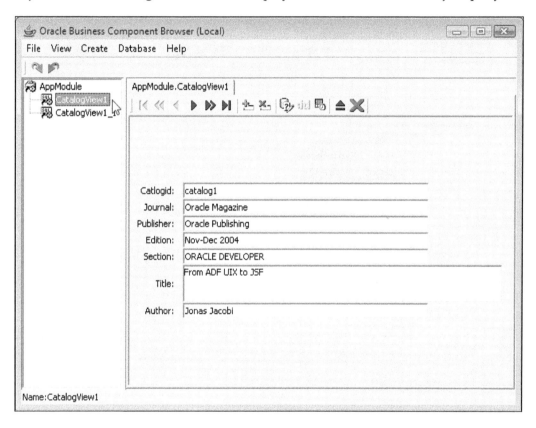

The **Go to next/previous record**, **Go to next/previous page**, and **Go to last/first record** links may be used to navigate through the view object query results. To add a new record, select the **Insert a new record** link.

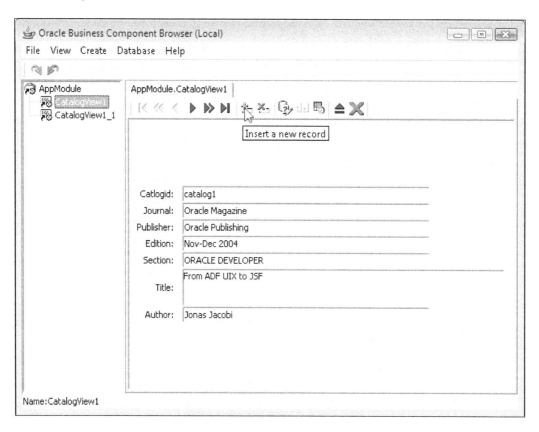

As an example, delete a record with the **Delete the current record** link. To commit the changes to a transaction, select **Database | Commit**.

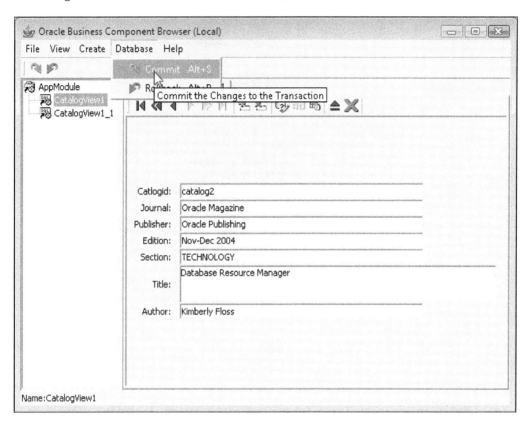

To view the data represented by a view object as XML select **View | Data As XML**.
A window for the view object XML data is displayed

The SQL query used to create a view object may be modified in the **View Object Editor**. Right-click on the view object node and select **Edit CatalogView**. In the **View Object Editor** window select the **SQL Statement** node. By default the SELECT list and the FROM clause of the SQL query are automatically defined. To override the default setting of the SELECT list and the FROM clause, check the **Expert Mode** checkbox. As an example, specify a WHERE clause for the SQL query. Click on the **Apply** button to apply the changes to the SQL query.

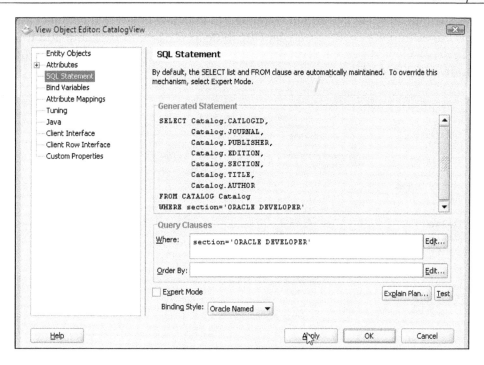

A window pops up to test the SQL query syntax. If the query syntax is correct, a **Query is valid message** is displayed. Click on **OK** in the **View Object Editor** window. Right-click on the application module node and select **Test** to the test the modified business components application. Click on Connect in the Connect window. In the **Oracle Business Components Browser**, the results of the filtered query are displayed. With the `WHERE` clause set to `section='ORACLE DEVELOPER'`, only the results with the `section` column value `'ORACLE DEVELOPER'` are displayed.

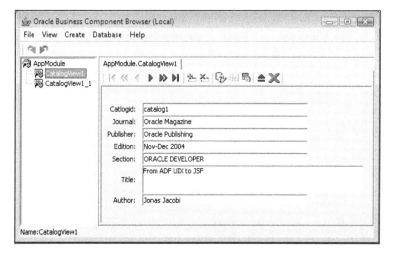

A new attribute may also be added/removed to the view object in the **View Object Editor**. For example, select the transient attribute `ArticleAbstract` and add it to the `CatalogView` view object. Click on the **Apply** button to apply the attribute additions or removals. Click on **OK**.

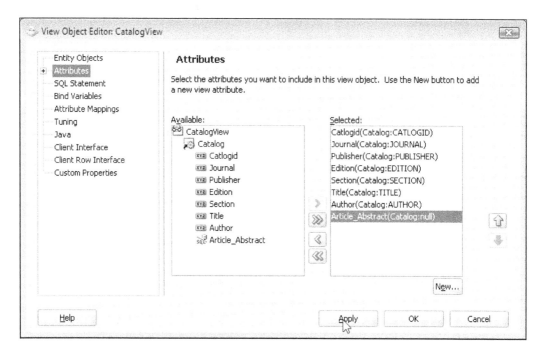

Right-click on the application module node and select **Test** to test the modified business components application. A new field **ArticleAbstract** is added to the results of the view object query. If the added attribute is a `transient` attribute, it does not get persisted to the database with the **Database | Commit** selection; only a `persistent` attribute is added to the database. A `transient` attribute does get displayed in the **View Object XML Data** window with **View | Data as XML** selection if a value is specified for the attribute.

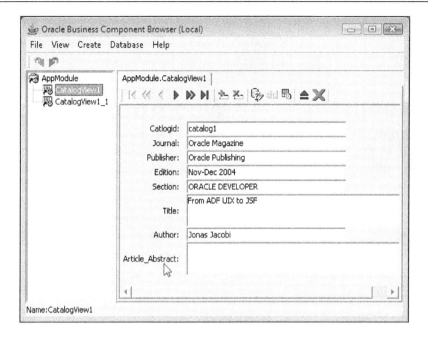

The updatable view object, `CatalogView1`, is updatable as explained in the previous section. Next, select the read-only view object instance node **CatalogView1_1**. The read-only view object instance only displays the results; the results from the view object query are not modifiable.

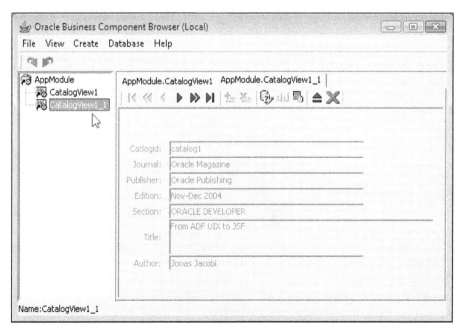

In this section, a business components application module was created and tested with the Oracle database. In the next section, we will create a web application for the business components.

Developing a BC4J Web Application

In this section a web application is created in the **ViewController** project of the Model-ViewController application. A web application JSP will invoke the business components in the **Model** project. Add the **Model** project business components to the classpath of the **ViewController** project. Select the ViewController project in the Applications Navigator. Select **Tools | Project Properties** in the JDeveloper IDE. In the **Project Properties** window, select the **Common | Dependencies** node. In the **Project Dependencies** window, click in the **Model.jpr** checkbox. Click on the **OK** button. The **Model** project gets added to the classpath of the View project.

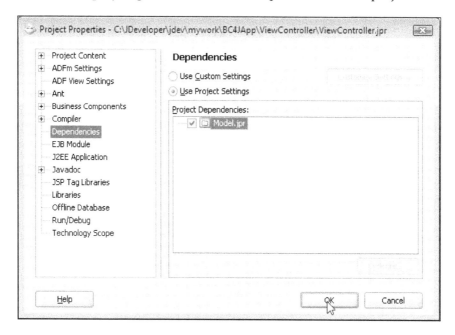

The JSP application will be integrated with the BC4J components in the **Model** project. To create a JSP right-click on the **ViewController** project and select **New**. In the **New Gallery** window, select **Web Tier | Java Server Pages**. Select **JSP Page** in the **Items** listed. In the **Create JSP** page, specify TestClient as the **File Name** and a **Directory Name** for the JSP page. The JSP page TestClient.jsp is added to the **ViewController** project of the BC4J application workspace. JDeveloper provides integrated support for the Oracle JDBC driver. For ADF/BC4J applications with a database other than Oracle database copy JDBC JAR file to BC4J/lib directory.

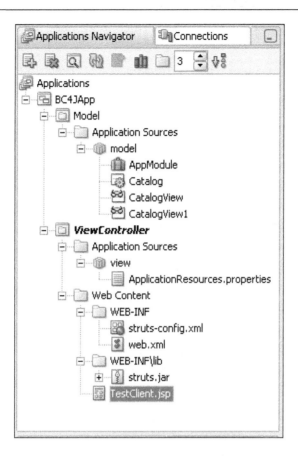

In the `TestClient.jsp`, import the `oracle.jbo` package and the `oracle.jbo.client.Configuration` class:

```
<%@page import="oracle.jbo.*, oracle.jbo.client.Configuration"%>
```

Create an application module name variable:

```
String appModule = "model.AppModule";
```

The application module name is specified in the `AppModuleJndiName`, element in the `<BC4JApp>\Model\src\model\common\bc4j.xcfg` configuration file. `<BC4JApp>` is the application workspace directory:

```
<AppModuleJndiName>model.AppModule</AppModuleJndiName>
```

Create an application module config name variable:

```
String cfg="AppModuleLocal";
```

The application module config name is specified in the `name` attribute of the `AppModuleConfig` element in the `bc4j.xcfg` file:

```
<AppModuleConfig name="AppModuleLocal"> </AppModuleConfig>
```

Create a view object instance variable:

```
String viewObject = "CatalogView1";
```

The view object instance is listed in the **View Object Instances** node in the application module **Structure** window in the JDeveloper. Create an `ApplicationModule` object from the BC4J application module using the `createRootApplicationModule()` static method of the `Configuration` class:

```
ApplicationModule applicationModule =(ApplicationModule)
    Configuration.createRootApplicationModule(appModule, cfg);
```

Obtain a `Transaction` object from the `ApplicationModule` object using the `getTransaction()` method. If the application module is not connected to the database connect to the database with the connect method.

```
Transaction transaction=applicationModule.getTransaction();
    if(transaction.isConnected()==false)
    transaction.connect("jdbc:oracle:thin:@<HOST>:<PORT>:<SID>", "OE",
                                          "<password>");
```

> `<HOST>` is the database host name.
> `<PORT>` is the database port.
> `<SID>` is the database instance.
> `<password>` is the password for the OE schema.

Obtain the view object instance from the application module using the `findViewObject()` method:

```
ViewObject vo = applicationModule.findViewObject(viewObject);
```

Iterate over the view object to output the attributes of the view object rows to the browser. A row in a view object is represented with the `oracle.jbo.Row` interface. Obtain the first row with the `first()` method of the `ViewObject` interface.

```
Row row = vo.first();
```

A row attribute is obtained using the `getAttribute()` method of the `Row` interface:

```
<% out.println(row.getAttribute(i++).toString());%>
```

Obtain the next row in the view object using the `next()` method:

```
row = vo.next();
```

Release and remove the application module using the `releaseRootApplicationModule()` method of the `Configuration` class:

```
Configuration.releaseRootApplicationModule(applicationModule, true);
```

`TestClient.jsp` JSP is listed below.

```
<%@ page
contentType="text/html;charset=windows-1252"%>
<%@ page import="oracle.jbo.*,
oracle.jbo.client.Configuration" %>
<html>
  <head>
    <meta http-equiv="Content-Type"
          content="text/html; charset=windows-1252">
    <title>BC4J Web Application</title>
  </head>
  <body>
  <%
  String appModule = "model.AppModule"; //App Module name
  String cfg="AppModuleLocal";//Config Name
  String viewObject = "CatalogView1"; //name of view object
 ApplicationModule applicationModule =(ApplicationModule)
  Configuration.createRootApplicationModule(appModule, cfg);
   //Establish connection with database
   Transaction
     transaction=applicationModule.getTransaction();
   if(transaction.isConnected()==false)
   transaction.connect("jdbc:oracle:thin:@localhost:1521:ORCL", "OE",
     "pw");
  // Find the viewobject included in the appmodule
    ViewObject vo = applicationModule.findViewObject(viewObject);
  %>
    <table border="1" cellspacing="0">
        <tr>
         <th>CatalogId</th>
         <th>Journal</th>
         <th>Publisher</th>
         <th>Edition</th>
         <th>Section</th>
         <th>Title</th>
         <th>Author</th>
        </tr>
        <%  Row row = vo.first();
            while (row != null)
          {   int i=0;
```

```
        %><tr>
        <td><% out.println(row.getAttribute(i++).toString());%></td>
        <td><%out.println(row.getAttribute(i++).toString());%></td>
        <td><%out.println(row.getAttribute(i++).toString());%></td>
        <td><%out.println(row.getAttribute(i++).toString());%></td>
        <td><%out.println(row.getAttribute(i++).toString());%></td>
        <td><% out.println(row.getAttribute(i++).toString());%></td>
        <td><%out.println(row.getAttribute(i).toString());%></td>
      </tr>
        <%
          row = vo.next();
        } %>
    </table>
  <%
    Configuration.releaseRootApplicationModule(applicationModule,
        true);
  %>
  </body>
</html>
```

In JSP `TestClient.jsp` the application module connects with the database with a JDBC URL. The application module may also be connected to the database with a data source. For a JDBC connection `DBConnection1` in the **Connections-Navigator** a data source with JNDI name `jdbc/DBConnection1DS` is available. An application module is connected to a database with a data source with the `connectToDataSource` method of the `Transaction` interface:

```
transaction.connectToDataSource(null,"jdbc/DBConnection1DS","OE",
    "<password>", false);
```

To run the `TestClient.jsp`, right-click on the JSP node in the **Applications Navigator** and select **Run**. The output of the JSP is displayed in the default browser.

CatalogId	Journal	Publisher	Edition	Section	Title	Author
catalog1	Oracle Magazine	Oracle Publishing	Nov-Dec 2004	ORACLE DEVELOPER	From ADF UIX to JSF	Jonas Jacobi
catalog3	Oracle Magazine	Oracle Publishing	March-April 2005	ORACLE DEVELOPER	Starting with Oracle ADF	Steve Muench

JDBC 4.0 Version

ADF Business Components use JDBC to access the database. OC4J server embedded in JDeveloper 10g or JDeveloper does not support JDBC 4.0. The new features in JDBC 4.0 may be availed in a JDeveloper version that supports JDBC 4.0. To use JDBC 4.0 in ADF Business Components configure a database connection with the Oracle database 11g JDBC 4.0 drivers JAR file `ojdbc6.jar`. We also need to set JDK version to JDK 6.0. To set the JDK version select **Tools | Project Properties**. In the **Project Properties** window, select **Libraries**. In the **J2SE Version** field, click on **Change** to select a JDK 6.0 Java executable.

We would be able to use those JDBC 4.0 features that are implemented by the OC4J server. Connection state tracking is implemented by the connection pool manager and is used to track unusable connections. Prior to the new feature of connection state tracking a connection pool manager would typically close all the connections and reinitiate a connection pool if some of the connections in the connection pool became unusable. Using the `isValid()` method of `Connection` interface in JDBC 4.0, the connection pool manager is able to determine if a connection is still valid. If a connection is not valid, the connection pool manager closes the connection.

```
if(!connection.isValid())
connection.close();
```

Summary

The ADF Business Components is a JDBC-based framework. The ADF Business components in JDeveloper may be configured with the Oracle database, as explained in this chapter or a third-party database by configuring a library for the JDBC driver for the database. A web application may be created with the ADF business components using the `oracle.jbo` package classes and interfaces. In a JDeveloper version that supports JDBC 4.0 we may also add the JDBC 4.0 features.

15
Hibernate

Hibernate is an open-source, JDBC-based object/relational persistence and query service. Hibernate is used to map data representation in a Java object to a database. Hibernate supports several databases including DB2, MySQL, Oracle, and PostgreSQL. With Hibernate, Java data types are mapped to SQL data types. Hibernate generates the required SQL to create, update, and delete database tables. Hibernate is used for generating tables from a Java Bean class and adding, retrieving, updating and deleting data to the tables.

Hibernate is preferred over other database persistence technologies, such as Castor, TopLink, and Entity EJB, because of lesser complexity, greater flexibility, open-source architecture, and support for different databases without the requirement to provide vendor-specific SQL code in the data access layer. Hibernate also provides classes for Ant build tasks, which may be integrated into an Ant build file. In this chapter, we will integrate Hibernate with the JDeveloper 10.1.3 IDE and the Oracle database 10g for developing an object/relational application.

The database persistence provided by Hibernate is based on a mapping file and a database properties file. The .hbm.xml mapping file consists of class definitions for database persistence, which specify the Javabean properties to be mapped to a database table, the database schema name, the database table name, and the table columns corresponding to the Javabean properties. The tables may be generated from the mapping file or prior to developing the Hibernate application.

The mapping file specifies the Java classes for database persistence, the different fields and field types in the Java objects, and the corresponding database table columns and column types. The Java classes for a database application may be generated from the mapping file or before developing the Hibernate application. The database properties file (a hibernate.properties file) specifies the database, the JDBC driver, and the connection URL for the database applications. The Ant task classes net.sf.hibernate.tool.hbm2java.Hbm2JavaTask and org.hibernate. tool.hbm2ddl.SchemaExportTask are used to map the mapping file to Java classes and database tables respectively. The Java classes are subsequently used to add/retrieve/update/delete data in the database tables. In this chapter, an example mapping file, (catalog.hbm.xml), consisting of properties for a journal catalog, is mapped to a database table, OE.Catalog, and to a Java class, Catalog.java.

Hibernate and JDBC

Hibernate is a JDBC-based database persistence framework. A Hibernate application's Java to SQL mappings are defined in the org.hibernate.cfg. Configuration object. The mappings are compiled from XML mapping files. A XML mapping file is added to a Configuration object as follows:

```
Configuration cfg = new
  Configuration().addResource("Catalog.hbm.xml");
```

Hibernate configuration properties, which include JDBC properties, are set using one of the following methods:

1. Set the configuration properties using setProperties() method of the Configuration object.
2. Specify the configuration properties in the hibernate.properties file.
3. Specify the properties as System properties.
4. Specify the properties in the hibernate.cfg.xml file.

A SessionFactory is used to create and pool connections. A SessionFactory is created from a Configuration object as follows:

```
SessionFactory sessionFactory = cfg.buildSessionFactory();
```

When a Session object is created a JDBC connection is obtained from the connection pool.

```
Session session = sessionFactory.openSession();
```

Hibernate creates and pools connections either using java.sql.DriverManager or a data source. If connections are to be created and pooled using a DriverManager, the JDBC connection properties discussed in the following table need to be specified.

Property	Description
hibernate.connection.driver_class	JDBC Driver Class
hibernate.connection.url	JDBC Connection URL
hibernate.connection.username	Database User Name

Property	Description
`hibernate.connection.password`	Database User Password
`hibernate.connection.pool_size`	Optional Property. Maximum number of pooled connections.
`hibernate.dialect`	The Dialect for the database. For the Oracle database specify `org.hibernate.dialect.OracleDialect`

To develop a Hibernate application in an application server, obtain connections from a data source with a JNDI name binding. The data source properties discussed in the following table configure a Hibernate application with a data source.

Property	Description
`hibernate.connection.datasource`	Datasource JNDI name
`hibernate.jndi.url`	JNDI provider URL (optional)
`hibernate.jndi.class`	JNDI InitialContextFactory class (optional)
`hibernate.connection.username`	Database Username
`hibernate.connection.password`	Database Password

JDBC connections obtained from a data source automatically participate in the container managed transactions of the application server. Arbitrary connection properties may be set using the `hibernate.connection` prefix. For example, connection property `hibernate.connection.charSet` sets a character set. Some of the other Hibernate, JDBC and connection configuration properties that may be set are discussed in the following table:

Property	Description
`hibernate.jdbc.fetch_size`	Specifies JDBC Fetch Size
`hibernate.jdbc.batch_size`	Enables Batch Updates
`hibernate.default_schema`	Specifies schema name for unqualified table names.
`hibernate.jdbc.use_scrollable_resultset`	Enables Scrollable ResultSets
`hibernate.connection.isolation`	Specifies JDBC transaction isolation level.
`hibernate.connection.autocommit`	Enables autocommit for JDBC pooled connections.

Property	Description
`hibernate.connection.release_mode`	Specifies when Hibernate should release JDBC connections to the pool. By default JDBC connections are released when a Session object is closed. The following values may be specified: `auto (default)` `on_close`- When a connection is closed. `after_transaction`- At the end of a transaction. `after_statement`- At the end of a statement.
`hibernate.jdbc.use_scrollable_resultset`	Enables Scrollable ResultSets
`hibernate.connection.<propertyName>`	Specifies a JDBC property to be used by `DriverManager.getConnection()`
`hibernate.jndi.<propertyName>`	Specifies a JDBC property for the JNDI `InitialContextFactory`.

If the JDeveloper OC4J server supports JDBC 4.0, the JDBC 4.0 features such as connection state tracking may be availed of. Connection state tracking is implemented by the connection pool manager to identify and close unusable connections.

In this chapter you will learn the following:

- Creating a Database Table using Hibernate
- Adding data to the Database Table using Hibernate
- Retrieving data from the Database Table using Hibernate
- Updating data in Database Table using Hibernate
- Deleting data from Database Table using Hibernate

Setting the Environment

The Hibernate API classes are required to integrate Hibernate with JDeveloper. Download the Hibernate 3.2 and Hibernate Extension 2.1.3 ZIP files from `http://www.hibernate.org/` and extract the files to an installation directory, `C:/Hibernate`. A `hibernate-3.2` directory is created for the Hibernate 3.2 and a `tools` directory is created for the extension classes. Also download Hibernate 2.1.6, which is required for the `net.sf.hibernate.tool.hbm2java.Hbm2JavaTask` tool.

Extract the Hibernate 2.1.6 ZIP file to the `C:/Hibernate` directory; hibernate 2.1.6 directory is created. Install the JDeveloper 10g IDE. Install the Oracle database 10g and create a database instance including the sample schemas.

Next, the Hibernate JAR files required to develop a Hibernate application will be integrated into a JDeveloper 10g project. First, select **File | New** in the JDeveloper IDE. In the **New Gallery** window, select **General | Applications** in the **Categories** listed and select **Application** in the **Items** listed. Specify a **Application Name** and **Directory Name** in the **Create Application** window with No Template as the Application Template. In the **Create Project** window, specify a project name and click on **OK**. A Hibernate application and project is added to the **Applications-Navigator**.

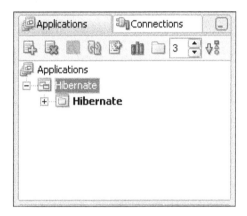

Next, add libraries required to generate a Hibernate application to the project. Select the Hibernate project node in the **Applications-Navigator**. Select **Tools | Project Properties**. In the **Project Properties** window, select the **Libraries** node. Select the **Add Library** button to create a new library. In the **Add Library** window select, the **New** button. In the **Create Library** window, specify `Hibernate` in the **Library Name** field and click on the **Add Entry** button. In the **Select Path Entry** window, select the `hibernate3.jar` file and click on the **Select** button. The selected JAR file is added to the **Class Path** node in the **Create Library** window. Click on the **OK** button in the **Create Library** window. Click on the **OK** button in the **Add Library** window. The Hibernate library gets created and added to the **Selected Libraries**. Similarly create libraries for the other JAR files required for a Hibernate application.

The libraries created and the corresponding JAR files are listed in the following table:

Project Library	Description	JAR/Zip File
Hibernate	The Hibernate API classes including the org.hibernate.tool. hbm2ddl.SchemaExportTask class.	<Hibernate>/hibernate-3.2/ hibernate3.jar
Hibernate-Extensions	The hibernate extension classes including the net. sf.hibernate.tool. hbm2java.Hbm2JavaTask class.	<Hibernate>/tools/ hibernate-tools.jar
Hibernate-Lib	The auxiliary Hibernate classes.	<Hibernate>/hibernate3.2/lib/ dom4j-1.6.1.jar,<Hibernate>/ hibernate-3.2/ lib/commons-logging-1.0.4.jar, <Hibernate>/ hibernate-3.2/ lib/commons-collections-2.1.1.jar, <Hibernate>/ hibernate-3.2/lib/ehcache-1.2.3.jar, <Hibernate>/ hibernate-3.2/lib/cglib-2.1.3.jar, <Hibernate>/ hibernate-3.2/lib/jta.jar, <Hibernate>/ hibernate-3.2/lib/asm.jar, <Hibernate>/ hibernate-3.2/ lib/antlr-2.7.6.jar
Oracle JDBC	The Oracle JDBC library. Delete orai18n.jar from <JDeveloper 10.1.3>\jdbc\lib.	

In previous table <Hibernate> is the directory in which the Hibernate is installed. <JDeveloper 10.1.3> is the directory in which JDeveloper 10.1.3 is installed.

The libraries created are listed in the **Libraries** window as shown in the following table:

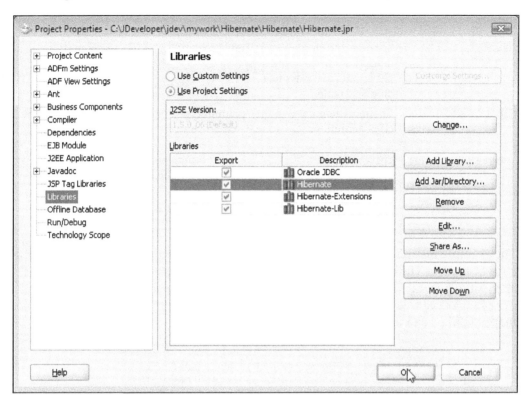

Developing Hibernate Mapping and Properties Files

The Hibernate mapping file (a `.hbm.xml` file) and the Hibernate properties file (`hibernate.properties` file) form the basis of a Hibernate application. The mapping file consists of class definitions. Each class definition consists of a set of properties to be mapped to a Java class and a database table. The field/column types and additional characteristics of the columns such as `length`, `not-null`, and `unique` are also specified with the properties. Some of the more often used tags in the mapping file are listed in the following table:

Tag Name	Description	Attributes	Sub Elements
hibernate-mapping	The root element	schema, package	class
class	Specifies the class definition for mapping a Hibernate Java class to a database table.	table,schema	id,property,set,list
id	Required element in a class definition.	column,type,length	column,generator
property	Specifies a class property, which corresponds to a table column and a Java class field.	type,column, length, not-null, unique	column

The example mapping file in this chapter consists of a class and class properties for a journal catalog. The element <generator class="native"/> is required in the <id> element to generate Java classes from the mapping file. The element <generator class="native"/> specifies the identifier generation strategy. The example mapping file, catalog.hbm.xml is listed below.

```
<?xml version="1.0"?><!DOCTYPE hibernate-mapping PUBLIC
    "-//Hibernate/Hibernate Mapping DTD 3.0//EN"
"http://hibernate.sourceforge.net/hibernate-mapping-3.0.dtd">
<hibernate-mapping>
<class name="hibernate.Catalog" table="OE.CATALOG">
<id name="id" type="string" column="ID">
 <generator class="native"/>  </id>
 <property name="journal" column="JOURNAL" type="string"/>
 <property name="publisher" column="PUBLISHER" type="string"/>
 <property name="edition" column="EDITION" type="string"/>
 <property name="title" column="TITLE" type="string"/>
 <property name="author" column="AUTHOR" type="string"/>
</class>
</hibernate-mapping>
```

Create a mappings directory in the C:/Hibernate directory and copy the catalog. hbm.xml file to it. The Hibernate properties file, hibernate.properties, specifies the database configuration for persistence to a database and query from the database. The properties file is a text file with properties specified in the <property>=<value>. The required JDBC connection properties of a hibernate.properties file are listed in the first table in this chapter.

In the `hibernate.properties` file for the example application in this chapter, the Oracle database example schema `OE` is specified for the username property. The Oracle Thin Type 4 driver is used with the driver class as `oracle.jdbc.OracleDriver`. The `hibernate.properties` file for the Oracle database is listed below.

```
hibernate.connection.driver_class=oracle.jdbc.OracleDriver
hibernate.connection.url=jdbc:oracle:thin:@localhost:1521:ORCL
hibernate.connection.username=OE
hibernate.connection.password=
hibernate.dialect=org.hibernate.dialect.OracleDialect
```

Create a `properties` directory in the `C:/Hibernate` directory and copy the `hibernate.properties` file to the `properties` directory.

Creating a Database Table

In this section, Java classes are generated from the example Hibernate mapping file (`catalog.hbm.xml`) and a Oracle database table is generated from the mapping file and the properties file (`hibernate.properties`). The mapping classes and database table are generated with a Ant build file. The Hibernate API provides the `net.sf.hibernate.tool.hbm2java.Hbm2JavaTask` task class to generate Java classes from a `hbm.xml` mapping file and the `org.hibernate.tool.hbm2ddl.SchemaExportTask` task class to generate a database table from a mapping file. First, create a Ant build file in Jdeveloper 10g IDE. Select **File | New**. In the **New Gallery** window select **General | Ant**. In the **Items** listed select **Empty Buildfile**.

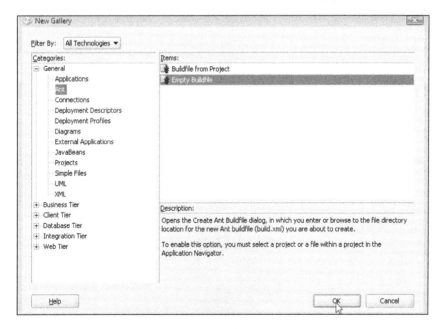

In the **Create Ant Buildfile** specify a **File Name**, **build.xml**, and a **Directory Name** for the build file. A `build.xml` file is added to the Hibernate project in the **Applications-Navigator**.

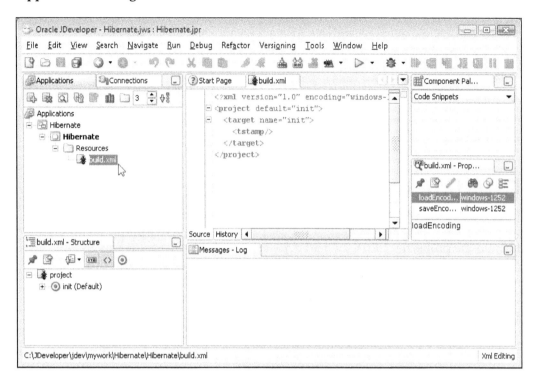

The example `build.xml` consists of targets for the following:

1. Generate Java classes from the mapping file.

2. Compile the Java classes.

3. Generate a database table from the mapping file and the `hibernate.properties` file.

We will discuss the structure of the `build.xml` file in detail. Add the `<project/>` tag, which specifies the project name, the default target and the `basedir` attribute. Add build file properties, which correspond to Hibernate directories. The directories are specified relative to the base directory, which is specified in the `basedir` attribute of the `project` element. The properties in the example `build.xml` are listed in the following table.

Property	Value	Description
src.dir	src	The directory in which the Java classes from the mapping file are generated.
classes.dir	classes	
hibernate-3.2	hibernate-3.2	
hibernate-2.1	hibernate-2.1	
hibernate.mappings	mappings	
jdbc	C:\oracle\ product\10.2.0\ db_1\jdbc\lib	The directory with the classes12.jar file and the ojdbc14.jar.
hibernate.extensions	tools	The directory with the hibernate-tools.jar file.
hibernate.properties	properties	The directory that has the hibernate.properties file.

In the `build.xml` file, add a `<path/>` element to specify the classpath for the `build.xml` file targets. The classpath includes the `hibernate3.jar`, `hibernate-tools.jar`, `ojdbc14.jar`, and the auxiliary Hibernate and Hibernate extensions JAR files. The `init` target generates the directories for the `build.xml` file. The `javaGenerator` target generates Java classes from the Hibernate mapping file with the `net.sf.hibernate.tool.hbm2java.Hbm2JavaTask` class. The `compile` target compiles the Java classes generated from the mapping file. The `schemaGenerator` target generates the database table from the mapping file and the properties file with the `org.hibernate.tool.hbm2ddl.SchemaExportTask` class. The example `build.xml` file is listed below.

```
<?xml version="1.0"?>
<project name="Hibernate"
default="schemaGenerator" basedir="C:\Hibernate">
  <property name="src.dir" value="src"/>
  <property name="classes.dir" value="classes"/>
  <property name="hibernate-3.2" value="hibernate-3.2"/>
  <property name="hibernate-2.1" value="hibernate-2.1"/>
  <property name="hibernate.mappings" value="mappings"/>
  <property name="jdbc"
     value="C:\oracle\product\10.2.0\db_1\jdbc\lib"/>
  <property name="hibernate.extensions" value="tools"/>
  <property name="hibernate.properties" value="properties"/>
  <path id="project.class.path">
  <pathelement location="${classes.dir}" />
```

```
<fileset dir="${hibernate-3.2}">
    <include name="hibernate3.jar"/>
</fileset>
<fileset dir="${hibernate-2.1}">
    <include name="hibernate2.jar"/>
</fileset>
<fileset dir="${hibernate-3.2}/lib">
    <include name="*.jar"/>
</fileset>
<fileset dir="${hibernate-2.1}/lib">
    <include name="commons-lang-1.0.1.jar"/>
</fileset>
    <fileset dir="${hibernate.extensions}/lib">
    <include name="*.jar"/>
</fileset>
<fileset dir="${hibernate.extensions}">
    <include name="hibernate-tools.jar"/>
</fileset>
<fileset dir="${jdbc}">
    <include name="ojdbc14.jar"/>
</fileset>
</path>
<target name="init">
<mkdir dir="${src.dir}"/>
<mkdir dir="${classes.dir}"/>
    </target>
<taskdef name="javaGen"
        classname="net.sf.hibernate.tool.hbm2java.Hbm2JavaTask"
        classpathref="project.class.path"/>
        <target name="javaGenerator" depends="init">
    <javaGen output="${src.dir}">
        <fileset dir="${hibernate.mappings}">
            <include name="catalog.hbm.xml"/>
        </fileset>
    </javaGen>
</target>
<target name="compile" depends="javaGenerator">
    <javac srcdir="${src.dir}"
        destdir="${classes.dir}">
        <classpath refid="project.class.path"/></javac>
</target>
<taskdef name="schemaGen"
classname="org.hibernate.tool.hbm2ddl.SchemaExportTask"
classpathref="project.class.path"/>
    <target name="schemaGenerator" depends="compile">
<schemaGen properties="${hibernate.properties}/hibernate.properties"
output="schema.ddl" create="true" quiet="no">
    <fileset
dir="${hibernate.mappings}">
        <include name="catalog.hbm.xml"/>
```

```
          </fileset>
      </schemaGen>
        </target>
      </project>
```

Copy the `build.xml` listing to the `build.xml` file in the JDeveloper Hibernate project. Build the targets in the `build.xml` file. Right-click on the **build.xml** file node and select **Run Ant**. In the **Run Ant** window, select the **schemaGenerator** target. The targets preceding the `schemaGenerator` target also get built as the targets are specified in the `depends` attribute.

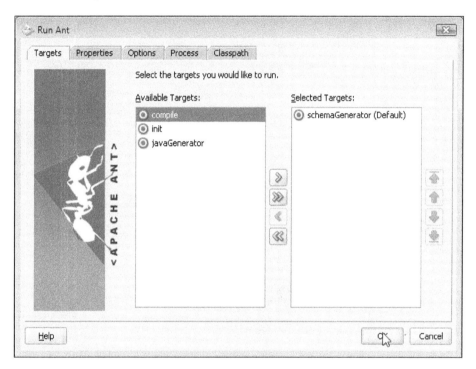

A Java class corresponding to the mapping file is generated. The Java class has getter and setter methods for each of the class properties specified in the mapping file. `Catalog.java`, the Java class, generated with Hibernate mapping file is listed as follows:

```
package hibernate;
import java.io.Serializable;
import org.apache.commons.lang.builder.ToStringBuilder;
/** @author Hibernate CodeGenerator */
public class Catalog implements Serializable {
    /** identifier field */
    private Integer id;
    /** nullable persistent field */
```

```
private String journal;
/** nullable persistent field */
private String publisher;
/** nullable persistent field */
private String edition;
/** nullable persistent field */
private String title;
/** nullable persistent field */
private String author;
/** full constructor */
public Catalog(String journal, String publisher, String edition,
   String title, String author) {
     this.journal = journal;
     this.publisher = publisher;
     this.edition = edition;
     this.title = title;
     this.author = author;
}
/** default constructor */
public Catalog() {
}
public Integer getId() {
     return this.id;
}
public void setId(Integer id) {
     this.id = id;
}
public String getJournal() {
     return this.journal;
}
public void setJournal(String journal) {
     this.journal = journal;
}
public String getPublisher() {
     return this.publisher;
}
public void setPublisher(String publisher) {
     this.publisher = publisher;
}
public String getEdition() {
     return this.edition;
}
public void setEdition(String edition) {
     this.edition = edition;
}
public String getTitle() {
     return this.title;
}
public void setTitle(String title) {
     this.title = title;
```

```
    }
    public String getAuthor() {
        return this.author;
    }
    public void setAuthor(String author) {
        this.author = author;
    }
    public String toString() {
        return new ToStringBuilder(this)
            .append("id", getId())
            .toString();
    }
}
```

A database table, specified in the table attribute of the class element in the mapping file, is generated as shown in the output from `build.xml`.

The CREATE TABLE script generated with Hibernate is as follows:

```
create table OE.CATALOG (ID varchar2(255) not null, JOURNAL
varchar2(255), PUBLISHER varchar2(255), EDITION varchar2(255), TITLE
varchar2(255), AUTHOR varchar2(255), primary key (ID))
create sequence hibernate_sequence
```

The structure of the `OE.Catalog` table generated is as follows:

```
SQL> DESC OE.CATALOG;
 Name                                      Null?    Type
 ----------------------------------------- -------- ------------------------------
 ID                                        NOT NULL VARCHAR2(255)
 JOURNAL                                            VARCHAR2(255)
 PUBLISHER                                          VARCHAR2(255)
 EDITION                                            VARCHAR2(255)
 TITLE                                              VARCHAR2(255)
 AUTHOR                                             VARCHAR2(255)

SQL>
```

In the following section table data will be added, retrieved, updated, and deleted with the Java class generated from the mapping file and the `hibernate.properties` properties file.

Modifying Table Data with Hibernate

In this section a middle-tier Hibernate Java application is developed to add/update and delete data to the table generated from the mapping file, `catalog.hbm.xml`. The Java application is not the JavaBean class generated from the mapping file. The Java application integrates the JavaBean class generated from the mapping file, the mapping file, and the properties file to provide a database persistence and query service.

Select **File | New** and in the **New Gallery** window select **General | Java Class**. In the **Create Java Class** window, specify a class name, HibernateDB.java, and a class package, hibernate. A Java class is added to the Hibernate project. Next, copy the mapping file `catalog.hbm.xml` and the `C:/Hibernate/src/hibernate/Catalog.java` java bean class to the `hibernate` directory. The directory structure of the Hibernate application is shown in following figure.

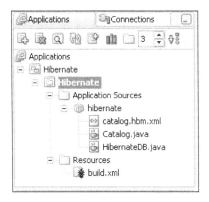

To the project libraries add the directory containing the `hibernate.properties` file. Also add the Commons lang JAR file from the `Hibernate 2.1.6` directory.

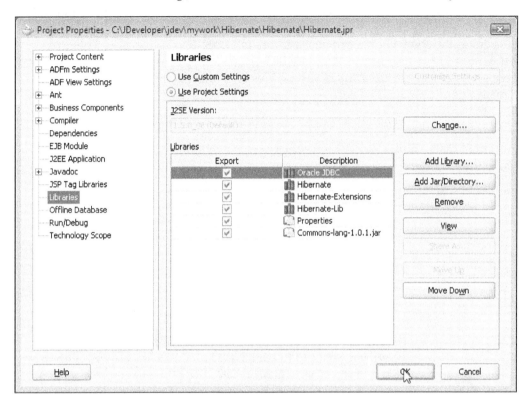

In the Hibernate Java application import the Hibernate API classes. Import the Java class that was generated from the mapping file.

Adding Data to the Database Table

Create a `Catalog` class object and set values for the different fields of the Java class with the setter methods.

```
Catalog catalog=new Catalog();
  catalog.setId("catalog 1");
  catalog.setJournal("Oracle Magazine");
  catalog.setPublisher("Oracle Publishing");
  catalog.setEdition("Jan-Feb 2004");
  catalog.setTitle("Understanding Optimization");
  catalog.setAuthor("Kimberly Floss");
```

Interface `org.hibernate.Session`, the main runtime interface between a Java application and Hibernate, is used to create, update, and delete data in a database. A `Session` object is obtained from a `SessionFactory`. The `SessionFactory` interface provides `openSession()` methods to create a database connection and open a session on the connection, or open a session on a specified connection. The `org.hibernate.cfg.Configuration` class is used to specify configuration properties, JavaBean persistence class and mapping files to create a `SessionFactory` object. Create a `Configuration` object:

```
Configuration config=new Configuration();
```

Add the JavaBean persistence class, `Catalog.class` to the `Configuration` object using the `addClass()` method.

```
config.addClass(example.hibernate.Catalog.class);
```

The mapping file, `catalog.hbm.xml`, which is copied to the same directory as the mapped Java class is configured with the `Configuration` object. The `hibernate.properties` file in the Class path of the Hibernate application gets configured as the properties file for the `Configuration` object. Create a `SessionFactory` object from the `Configuration` object using the `buildSessionFactory()` method.

```
SessionFactory sessionFactory=config.buildSessionFactory();
```

The `SessionFactory` creates and pools JDBC connections for the Hibernate application. First, we will add data to the database table that was created with the hibernate mapping file and the hibernate properties file. Obtain a `Session` object from the `SessionFactory` object using the `openSession()` method.

```
Session sess = sessionFactory.openSession();
```

A JDBC connection gets obtained from the connection pool when a `Session` is opened. Hibernate obtains and pools connections using `java.sql.DriverManager`. Obtain a `Transaction` object from the `Session` object using the `beginTransaction()` method to add data to the database table.

```
org.hibernate.Transaction tx = sess.beginTransaction();
```

Store the JavaBean object, created earlier, in the database with the `save()` method and commit the transaction using the `commit()` method:

```
sess.save(catalog);
tx.commit();
```

The values specified in the `Catalog` object get stored in the database table. Close the `Session` object using the `close()` method:

```
sess.close();
```

Retrieving Data from the Database Table

Next, we will retrieve the data stored in the database table. Create a query to select data from the table. The query is defined in Hibernate Query Language (HQL) syntax which is similar to SQL.

```
String hqlQuery ="from example.hibernate.Catalog";
```

If the `Select` clause is not specified in the query all of the fields selected in the `From` clause are selected from the mapped class. The `From` clause is specified with the mapped Java class, `example.hibernate.Catalog`, not the database table. The Java class object to database mapping is performed by the mapping file and the properties file. Open a `Session` object from the `SessionFactory` object using the `openSession()` method:

```
Session sess = sessionFactory.openSession();
```

Create a `Query` object with the `createQuery(hqlQuery)` method of the `Session` object:

```
Query query = sess.createQuery(hqlQuery);
```

Obtain a `List` from the HQL query with the `list()` method of the `Query` object:

```
List list = query.list();
```

Iterate over the `List` and output values for the specified HQL query. For example the `Journal` column value is output as follows:

```
for (int i = 0; i < list.size(); i++) {
Catalog catalog = (Catalog) list.get(i);
            System.out.println("CatalogId " + catalog.getId() +
                + " Journal: " + catalog.getJournal());
 }
```

Updating the Database Table

Next, we will update table values with the Hibernate Java application. Create a query to select data, which is to be modified, from the table

```
String hqlQuery="from Catalog";
```

Obtain a `Session` object from the `SessionObject`.

```
Session sess = sessionFactory.openSession();
```

Obtain a `Transaction` object from the `Session` object.

```
Transaction tx = sess.beginTransaction();
```

Create a `Query` object from the HQL query using the `createQuery()` method of the `Session` object. Obtain a `List` result set with the `list()` method. Obtain the JavaBean object to be modified.

```
Query query = sess.createQuery(hqlQuery);
 List list = query.list();
Catalog catalog = (Catalog) list.get(0);
```

As an example, set the value of the `publisher` field to `"Oracle Magazine"`.

```
catalog.setPublisher("Oracle Magazine");
```

Begin a `Session` transaction using the `beginTransaction()` method of the `Session` object.

```
Transaction tx = sess.beginTransaction();
```

Update the database table with the `saveOrUpdate()` method of the `Session` object and commit the transaction:

```
sess.saveOrUpdate(catalog);
tx.commit();
```

Deleting Data

Next, delete a table row with the Hibernate API. As an example, delete the table row for edition `"March-April 2005"`. Create a HQL query which selects a database table row to delete.

```
String hqlQuery="from Catalog as catalog where catalog.edition='March-
April 2005'";
```

Open a database session with the `openSession()` method of the `SessionFactory` object:

```
Session sess = sessionFactory.openSession();
```

Create a `Query` object with the HQL query. Obtain the result set `List` for the HQL query. Obtain the result set item to be deleted:

```
Query query = sess.createQuery(hqlQuery);
List list = query.list();
Catalog catalog = (Catalog) list.get(0);
```

Begin a session transaction using the `beginTransaction()` method:

```
Transaction tx = sess.beginTransaction();
```

Delete the row specified in the HQL query with the delete() method of the Session object and commit the transaction:

```
sess.delete(catalog);
tx.commit();
```

The example Java application, HibernateDB.java, has the addToCatalog method to add data, retrieveFromCatalog method to retrieve data, updateCatalog method to update data, and deleteFromCatalog method to delete data. The following list contains HibernateDB.java:

```
package hibernate;
import hibernate.Catalog;
import org.hibernate.Session;
import org.hibernate.SessionFactory;
import org.hibernate.Transaction;
import org.hibernate.cfg.Configuration;
import org.hibernate.Query;
import java.util.List;
public class HibernateDB {
  Transaction tx;
  Session sess;
  Configuration config;
  SessionFactory sessionFactory;
  public void addToCatalog() {
    try {
      Catalog catalog = new Catalog();
      catalog.setId("catalog 1");
      catalog.setJournal("Oracle Magazine");
      catalog.setPublisher("Oracle Publishing");
      catalog.setEdition("Jan-Feb 2004");
      catalog.setTitle("Understanding Optimization");
      catalog.setAuthor("Kimberly Floss");

      Catalog catalog2 = new Catalog();
      catalog2.setId("catalog 2");
      catalog2.setJournal("Oracle Magazine");
      catalog2.setPublisher("Oracle Publishing");
      catalog2.setEdition("March-April 2005");
      catalog2.setTitle("Starting with Oracle ADF");
      catalog2.setAuthor("Steve Muench");

      config = new Configuration();
      config.addClass(Catalog.class);
      sessionFactory = config.buildSessionFactory();
      sess = sessionFactory.openSession();
      tx = sess.beginTransaction();
```

```
            sess.save(catalog);
            sess.save(catalog2);
            tx.commit();
        } catch (Exception e) {
            try {
                if (tx != null) {
                    tx.rollback();
                }
            } catch (
                org.hibernate.HibernateException excp) {
            }
        } finally {
            try {
                if (sess != null) {
                    sess.close();
                }
            } catch (
                org.hibernate.HibernateException excp) {
            }
        }
    }
    public void retrieveFromCatalog() {
        try {
            String hqlQuery = "from Catalog";
            config = new Configuration();
            config.addClass(Catalog.class);
            sessionFactory = config.buildSessionFactory();
            sess = sessionFactory.openSession();
            Query query = sess.createQuery(hqlQuery);
            List list = query.list();
            for (int i = 0; i < list.size(); i++) {
                Catalog catalog = (Catalog) list.get(i);
                System.out.println(
                    "CatalogId " + catalog.getId() +
                    " Journal: " + catalog.getJournal());
                System.out.println(
                    "CatalogId " + catalog.getId() +
                    " Publisher: " + catalog.getPublisher());
                System.out.println(
                    "CatalogId " + catalog.getId() +
                    " Edition: " + catalog.getEdition());
                System.out.println(
                    "CatalogId " + catalog.getId() + " Title " +
                    catalog.getTitle());
```

```
        System.out.println(
          "CatalogId " + catalog.getId() +
          " Author: " + catalog.getAuthor());
      }
      if (sess != null) {
        sess.close();
      }
    } catch (org.hibernate.HibernateException e) {
    }
  }
  public void updateCatalog() {
    try {
      String hqlQuery = "from Catalog";
      config = new Configuration();
      config.addClass(Catalog.class);
      sessionFactory = config.buildSessionFactory();
      sess = sessionFactory.openSession();
      Query query = sess.createQuery(hqlQuery);
      List list = query.list();
      Catalog catalog = (Catalog) list.get(0);
      catalog.setPublisher("Oracle Magazine");
      tx = sess.beginTransaction();
      sess.saveOrUpdate(catalog);
      tx.commit();
    } catch (Exception e) {
      try {
        if (tx != null) {
          tx.rollback();
        }
      } catch (
        org.hibernate.HibernateException excp) {
      }
    } finally {
      try {
        if (sess != null) {
          sess.close();
        }
      } catch (
        org.hibernate.HibernateException excp) {
      }
    }
  }
      public void deleteFromCatalog() {
          try {
```

```
                String hqlQuery = "from Catalog as catalog WHERE
                  catalog.edition='March-April 2005'";
                config = new Configuration();
                config.addClass(Catalog.class);
                sessionFactory = config.buildSessionFactory();
                sess = sessionFactory.openSession();
                Query query = sess.createQuery(hqlQuery);
                List list = query.list();
                Catalog catalog = (Catalog) list.get(0);
                tx = sess.beginTransaction();
                sess.delete(catalog);
                tx.commit();
            } catch (Exception e) {
                try {
                    if (tx != null) {
                        tx.rollback();
                    }
                } catch (
                    org.hibernate.HibernateException excp) {
                }
            } finally {
                try {
                    if (sess != null) {
                        sess.close();
                    }
                } catch (
                    org.hibernate.HibernateException excp) {
                }
            }
        }
    public static void main(String[] argv) {
        HibernateDB hibernateDB = new HibernateDB();
        hibernateDB.addToCatalog();
        /*hibernateDB.retrieveFromCatalog();
        hibernateDB.updateCatalog();
        hibernateDB.deleteFromCatalog();*/
    }
}
```

Copy `HibernateDB.java` to the Hibernate project. To add data to the `Catalog` table, comment out all the methods except `addToCatalog()`. To run the Java application, right-click on the application node and select **Run**. To retrieve data from the database, comment out all the methods in the `HibernateDB.java` class except `retrieveFromCatalog()` and run the application. The Hibernate application retrieves the `Catalog` table data.

```
CatalogId 1 Journal: Oracle Magazine
CatalogId 1 Publisher: Oracle Publishing
CatalogId 1 Edition: Jan-Feb 2004
CatalogId 1 Title Understanding Optimization
CatalogId 1 Author: Kimberly Floss
CatalogId 2 Journal: Oracle Magazine
CatalogId 2 Publisher: Oracle Publishing
CatalogId 2 Edition: March-April 2005
CatalogId 2 Title Starting with Oracle ADF
CatalogId 2 Author: Steve Muench
```

To update the database table, comment out all the methods except `updateCatalog()` and run the `HibernateDB` application. To delete from the `Catalog` table, comment out all the methods except the `deleteFromCatalog()` method and run the `HibernateDB` application.

Summary

Object/relational mapping without a database persistence and query service requires JDBC API and vendor-specific SQL scripts to create, update, delete database tables. With Hibernate the JDBC API and the SQL scripts are not required. Hibernate generates the SQL script to add, retrieve, update, and delete data from a database. Hibernate provides the `net.sf.hibernate.tool.hbm2java.Hbm2JavaTask` Apache Ant build task to generate a JavaBean class from a `hbm.xml` configuration file and the `org.hibernate.tool.hbm2ddl.SchemaExportTask` Apache Ant build task to generate a database table from a `hbm.xml` configuration file.

Index

getConnection() method 8
getDrivers() method 8

E

evironment
setting 50
Excel spreadsheet, creating with Apache
 POI HSSF 363
Excel spreadsheet, creating with
 JasperReports 353
Extensible Markup Language. *See* XML
Extensible Stylesheet Language
 Transformation. *See* XSLT

F

factory class, JDeveloper 62
first method 14

G

getClientInfo() method 9
getClientInfoProperties() method 21
getColumns(String catalog,String
 schemaPattern,String
 tableNamePattern,String
 columnNamePattern) method 20
getConnection() method 8
getDriver() method 8
getFunctionColumns() method 21
getFunctions() method 21
getMaxColumnsInSelect() method 19
getProcedures(String catalog,String
schemaPattern, String
procedureNamePattern) method 20
getRowIdLifetime() method 20
getSchemas() method 21
getTables(String catalog,String
schemaPattern,String tableNamePatte
rn,String[] types) method 19
getTypeInfo() method 18
getConnection() method 8
getDrivers() method 8
getHoldability() method 16
getNCharacterStream() method 16
getNClob() method 16

getNString() method 16
getRowId() method 16
getSQLXML() method 16
getSavepointId() method 11
getSavepointName() method 11
getCause() method 21
getErrorCode() method 21
getMessage() method 21
getNextException() method 21
getSQLState() method 21
getMoreResults() method 12
getResultSet() method 12
getUpdateCount() method 12

H

Hibernate
 about 401
 data, adding to database table 417, 419
 data, deleting 420-425
 data, retrieving from database table 419
 database table, creating 409-416
 database table, updating 419
 data table, modifying 416, 417
 directory structure 416
 environment, setting 404
 mapping file 407, 408
Hibernate and JDBC 402
 connection configuration properties 403,
  404
 data source properties 403
 JDBC connection properties 402, 403
Hypersonic Database (HSQLDB) 105

I

IBM DB2 9 161
installing, JasperReports 342
insertRow() method 15
isAfterLast() method 15
isBeforeFirst() method 15
isClosed() method 13, 16
isFirst() method 15
isLast() method 15
isPoolable() method 13
isValid() method 9

J

WebSphere
about 161
data source, configuring 167-176
environment, setting 162
JDBC provider, configuring 162-167
web application, deploying from
JDeveloper 176-186
wrapper interface
extending 31
isWrapperFor() method 31
unwrap() method 31

X

XML 191
XML document
data, accessing 29
database table updating, XSU used 200, 201
generating 26, 28
mapping to SQL database, XSU used 196-200
retrieving 29
storing 28
XML SQL Utility. *See* **XSU**
XSLT 191
XSQL
about 209
connection, configuring 215
connection, configuring in embedded OC4J server 217, 218
database connection, creating 216
environment, setting 214
JDBC 4.0 version 234
page processor, steps 209, 210
XSQL output transforming, XSLT used 231, 232, 233
XSQL page, creating 219-226
XSQL queries, creating 219

XSQL query attributes, demonstrating 228-231
XSQL tags, overview 210
xsql-query tag, XSQL
bind-params attribute 227
date-format attribute 227
error-statement attribute 227
id-attribute 227
id-attribute-column 227
include-schema attribute 227
max-rows attribute 227
null-indicator attribute 227
row-element attribute 227
rowset-element attribute 227
skip-rows attribute 227
tag-case attribute 227
XSQL queries, creating 219
XSQL query attributes, applying 228
XSQL tags
xsql.delete-request 213
xsql.include-request-params 212
xsql.include-xml 212
xsql.include-xsql 212
xsql.insert-param 213
xsql.insert-request 213
xsql.query 211
xsql.set-cookie 214
xsql.update-request 213
XSU
about 191
database table from XML document, updating 200, 201
environment, setting 193-195
SQL database to XML document, mapping 202-207
XML document to SQL database, mapping 196-200

Learning PHP Data Objects

ISBN: 978-1-847192-66-0   Paperback: 200 pages

A Beginner's Guide to PHP Data Objects, Database Connection Abstraction Library for PHP 5

1. An overview of PDO

2. Creating a database and connecting to it

3. Error Handling

4. Advanced features

Service Oriented Java Business Integration

ISBN: 978-1-847194-40-4   Paperback: 414 pages

Enterprise Service Bus integration solutions for Java developers

1. Enterprise Service Bus (ESB) for integrating loosely coupled, pluggable services

2. See Enterprise Integration Patterns (EIP) in action, in code

3. ESB integration solutions using Apache open source tools

4. JBI features explained with the help of real world examples

Please check **www.PacktPub.com** for information on our titles

www.ingramcontent.com/pod-product-compliance
Lightning Source LLC
Chambersburg PA
CBHW081459050326
40690CB00015B/2853